Human Values and Health

Compiled and Written by

Dr. (Mrs.) Charanjit Ghooi

M.B.B.S.; F.P.L.S. (England), Allopathy
D.H.B.; D.M.; D.Pre (Germany) M.D. Homeopathy
Ayurveda Ratna; D.Ac (I.N.I.R.) and Yoga
F.W.A.I.M. (USA), F.I.H.H.A. (USA)

Edited by

Mrs. Zeba Bashiruddine, Julia Hall
Joan Powers and Joan Riggi

PRASANTHI NILAYAM

SRI SATHYA SAI BOOKS & PUBLICATIONS TRUST
Prasanthi Nilayam – 515 134
Anantapur District, Andhra Pradesh, India
STD: 08555 ISD: 91 – 8555
Phone: 287375 Fax: 287236
enquiry@sssbpt.org

International Standard Book Number:
978-81-7208-507-0

First Edition: June 2007

Cover Illustration by Author

Published by
The Convener,
Sri Sathya Sai Books & Publications Trust,
Prasanthi Nilayam – 515 134,
Anantapur District, Andhra Pradesh, India.
STD: 08555 ISD: 91 – 8555
Phone: 287375 Fax: 287236
enquiry@sssbpt.org

Printed at : **Omkar Offset Printers**
No. 3/4, N T Pet, Bangalore - 560 002
Phone : 080 - 2670 8186
Email : omkaroffset@gmail.com

Publisher's Note

This third book of Dr. (Mrs) Charanjit Ghooi's, **Human Values And Health**, is a happy harmonizing of the teachings of *Bhagawan* Sri Sathya Sai Baba on Human Values and health with modern research on neurophysiology. Her earlier works, ***Bhakti* And Health** and **Spirituality And Health,** were well received by the public. Dr. (Mrs) Charanjit Ghooi has spent over twenty years in the making of this volume and it is a fitting fruition of *Bhagawan's* grace and her efforts.

Sri Sathya Sai Books and Publications Trust is happy to bring out the present volume which is insightful with modern research and *Bhagawan's* pronouncements on Human Values relating to health and healing.

Convener
20 April 2007
Prasanthi Nilayam

Virtue is the panacea for both body and mind. The virtuous person can be both healthy and happy.

~ **Sri Sathya Sai Baba**

CONTENTS

INDEX OF DIAGRAMS AND CHARTS

Union Of *Jiva* With *Purusha*

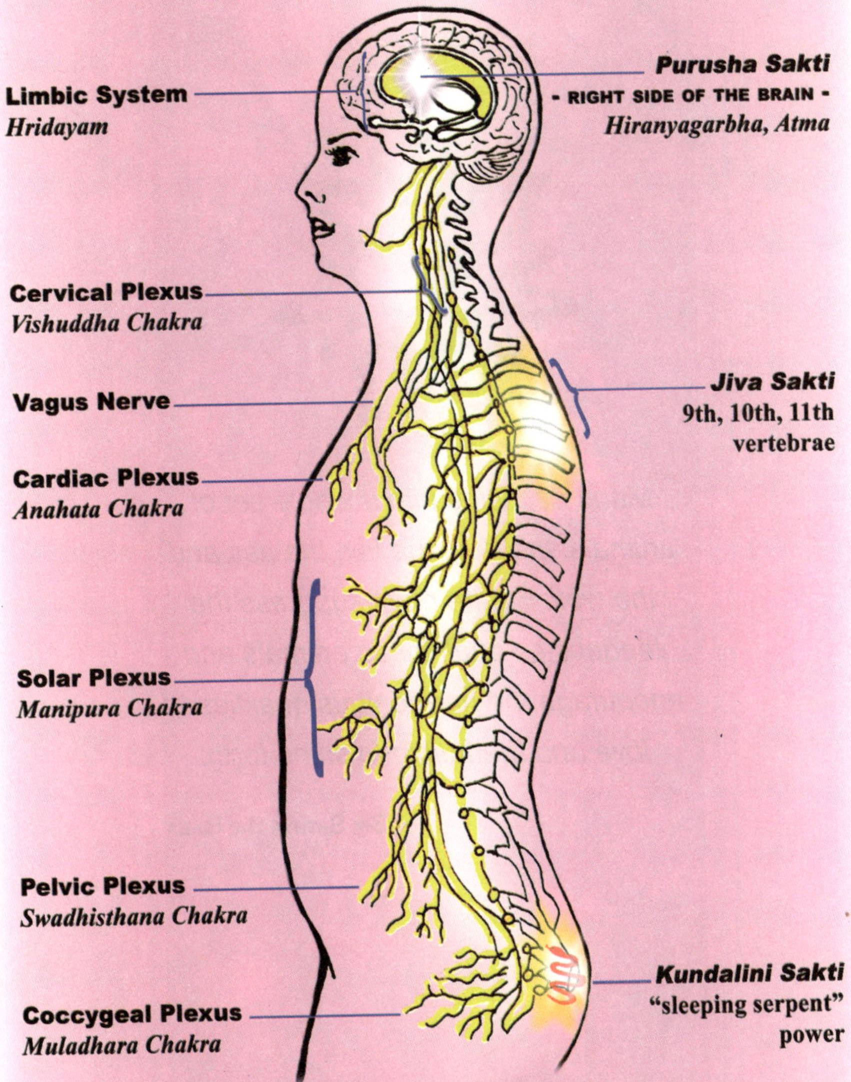

Human Values And Health ~ Cover Diagram

SOURCE: Divine Discourses of *Bhagawan* Sri Sathya Sai Baba

Man has inside him a whole set of animals: the dog, the fox, the ass and the wolf. But he must suppress the tendencies of all these animals and encourage the harmonious qualities of love and friendship to shine forth.

~ **Sri Sathya Sai Baba**

acknowledgements

It is with great reverence and love that I dedicate this book to *Bhagawan* Sri Sathya Sai Baba, who has been teaching Human Values since His childhood, through songs, poems, lectures and the message of His Life. This book is primarily a compilation of His Divine discourses. Millions and millions of people on this earth are being looked after by Sri Sathya Sai Baba, the *Avatar* of the *Kaliyuga*. In one form or another, He attends to the needs of all His children and when called upon, *Swami* goes "door to door" (or heart to heart). You might have already read about some of His innumerable *Leelas* (divine games) and the blessings given to *Bhaktas* (devotees) that have been described in various books.

Baba says there are many Ravanas and Kamsas[*1] in this *Kali* age. This Incarnation (Sai *Avatar*) will not kill these demons and wicked ones. Instead Baba will transform their *Hridayam* (spiritual heart) through His teachings on Human Values, which He demonstrates and exemplifies in His life. This is the subject matter of this book. It has been conveyed to me from His *Hridayam* to my *Hridayam*. I am very grateful to *Bhagawan* for making me His humble instrument in gathering all this information together.

I am so very thankful to Dr. Alreja, the Superintendent of the Sri Sathya Sai General Hospital in *Puttaparthi*, who took the diagrams for this book to *Swami* in Brindavan for His blessings. With deep humility in my heart, I mention that *Swami*, Himself, corrected several of the diagrams and blessed them all three times. Dr. Alreja is the liaison between the hospital doctors and *Swami*. I fondly see him as "Uddhava".[*2]

---

* 1 Ravana and Kamsa were demonic personalities during the times of Rama and Krishna respectively.

* 2 Dear friend of Krishna who used to take Krishna's messages to the Gopikas and vice versa.

There are no words sufficient to convey my deepest gratitude to the late Dr. V. K. Gokak, "my Papa," who insisted, upon Baba's instructions, that I compile Baba's medical lectures in a book form. Dr. Gokak also contributed a great deal of literature on Human Values during the period from 1982 to 1986, which I have quoted throughout the book. Papa used to say Baba is very specific regarding Human Values and tells us that **if people adopt Human Values in practical life it will cure 90% of the diseases in humanity**. Physical, mental, emotional, and social health is acheived only through the practice of Human Values. Because Human Values purify the nervous system and *Hridayam*, which is the seat of *Atma* (soul), they enable the *Atmic Sakti* (cosmic energy) to travel through the nervous system giving *Prana* (vital energy) to every organ, tissue, and cell of the body. This in turn creates a healthy body.

My heartfelt thanks is also extended to Mrs. Zeba Bashiruddine, Head of the Department of English in Sri Sathya Sai Institute of Higher Learning, Boys College, Prasanthi Nilayam, Puttaparthi, for editing the first drafts of this book. I am very thankful to her, as she is a non-medico who under my guidance has not only edited the text, but also prepared most of the original diagrams.

I would also like to give my thanks, through my *Hridayam* to Joan Riggi and Joan Powers of the U.S.A. who, under time constraints, assisted in formatting and typing the manuscript and worked tirelessly day and night editing the text which was presented to Baba in 2000. Only *Swami* knows how they have finished such an undertaking.

Many thanks also go to my granddaughter, Ananya Juneja, who when she was just nine years old, taught me the fundamentals of using a computer, and also typed important additions for me. At this writing she is now 16 and continues to encourage my efforts to use computers.

I also humbly give thanks to the scientists, saints, teachers, writers, researchers, medicos and spiritual seekers from whom I have complied additional information for this volume. Their names are many and can be found in references throughout and in the Bibliography.

This book was first presented to *Bhagawan* as a 75th Birthday present, through Dr. Alreja. The conditions were that He will give the Foreword and He will print. He accepted these conditions and kept the book with Him from 2000 to 2006. In the beginning *Swami* said, "The public is not ready for this." I waited patiently. In 2004, one of my friends who went in for interview asked, "*Swami* what is happening with Dr. Ghooi's book?" *Swami* answered, "I will do it, do it, do it!" And still He did not do.

On the 9th of December 2005, *Swami* granted me an interview. About the book, He said, "Expand Chapter 19 and review the book." How to do this? In Puttaparthi I knew no computer people. My life was lived in the small circle between the hospital, *darshan,* my flat and back again. I sat before my *puja* (altar) and prayed, "*Swami* in Bhopal it is easy for me to work, but here I know no one."

Then my friend, Julia Hall, who for many years helped to edit the *Canadian Sathya Sai Newsletter,* came to visit. I requested her to assist in reviewing this book. She willingly and reverentially took this job and completed the re-edition and preparation of the book and diagrams for the next presentation to *Swami.* There are no words to thank her for her efforts. Only *Swami* can bless her.

May my *Swami* (Divine Partner) bless them all with Health, Prosperity, Spiritual Wealth and most of all – a life lived with Human Values that leads to realisation of Oneself.

With Love,

Dr. (Mrs.) Charanjit Ghooi
Gynaecologist,
Sri Sathya Sai General Hospital
Prasanthi Nilayam
August 2006

Most humbly this book is dedicated to

My Beloved Lord, ***Bhagawan*** *Sri Sathya*

Sai Baba, the King of the Cosmos.

The greatest obstacle on the path of Surrender is ***ahamkara*** *(egoism) and* ***mamakara*** *("mine-ness" or possessiveness). It is something that has been inhering in your personality since ages, sending its tentacles deeper and deeper with the experience of every succeeding life. It can be removed only by the twin detergents of discrimination and renunciation.* ***Bhakti*** *is the water to wash away this dirt of ages and the soap of* ***japa, dhyana*** *and* ***yoga*** *(repetition of God's name, meditation and union with God) will help to remove it quicker and more effectively.*

~ **Sri Sathya Sai Baba**

Good character is a source of health. Be good; be joyful; be bold; be honest; be temperate; be patient. These are all rules of health. Good character is the most valuable source of health.

~ **Sri Sathya Sai Baba**

preface

In 1975, for the first time, I visited the ashram of *Bhagawan* Sri Sathya Sai Baba, known as *Prasanthi Nilayam*, in the South Indian town of Puttaparthi. I went to join the celebration of His 50th Birthday. After physically seeing Sai Baba with my own eyes, I was astonished to realise that He was none other than Guru Nanak, Lord Krishna, and *Purushotthama* Rama. Since then, I visited the *ashram* during every birthday of *Swami* 's and have been working in the Medical Camp which is conducted during large festivals. The doctors, who are volunteers, are requested to arrive by 14th November and stay until 26th November. They attend to the medical problems of Baba's devotees who come to *Puttaparthi* from far off to join the birthday celebrations. Since 1975 I never missed an opportunity to do service at the Medical Camp.

I also made sure to allot time for a visit with my ""Papa"", Dr. V. K. Gokak, whom many may know as the first Vice-Chancellor of *Swami's* Institute of Higher Learning. Since 1975, when Sai Baba literally ordered him to embrace me as his adopted daughter, I have accepted Dr. Gokak forever as ""Papa"," and was in the habit of writing and speaking to him on a regular basis.

In 1984, although I was physically ill, I could not restrain myself from going to *Puttaparthi* for the Medical Camp. As per the *ashram's* strict schedule, I arrived at *Puttaparthi* on 14th November. Before my arrival, I notified Dr. V. K. Gokak of my programme to attend the 1984 Birthday Celebration. The desire to have Sai Baba's *darshan* (site of a holy person or God), as well as have an opportunity to stay with Dr. and Mrs. Gokak was all too compelling. On the day of my arrival, however, I was unable to visit my "Papa" because I was running a high temperature caused by the flare up of arthritis. The following day, Dr. Gokak, not being aware of my condition, sent a *sevadal* volunteer to inquire of my whereabouts and ordered that I must visit him. Assisted by my nurse, who had come with me from Bhopal, I went to his flat. As soon as I stepped onto the veranda, I could see "Papa" was busy talking to someone. I quietly bowed to touch his feet, whereupon he gave me his blessing, and indicated that I may go inside the flat. When I stepped inside, *Amma*, Mrs. Gokak immediately approached me from the kitchen and inquired as to when I had reached *Puttaparthi*. I told her of my arrival on 14th November and of my sickness. At that time, I was shivering and *Amma*, noticing this, lovingly wrapped me in a blanket and insisted that I should lie on the bed. She offered tea, which was perhaps the first need of mine. While I was sitting quite comfortably on the bed with my back against the wall sipping tea, Dr. Gokak entered the room and with great concern inquired about my sickness. While telling him of my high fever, I asked him to give me a paracetamol tablet, which was available in his cabinet. "Papa" was not at ease seeing my gloomy face. I then came forward and requested that he and Amm partake of their dinner, as it was already late.

After dinner, "Papa" said, "I have collected certain books, along with other literature on human values during my lecture trips outside India. I am happy to entrust them to you to help you in writing your next book, after you complete the current one, **Spirituality And Health**."

It was surprising that he knew so many years in advance that one day I would need such literature. Today, after making a humble effort and through the encouragement of my well wishers and dear readers, and above all inspired by my Beloved *Swami*, I have finished this, my fourth book, **HUMAN VALUES AND HEALTH**. The literature that I obtained from Dr. Gokak, my dear "Papa", helped me considerably in writing this book.

I can recall, during that time, how physically helpless I felt due to my illness. I told "Papa" how much I was suffering and how seriously sick I felt from a number of diseases. I remembered questioning him as to whether he had hopes of my writing any more books. While telling "Papa" of my poor state of health, it was only natural for the tears to cascade down my cheeks. In a fatherly and affectionate manner, he consoled me and said, "My child! You need not condemn yourself and your health. Baba has told me that you will write His medical books, such as the one you wrote, **SPIRITUALITY AND HEALTH,** and they will be published. Remember one thing. What Baba says has to happen. I you are His chosen instrument ...

He will refine you with Love,
He will chisel you with Love,
He will hammer you with Love,
He will burn you with Love,
Then He will make you cry for His Love.

It is better that you write Baba's medical lectures and compile them in a book form. You are a well qualified medical practitioner, and why should you not believe that you will write these books?"

I said to Dr. Gokak, ""Papa", I understand that a doctor can only give the best medicine to the patient, but he cannot guarantee to heal the patient. In fact, healing is purely in the hands of the Almighty God. I, myself, have tried Allopathic, *Ayurveda* and Homeopathy treatments, but what to say of healing? My problems have slightly increased. It is evident that Baba's Grace has not yet been showered on me; that is why I am not getting cured."

Dr. Gokak sharply answered me, "Baba's Grace is like sunlight that is showered on all. What is needed, in fact, is that the person in question – namely you! –develops sincere faith in Him. Prayers have to emerge from the depths of a pure heart. To achieve a pure heart, one needs to practise many types of *yoga* regularly. Diseases arise from one's stress. Therefore, to relieve stress one should make an effort to practise *yoga*." He then proceeded to list five types:

1. ***Hatha Yoga*** (*asanas* and *pranayama*)
2. ***Laya Yoga*** (meditation)
3. ***Bhakti Yoga*** (devotion to God through *namasmarana*, *kirtanam* and singing *bhajans*)
4. ***Nava Vidha Bhakti*** (nine forms of devotion)
5. ***Bhava Bhakti*** (intense love of God).

"One may adopt either one or more of the different types of *yoga*," "Papa" continued. "It is also essential to develop in oneself *Prema* (love) for God. This will certainly relieve a person from stress and diseases will automatically start disappearing." As Dr. Gokak was telling me all this, I watched his face without blinking an eye.

While the three of us dined together, I observed that Mrs. Gokak, my dear *Amma*, had a very fair complexion with sharp features. They were both watching me closely to see whether I had recovered. Suddenly I asked, ""Papa", you have three children of your own, two daughters, and one son – do you love me like your other children?"

"Yes, Baba asked me to adopt you and I love you in the same way as I love my two other daughters and my daughter-in-law."

"Why?", he continued, "The reply is only with Baba. Besides, my third daughter, whom I had lost, would have been the same age as you are now. So, when I saw you, I found my daughter in you. Apart from this, you yourself are a charming child. I would like you to learn *Vedanta*. If needed, I will help you. What I foresee is that Baba wants some good and big acts to be done by both you and me. We should believe in the saying of Baba: **The Fatherhood of God and the Brotherhood of Man**." Dr. Gokak had spoken to me both as a philosopher and as a father.

I spent a moment and probed into the meaning of his words. I realised that I never knew the type of love a father gives his child because I had lost my father when I was hardly an year old. I told Dr. Gokak that from the depths of my heart I considered him as my "Papa", my Divine Father. I wept with happiness. Just as a father would console a crying child, Dr. Gokak consoled me as he handed me some books. Since I was so ill, he gave me a VIP pass that enabled me to be excused from working in the Medical Camp. "Papa" also invited me to join him anytime for breakfast and dinner.

The next day I received a fatherly scolding. My dear "Papa" warned me not to be so worried because stress is the root cause of all my ailments. After hearing this, I revealed to him that since the death of my husband, Dr. A. M. Ghooi the previous year, I found myself quite alone. Two of my three children were already in Medical College and the third awaiting admission. I also explained that Ghooi Hospital in Bhopal was a big one and it was not possible for me to manage it alone. I questioned him about my sudden feeling of loneliness, wondering if it had created so much stress that it caused a rapid development of so many diseases.

A Partnership With God

Dr. Gokak listened to me so peacefully and then explained that Baba is my **Divine Partner (*Adipati*)**. He said that Baba is always with me and I should surrender all my burden to Him, which in turn would relieve me. At that time, it was not easy for me to digest what Dr. Gokak had advised me: a partnership with God! In order to fully understand I questioned him; on one hand, I had worshipped *Swami* as *Avatar* (divine incarnation) and on the other, how could I dare involve Him in my day-to-day work? It appeared as though Dr. Gokak was expecting me to ask a question like this because he responded without hesitation. His answer is forever burning in my mind. He said . . .

> **". . . whether devotee or non-devotee, no one can ever consider maintaining a physical relationship with *Swami*, since He has long ago relinquished His parents, family and all other worldly ties . . ."**

"There is only one way for devotees to maintain a relationship with *Swami* (the God) and it is through an emotional relationship," continued "Papa". "A devotee is free to establish a relationship of mother, father, brother, husband, beloved, friend or even a child with God. These emotional relationships with God are categorised as ***Bhakti*** (devotion) and the devotee, at heart, feels ecstasy through the closeness to his Beloved God."

Dr. Gokak looked at me and paused. Feeling assured that I was avidly listening, he proceeded to tell me that since I lost my husband, I have found myself very lonely on this vast earth. He reiterated that I must adopt one of the forms of *Bhakti* that he had already mentioned and become involved emotionally with God. Maintaining the desired relationship would then make God my Divine Partner. He added that, thereafter, I might shift all my liabilities to God's shoulders and, at the time of need, I should stretch my hands before Him, the Giver of Givers. He will save and give protection against evil-doers.

Dr. Gokak continued to say that more devotion is followed by more faith and more faith is followed by more showers of favour. Purification of the ***Hridayam*** (spiritual heart) requires ***prema*** (love). *Prema* followed by ***dharma*** (right action) not only characterises religion and duty but also, all good acts necessary to develop the personality. This leads to ***santi*** *(*mental peace*)* and a clear conscience. One who has peace of mind and a clear conscience practises ***ahimsa*** (non-violence). This is the way to evaluate Human Values. *Hridayam* is the temple where God is enthroned. Therefore, this temple and the roads leading to the temple must always be kept neat, clean, and pure.

I objected, "But "Papa", it is very difficult to adopt this way of life. As far as Baba is concerned, He is always happy, lovable and merciful. He knows our faults, yet He forgives and loves us. He works physically and mentally day and night. He is always cheerful. Adding the burden of our problems to Baba, by shifting them to Him, will perhaps not be justified."

"He is happy to take up your burden, but before shifting your burden, you will have to uplift yourself from the human and chase the Divinity. Look with love at Him and all His creation," Dr. Gokak said smilingly.

I looked within for some guidance to make a decision. After sometime, I found myself quite relaxed and light hearted. In a decisive tone I said, "Well! This is perhaps *Prabhu-ichcha* (God's Will) that I must take shelter in Him and accept Him as my Divine Partner (*Adipati*) for the remaining life of mine."

Dr. Gokak, my dear "Papa", sighed with relief and said, "My dear child! **God needs only pure *prema*.** Your Guru Nanak sang a number of *bhajans* depicting deep love for God. Mira worshipped God and treated Lord Krishna as her husband. Kabir also did the same. I recall in the year of 1981, when you teased me by singing the songs of some saint, though I don't remember his name." I reminded Dr. Gokak, ""Papa", he is Bulle Shah of North India, renowned Sufi Saint who treated God as his best friend and beloved partner. Bulle Shah expressed his love to God in terms of love songs, which he sang and composed in the style of *rubaiyas*, which are popular now too."

I asked Dr. Gokak why it was only Mira who was harassed and tortured by the members of her royal family because of her intense and immense love towards Lord Krishna, even though physically He did not exist in that era. Dr. Gokak responded by saying, "The only reason behind Mira's torture and harassment was due to the perverted minds of the ignorant men of that age. Even today, this mentality exists because many people do not understand the inner divine love, the pure *prema* – that of a devotee, a *jiva* (individual soul) of the higher level, to his *Aradhya* (chosen God). In fact, each *jiva* ultimately has to merge with God, Lord Vishnu. You must know that Vishnu is the only *Purusha* (Supreme Lord, masculine); whereas all *jivas* are *narees* (female). God is the only *Adipati* (Divine Partner) for everyone. He reflects, reacts and resounds to the *jiva's* emotions. Take the example of Lord Krishna, who had *Satwika Prema* (pure love) towards His *Gopikas* (devotees). In fact, all those *Gopikas* reached a higher level of devotion. This is called *Madhura Bhakti* (sweet devotion). Baba tells us of the stories of Lord Krishna and the *Gopikas*. The *Gopikas* were fascinated by Krishna's pure love. The love that originally vibrated around Lord Krishna created an alluring charm and bright aura, which reflected on the *Gopikas's* faces and bodies. Krishna's love reflected, reacted and resounded from the *Gopikas*."

Divine Love Is Healing

It seemed as if **Divine Love** originated from the body of *Bhagawan* Baba and was reflected all over *Puttaparthi*. I told Dr.

Gokak that even though I had never physically seen Lord Krishna, I could see His beauty in BABA, who Himself is extremely lovable, handsome and charming. After setting your gaze upon BABA, it is very difficult to move your eyes away from him. The heavenly love constantly flows from Him to all around. What the poet Khusro had said is true:

Lali Mere Lal Ki,
Lali Lal Gulal,
Lali Dekhan Main Gayi,
Main Bhi Ho Gai Lal.

(The colour of my Beloved, colours me in the same colour, when I go near my Beloved.)

Dr. Gokak said to me, "The matter does not end here. It is the experience of mine that when we talk about BABA, we draw in the vibrations of love, which others can easily observe. This happened to you when you and your husband, Dr. A. M. Ghooi, came to Mira Cottage in Bangalore in 1979. It was apparent from his face that he was not happy with the changes that occurred in you when we spoke about Baba. He looked quite jealous of Baba. At the time, I advised you not to be emotionally involved with *Swami*. Now, I am recommending it to you because **it is only through an emotional relationship with God that you will get relief from your stress.** This will trigger a physiological change that will cure your body of the diseases from which you suffer. This involvement will certainly uplift all aspects of your body, mind and soul."

I said to myself that I must develop that sort of involvement with *Swami*. I wished to be cured of my diseases and live with my children for a minimum of ten more years.

The Work

Dr. Gokak gave me two books, **Sai *Chandana*** and **The Beacon**, which were published by the World Council of Sri Sathya Sai

Organisation. He told me that Baba has placed a great deal of significance on Human Values. He tells us that most of the problems of the existing world would be solved if people merely followed Human Values, because there is a strong correlation between Human Values and mental health.

The next day Dr. Gokak asked me if I had read his articles in **SAI *CHANDANA*.** I told him that his articles had a profound effect on me and that what surprised me the most was that I felt as if the contents had been written solely for me. "You are looking much better now – free from fever and are light in mind too," said Dr. Gokak. Since his judgment was based on close observation, I accepted it. I told him that I felt as though my burden had been lifted and my inner calm and comfort were restored.

Dr. Gokak said, "If you have faith in Baba and have trust, God is always with you at every step of your life. This will have a direct effect on your mind and body. Your negative thoughts will be replaced by positive thoughts. Enemies will become friends. Your surroundings will become full of life. Your own thoughts will cure you from long pending diseases without medicine."

I virtually started feeling all this within me and was twinkling with joy. ""Papa", if you permit, I would like to comment on a reference in your articles," I said to Dr. Gokak. He was perhaps not ready to hear such a remark from a person like me. However, he looked at me with interest and said, "Go ahead."

"In your article, 'A Sathya Sai Addition to Sathya Sai Theory of Integral Education,' you made a correlation with Human Values and the brain. Typically, people do not know from where the intuition comes. Most of the cerebral cortex functions are not yet known. The emotional part of the brain does not exist in the cerebral cortex but, rather, in the mid-brain and **Limbic System**, which is hidden under the cerebral cortex. The mid-brain, hypothalamus, thalamus, and limbic system, in combination, form the Emotional Centre, which Baba calls ***Hridayam*** (spiritual heart). This is the portion of the brain responsible for all instincts, emotions and motivations such as love, compassion, sex, anger, hatred, shame and jealousy. It is very clear that purity of thought, emotions and actions clear up the *Hridayam* which is the seat of *Sat-Chit-Ananda* (cosmic energy in the brain)."

"I never knew that you knew so much about Human Values. I am happy that you have sufficient knowledge of the subject. I am surprised that you have been delaying the work of compiling the medical aspects of Baba's lectures in a book. Hence, you must do it as soon as possible. I will edit your book," said Dr. Gokak.

"My best efforts will be to fulfill your desire, "Papa"," I replied. However, within my mind, there was a storm of thoughts. Being a medical doctor, I knew that my body was suffering from a number of diseases, which were day-by-day shortening the span of my life. The undertaking of writing a book seemed to be an impossible venture. I also cursed myself for thinking that right from 1975, I had been disappointing my "Papa" who placed false hopes in my abilities. It seemed as if he had x-ray eyes that could penetrate my mind and allow him to read my thoughts.

"Cheer up my child. Be happy under all circumstances. Feel that God is always with you. Baba will solve all your problems. Do not think that you are alone. Your *Swami* is always with you," said Dr. Gokak as he consolingly gazed at me with eyes filled with love.

Renewal Of Health

After returning from my trip to *Puttaparthi*, I changed my daily routine and started practising *Yoga*. This improved my health without the use of medicine. It took some time, but the improvement in my health became permanent. Today, I find myself fully energetic and free from most of my diseases. During this span of time, my three books were published:

- **SPIRITUALITY AND HEALTH** published by the Sri Sathya Sai Books & Publication Trust.
- ***BHAKTI* AND HEALTH** published by the Sri Sathya Sai Books & Publication Trust.
- ***VEDANTIC* METHODS AND VIRTUOUS CHILDREN**, published privately.

From September 1991 onwards, I had to face many situations, which were very disturbing and yet created in me more faith in the omnipresence of Sri Sathya Sai Baba. I learned to trust His timely and unexpected Divine help in solving my seemingly insurmountable problems. I was first shocked in 1991 when my elder son, Dr. Anand Ghooi, was on his deathbed with an extremely remote chance of recovery. My second shock was in 1992 when Dr. V. K. Gokak, my divine father, died on the 28th of April. The third shock was due to the passing away of his wife, Mrs. Sharada Gokak, my divine mother. I was devastated for the fourth time in April of 1995 when my elder son was again on his deathbed, yet was miraculously saved. It is worth mentioning here that it was only *Swami*, who by His Divine Grace had twice brought life to my ailing son. On April 30, 1995, my biological mother died. In 1998, I lost my elder son from this worldly existence. Only with the help of my *Adipati*, Sai Baba, I was able to handle these series of painful events. *Swami* continues to send me all the necessary love and energy to bear with these ups and downs of life.

Through all my early years with *Swami* I was never physically close to Him, either through interviews or physical interactions, but He was looking after me very well. Lovingly, He was seeing to it that all my daily needs were beautifully met, as well as chiselling me and refining me, making me what I am today. What I did have was the good *karma* to know many blessed souls, such as the late Dr. V. K. Gokak, Dr. Bhagwat, cardiologist, Dr. Alreja, the present superintendent of the Sri Sathya Sai General Hospital, and other friends whom *Swami* called for interviews. They became the direct physical link between *Swami* and me, delivering my letters to *Swami* and His responses back to me. Time and again, *Swami* used them to let me know that He was aware of my every thought and my every need and was looking after me all the time. After my eldest son died, this became even more pronounced. I was alone, my husband had passed away and my other children were overseas. Alone physically, but truly, never alone – *Swami* knew of my needs. It was then that He called me into His presence to serve at the Sri Sathya Sai General Hospital. If you can imagine, I refused three times! Finally *Swami* sent a direct order I could not refuse, "Tell her to lock the hospital and come. She is alone and unsafe!" Needless to say I hurried to Puttaparthi.

When I arrived in Prasanthi Nilayam to begin work, *Swami* ignored me completely. I expected some familiar interaction from His physical form. But for five long years He didn't talk to me at all. There was not even a glance at darshan to let me know He knew I had come. I started feeling as if He didn't know me at all. However, I learned from other sources that He was quite aware of me. In addition, I did not want anything and whatever I needed literally arrived at my doorstep. Only God could have such intimate knowledge of my needs and how to meet them. If people will take Him to heart and believe, they will realise that *Swami* is fully omnipresent and the true ***Adipati*** (Divine partner) – not just for me, but for every one.

With Love,

Dr. (Mrs.) Charanjit Ghooi
Prasanthi Nilayam,
Puttaparthi, India

It is when you relinquish your limited individuality and recognise the principle of Divinity which is inherent within you that all your weaknesses will leave you and you develop broadness of mind that will finally culminate in your mergence with the Lord. How can you gain this understanding of your Divine nature? It is only through steady practice that you will acquire realisation.

~ **Sri Sathya Sai Baba**

introduction

Bhagawan Sri Sathya Sai Baba, *Avatar* of the *Kaliyuga,* has taken birth on earth to lead humankind toward humanness. Today, though man is born as a human being, he has descended to the animal level. "The word 'HUMAN'," Sai Baba tells us, "is full of significance:

'H' stands for 'high Human Values'.

'U' stands for 'understanding of human sanctity.'

'M' stands for 'mindful of one's duty'.

'A' stands for '*ananda*' (bliss).

'N' stands for the name of God'."[1]

As a humble servant of my Beloved *Swami*, I have created this compilation of His teachings on Human Values that relate to health. This I have intermingled with information on human anatomy, physiology and psychology, in the hopes that readers grasp the inter-relatedness of body, mind and spirit. According to Sai Baba, "Human Being is a combination of Body + Mind + *Atma* (Divine Soul)."

Sri Sathya Sai Baba says:

"What are these Human Values? People simply utter the names of Human Values: *Sathya, Dharma, Santi, Prema, Ahimsa.*

These come only from the lips, but true Human Values come from birth.

- ***Sathya*** (Truth) is that which must be said.
- ***Dharma*** (Righteousness) is that which has to be practised.
- ***Santi*** (Peace) is that which has to be experienced.
- ***Prema*** (Love) is our true nature it should be practised and shared.
- ***Ahimsa*** (Nonviolence) is staying away from violence. [2]

"Human Values are born with man," says Baba. "They are not got from outside. Man in his ignorance is not aware of these Values. When man sheds his ignorance, he will experience his divine nature." [3]

Making The Most Of This Book

The purpose of **Human Values And Health** is to aid readers in creating and maintaining health through the adoption of Human Values as a way of life, thereby creating a pure mind, which is necessary for the realisation of the *Atma*. It is not intended to be a medical compendium, but rather a collection of *Bhagawan* Sri Sathya Sai Baba's teachings that correlate Human Values with the establishment of health.

Readers who are familiar with my previous books, **Spirituality And Health** and ***Bhakti* And Health** will note that many of the chapter titles here are similar or the same. What to do? The human body is what it is. But, whereas those books dealt with *Bhagawan*'s teachings on health as they related to spirituality and *bhakti* respectively, this book explores the impact that the practice of Human Values has on human health. So while some chapter titles remain unchanged, the material is presented in a different way.

Gracious *Swami* offers His teachings to us in a variety of ways, giving us many opportunities to practise them and be transformed. Readers may find either repetition or omissions in the text; please accept my humble apologies. I lack the courage to change *Swami's* words. How grateful we have to be to Him, who gives us so much.

Scientific information has been interwoven to enhance the understanding and practice of Human Values. This book is not meant to be theoretical only. I hope it will become for others what it has been for me – a useful tool for daily refinement of character. I say from personal experience that the practice of Human Values transforms poor health to good health at all levels – spiritual, mental, emotional, physical and social.

The text includes both *Sanskrit* and medical terms. These have been defined when they first appear. Thereafter, I hope the readers will refer to the glossary that has been included in the back of the book.

Hridayam And Limbic System

A major focus of this book is on purification of the ***Hridayam,*** Sri Sathya Sai Baba's name for the spiritual heart in man, through the practice of Human Values. Medically speaking, *Hridayam* correlates to the **Limbic System** in the human brain which is the collective name for the **corpus callosum, thalamus, hypothalamus, amygdala, hippocampus, olfactory lobe, right frontal lobe, right inferior temporal lobe** (of the brain) and **pituitary** and **pineal bodies.** Although from different systems of the human anatomy, these structures are interrelated and together are responsible for behaviour and emotions. The limbic system forms a sort of a borderland between the older, less evolved parts of the brain, mainly involved with instincts, drives and automatic regulation of body processes, and the highly evolved, uniquely human brain areas, associated with the cerebral cortex, which permit advanced reasoning and planning. The nuclei that cognise love, hatred, compassion, envy, jealousy, anger, lust, greed, patience, forbearance, sex and other emotional states are situated in the limbic system. Purification of these nuclei is very important to the development of humanness and spirituality.

Human Brain, The Seat Of The Soul

The human brain is the seat of the ***Atma*** and the ***Hiranyagarbha*** (womb of pure creation, the birthplace of the cosmos). The *Atma* is a spark of the same effulgence as the *Paramatma* (Universal Soul) and it contains the same qualities, or characteristics, which are:

- *Nirmal* (eternally pure)
- *Buddhi* (wisdom)
- *Mukta* (internally liberated)
- *Nirajana* (eternally content)
- *Sanathana* (eternally existing)
- *Sathyaswarupa* (embodiment of truth)
- *Nikethana* (dwelling everywhere and nowhere)
- *Nirgunam* (without attributes)

When the embodied *Atma* is separated from God, it remains linked with Him through a silver cord. Life energy flows through this cord, sustaining man's life and health.[4]

Only when the brain and nervous system have been purified by Human Values will you be able to manifest these *Atmic* qualities and reach a state of total health. In Sanskrit, the term for this is *Atmajnana* (awareness of the *Atma* or self-realisation), but it is also a physiological event, as modern science has discovered. The study of the brain and nervous system is very important since they conduct our thoughts and emotions as well as the life force energy, called ***Prana Sakti*** (*chi* in China, *ki* in Japan, *manna* in Hawaiian and *Holy Spirit* to Christians). Efficiently inter-linked nerve fibers supply every cell in the body with *prana*. This vital energy permeates all living beings and is truly the sustainer of life in the body.

Seat Of Divine Guidance

Atma resides in the *Hridayam,* where it is also referred to as *Purusha*, *Neotis, Sai Tathwa* and *Sat-Chit-Ananda.* In English the word is **Soul**. *Hridayam* is situated behind the mid-brow and interpenetrates the limbic system on a subtle level. This area also corresponds to one of the energy centres in the subtle body called ***Chakras*** (literally "wheel"). The name of this *chakra* is "*Ajna*", which in Sanskrit means, "Command of the *Guru* or Lord". This is our control centre, our **conscience**, the seat of the soul and the direct recipient of Divine guidance. If this area is muddied or blocked by negative thoughts, impure speech or unhealthy actions, so too is our channel of communication with our Highest Guru, God.

Therefore, purification of the *Hridayam* through the practice of Human Values is essential. A purified *Hridayam* allows light from the Higher Self to reach the limbic system, which in turn sends messages of health and wholeness throughout the physical body. This impacts not just our own health, but also the environment through which we move. To paraphrase Baba:

> **When there is Purity in the *Hridayam*,**
> **There is Beauty in the Character,**
> **When there is Beauty in the Character,**
> **There is Harmony in the Home,**
> **When there is Harmony in the Home,**
> **There is Order in the Nation,**
> **When there is Order in the Nation,**
> **There is Peace in the World.**

Akasa (Ether Or Space)

The element related to *Ajnachakra* is ***Akasa*** and it is through *akasa* that thought waves move. Thought waves are energy and the all-pervasive *akasa*, also known as space or ether, is the substance through which all the elements draw the life force energy, the *prana sakti*. *Akasa* is not visible to the naked eye and no scientist has been able to make an instrument enabling us to see *akasa*.[5] However, if you understand how transmitted radio waves and cell phone signals can be received across long distances, you can easily grasp how a thought wave, moving through *akasa*, can have impact on a material object. *Akasa* is one of the *Panchamahabhutas* (five basic elements), which are discussed below.

Sai Baba's teachings tell us that there are many unknown subtle energies in the *akasa*. Some of the known energies are magnetism, gravitation, radiation, radio and television waves and, of course, *prana sakti*. There are actually trillions upon trillions of vibrations found in the *akasa*, including the vibrations emanating from the rays of the many suns, planets and moons. Vibrations, which are subtle in nature, permeate the atmosphere and affect the human body, making it healthy or sick.[6]

The *Panchamahabhutas*

The *Panchamahabhutas* (five basic elements) are other carriers of energy. In addition to ***Akasa*** (ether or space), there are ***Vayu*** (Air), ***Agni*** (Fire), ***Jala*** (Water) and ***Prithivi*** (Earth). Further, these *Panchamahabhutas* make up the animal kingdom, plant kingdom, mineral kingdom and the human body. As Guru Nanak said, *"Jo Brahmande Soyee Pinde* (Macro-cosmos is in Micro-cosmos)". In turn, the human body is made up of trillions of cells whereby a single cell represents the whole body. Scientists have proved this fact with genetic engineering by the successful cloning of sheep.[7]

About the five elements Sri Sathya Sai Baba says, "Wherever you look, whether it be here on earth or in heaven, or even in the netherworld, everything that you can ever find anywhere is made up of some combination of the five elements and only the five elements. Nothing else exists."[8]

These five elements take a subtle form when they enter the human body, becoming **sound, touch, form, taste** and **smell**. It is the human sense organs (**ear, skin, eye, mouth** and **nose**), which perceive the *panchamahabhutas* in their subtle forms, and hence create a bridge between the inner and outer experience of man. One of the great challenges of life is maintaining a healthy balance of these elements in our body, mind and environment. It is the imbalance of the elements in either their gross or subtle forms that produce disease. More details can be found on this in Chapter 2.

The five elements, Sathya Sai Baba tells us, "are the vesture of God as well as man. Use them with wisdom, fear and humility[9]... use them intelligently to promote the welfare of yourself and others; use them with moderation and with the ideal of loving service to the community, to all. They are all free and full of precious potentiality. Appreciate the plenty and the preciousness. You know from experience that excessive quantities of wind or fire or water are injurious to health. Drinking more water than is needed is a torture; inhaling more air is suffocating; fire in moderation can warm or serve to heat and melt but beyond a certain limit, it is a holocaust. Even sound and light, beyond certain limits is a calamity; they are weapons which can distract and drive people mad. So efficient use of these is itself a form of worship."[10]

Total Health

In order to understand health, one must know the definition of health. Health is man's normal condition, living in accordance with the natural laws pertaining to the body, mind, soul and environment. The World Health Organisation (WHO) has said that man should be healthy Physically, Mentally, Emotionally, Socially and Spiritually. Mere absence of disease is not health. Man should have complete wellbeing in all these areas.

Sri Sathya Sai Baba says:

"For the achievement of the four main goals of life (right conduct, wealth, fulfillment of desires and liberation) health is essential. Without good health man cannot accomplish even the most trivial thing. Hence, health is wealth. For every man two things are essential: Good health and bliss. Health for the body and bliss for the spirit. With these two wings you can soar to any height." [11]

There is a parallel between the theory of total health and the principles of Human Values found in the teachings of Sri Sathya Sai Baba and the fundamental teachings of Lord Rama, Lord Krishna, Jesus Christ, Lord Buddha, Guru Nanak, Zoroaster, Shirdi Sai Baba and Mohammed. Human Values not only make up the very fabric of a healthy body, but also a healthy society. It is essential that one lives according to healthy Human Values or else psychological disorders, which cause **75%** of all physical disease, will result. Previous *karmas* (actions) too, play an important role in determining one's fate. Many congenital diseases are caused from the effects of the bad *karmas* done in prior births.

The psychic area of the brain, the Mind, is responsible for self-realisation and it is also to blame for physical as well as psychological diseases. Let me describe the characteristics of the human body and the way to achieve total health. Basically, man should be healthy at the following levels:

1. **Mental** and **Spiritual**
2. **Emotional**
3. **Physical** (including sleep, sex, food & the five senses)

These levels are not in reality separate and distinct but rather, there is complete interaction among them. As Sai Baba says, "People are made up of awareness, the vital force, and the body, the material substance. Vibration is the expression of the vital force. **In every action there is a vibration, which is between the consciousness and the physical body.**" [12]

The degree of health or disease of the individual can be evaluated as follows:

1. The Mental And Spiritual Levels

The highest and the most important levels through which the human being functions are the mental and spiritual. As a general definition, we can say that the mental level of an individual registers changes in understanding or consciousness through thinking, criticising, comparing, calculating, classifying, creating, synthesising, conjecturing, visualising, planning, describing, communicating, and so forth. Disturbances of these functions, in turn, constitute symptoms of mental illness.[13]

The mental level is the most crucial for the human being. **It is the mental and spiritual content of a person, which is the true essence of that person**. If the inner tools of attaining a higher consciousness on the mental or spiritual levels are disturbed, the possibility of an evolution in consciousness is lost. Where then is the meaning of human life? A person can live happily and be of creative service to himself and others, being physically impaired, no matter how crippled the body is – even with loss of limbs, loss of sight, or loss of hearing. Although the physical body is the medium through which the higher faculties can manifest themselves in this material world, its maintenance in health cannot become an end in itself. If it were possible to have an absolutely healthy mind, we would see people who live continually in spiritual bliss, daily revealing new creative ideas expressed in a very clear way and who are always of service to others. Such people would be living constantly in the clearness of light and never be in the confusion of spiritual darkness.

The **three indispensable qualities** that should accompany the different aspects of Mind are:

- Clarity
- Rationality, coherence and logical sequence
- Creative service for the good of others as well as for the good of oneself

All these three qualities must be present, but the third is of prime importance, which is the quality of creative service. Take the example of a master criminal who is highly intelligent and plans a theft or murder with the utmost degree of clarity and rationality. Yet, this person is ill in the deepest regions of his being because he is pursuing selfish goals at the expense of others, instead of pursuing good creative service for them. Such mentality pervades our modern world to an extreme degree and is the root cause of the problems of competition, violence, alcohol and drug abuse, poverty and war. Rather, there is a continuous degradation – a mental degeneration starting from selfishness and possessiveness, leading to insanity.

Disturbing thoughts or **feelings** can completely disrupt the health of a person. An unexpected grief, a sudden fear, an abrupt communication of bad news can lead an individual into extreme suffering that may even incapacitate that person for an entire lifetime. When we examine the source of mental or emotional suffering, we find that such suffering arises from two basic sources, unfulfilled ambitions and broken attachments. It may also be referred to as selfishness and acquisitiveness (greed). In order for a person to avoid mental and emotional suffering, he or she should cultivate selfless, humble and altruistic qualities and, as Sathya Sai Baba says,"**Love All and Serve All with Love".**[14]

2. The Emotional Level

This is the level of human existence which registers changes in emotional states. Emotions have a wide range of expression: love/hate, joy/sadness, calmness/anxiety, trust/mistrust, courage/fear, etc. The emotional level is unique to each individual, as feelings play a very important role in the life of every human being. According to their quality, feelings can be defined as positive or negative.

- **Positive Feelings:** Those that tend to draw the individual towards a state of happiness.
- **Negative Feelings:** Those that tend to draw the individual towards a state of unhappiness.

There is a correlation between the experience of positive and negative feelings and the state of one's health. The more an individual feels or experiences negative feelings, the more unhealthy he or she becomes. In order to measure the degree of emotional disturbances of a person, find out how much in his waking state he is occupied with negative feelings such as apathy, irritability, anxiety, anguish, depression, suicidal thoughts, jealousy, hatred, envy, etc. The individual who is more highly evolved emotionally experiences some of the most profound states known to mankind such as mystical experiences, bliss, pure love, compassion, devotion and a wide range of sublime feelings.

Generally, imbalances on the emotional plane manifest themselves as a heightened sensitivity to the sense of oneself as being vulnerable and separate from the rest of creation. Emotionally disturbed states tend to revolve around egoistic issues of personal comfort, personal survival and personal expression. On the other hand, the most evolved emotional states tend to involve feelings of Oneness with all creation resulting in feelings of love, bliss and devotion. Thus, positive feelings in an individual will always tend to create a sense of unification with the whole world, whereas negative feelings tend to produce a sense of isolation and separation from it.

As one can suffer from negative thoughts on the Mental Level one can have negative feelings on the Emotional Level. If we strengthen the inner emotional state and create a positive condition, it will enhance our communications with people and in turn serve the community. When someone expresses trust in another, this very act facilitates that person's spiritual growth and creates harmony between the two individuals. On the other hand, an expression of anger or mistrust creates a disharmonious emotional state for everyone and, in this way, adds to the unpleasant environment. One who lives with feelings of inner calm, joy, bliss, etc., provides the best possible emotional environment for the nourishment of himself and others. Conversely, one who lives with feelings of anxiety, sadness, or fear provides an emotionally poisonous environment with toxic sustenance for him and others. The result of these two types of feelings is obvious. Feelings of joy enhance life, whereas feelings of anxiety reduce it.

3. The Physical Level

In the physical body, freedom from pain is a sign of a state of wellbeing. The gross physical body and its organs constitute the least important plane of the human being. **The body itself maintains a hierarchy of importance in its organs and functions.** The diseases of the brain are more serious than that of the heart. An infarct (blockage) of the brain will be more significant than an infarct of the heart, which in turn is more significant than a thrombosis (blockage) of an artery in the leg. The organism will always try to keep disturbances away from important organs, the brain, heart, pituitary gland, liver, lungs, kidneys and spinal cord. The least important organs are the muscles and skin.

The physical body has been well explored by Allopathic doctors through surgery, electron microscopes, ultra-sonography, Electroencephalography (E.E.G.), Electrocardiography (E.C.G.), X-ray, and even Kirlian photography. Acupuncture, Acupressure, and Homeopathy explore the body by the analysis of mental symptoms. Magnetotherapy, too, has its own curative field. Various methods of *pranic* healing have become popular and hypnosis is being utilised for many ailments including insomnia and psychological disorders. But *avatars* deal expertly with the state of human health through devotional practices that purify the mind, leading to purity of the body. *Japa* (repeating the name of God), *Dhyana* (meditation), *Bhajans* (devotional singing), *Satsang* (good company), any of the *Yogas – Jnana, Karma, Bhakti* or *Hatha* – are examples of such practices.

The reading of traditional books written by *avatars*, *gurus*, and *rasuls*, such as the ***Ramayana, Bhagavad Gita, Adi Guru Granth Sahib,*** the ***Holy Quran*** and the ***Holy Bible*** primarily teach Human Values and promote good mental health. All the Saints and Sages who have seen Godly Light or achieved Self-Realisation, have emphasised the same path of Human Values in different languages – love all, be truthful, do not fight or kill anyone, love your neighbours, respect your parents, country, friends and relatives, and help all in need.

- Freedom from Negative Thoughts is Mental Health.
- Freedom from Negative Feeling is Emotional Health.
- Freedom from Pain is Physical Health.
- Freedom from Ego is *Bhakti*.
- Freedom from Desire is Liberation. [15]

The Nervous System And Other Systems

The nervous system is the conduit for cosmic energy from the *Atma* to the physical body's master control centres in the brain, hence the study of its inter-relatedness to the other systems of the body is of great importance.

NERVOUS SYSTEM: The nervous system may be compared to a big powerhouse that generates electricity and has a network of wires that distributes the electricity to the different machines in a factory. The brain, the spinal cord and the sympathetic nerve cords constitute the powerhouse. The nerves, as they start from the brain and proceed through the spinal cord and sympathetic nervous system, act like electrical wires in a factory. In a regular factory, every piece of machinery is set in motion by the electric current carried to it through the wires from the powerhouse. Similarly, in the factory of the human body every physical movement depends upon the impulses carried by the nerves from the brain and sympathetic nervous system. Let the powerhouse go out of order, or let there be an obstruction, and all the machinery will come to a standstill. Similarly, if the brain or the spinal cord is damaged, or the nerves are so degenerated that they do not convey the impulses, then physical movement will cease. The cessation of physical movement has a deeper effect than we might first imagine. Our digestive system, circulatory system, renal system, respiratory system and our endocrine system are all controlled and maintained by nerve impulses brought to the organs responsible for these systems via the brain and the nerves. **If the nerve impulses do not start or do not reach their destination, all life processes will cease, and even death will result.**

LIMBIC SYSTEM/*HRIDAYAM:* Situated as it is behind the mid-brow, the *Hridayam* may also be compared to a powerhouse that generates electricity, with wires that conduct that electricity to their terminals. It, too, must have electrical current that is of sufficient strength to run its machinery. The electrical current that powers the *Hridayam* is *prana sakti* – and that comes from the *Atma*. In a *Hridayam* purified by Human Values, the wires conduct smoothly and this *prana* streams forth into its correspondent in the brain, the limbic system, thereby purifying it. A purified limbic system leads to better secretion of the pituitary gland, the master gland of the endocrine system. The whole nervous system may be in perfect order physiologically, and yet if the *prana sakti* of the *Atma* cannot get through to the limbic system to signal the appropriate endocrine secretions, the strength of the nerve impulses and eventually the nerves themselves will degenerate. Consequently, physical movement and life processes will become slow and eventually even cease.

ENDOCRINE SYSTEM: This is the regulatory system of the body, which secretes hormones through the bloodstream from seven ductless glands, each of which corresponds to seven *chakras* (energy centres in man's subtle bodies). However, for our discussion, let us stay on a physical level and consider the example of the thyroid gland; it is the most well known of the endocrine glands. Remove the thyroid from the healthy person and his eyes become pale, his cheeks begin to sink, his muscles become flabby or lean, his hair begins to turn gray and he becomes subject to premature aging. Restore the thyroid and the man begins to show all the signs of youthful enthusiasm. The symptoms of old age disappear, the person begins to walk erect, his outlook brightens up, and life again becomes a pleasure. Thus, it becomes apparent that the endocrine system stands on the same level of physiological importance as the nervous system. From the direct connection of endocrine glands with man's subtle bodies through the *chakras*, it is clear that the endocrine system responds very quickly to an influx of *prana sakti*.

CIRCULATORY SYSTEM: The study of human physiology clearly indicates that these two systems, endocrine and nervous, are of infinite importance in the human organism. Yet, they have to depend upon the circulatory system for getting the necessary supply of blood and upon the respiratory and the digestive systems for getting the necessary quality of blood. The circulatory system consists of the heart, the arteries, the veins and the capillaries. It is the duty of the circulatory system to carry the blood supply and if it degenerates in its functions, the results are disastrous. It is, however, of no practical use to have the circulatory system in an efficient condition, if the quality of the blood that is being circulated through it is not rich. If the blood is loaded with toxins, the efficiency of the circulatory system will be of little consequence.

RESPIRATORY & DIGESTIVE SYSTEMS: In order that the blood may be rich in quality, it must carry the necessary quantity of oxygen and contain the elements of nutrition for the tissues. The blood gets oxygen from the air inhaled and the elements of nutrition from food and drink. The quantity of oxygen in the blood depends mainly upon the efficiency of the Respiratory System. With defective respiration, the absorption of oxygen into the blood is deficient and the tissues supplied by the blood will be starved of oxygen. One may ingest rich food and luxuriant drinks, but if the digestive apparatus is not in order, there will be little digestion and absorption and most of the food will be wasted, resulting in blood that contains very little nutrition. If both the respiratory and digestive systems are malfunctioning, they also load the blood with waste matter that is poisonous.

ELIMINATORY SYSTEMS: The efficiently working circulatory system carries carbon dioxide to the lungs where it is released through exhalation. If, however, the efficacy of this system suffers, waste matter accumulates in the different tissues and causes dangerous toxicity. Similarly, food leaves large amounts of waste for the bowels to excrete. **The poorer the quality of digestion and absorption, the larger the amount of waste.** And if the bowels, which are a part of the digestive track, do not work efficiently, the waste matter remains lodged in the colon or even in the small intestine for several days, also giving rise to other highly dangerous toxins. The toxins get into the blood through the walls of the bowels and poison the blood circulated throughout the body, leading to the degeneration of the whole organism.

The kidneys too are organs of elimination. Some of the poisonous waste products are also carried out of the human organism with the urine. If the kidneys do not function satisfactorily, poisons are retained in the body and settle primarily in the different joints. People suffering from gout invariably have defective kidneys.

Thus far, we have reviewed some of the broadest features of the most important physiological systems on which the health and harmonious functioning of the human body depends.

NERVOUS SYSTEM AND *VEDANTA*

During the compilation of this book, **HUMAN VALUES AND HEALTH,** I tried to gather all I could from *Vedpurusha* (God of the ***VEDAS***) *Bhagawan* Sri Sathya Sai Baba's Divine Discourses. I am humbly relating relevant excerpts in this section on the Brain and Nervous System.

Sri Sathya Sai Baba says:

The ***Hridayam*** resides behind the mid-brow [at the limbic system level of the brain – **SEE COVER DIAGRAM, PAGE IX**]. A*vatars, rasuls*, seers and sages of India and throughout the world have all given names to the spark of cosmic energy. *Atma, Purusha, Hiranyagarbha, Sat-Chit-Ananda, Neotis, Tao* or *Sai Tathwa* are just a few. The nuclei of emotions, behaviour and ideas lie within this area of the brain. It is a place of Effulgent Light. When meditating, *yogis* experience this light, which is extraordinarily soothing and much more luminous than the sun. It can be called the cosmic power supply station or the seat of the *Atma* or Divine Soul and is on the right side of the brain. The Soul radiates cosmic energy first to the brain, which then pulsates it to the entire body through the rest of the brain, nerves and nerve fibers to give *prana sakti* to all the organs of the body.[16]

The area that surrounds this system where vibrations start is called *Buddhi* (or *Vijnanamaya Kosa* [*Kosa*=sheath], a field of energy functioning as intellect or wisdom) which takes light from the *Atma* (*Sat-Chit-Ananda*). After *Buddhi*, the cosmic energy is surrounded by a mental and emotional field of energy called *Manomaya Kosa.* The *Manomaya Kosa* is vibrating according to the individuated thoughts, sensations, emotions and *karmas* of a person. It is made up of thoughts, good and bad, of which man is capable of fifty million. Each individual brain cell cannot be acquainted with all the thoughts, which are passing through the brain as a whole. Man's thoughts come and go like passing clouds having no effect on the human brain. But when they are allowed to stay and stir things up for long periods of time, these prolonged thoughts form definite grooves in the brain that produce different types of **neuropeptides**, leading to different types of behaviour and actions by the human body, causing good and bad *karmas*. It is, therefore, essential that man purifies himself on the thought level. Thoughts are the real psyche of man and form the Mind of human beings.[17]

The Human Mind

The Mind operates at many levels of the human brain as follows:

1. **THE REPTILE LEVEL** of the brain is called the Subconscious Mind (*Chittha*) and it functions below waking consciousness. Circulation, digestion and respiration are all part of the automatic system of the body, which operates through this part of the Brain.

2. **THE LIMBIC SYSTEM** is the level where the Ego Mind functions. It gets sensations from the external world through the *Pancha Jnanendriyas* (sense organs: eyes, ears, nose, mouth, hands, skin) and the *Pancha Karmendriyas* (working organs: vocal organs, hands and legs, genitals, bladder and anus), which in turn feed this system. Impulses and sensations arise from the higher brain, the Cerebrum, and feed the limbic system. Human emotions and behaviours function in this mind. All this together creates the *Ahamkara* (ego mind).

3. **THE CEREBRUM LEVEL** of the human brain is more highly developed than any other level of the brain. It has qualities of the Higher Mind; this portion of the Brain is connected with what is called Super Mind, Illuminated Mind, or Over Mind.

Cosmic energy is distributed from the brain to the nerves, providing *prana* to every organ and cell of the body, thus *prana* keeps the body alive. There is a wireless system supplying *pranic* energy to the body through the channels called ***Nadis***. These are energy channels in the subtle body that connect the vast network of great and tiny *chakras*.

All the sensations from the *Pancha Jnanendriyas* and the *Pancha Karmendriyas* go to the thalamus level and fill the entire limbic system. These sensations are then fed into the cortex of the brain and stored there, forming impulses which come back from birth to birth. The good impulses are found in the higher area of the mind called *Buddhi*.

The Impact Of Thoughts On Human Body

Sri Sathya Sai Baba says:

When thought impulses and ideas come from *Paramatma* (supreme soul) to the cerebrum, they are called intuitions. [AUTHOR'S NOTE: A good clean limbic system, which is the seat of the *Hridayam*, is capable of catching those intuitions from *Paramatma.*] When the stored thoughts or the impressions from the five senses lead to emotions such as anger, hatred, jealousy, envy, fear, love and compassion, they cause different colours of the **aura** (energy field) around the physical body, called the **Bioplasmic Body** (subtle body, also called astral body) **[See Diagram No. 1]**. The *prana sakti* is either discharged through bad thoughts or charged with good thoughts. The impact of good and bad impulses can be observed by the effect they have on the faces of individuals – making them appear either ugly or beautiful depending upon their thoughts. A person entertaining negative thoughts creates holes or leaks in the Bioplasmic Body through which *prana sakti* is lost, inducing illness. Bad thoughts attract bad vibrations from the atmosphere and promote psychological disorders, even to the extent of schizophrenia, thoughts of suicide, murder and other crimes.[18]

The Bioplasmic Body Of Man

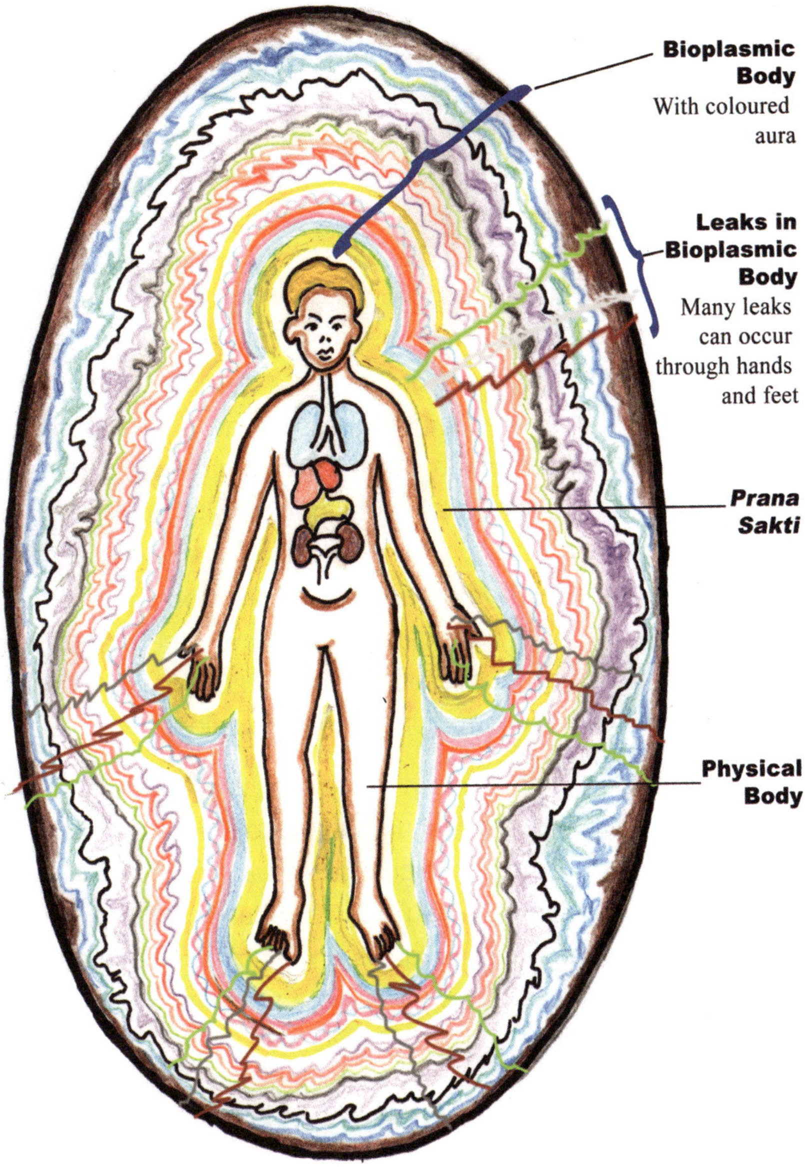

Human Values And Health ~ Diagram No. 1

Source: Bhagawan Sri Sathya Sai Baba, **Summer Showers In Brindavan, 1990.**

Likewise, good thoughts will draw forth good and vital *pranic* energy from the atmosphere and from deep within your own soul. This good energy is also discharged into the environment. Hands and feet are big transmitters of energy and while they leak negativity from a negative person, they also radiate love and positive vibrations from a good person. This is the reason why devotees yearn to touch the hands and feet of their guru and even the ground they walk upon.

Sri Sathya Sai Baba continues:

The body is a world in itself. It is not merely the outer form. It is the collective assemblage of many organs and limbs. Each organ has its own beauty, which has to be fostered. A weak and unhealthy body is incapable of any resolute action. Pure, noble, and sublime ideas can emanate only from a strong and healthy body. All religions are agreed on this point. Although you may have body-consciousness, your lives should be guided by the *Atmic* awareness. The **body,** the **senses,** the **mind,** the **intellect** and the ***Atma*** are to be considered as your five-breaths *(pancha pranas)*. Once you have understood the mysteries or subtleties of each of them you need no other spiritual discipline.[19]

Health does not depend on medicines. Good words, good manners, good sights, good thoughts – these are essential. What can even powerful or costly medicines do if one is ill with bad thoughts and bad feelings? On the other hand, virtuous living, beneficial thoughts, elevating ideals and righteous conduct can confer not only health, but what is more precious, *Atmananda*, the ecstatic awareness of the Reality itself.[20]

Love All, Serve All, Realise All

Human Values, then, has a great role to play, not just in helping individuals develop Total Health and humanness, but in bringing out the Total Health in society. On a deeper level, I pray that as we practise "Love All, Serve All" we can discover that ***we are ALL***. It is my humble wish that this book will provide some inspiration for readers to accelerate their efforts to this end.

Sri Sathya Sai Baba says:

> *What the world needs today is neither a new order nor a new education nor a new system nor a new religion. The remedy lies in a new mind, in a heart filled with holiness. Holiness must take root and grow in the minds and hearts of people everywhere. The good and Godly must endeavour to promote this task as the one great spiritual work they have to undertake.*[21]

---

1 *Bhagawan* Sri Sathya Sai Baba, Divine Discourse, 10/03/1994.
2 *Bhagawan* Sri Sathya Sai Baba, Divine Discourse, 20/11/1993.
3 *Bhagawan* Sri Sathya Sai Baba, ***Santhana Sarathi***, May 1995.
4 Aurobindo, Sri, **The Life Divine**.
5 *Bhagawan* Sri Sathya Sai Baba, reference unknown.
6 Vivakananda, *Swami*, ***Raja Yoga.***
7 *Bhagawan* Sri Sathya Sai Baba, reference unknown.
8 *Bhagawan* Sri Sathya Sai Baba, **Discourses on the *Bhagavad Gita***, Ch. 17, 1984.
9 *Bhagawan* Sri Sathya Sai Baba, **Sathya Sai Speaks – Vol 6,** Ch. 27.
10 *Bhagawan* Sri Sathya Sai Baba, **Sathya Sai Speaks – Vol 5,** Ch. 45.
11 *Bhagawan* Sri Sathya Sai Baba, Divine Discourse, 03/06/1995.
12 *Bhagawan* Sri Sathya Sai Baba, **Sathya Sai Newsletter, USA**, Spring 1994.
13 Hahnemann, Dr. Samuel, **Organon of Homeopathy**.
14 Author, **Spirituality & Health**.
15 Author, **Spirituality & Health**.
16 *Bhagawan* Sri Sathya Sai Baba, reference unknown.
17 *Bhagawan* Sri Sathya Sai Baba, reference unknown.
18 *Bhagawan* Sri Sathya Sai Baba, reference unknown.
19 *Bhagawan* Sri Sathya Sai Baba, **Summer Showers, 1990**, Ch. 3.
20 *Bhagawan* Sri Sathya Sai Baba, Divine Discourse, 20/11/1982.
21 *Bhagawan* Sri Sathya Sai Baba, Divine Discourse, reprinted in ***Sanathana Sarathi,*** December 1981, P. 274.

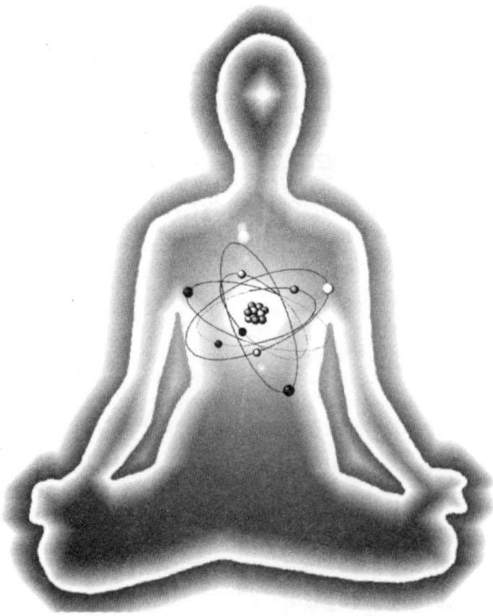

Subtler than the subtlest and vaster than the cosmos, the ***Atma*** *is the atom, and atom is the* ***Atma****.*

~ **SRI SATHYA SAI BABA**

chapter - 1

THE COSMOS AND DIVINE ENERGY

Sri Sathya Sai Baba says:

> *Where is the Cosmic Energy? The Cosmic Energy is all pervasive. It is in you, above you, below you and around you. You yourself are the Cosmic Energy, but you are not able to realise it.*[1]

The entire creation is a conglomeration of subatomic particles. These particles are waves of energy. All of them emanate from the same source of energy. Even the scientists, who know all about electrons, do not seek to find the primary source of all energy - the *Paratathwa* (the Supreme Principle). The power of *Sakti* (Divine manifested energy) is incalculable. A small stone cast in a tumbler of water causes a ripple on the surface. A storm in the sea has the power to sink a ship. Both are manifestations of the power of atomic particles under varying conditions.

Different combinations of atoms result in objects of different kinds like copper, gold or silver, which have varying utility and value. But, the primary energy, which manifests itself in different kinds of atoms and objects, is the same. The ***Vedas*** indicated this truth when they declared, "The One willed to become the many (*Ekoham Bahusyam*)... The Reality is one, the wise call it by many names (*Ekam Sat Viprah Bahudha Vadanti*)."

If the universe is itself the manifestation of one primary energy, everything in it is also an expression of that energy. For instance, a wall which you see as a solid block can be seen as a vast congregation of minute particles when it is viewed through a microscope. Empty space between different particles can also be noticed. Thus, there is a difference between the appearance of objects as we observe them in daily life and their inner reality. But the external appearance is based on the inner reality. **It is the basic truth of the internal which enables us to experience the external.** The basic truth is the power of the primal energy, which is matter. This basic truth was proclaimed in the *Vedic* statement: "It is Absolute and is subtler than the subtlest and vaster than the vastest." (*Anoraniyan Mahatno Mahiyan*) — This means that what is subtle can become immense.

All experiences in daily life are variations in form of the Basic Reality and not different from it. Experience of this Basic Reality will reveal how the changes in the primary energy bring about the emergence and the disappearance of the material substances. It should be clear from all this that there is one primordial power which is the basis of all that is.[2]

Generation, Organisation, Destruction

God is the primordial cause for Creation, Organisation and Destruction. The same Divine power assumes different names and forms. The whole world rests upon these three basic activities. The Creation aspect is governed by Brahma (Divine), Organisation by Vishnu, and Destruction by Siva. This division of powers is essential for smooth functioning of the world. The collective aspect of the three is God. The word God comprises three letters - **G**, **O**, **D**:

'**G**' stands for **G**eneration,
'**O**' stands for **O**rganisation,
'**D**' stands for **D**estruction.

These three aspects of Brahma, Vishnu, and Maheswara (Siva) constitute God. None can deny the existence of God. If someone argues by saying that there is no God, tell him that he has no right to question your conviction. God may not exist for those who deny His existence, but He exists for those who have faith in Him. One may say 'God is nowhere.' Take the letter 'w' away from the word 'where' and join it to 'no', which will make it, **'God is now here'**. All this is word building, but its essence is significant.[3]

The Atom And The *Atma* – Effulgent Energy

Sri Sathya Sai Baba proclaims:

The whole cosmos is based on the *Anu* (atom). Whether an object is microcosmic or as vast as the cosmos, it is built based on atomic energy. Few can realise fully the power of the atom. The atom is constituted of the energy in all its forms. The words you speak by mouth, the objects you see with eyes, the sounds you hear with ears, the activities you undertake with hands and legs are all based on the power of the atom. **Every movement of every being is based on atomic power.** It has taken scientists thousands of years to discover this Truth. To a man with pure *Hridayam* (spiritual heart) the Truth reveals itself spontaneously. "Subtler than the subtlest and vaster than the cosmos, the *Atma* is the atom, and atom is the *Atma*." When this truth is recognised, the whole cosmos will be seen as permeated by the Divine and as a manifestation of the Divine.

In every object there is the power of the atom. One cannot find any object or any place in which the atom is not present. All objects are composed of atoms. All forms of energy are manifestations of the atom. The whole earth is made up of atoms. In this world, every human being is a kind of small generator [of energy]. The magnetic power in him becomes electrical energy. It is because of this energy that man is able to walk, see, hear and do many other things.

ONE ENERGY, MANY FORMS

Sri Sathya Sai Baba explains:

The *Hridayam* in every man is like a radio station. There are light waves. These generate magnetic energy. Recognising the connection between matter and energy, **Albert Einstein** affirmed their convertibility. These findings of the scientists confirm the *Vedantic* view that the *Brahman* (Divine) permeates the whole cosmos. Only the terms used are different. The scientists declare that the cosmos is constituted of atoms. The *Vedanta* (philosophy of the ***VEDAS***) declares that the cosmos is permeated by the *Brahma Mayam* (Supreme Reality). They include the all-pervading cosmic vibrations, the power latent in all animate and inanimate objects, as the effulgence of the all-pervading Light. God is the energy that animates every being. There is electromagnetic energy in every body. Nature is the embodiment of the same energy. **This energy may assume different forms, but its essential character is one and the same.** A lighted bulb, a revolving fan and many other things working through electrical power depend on the same current. The energy may manifest itself in the form of light, heat, or magnetic energy, but it proclaims the power of the Divine that is the source of all energy.

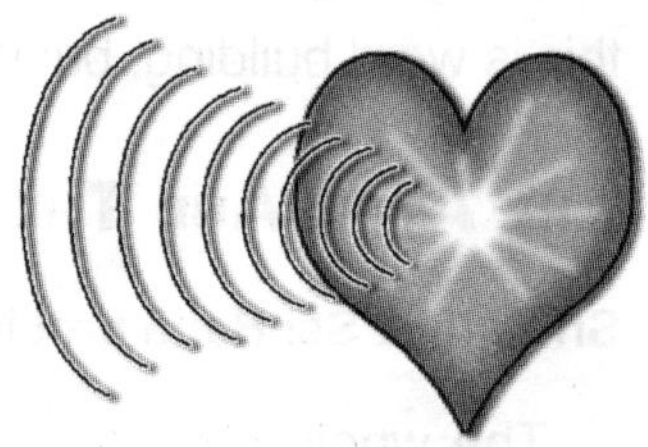

The electro-magnetic energy in man expresses itself in the form of **Radiation.** It is also called reflection of the Inner Being. The power of sight, hearing, speech, digestion and movement of limbs are derived from this energy. Water also contains this energy. In fact, the entire cosmos is permeated by this Divine energy. On this basis, the *Vedas* have declared "*Sarvam Vishumayam Jagath*" (the cosmos is permeated by God).[4]

God Is Omnipresent And Omnipotent

God is all-powerful and all-pervasive, "*Sarvam Khalvidam Brahma*" (Verily all is Divine). An enquiry into science and spirituality will reveal that both affirm the same truth. The existence of God is visualised by science in the form of **electric**, **magnetic**, **laser**, **radio, heat** and **light waves,** which are all-pervasive. This is the direct evidence for the existence of God. Divinity is present in the food you eat, the water you drink and the air you breathe.

MAGNETISM, THE POWER OF ATTRACTION: There is no place in this world devoid of magnetism. What is a magnet? It is not merely the one that attracts iron filings; everything in this world is suffused with magnetism. Mother is a magnet for the child and vice-versa. Similarly, husband and wife are attracted to each other. Grass is a magnet for the cow. The flower is the magnet for the honeybee. When we investigate on these lines, it is evident that everything is governed by the principle of magnetism. *Vedanta* declared, "*Ramayathi ithi Ramah*" (that which attracts is the principle of Rama [God]). The magnetic power acts as a link between that which is manifest and that which is unmanifest. The philosophers term it Divine magnetic power, whereas the scientists term it **bio-cosmic** or **super power**. Therefore, scientists as well as V*edantics* experience the same Divine power with different names and forms.[5]

Nature has immense magnetic power. Every object is affected by magnetic power. The object also gets magnetised in the process and acquires magnetic power. Today scientists are trying to understand this power of attraction in Nature. Take for instance, a temple. Thousands of people go to the temple for worship. The magnetic power in the earth extends to the idol in the sanctum. The thoughts of the worshipers are also attracted by the idol. Thereby the power of attraction in the idol intensifies. The rituals performed for the idol also enhance its power of attraction. This process can be noticed if a couple of nails are kept near a magnet. After two days it will be found that the nails have also been magnetised. In the same manner when worshipers go to a temple, the power goes forth from thousands of worshipers, the power of attraction in the idol gets immensely intensified. The idol surcharged with this power is able to energise worshipers.

ELECTRICITY: All of you are endowed with electro-magnetic energy, atomic energy, heat and other forms of energy. The magnetic energy is the most important power in man. From this magnetic energy comes electrical energy. The strength of electrical energy is related to the strength of magnetic energy. When the electrical energy and the magnetic energy come together, the Divine power operates. This Divine power does not come from outside. It is within all human beings.[6]

MYSTERIOUS POWERS: In this visible fleeting world, there are many mysterious powers unknown to man. These are referred to as transcendental and hidden powers; not all can understand them. Every creature is endowed with Divine power. That is why I always address you as *Divyatma Swaruplara* (embodiments of Divine *Atma*). Doctors are unable to comprehend the secrets and mysteries of the human body. Take, for example, the tongue. There are forty thousand (40,000) taste buds in the tongue and twenty thousand (20,000) of these generate heat in the tongue. The eye, which is hardly an inch in size, can recognise thirteen *crore* (130,000,000) types of light rays. There are millions and millions of cells in your body. Each cell is Divine and contains your complete form. Is it not awe-inspiring? Whose creation is this? This is the transcendental power of Divinity.[7]

The energy with which the most elementary and subtle particles are bound with each other is Divine. The individual separation of these individual particles is absolutely precise and cannot be altered by anyone. Any separation or merger would mean the non-existence of Creation. This Divine Energy is God.[8]

Power Of Love

Everything is contained in the self. Self means *Atma*, the spirit. Use this *Atmic* principle to acquire spiritual knowledge. The power in spirituality is limitless. The power of love (which is *Atmic* power) far exceeds the power of the atom bomb. It transforms even those who hate. Develop such sacred love. Only then there will be harmony among the *Bharatiyas* (people of India). Violence is rampant everywhere. The wicked thoughts in men are responsible for this. Once man develops love, there will be no hatred in the community.[9]

There is no greater power than *Prema* in this world because it is selfless and pure. Sages spent their time in the forests amidst wild animals. They lived amicably side by side with them. The animals did not harm the sages. What was the reason? The sages had no weapons at all. They had the sole weapon of love. With this weapon they were able to tame wild animals.[10]

The Divine power has neither birth nor death. I do not feel elated when praised nor depressed when blamed. I treat these dualities of life with equanimity. I am happy both in pleasure and pain. There is only love in Me. My love lives by giving and giving. It never receives. This is the difference between My love and worldly love, which believes in receiving alone. That is why My love is ever expanding. A small seed becomes a gigantic tree with many branches and fruits. All of them have their origin in the seed. Likewise, **out of love has emerged creation**.[11]

The path to God lies through love. With love, one can go anywhere. Love is God. Live in Love. Never forget God. God alone is everlasting. That is the only Truth. Your parents will pass away sometime or other. But God will remain forever. God is eternal. Always adore God. Love is present in all beings. You are all manifestations of the Divine. Consider yourselves as Divine. There is nothing wrong in that. In terms of the body, you are a human being. But spiritually you are Divine.[12]

Vibrations And The Scientists

Seers of the truth are not absent in the world of science. These great scientists have examined, explored and declared that truth is the basis of the cosmos. They are like ancient *saptarishis* (seven sacred sages). **Isaac Newton** declared that the universe is a manifestation of God and everything revolves through the power of God. **Fritjof Capra**, a modern day physicist, explored the link between the atom and vibrations in nature. In ancient times, Sage Vyasa declared that the universe emanated from the vibrations of the sound ***"Sita"***, and all things in creation, i.e. living and non-living, were the outcome of these vibrations.

It is a welcome sign that there are open minded scientists today who are prepared to explore the truths declared by our ancient sages and to seek their link between science and spiritually. On the other hand, it is a pity that people born in this great country with such a precious heritage are leading lives contrary to its ideals and wasting their opportunities.

The American astronaut, **Edgar Mitchell,** after landing on the moon, had a look at the earth. He saw the earth as a huge brilliant diamond set against a vast carpet of blue velvet. Experiencing this spectacle, he shed a few tears. He was stricken by the feeling: "Born on such a beautiful and brilliant land, why are men behaving like ignorant, evil minded beings?" Only a diamond can come out of a diamond and not a mere piece of stone. Why should evil men arise from the pure, holy soil of Mother Earth? He wanted to know, and he found the answer in man's fascination for material things, ignoring the cultivation of good qualities.[13]

The Power Of Eternal Truth

All kinds of power, whether physical, intellectual, monetary, military or political have to bend before Truth and Righteousness; but the latter will yield to none. Truth and Righteousness will always triumph.[14]

Even today, some noble minds are exploring spiritual truths, analysing them, and trying to see how these can be used for transforming man. **Sir Isaac Newton**, for instance, after discovering the gravitational power of the earth, declared: "Although I have discovered the force of gravity, the gravitational force itself has always existed before my discovery." He also admitted, "While I have been able to identify the force of gravity, I did not create it." He was convinced that there was a creator for the force of gravity. **Albert Einstein** too, after his scientific studies of the working of nature, turned his mind to spiritual matters. He realised that for spiritual pursuits, the company of good men was necessary, and that the association of good men can transform the human condition. Therefore, he declared, "Tell me your company and I shall tell you what you are." It shows that what we are is determined by the character of the people with whom we are associated.

Werner Heisenberg, a great physicist, after studying various sciences, embarked on an investigation of the link between the physical sciences and spirituality. He discovered the great secrets contained in the *Yoga-sastras* (records of *Yogic* philosophy). He observed, "Master the mind, be a mastermind." Another great scientist, **Erwin Schrodinger**, found that science and spirituality were integrally connected and that, in fact, spirituality was the basis for science. He also noted that the growth of science had led to a multiplication of wants, which has brought about a weakening of man's will and intelligence. He declared: "More Desires, More Despair."

Another great physicist and thinker, **Paul Dirac,** sought to know the connection between science and spirituality. He tried to discover the one entity underlying all things in creation and conducted experiments for this purpose. He found the truth that consists in the statement: "Love Ever, Hurt Never." Dirac's conclusion is nothing but an echo of Sage Vyasa's pregnant pronouncement, after completing his works on eighteen ***Puranas:*** **"To help others is meritorious; to hurt others is sinful."** We have yet another physicist and modern thinker, **Louis de Broglie.** Having begun as a critic of spirituality, after serious enquiry, de Broglie confessed that his criticisms were due to ignorance. He proclaimed, from this own experience, that Divinity was at the core of everything in the universe.[15]

God Is The Director Of Cosmic Drama

One may ask a question: Who is the director of the cosmic drama? The answer will be, it is the Divine. Every human being is a manifestation of the Divine Will. He has taken birth, as a human being to fulfill his duty. He has to manifest His humanness. Every individual has to play his role well and acquit himself worthily.

In the drama of life, there is a mixture of good and bad. Humanness is present in this mixture. They are known as:

- ***Marakam*** implies that one acts on the basis that nothing belongs to him and that whatever words he utters or whatever action he does, all belong to God and nothing of his own. He plays his role in this spirit, ascribing nothing to himself.

- ***Tharakam*** represents the attitude of the actor, who is conscious of the role he is playing and does not forget his individuality in his actions. He does not consider himself as merely acting a part, but regards himself as the doer.

The difference between the two is that the former realises the temporary nature of the part he is playing and is not attached to the things connected with the role. The *tharaka* develops attachment to the role, which he plays and does not wish to part with things connected with it. In the concept of *marakam* there is no sense of possessiveness. But in *tharakam*, one is attached to what he considers as his.

Modern man suffers from the sense of possession (*tharakam*). This is a negative attitude. He is obsessed with the idea of "my" and "mine". He attaches excessive importance to the body, forgetting the most precious *Atmic* principle that is within it and which will give him enduring bliss. The reason for this attachment is the failure to use the senses properly and to become a slave of the desires promoted by the senses.

Man is wasting his life with narrow-minded feelings. He is concerned about himself and his family alone; this is contraction of love. Consider the whole world as one family; that is expansion of love. Different countries are like different rooms in the mansion of the world. Consider all those that live in these rooms as your brothers and sisters. When you develop such a relationship with your fellow human beings, you will not hate anybody.

Try to understand the principle of Divinity. In this world there is none other than God. Some may say that the world consists of matter and energy. **Truly speaking, there is only energy, not matter. Whatever matter you see will be transformed**

into energy after some time. Similarly, name and form vary, but there is only one fundamental principle; that is Divinity. [16]

Form And Formless Aspects Of Divinity

In the Divine Drama, God takes many forms. This gives man the opportunity to experience good or bad, joy or sorrow, birth and death. All these come and go, but they do not affect the *Atma*.

Sri Sathya Sai Baba stresses this fact:

In the cinema of life, the screen is *Atma*. It is *Sankara* and it is Divinity. When one understands this principle, one will be able to understand, enjoy and find fulfillment in life.

Sankara (a name for God) refers to the one who is endowed with all types of *Aishvarya* (prosperity or wealth). The types of wealth that we enjoy in the worldly sense are not what one means by *Aishvarya*. Everything in the phenomenal world, every person, every bit of matter that one sees has this principle of *Aishvarya* in it. This *Aishvarya* is nothing other than *Easwara* (a name for God). In other words the entire phenomenal world is made up of *Easwara*. This has also been described as *Sathamatra Chaitanya* or Pure Consciousness. This principle of *Chaitanya* cannot be directly seen. It exists unseen. It is eternal; it is permanent; it is all-pervasive. It is the *Aishvarya* (wealth principle) that permeates and fills this world. For this principle of *Easwara* there are two aspects.

- *Saguna* or *Sakara* (attributeful or formful)
- *Nirguna* or *Nirakara* (attributeless and formless)

The *saguna* (formful) aspects of *Easwara* are associated with the mind and thoughts, and respond to the joys and sorrows, the pain and sufferings of human beings.

These are visualised as the various forms of Divinity. We have the trinity, Brahma, Vishnu and Maheswara. These are associated with the three ***gunas*** or attributes:

- *Raja* with Brahma = 'A'
- *Satwa* with Vishnu = 'U'
- *Tamas* with Siva = 'M'

These three forms, comprising the Trinity, are not permanent, because they have taken form. **Anything that has a form cannot be permanent.** In the worship of the Divine with attributes, the Trinity exists in each individual as auspicious Witness.

There is one syllable consisting of 'A', 'U' & 'M', which is the one underlying all the three forms: that is the *Omkara.* It is an expression of the *Nirguna,* the attributeless Divine principle. Whatever number of births we may take and however long we may go worshipping these three forms, we will never be able to free ourselves from the cycle of birth and death. If one wants to get rid of birth and death forever, one has to worship the *Nirguna Nirakara,* the formless and attributeless principle, which is represented by the *Omkara.*

FROM *SAGUNA* TO *NIRGUNA*

Only when we get rid of action, we will be free from the delusion that the world is real. When we are rid of delusion, we will also be free from *Maya* (illusion of the form world). Only then we will be free from sorrow and will finally be able to reach the *Paratathwa* (the transcendent principle). This may also be described as *Paramatma,* (supreme soul) the transcendent principle within us. As long as we have the mind and the tendencies, we can only be described as *Jivatma* (individual, unaware soul).

Jivatma and *Paramatma* are not two different entities. The characteristic of *Jivatma* is to waste the entire life in worldly things and associate the mind with this phenomenal world. This is the externalised vision, which is full of illusion and delusion. If you turn your mind inwards, it will be free from delusion. When it is associated with delusion, it is *Jiva.* When it is free from delusion and illusion, then it is one with the principle of *Paramatma.*[17]

The Human Body And Cosmic Power

Sri Sathya Sai Baba says:

Man possesses within himself all potencies. Man's powers are limitless and astonishing. Nothing in the world is beyond his comprehension. Man today appears as a highly knowledgeable and vastly capable being. But these capacities only proclaim his powers over the physical forces of Nature.

There is, however, an unseen, unknown, unmanifested infinite power within him. This is the Cosmic Power in man. It is all-pervasive. It is in every human being. Only when one goes beyond the form, one finds that there is an apparent distinction between the microcosm and the macrocosm, like the difference between the air in a balloon and the air in the vast atmosphere outside. But when the balloon bursts, the small air inside becomes one with the infinite air outside.

Human body is like a balloon. The infinite potency within each body is regarded as imperceptibly small. But the power of air both outside and inside the balloon is the same. This potency is a part of the Universal Cosmic Power. *Anuraneyan Mahathomaheyan* declare the *Upanishads* (*Vedic* texts): "More minute than the atom and vaster than the vastest." [18]

Divinity Is Omnipresent

The true devotee sees the Divine in everything. The power of the Divine permeates every atom in the cosmos. How is this to be recognised? The Divine is effulgent. The devotees envisage the Divine in different ways and express their adoration in various forms.[19]

Each Has His Own Faith

It is foolish to consider Divinity to be non-existent. Those who are not able to understand this transcendental power deny the existence of God. Do not pretend to know what you do not know in reality. No one has any right to deny the existence of God. "*Munde Munde Mathir Bhinnah*" (opinions differ from person to person). Each has his own faith.

'NO' is the reply for those that say 'no',
'YES' is the reply for those who say 'yes',
'NO' and 'YES' pertain to you,
But for Sai it is always 'yes', 'yes', 'yes'.

People tend to deny the existence of all that is formless. The fact that radio waves are invisible does not mean that they are non-existent. The programme that is being broadcast at the Delhi Radio Station can be heard anywhere if the radio is tuned to that frequency. The human body can be compared to a radio. It has to be tuned to the formless God in order to experience Him. Human body is like a computer, which has so many hidden secrets. The Mind is like a television set. Many names and forms are displayed in it. The Body is a generator. The sum and substance of all this is that all powers are latent in man. **Albert Einstein** showed that matter could be converted into energy and energy into matter. Energy is all encompassing. **Sir Isaac Newton** said that energy could neither be created nor destroyed. However, energy could be converted from one form to another. Philosophers explained this in various ways:

God has neither birth nor death,
He has neither beginning nor end,
He is present everywhere,
He is the Eternal Witness.

Modern scientists are not able to comprehend this truth. What they have known and understood is just a fraction of the totality. What is awareness? It is total understanding. Total understanding denotes knowing and experiencing the omnipresence of Divinity. *Moha Kshaya* is *Moksha* (absolute detachment is liberation). What does this mean? Air mixes with air, fire mixes with fire, water mixes with water easily. Similarly **God is the very form of light, and becomes light in yourself.** You will become one with the cosmic light. God is formless. In order to merge in the formless God, you have to give up identification with the body. Concentrate on the principle of *Atma.* When you are always attached to the body, how can you realise the *Atma,* the Cosmic Principle? Concentrate on the *Atma.* Only then your conscience will merge with the Cosmic Consciousness.[20]

Power Of Divine Consciousness

One can proceed to the awareness of a Cosmic Divine. This realisation comes out of the recognition that the Divine Consciousness experienced by the individual is also present in all other individuals. This is the Cosmic Power. The all-pervading Divine Power is one and the same. There is no second power. Bodies may be multifarious like electric bulbs. But the energy that makes them shine is one. When this truth is realised one has the awareness of the Cosmic Divine. It is not enough for one to realise his true Self. He cannot seek his individual salvation. He must experience the oneness that underlies the multiplicity in creation. Only when that oneness is realised can the true meaning of humanness be understood.[21]

Experiencing God

The Cosmos is a manifestation of the Divine. They are foolish men who, while seeing the handiworks of the Divine everywhere, think that there is no God. Without recognising the omnipresence of God, men seek God somewhere outside themselves. This reflects the dualistic attitude of persons who identify themselves with the body and alienate themselves from God. While God is omnipresent and can be recognised in the Divine manifestation of Nature, the body consciousness prevents men from experiencing oneness with the Divine. How is God to be experienced?

- The first requisite is purity of the *Hridayam*. All religions have affirmed the basic importance of such purity.
- The aim of all *sadhana* (spiritual effort) is to achieve peace of mind.
- Compassion towards all beings is devotion to God. God cannot be experienced through observance of rituals and worship. Where there is pomp and show there can be no Divinity. The bliss of the Divine cannot be found there. As a seed will not sprout on rocky ground, the bliss of the Divine cannot be realised by worship devoid of humility and sincerity.
- All *sadhanas* are not pursued for realising the *Atma*. In fact, there is no need to seek the *Atma*, which is all-pervasive and present everywhere. ***Sadhana* must be performed to get rid of the *anatma* (that which bars the vision of the *Atma*).**

Man forgets his real nature and loses himself in the consciousness of what he is not. He forgets that he is the *Atma* in reality. Man identifies himself with a particular name and form and builds up all relations on that basis. But how real and permanent are these names and forms? They are all projections of the mind and have existence only as long as the mind and the body remain. The *Hridayam* represents the *Atma*. It is self-effulgent. The light from the *Hridayam* (*Atma*) illumines the mind and enables it to see the external world. Without this illumination, the mind cannot comprehend the world. **The mind is like the moon which receives its light from the sun. It has no light of its own. It shines because of the light from the *Atma*. When the sun shines, the moon is hardly visible.**

Likewise, when there is awareness of the *Atma*, the mind is not perceivable. In the world, *Atma* is the basis for everything. Men are naïve in imaging that the *Atma* is in the body. **The truth is that the body, the mind and the entire cosmos are in *Atma*.** The *Atma* cannot be inside anything else. It is the All. It is everything.[22]

Realise Divinity In The World

You have to stick to Divine Consciousness even while you are engaged in worldly activities. In spite of a lapse of millions of years, man is not yet able to understand his reality. How can he realise Divinity? If you develop human qualities you can easily realise Divinity. *Vedanta* teaches *Sathyam vada: Dharam chara* (speak the truth, adhere to righteousness). Now, people kill Truth and ignore righteousness. *Santi* (peace) and *Prema* (Love) are reduced to the narrowest possible limits. All the four *Sathya, Dharma, Santi* and *Prema* must be put in unison for the world and humanity to thrive. If you study how these electric lights here are functioning, you will find that the current passes through the wire and illuminates the bulb.

Likewise *Sathya* (Truth) is the current, *Dharma* is the wire and *Santi* is the bulb. When the current flows to the bulb, it burns brightly. This light is love (*Prema*). You will see that *Sathya, Dharma, Santi* together form the constituents for *Prema*.[23]

God, who is everywhere, has to be enshrined in the *Hridayam*. Turn the milk into curds by good deeds and churn by *sadhana*. Then there will be direct experience of the Divine. The discharging of duties in a spirit of detachment is the basic obligation of everyone from a student to a scholar. Thereby, you can manifest the Divinity within you. But, if you cannot recognise your humanness, how can you recognise your Divinity? The first requisite is purity of *Hridayam* and the Mind, which has to be free from all desires.[24]

Meditate On God All The Time

Many undertake meditation as a spiritual exercise and spend many hours a day on it. **In fact, meditation (*dhyana*) must be implicit in almost every act that is done from morning till night.** Meditation (in the sense of concentration) is implied in all the daily chores like eating, going to work, attending to business, etc. One is meditating while reading, playing or shopping. Without concentration no activity of any kind can be done. **When the concentration is on God, it becomes spiritual meditation.** Does such meditation call for a specific time or place? There is no special technique needed for such meditation. By giving meditation some special names, they forget its real significance. For instance, if people do not listen with *dharana* (one pointed attention) to *Swami*'s discourse, they will not remember what *Swami* has said. Even listening calls for *dhyana*. It has no specific form. No *dhyana* is possible with a wandering mind. Today in the name of *dhyana*, several stunts are being practised. Instead of spending hours in so-called meditation with a mind restlessly hopping from one thought to another like a monkey, it would be better to concentrate on the performance of one's household, official and social duties with earnestness and dedication. Is that not meditation? Of what use is it to sit in "Meditation" for an hour, when you cannot keep your mind still for a minute?

Think about God while carrying on your regular duties. Regard all work as sacred offering to the Divine. **See God in everything you do**. Instead of following this simple and easy path, people are engaged in all forms of gymnastics and subjecting themselves to various hazards. Devote yourselves to your duties. **Meditation is not confined to any one thing. It should permeate every action you do**.

Solitude: Turn Thoughts Towards The Divine

Some aspirants wish to seek solitude (*ekantham*). But being alone is not solitude. People go to Hrishikesh, Haridwar or Tapovanam in search of solitude. Only those who have not understood the real meaning of solitude will resort to such things. **There is real solitude only when the mind is completely stilled**. While sitting alone in a forest, if your mind is ruminating on affairs of the world, how can it be called solitude? Without curbing thoughts, loneliness cannot be found anywhere. Thoughts either have to be eliminated, or all thoughts should be turned towards the Divine.

Many imagine that they are deriving happiness by enjoying the things of the world. They should examine who is 'enjoying' whom. In reality, far from their 'enjoying' the things they possess, their possessions are enjoying them. **Hatred, anger, envy and other evils bred by possessions only lead to disease and misery.** Why should the body suffer from ills if real possessions are the source of happiness? Man is losing real happiness by attachment to things, which cannot give him happiness.

Those who have faith in ***Bhagavad Gita*** should note that it has clearly declared that this world is ephemeral and "a veil of tears" and enduring peace and bliss are not to be found by attachment to it. The source of lasting peace and happiness is within ourselves.

That is the *Atma* (the Omniself). It is by realising it that peace and bliss have to be secured.

One must constantly develop the consciousness that the *Atma* is everything – the doer, the deed, and the outcome thereof. When the consciousness is broadened in this way, in due course it leads to Self-realisation. If your vision is broad, your destination will also be of the same magnitude. A narrow outlook can lead only to a narrow alley. If you are immersed all the time in the petty trifles of mundane existence, when will you ever understand the Reality which is beyond the physical and the mental? Set your sight on the Supreme. Illumination will come in a flash.

Enquire "Who Am I?"

The physical body that performs *japa* or *dhyana* or the various other spiritual practices is but a water-bubble. The mind, which is based upon this physical body, is but a mad monkey. With the help of this mad monkey mind and this water bubble body, how can you hope to achieve the permanent *Atma*? *Japa*, *dhyana, bhajans*, austerities and sacrifices are from the mind. But there is one practice that will have a permanent effect, and that is enquiry. **You should go on enquiring, 'Who am I? Who am I?' Until you reach the stage where you find out who you really are.** The enquiry should go on like this:

> **"Here is my body, and here is my mind, my heart, my feelings, my intellect and my memory power; I am not any of these. Someone has praised me, someone has censured me, but to whom does this pertain? Only to this physical body."**

In this way, you have to develop a sense of detachment and a sacrificing nature. How can a physical body abuse another physical body? Both are inert. How can inert things criticise or admonish?

They cannot. How can they even worship anything? They cannot. But then can *Atma* criticise another *Atma*? That also is absurd.

What Is Devotion?

Many people aspire for grace, love, devotion and humility. All these are forms of the *Atma*. God is not different from faith. Faith and God are one and the same. Love is God, devotion is God; they are not different entities. What is the meaning of devotion?

> **Devotion is that which enables the unmanifested Divine principle to manifest itself if the inner vision of the devotee is pure.** ~ Sri Sathya Sai Baba

Then for that devotee nothing else exists than He. To reach that stage you must discharge your duties, keeping the permanent entity constantly in mind. You can cross the vast, deep ocean of worldly existence and enjoy the infinite Divinity that is its Reality, with the help of a small boat. That boat is the name of God. In the beginning of the spiritual journey the name is the basis for the progress, but it should not become a life-long support, depending entirely on it alone.

Whatever service you are rendering you should not feel that you are serving others, but that you are serving God Himself. While taking a bath or giving one to the children, consider that you are doing the purification ritual of washing God Himself. While serving food, consider that you are offering it to God Himself. When giving food to a beggar, consider that God has come in this form and you are serving Him. Although it appears to you that the beggar is asking, it is really the *Atma* enjoying the food you give.

When you are cutting some vegetables for cooking, consider that you are cutting away your desires and ego with the knife of wisdom. While sweeping the floor at home, do not lament saying, "Oh, it keeps getting dirty again and again." Think rather that you are cleaning your own *Hridayam*. If you are rolling *chapatis* at home, consider what joy it is to roll and expand your *Hridayam*. In this way, you can consider every activity you undertake as being done for the sake of God. Then where is the need for any separate meditation, separate penance, or separate worship?

The Seat Of *Atma* Is Your *Hridayam*

Consider your *Hridayam* as *Atma.* Soften it and make it full of compassion. That is the only spiritual exercise you need to perform. It is only because of love that it is here and felt from *Hridayam* to *Hridayam*. Through love you can accomplish anything in the world. **Consider love as the *Atma* itself.** You may read many scriptures and do many spiritual exercises, but if you do not allow your *Hridayam* to melt with compassion your life will be a sheer waste. All practices have to be directed towards softening your *Hridayam* so that it will flow with kindness and love. Develop this feeling of compassion and allow it to flow fully and spread among all the people of the world. Steps to realise *Atma*:

1. *Namasmarana, kirtanam, nagarsankirtanam.*
2. See God in all, and serve all with love.
3. Clean your *Hridayam* all the time.
4. Expand your *Hridayam* by loving all.
5. Cut your desires and ego.
6. Be compassionate to all.
7. Remove hatred, jealousy, greed and envy from your *Hridayam* and make it a pure seat for Divinity.[25]

Realise Your Divine Potency

The primary requisite for man is to realise the divine potency in him that is the source of all the faculties and talents in him. That is true whether one is an atheist, a theist or an agnostic. No one in the world can get on without the energy. It may be called by different names. Names are not important. The energy is one. It is this divine energy which directs mankind on the right path. Men should strive to recognise the presence of the Divine even in small things.[26]

---

1 *Bhagawan* Sri Sathya Sai Baba, **Summer Showers**, 1993.
2 *Bhagawan* Sri Sathya Sai Baba, ***Santhana Sarathi,*** March 1986.
3 *Bhagawan* Sri Sathya Sai Baba, Divine Discourse, 23/12/1998.
4 *Bhagawan* Sri Sathya Sai Baba, ***Santhana Sarathi,*** March 1986.
5 *Bhagawan* Sri Sathya Sai Baba. Divine Discourse, 23/11/1998.
6 *Bhagawan* Sri Sathya Sai Baba, ***Sanathana Sarathi,*** March 1995.
7 *Bhagawan* Sri Sathya Sai Baba. Divine Discourse, 23/11/1998.
8 *Bhagawan* Sri Sathya Sai Baba, ***Sanathana Sarathi***, September 1994.
9 *Bhagawan* Sri Sathya Sai Baba. Divine Discourse, 23/12/1998.
10 *Bhagawan* Sri Sathya Sai Baba, ***Sanathana Sarathi***, June 1995.
11 *Bhagawan* Sri Sathya Sai Baba. Divine Discourse, 23/11/1998
12 *Bhagawan* Sri Sathya Sai Baba. Divine Discourse, 25/08/1998.
13 *Bhagawan* Sri Sathya Sai Baba. Divine Discourse, November 1985.
14 *Bhagawan* Sri Sathya Sai Baba. **Summer Showers**, 1990.
15 *Bhagawan* Sri Sathya Sai Baba. Divine Discourse, November 1985.
16 *Bhagawan* Sri Sathya Sai Baba. Divine Discourse, 23/12/1998
17 *Bhagawan* Sri Sathya Sai Baba. Divine Discourse, 14/01/1985.
18 *Bhagawan* Sri Sathya Sai Baba. Divine Discourse, 19/11/1998.
19 *Bhagawan* Sri Sathya Sai Baba. Divine Discourse, 25/08/1998.
20 *Bhagawan* Sri Sathya Sai Baba. Divine Discourse, 23/11/1998.
21 *Bhagawan* Sri Sathya Sai Baba. Divine Discourse, 19/12/1985.
22 *Bhagawan* Sri Sathya Sai Baba. Divine Discourse, 30/03/1987.
23 *Bhagawan* Sri Sathya Sai Baba. Divine Discourse, 01/04/1998.
24 *Bhagawan* Sri Sathya Sai Baba. Divine Discourse, 15/02/1998.
25 *Bhagawan* Sri Sathya Sai Baba. Divine Discourse, 30/03/1987.
26 *Bhagawan* Sri Sathya Sai Baba, ***Sanathana Sarathi,*** February 1995.

chapter - 2

THE DIVINE AND *PANCHAMAHABHUTAS*

Listen to the melodious music of the divine poet. He plays upon the flute of love, the notes soar to high heaven and reach the distant stars and dance on the raging waves of the sea. The earth, the sea, the sky, the stars are all woven together by the soft strains of the divine music. Its vibrations echo through the corridors of time in the endless canopy of the sky.

~ ***Samaveda*** **446**

Sri Sathya Sai Baba says:

Wherever you look, whether it be here on earth, or in heaven, or even in the netherworld, everything that you can ever find anywhere is made up of some combination of the five elements and only the five elements. Nothing else exists. Whatever you have ever desired, whatever you have ever used, whatever you have ever lost, all these myriads of things are nothing but changes in manifestation of the five elements. All these countless variations of the five elements have been and are forever changing with time; they are all temporary, endlessly cycling from one name and form to another.[1]

Whatever forms these elements take, their basis and support is always God. These five elements are five aspects or reflections of the one Divinity. Except for these five reflections of divinity, nothing else exists in the whole universe. In all these five, the divinity is the same. It is one.[2]

THE *PANCHAMAHABHUTAS* (FIVE ELEMENTS)

Sri Sathya Sai Baba continues:

1. Earth *(Prithivi)*

Among the five elements, the primary one is the earth. It is all-pervasive. All the mountains, rivers, villages, towns, etc. are outcomes of the earth. The scientists have found earth revolving round itself. In that case, all the objects on the earth should also be revolving. But that is not so. The earth has a Divine power of attraction. This power of attraction holds all the objects together. Hence, the earth alone cannot be regarded as the basis for all the objects. If we enquire more deeply, it will be found that even the earth is supported by something else. The earth is based on a higher power, the Divine power.

Thus, the Divine is firm, pure, and changeless. Without this Divine power, nature and the physical world cannot function systematically. If, for instance, the rails on which a locomotive run were also to move along with the train, the results will be disastrous. Likewise, if the road were also to move along with the car running on it, there would be accidents. It is the car that moves and not the earth. In this manner, many objects are in motion in the universe, but the Divine remains steady and unchanging.

2. Water *(Jala)*

The next element is called water, which is present everywhere whether we perceive it or not. Life is impossible without water. It is vibrant with vitality (*Prajnana*). When one is prostrate with thirst or weakness, a cup of cold water can restore him to activity.[3]

A large part of the water we drink is expelled as urine. A minute part of the water consumed becomes *prana*. Therefore the nature of the food and water that we take in decides our character.[4]

Water is getting scarcer every day. What is the reason? Because of the decline in morality among men, water is getting scarce in the world. For human life morality is the life breath. Morality makes humanness blossom. Because morals have been lost, water is getting scarcer.[5]

About water the ***Rig Veda*** says, "Waters contain all disease-dispelling medicaments useful for the upkeep of our body so that we may live long to enjoy the bright sun. That there is ambrosia in waters, that there is healing balm in them, and there are medicinal herbs, know this all, and by their proper use, become wiser." From the following prayer, also in the ***Rig Veda***, we know water is a great purifier: "The divine waters, the purifiers of hundreds, rejoicing in their innate nature, pursue the paths of nature's forces. They never violate the sacred ways of the Resplendent Lord. May you offer to rivers your tribute rich in affection and love! ... Oh, powerful water! I might have violated the laws of nature knowingly or unknowingly, foolishly or impudently. Take away whatever is wrong or deficient in me."[6]

3. Fire *(Agni)*

Sri Sathya Sai Baba says:

The next one is Fire. This fire element is present in every living being, including man, as the digestive fire (*jataragni*). This fire is not only on the earth, but is even in space. When clouds clash against each other, fire is generated. Man is bound intimately with fire throughout his life in many ways. Man is a warm-blooded creature; warmth promotes intellect and intuition. Calling upon God and placing the offerings in the fire are acts which bring about rain to provide rich harvests. Fire is thus a valuable medium for gaining safety and security, for preserving morality and goodness. The ocean too has *Agni* latent in it. So, also, there is fire in the body.

Man has in his stomach the latent fire that digests food. God resides in man as this Fire. *Aham Vaishwanaro Bhuthva Praninam Deham Ashrithah*, says Krishna. "Having become the *Vaishwanara* (the Lord as the digestive fire), I enter the body of living beings." So, it is God who keeps all the limbs trim and makes keenness and knowledge possible. This latent fire has eight functions:

1. It hardens and strengthens the muscles.
2. It develops energy.
3. It ensures healthy progeny.
4. It gives one patience and therefore makes them a better instrument.
5. It increases the duration of life.
6. It sharpens and deepens memory.
7. It confers boldness of thought and action.
8. It consumes. In order to light the Fire in the sacrificial enclosure, a churning rod of hardwood is used on a

block of similar hardness. The timber has to be banyan or *peepul.* The block is the mother and the churner is the father. *Agni* or Fire is the child. It consumes the parents — the mother and the father when born. They are reduced to ashes; that is to say, that the child becomes one with them and they become one with their progeny. All the three are inseparably related. The Son of God, Jesus, declared, "I and My Father are one." The religion of the *Parsis* also considers the highest truth as "I am the Light" and "The Light is in Me."

The ***Yajur Veda*** has a name for *Agni,* **Tiger**. When *Agni* is treated without faith and reverence, it destroys the very person who feeds it, just as the tiger when angry tears its own cubs with its deadly claws. Another characteristic of *Agni* is its presence everywhere. The scientists and technologists today are proud that they have grasped the secrets of the five elements — sky, wind, fire, water and earth. But they are still unaware of the intimate kinship each of them has with man and his daily life. The sages of the past have delved into the mystery and revealed it to the world. Notice, for example, that birds do not rest on the ground at night. They prefer treetops. Why? The *Rishis* (sages) of *Vedic* times have explained that they seek to avoid the heat latent in the earth but potent in them. Man is unaware of this fact but the birds know it.

The inner meaning of *yajna* is renunciation, sacrifice, or giving up. For whom? For the Divine, the Lord. The *Hridayam* is that organ wherein the renunciation takes place. The *Hridayam* the Lord has given, the feelings He evokes, the wealth He has conferred, the fame He has awarded — these have to be gladly offered back. As part of these *yagnas,* what is recommended is sacrifice of the wayward mind, dedicating it to God, so that it becomes stable and calm by selfless, pure and joyful concentration. Treasure them in the *Hridayam* for practice in daily life and for sharing with other earnest souls.[7]

4. Air *(Vayu)*

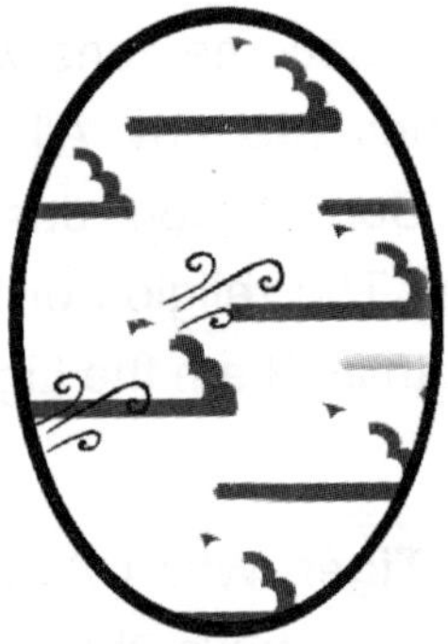

It pervades everything. There is Air (*Vayu*). There can be no life without air. One experiences the presence of air during a storm or a whirlwind. But air is present all the time everywhere. Air carries the life principle, the aroma, the *prana sakti.*

The life force (*prana*) is subtle and separate and different from the body; it is activated by air and is saturated with it. It pervades and subsumes the entire physical body. You can say that the *prana* is the soul of the physical body, for it makes it function from head to foot.[8]

No one can escape the influence of the pollution in the air he breathes. The sounds that we produce, with good intent or bad, spread throughout the air around us. When we fill the air with harshness, we become harsh in nature. When we saturate the air with sounds of reverence, humility, love, courage, self-confidence and tolerance, we benefit from those qualities ourselves.[9]

5. Space Or Ether *(Akasa)*

Sri Sathya Sai Baba says:

There are three types of *Akasas* which can all be considered universes or worlds. These are:

A. *BHUTAKASA* is the gross physical universe. It contains billions of suns, each with its own world; there are countless planets, big and small and innumerable beings; and in this entire vast universe the earth is smaller than even a tiny drop. All things found in *Bhutakasa*, in the physical world, are impermanent and subject to continuous change. Everything is in constant motion.

B. ***CHITTHAKASA,*** the subtle universe of the mind, is made up of the elements in their subtle aspect of sound, touch, sight, taste and smell.

C. ***CHIDAKASA,*** the subtlest and the most extensive of all the three, is referred to as the causal universe. All the apparent luster of objects in the world arises from *Chidakasa*, the causal world and is then reflected by the *Chitthakasa* and *Bhutakasa*, which act as mirrors. Just as the effulgence of the sun gets reflected by the moon, the effulgence present in the causal state of *Chidakasa* gets reflected in the subtle mental state of the *Chitthakasa* and then in the gross physical state of the *Bhutakasa*.

Beyond these and serving as the basis for all three of them is the divine principle, what has been called *Brahman* or God, and what has also been called *Atma* - the immortal Self.[10]

Panchamahabhutas And The Five Senses

The human being has five *Jnanendriyas* (sense organs of knowledge): ears, skin, eyes, tongue and nose. With these senses he perceives the external world in five different ways. The external object is not only perceived using the senses, it is also absorbed into the human body in the form of energy. These five senses correspond with the five elements, the *Panchamahabhutas*, and are the basis on which the entire universe is divided or classified.

The ***Atharvaveda, Rigveda, Samveda***, the ***Puranas*** and *Bhagawan* Baba outline this as follows:

Chart No. 2 ~ The *Panchamahabhutas*

Element	Originates	Gross Sense	Property (Subtle)	Formation In the Body
Akasa (ether or space) *PREMA*	**FIVE SUBTLE ETHERS** • *Jnatha* (cogniser) • *Manas* (mind) • *Buddhi* (intellect) • *Ahamkara* (ego) • *Panchakarma* (five inner senses)	Ear	***Sabda*** (Sound)	• Lust • Pride • Anger • Envy • Greed
Vayu (air) *SATHYA*	**FIVE PRANAS** • *Samana* (balanced breathe) • *Vyana* (entire body) • *Udhana* (throat and head) • *Prana* (breath, vital airs) • *Apana* (down breath, anus)	Skin	***Sparsa*** (Touch)	• Activities • Movements • Speed • Shame • Fear
Agni (fire) *DHARMA*	**FIVE SENSES *(Jnanendryas:*** organs of knowledge) • Ears • Skin • Eyes • Tongue • Nose	Eyes	***Rupa*** (Sight or Form)	• Hunger • Thirst • Sleep • Sloth • Comrade-ship
Jala (water) *SANTI*	**FIVE SUBTLENESSES *(Tanmatras)*** • *Sabda* (sound) • *Sparsa* (touch) • *Rupa* (form) • *Rasa* (taste) • *Gandha* (smell)	Tongue	***Rasa*** (Taste)	• Blood • Urine • Saline • Phlegm • Brain

Element	Originates	Gross Sense	Property (Subtle)	Formation In The Body
Prithivi (Earth) *AHIMSA*	**FIVE WORKING ORGANS *(Karmendriyas:*** organs of action**)** • Vocal organs • Hands • Legs • Genitals • Excretory organs (bladder & anus)	Nose	***Gandha*** (Smell) →	• Bones • Skin • Flesh • Veins • Hair
Source: *Bhagawan* Sri Sathya Sai Baba, ***Prasnottara Vahini,*** Chapter 1.				

We use both the gross and subtle senses to experience the world outside our bodies, as the above chart clearly illustrates. From there we can infer the beautiful interconnectedness of the human being with all of life. Sathya Sai Baba reminds us over and over again of the power of our thoughts to transform our health and environment. Our every experience, in fact, is merely a reaction, reflection and resound of our inner reality. By changing our thoughts through the practice of Human Values, we impact the elements and improve our total health as well as add value to the world around us.

Lost In The Translation

Understand that English equivalents of these terms do not connote the correct and full meaning. For example, ordinary water does not contain *jala mahabhuta* alone, it is composed of all the five *mahabhutas*. It is the force of cohesion or the power of attraction that is inherent in *jala mahabhuta*. Similarly, air is not *vayu mahabhuta* alone, it contains the elements, which belong to other *mahabhutas* also. For example, oxygen will be nearer to *agni mahabhuta* and hydrogen nearer to *jala mahabhuta*.

Modern Science And Philosophy

Modern physics and chemistry have divided all the matter available in the universe into a basic table of elements familiar to most secondary school students. These elements differ from each other on certain points. Still all of these elements can be classified into one of the five categories of *mahabhutas.*

On the other hand, each atom has the characteristic features of all the five *mahabhutas* in it:

- The electrons, positrons, neutrons, etc., present inside the atom represents ***prithivi*** *mahabhuta.*
- The force or cohesion that causes them to remain attracted towards each other is the characteristic attribute of ***jala*** *mahabhuta*.
- The energy that is produced inside the atom when it is broken and the energy, which remains latent in it in its unbroken form, represents the attributes of ***agni*** *mahabhuta*.
- The force of movement of the electrons represents the characteristic feature of ***vayu*** *mahabhuta*.
- The space in which they move is the primary attribute of ***akasa*** *mahabhuta*.

Like the scientific community, various schools of philosophy have tried to explain the *Panchamahabhutas* theory in different ways. However, all schools of theistic philosophy have a common ground in their belief in the creation of this universe through the *Panchamahabhutas*. Some atheist schools of philosophy like the one in *Charvaka* do not believe in the existence of the fifth *mahabhuta*, i.e., *akasa,* because it is not perceptible to the ordinary eye. However, *Ayurveda* is very clear about it and believes in the *Panchamahabhutas* theory.

PANCHAMAHABHUTAS AND AYURVEDA

According to *Ayurveda*, the body of an individual is composed of five *mahabhutas*. Similarly, in other extraneous matters, there are also five *mahabhutas*. In the human body, these five *mahabhutas* are represented in the form of:

- ***DOSHAS:*** Combinations of the *panchamahabhutas* govern the physiochemical and physiological activities of the body. When these elements are in balance there is health. Imbalance in these elements causes disease.
- ***DHATUS:*** Elements which help in the formation of the basic structure of a body cell.
- ***MALAS:*** Substances which are partly utilised in the body and partly excreted in a modified form after serving their physiological functions. Waste products of the body, i.e., stool, urine, sweat.

Outside the body the five elements form the basic ingredients of the drugs and food ingredients. The characteristic attributes of these five *mahabhutas* are explained in terms of . . .

- ***Rasa*** (taste)
- ***Guna*** (quality)
- ***Virya*** (potency)
- ***Vipaka*** (the taste that arises after the digestion and metabolism of a substance)

In a normal body of a living being, these substances remain in a particular proportion. However, because of enzymatic action inside the human body, this ratio of five *mahabhutas* or their equilibrium inside the body gets disturbed. The body has, however, a natural tendency to maintain equilibrium. It eliminates portions of the *mahabhutas* which are in excess and takes on some of the *mahabhutas*, which are in shortage. This shortage of *mahabhutas* is replenished through the ingredients of food, drink, air, heat, sunlight, etc.

Even during the process of death, these five *mahabhutas* play a very important role. They have two different forms, namely gross and subtle **[See Chart No. 2]**. The five categories of subtle *mahabhutas* inside the body are sound, touch, form, taste and smell, called ***Tanmatras*** (the five subtlenesses). They impregnate the five *Jnanendriyas* while there is life in the body, but detach from the subtle and gross senses when death occurs. The dead body, then, loses the five *Tanmatras* and *Jnanendriyas* and is composed only of the five *mahabhutas*.

***Tridosha* Concept**

As already expressed, the human body, according to *Ayurveda*, is composed of three fundamental elements called *doshas*, *dhatus* and *malas*. These three elements are said to be in a dynamic equilibrium with each other for the maintenance of health. Any imbalance of their relative prevalence in the body results in disease and decay.

The *doshas* govern the physiochemical and physiological activities. These three *doshas* are *vayu (vata)*, *pitta* and *kapha*. The nearest English equivalents of these terms will be air, bile and phlegm.

As has been stated before, all the constituents of the body are derived from the five *mahabhutas*. Therefore, the *doshas* are also composed of five *mahabhutas*. The ***vata*** *(vayu) dosha* is dominated by *akasa mahabhuta* and *vayu mahabhuta*. In

pitta, *agni mahabhuta* is predominant, and ***kapha*** is primarily constituted of *jala* and *prithivi mahabhutas*.

The doctrine of the *doshas* plays an important part in *Ayurveda* in as much as it forms the basis for the maintenance of positive health as well as the diagnosis and treatment of diseases. A correct appreciation of this doctrine is, therefore, essential for proper comprehension and appreciation of the theory and practice of *Ayurveda*.

When the *doshas* are in their normal state, they sustain the body and any disturbance in their equilibrium results in disease and decay. These three *doshas* pervade the entire body, although one may be more dominant in certain elements or body organs than others. For example:

- The urinary bladder, the intestines, the pelvic region, the thighs, legs and the bones are the primary seats of ***vayu (vata)***.
- The seats of ***pitta*** are the sweat glands, the lymph, the blood and the stomach.
- The seats of ***kapha*** are the thorax, the head, the neck, the joints, the upper portion of the stomach, and the fatty tissues of the body.

Each *dosha* is divided into five qualities. These divisions represent only five different aspects of the same *doshas* and it should be made clear that they are not five different entities in the body.[11] In fact, the *doshas* and their division are located in almost all the vital organs of the body and regulate all the functions of both the body and the mind.

Locations and functions of these divisions of *vata*, *pitta* and *kapha* are given in the following chart of the ***Tridoshas***:

Chart No. 3 ~ The *Tridoshas* of *Ayurveda*

DOSHA	LOCATION	NORMAL FUNCTIONS	AILMENTS CAUSED BY ITS DEFICIENCY
VAYU (VATA) Elements: Air and Space			
1- ***PRANA***	All pervading	Breathing and swallowing of food	Hiccup, bronchitis, asthma, cold, hoarseness of voice
2- ***UDANA***	Throat	Speech and voice	Various diseases of the ear, eye, nose and throat
3- ***SAMANA***	Stomach and small intestine	Help in the action of digestive enzymes, assimilation of end products of food and separation into their various tissue elements	Indigestion, diarrhoea and defective assimilation
4- ***APANA***	Colon and organs of the pelvis	Elimination of stool, urine, semen and menstrual blood	Diseases of bladder, anus, testicles, obstinate urinary diseases including diabetes
5- ***VAYANA***	Heart	Helps in circulation of channels like blood vessels	Impairment of circulation and diseases like fever, diarrhoea

PITTA Elements: Fire			
1- ***PACHAKA***	Stomach and small intestines	Digestion	Indigestion
2- ***RANJAKA***	Liver, spleen and stomach	Blood formation	Anemia, jaundice, etc.
3- ***SADHAKA***	Heart	Memory and other mental functions	Psychic disturbances
4- ***ALOCHAKA***	Eyes	Vision	Impairment of vision
5- ***BHRAJAKA***	Skin	Colour and glaze of the skin	Leucoderma and other skin diseases
KAPHA Elements: Earth and Water			
1- ***KLEDAKA***	Stomach	Moistens food, which helps in digestion	Impairment of digestion
2- ***AVALAMBAKA***	Heart	Energy in limbs	Laziness
3- ***BODHAKA***	Tongue	Perception of taste	Impairment of taste
4- ***TARPAKA***	Heart	Nourishment of sense organs	Loss of memory and impairment of the functions of the sense organs
5- ***SHLESHAKA***	Joints	Lubrication of the joints	Pain in joints and the impairment of the functions of the joints.

SOURCE: *ATHARVA VEDA*, Modern Textbooks of *Ayurveda*

Concept Of *Sapta* (Seven) *Dhatu*

The *dhatus* are the basic tissue elements of the body. The term *dhatu* etymologically means "one which assists the body or which enters the formation of the basic structure of the body as a whole". The *dhatus* are seven in number and they are:

1. ***Rasa*** (chyle, including lymph)
2. ***Rakta*** (hemoglobin fraction of the blood)
3. ***Mamsa*** (muscle tissue)
4. ***Medas*** (fat tissue)
5. ***Asthi*** (bone tissue)
6. ***Majja*** (bone marrow)
7. ***Shukra*** (sperm in male and ovum in female)

These seven *dhatus* are composed of the five *mahabhutas.*

1. ***Prithivi*** *mahabhuta* predominates in muscle and fat tissues.
2. ***Jala*** *mahabhuta* predominates in the lymph and chyle.
3. The hemoglobin fraction of the blood is primarily constituted of ***Agni*** *mahabhuta.*
4. The bone is composed of ***Vayu*** *mahabhuta,*
5. The pores inside the bone are dominated by ***Akasa*** *mahabhuta.*

It should be made clear here again that all the seven *dhatus* are composed of all the five *mahabhutas* and only the dominating *mahabhutas* are described above. The *dhatus* remain inside the human body of the individual in a particular proportion. And any change in their equilibrium leads to disease and decay.

CONCEPT OF *MALA*

Stool, urine and sweat are the three important *malas* recognised in *Ayurveda*. They are waste products of the body and their proper elimination is essential for the maintenance of the health of the individual.

STOOL: Stool is not only the refuse of the food taken by the individual as is commonly believed; it also contains substances which are eliminated from the tissue cells of the body. Proper evacuation of stool is essential for maintaining the tissue cells in their state of excellent health. If there is improper evacuation, diseases occur, not only in the gastro-intestinal tract, but also in other parts of the body. In diseases like lumbago, rheumatism, sciatica and paralysis and even bronchitis and asthma, taking precautions to ensure proper evacuation of the stool is essential before starting any *Ayurvedic* treatment. If not properly evacuated, it provides a congenial atmosphere for the growth of different kinds of intestinal worms. This affects the growth of the friendly bacteria in the colon, which help in the synthesis of nutrients which are useful for the body.

URINE: This is another waste product through which body wastes are eliminated. Even though excessive passage of urine is considered a disease, in *Ayurveda* it is always advised that the person should take adequate quantity of water, both in summer and winter, so as to pass urine a minimum six times during the daytime.

SWEAT: Sweating is essential for the maintenance of health of the skin. Proper exercise and therapies like fomentation, as well as certain drugs, help the individual to sweat, enabling many bodily wastes to be eliminated.

Normally stool, urine, and sweat have a foul smell. At times, the smell becomes intolerable and the individual has to take certain medicines for correcting these foul odours.

The Five Elements Are Based On Truth

Sri Sathya Sai Baba says:

When the five elements have such immense power, can you imagine what must be the potency of the Divine, which sustains them? The five elements are manifestations of the *Paramatmaswarupa* (Supreme Omniself). No one can deny its existence, whether one is a theist, an atheist or an agnostic. Today, these five elements are not being properly used. Instead, they are very much misused. Their misuse is the root cause of all the travails of the world. As the five elements are based on Truth, the ancient *rishis* observed restraint in speech so that they could adhere to the maxim, **"Restraint in speech nourishes the Truth"**. Excessive speech is the cause of great unrest. It is essential, therefore, for everyone to recognise the basic role of the five elements and live in consonance with that awareness.

The mind demonstrates the nature of the five elements. Belief (*mathi*) has emerged from the mind. Religion (*matham*) is a reflection of belief. Religion is not what it is normally understood to be; it is based on misbelief. Many are engaged in destruction of religion. If religion is destroyed, belief (or faith) will be destroyed and then the mind itself will be destroyed. Religious hatred has to be gotten rid of, not religions as such. Adherents of all faiths recognise the power of the five elements and therefore worship them. Based on the source of the five elements, ***Vedas*** have conceived the oneness of God.

When the *Hridayam* is filled with compassion, when the hands are dedicated to the service of others, when the body is engaged in constant help to others, then the life of such a person is sacred, purposeful and noble. The entire Cosmos is based on this bedrock of Truth. Wealth and welfare and all comforts and pleasures are dependent on truth. Wherever you turn, truth shines effulgently. The goddess of wealth, Lakshmi, dwells in the abode of truth. The world cannot exist without truth, just as the rays cannot exist without the sun. Truth is the Cosmos and the Cosmos is Truth. The entire Cosmos is permeated by the Divine (*Isavasyam Idam Jagat*). It is foolish to imagine that the natural, physical and mundane world is real and nothing else sustains it.

Proper Use Of The Five Elements

Man must realise that true humanness can be achieved only when the five elements in the universe are properly used. The other four elements are superimposed on the first, Earth. Without the base, the other elements will be functionless. Hence, all human beings living on Earth should cooperate with each other, engage themselves in socially helpful activities, and redeem their lives. Every man has duties to perform, but can claim no rights. Duties and rights go together. Today, people tend to assert their rights without regard to their responsibilities or duties. This has become a kind of epidemic in all spheres of life today. When you discharge your responsibilities, your rights will be automatically ensured.

Be Good, Do Good, Speak Good

All of you are embodiments of the Spirit (*Atma*). You are all manifestations of the Divine. The Indwelling Spirit is one and the same in all beings irrespective of their external difference, like the current that illumines bulbs of different wattage and colour. Fill your *Hridayam* with love. Then you can experience real bliss. With a narrow mind and impure *Hridayam* if you pontificate, no one will care to listen to you. First of all "Be" – be good yourself. Then "Do" – act likewise. Then "Speak" – tell others (what is good). Only thus you will be setting an ideal example. **Do not entertain bad feelings about anyone.** They do you more harm than they do to others. As the saying goes: "One's own anger is one's enemy and one's peace is one's friend and kinfolk. One's happiness is heaven and one's sorrow is hell." Develop sacred and pure feelings. We claim to celebrate the birthday of people. But the birthday is only truly celebrated when there is the birth of pure ideas in *Hridayam*.

Purity Is Most Important

Purity is the most important. Today everything is polluted. Water, air and all the five elements are polluted. As a result the mind of man is also polluted. How is purity to be achieved? Fill your minds with thoughts of God, dedicate all your actions to God, and consider God as the inner motivator. Contemplation of God is not a matter for derision. You need have no fear on that account. You must have full faith in God, who is the universal sustainer. He is the protector, but not the punisher. The punishment you get is the consequence of your own actions. Therefore, chant the name of God, sing *bhajans,* perform good deeds, and engage yourselves in service of your fellow beings. Nourish love in your hearts. Love will drive away all bad thoughts. It will promote the spirit of forgiveness.[12]

---

1 *Bhagawan* Sri Sathya Sai Baba, **Discourses on the *Bhagavad Gita,*** Ch17, 1984.

2 *Bhagawan* Sri Sathya Sai Baba, **Discourses on the *Bhagavad Gita,*** Ch 28, 1984.

3 *Bhagawan* Sri Sathya Sai Baba, Divine Discourse, 23/11/1993.

4 *Bhagawan* Sri Sathya Sai Baba, recorded in **Vision of Sai** by Rita Bruce.

5 *Bhagawan* Sri Sathya Sai Baba, ***Sanathana Sarathi,*** August 1995.

6 Vidyalankar, Pandit Satyakam, **The Holy *Vedas,*** Clarion Books, Delhi, Reprint 1998.

7 *Bhagawan* Sri Sathya Sai Baba, Divine Discourse, 21/10/1982.

8 *Bhagawan* Sri Sathya Sai Baba, ***Upanishad Vahini,*** Ch. 11.

9 *Bhagawan* Sri Sathya Sai Baba, **Sathya Sai Speaks, Vol 10,** Ch. 14,

10 *Bhagawan* Sri Sathya Sai Baba, **Discourses on the *Bhagavad Gita,*** Ch 22, 1984.

11 ***Charvaka Sastra.***

12 *Bhagawan* Sri Sathya Sai Baba, Divine Discourse, 23/11/1993.

In an ocean, there are huge waves like mountains, then smaller waves and still smaller ones down to little bubbles, but in back of all these is the infinite ocean. The bubble is connected with the infinite ocean at one end and the huge wave at the other end. Likewise, everyone, no matter how gigantic, small, or different in any way, is connected with that infinite ocean of energy, which is the common birth right of every man, animal and plant that exists.

~ **Sri Sathya Sai Baba**

chapter - 3

THE *AKASA*, *PRANA* AND VIBRATIONS

According to the philosophers of India, the whole universe is composed of two materials, one of which they call ***Akasa*** **(Ether)** and the other is ***Prana*** **(Energy)**. The *akasa* is omnipresent, all-penetrating existence. Everything that has form, everything that is the result of combination, is evolved out of this *akasa*. It is the *akasa* that becomes the air, that becomes the liquids, that becomes the solids; it is *akasa* that becomes the sun, the earth, the moon, the stars and the comets. It is the *akasa* that becomes the human body, the animal body, the plants and the minerals. It becomes every form we see, everything that can be sensed, and everything that exists. It cannot be perceived. It is so subtle that it is beyond all ordinary perception and can only be seen when it has become gross and taken on a form. At the beginning of creation there is only this *akasa*. At the end of the cycle solids, liquids and gases all melt into the *akasa* again. The next creation similarly proceeds out of this *akasa*.

Sri Sathya Sai Baba says:

That which cannot be seen by the eye, or cannot be heard by the ear or cannot be expressed by words characterizes the realm of *akasa*. It cannot be comprehended by the mind either. The sun and the moon, the clouds and the stars belong to the realm of *akasa*. There are three different *akasas*:

1. ***BHUTAKASA*:** This is the one you think you are because it contains all that you see, hear and experience. *Bhutakasa* envelops the visible and the invisible phenomena. For example, some stars are visible in the sky; but there are many more that remain invisible. The light emanating from the stars is stupendous in its intensity. The brilliance cannot be withstood by anything or anyone on the earth. Our sun imparts only a portion of its radiance to earth. Neither the huge stars nor the sun and the moon are capable of generating this effulgence on their own. There is a fundamental power that is the basis of all this. It is the basic illumination from which the rest of the brilliance originates. This primordial power is that of the *Atma*. It allows the stars, sun and moon to shine. All these mentioned are encompassed in the *Bhutakasa*. The *Bhutakasa* spreads over an extent that is impossible to calculate.

2. ***CHITTHAKASA*:** This is the one that others think you are because it reflects in your mind's eye whatever you contemplate on. In it is reflected or imprinted everything that is seen in *Bhutakasa*. The span of *Chitthakasa* is very small and subtle. On the other hand, the gross *Bhutakasa* spans a terrific event. **Yet the entire contents of *Bhutakasa* appear in the *Chitthakasa* as small blips.** For example, you see a huge mountain. When you close your eyes after seeing it, you will be able to visualize the image of the mountain from *Chitthakasa*. Similarly, the stars and sky and all that is seen are permanently etched on the *Chitthakasa*. The entire creation is stored in *Chitthakasa* in a subtle form. *Bhutakasa* is physically perceptible; that which is mentally perceptible is *Chitthakasa*.

3. ***CHIDAKASA*:** This is the one you really are or the principle of the *Atma* – your true nature. It has no form. It has no movement. It is attributeless, pure, the final abode, eternal, unsullied, enlightened, free and the embodiment of sacredness. He who

has seen this *Chidakasa* is one who has had the experience of *Atma*. It has nothing to do with reflections, reactions and resounds. It is beyond all the three. [1]

The whole vast world, the *Bhutakasa* is something like an atom in the *Chitthakasa*, the mental world, just as your body is like an atom in the *Bhutakasa*. And this incredibly huge *Chitthakasa* is only the size of an atom in the *Chidakasa*, the causal world. The *Bhutakasa*, being made up of the five gross elements (*akasa*, air, fire, water, earth), can be apprehended by the five senses of perception (ears, skin, eyes, mouth, nose). But since everything in the *Bhutakasa* is made up of the five gross elements and only the five elements, the *Bhutakasa* is inert and insentient.

Similarly, this divine principle is also to be found in the *Chitthakasa*; however, although the *Chitthakasa* is made up of the same five elements in their subtle aspects (sound, touch, form, taste, smell), it is inert and insentient. But, just as the divine principle as the indweller is inherent in the inert body, vitalizing and activating it, so also, it is inherent in these physical and mental worlds, the *Bhutakasa* and *Chitthakasa*. The divine principle shines forth from the *Chidakasa*, the subtlest of these infinite universes.

In order to understand this, consider a reflection in a mirror. The image or reflection has no independent existence of its own. It moves only when the object which is being reflected moves. All the apparent luster of objects in the world arises from the *Chidakasa*, the causal world, and is then reflected by the *Chitthakasa* and *Bhutakasa*, which act as mirrors. Just as the effulgence of the sun gets reflected by the moon, the effulgence present in the causal state of *Chidaakasa* gets reflected in the subtle mental state of the *Chitthakasa* and then the gross physical state of the *Bhutakasa*. [2]

Sai Baba concludes by saying, "True *akasa* is *'Hridayakasa'* – the heart."[3]

Prana And Manifestation

Sri Sathya Sai Baba continues:

By what power is *akasa* manufactured into this universe? By the power of *prana*. **Just as *akasa* is the universe, so is *prana* the infinite, omnipresent manifesting power of this universe.** At the beginning and end of a cycle everything becomes *akasa,* and all the infinite forces of power in the universe resolve back into the *prana*. In the next cycle, out of this *prana* is evolved everything that we call energy, everything that we call force. It is the *prana* that is manifesting as motion; it is the *prana* that is manifesting as gravitation and magnetism. It is the *prana* that is manifesting as actions of the body, as the nerve currents and thought force. From the thought down to the lowest force, everything is but the manifestation of *prana*. The sum total of all forces in the universe, mental or physical, when resolved back to their original state, is called *prana*.

Aim Of *Pranayama*

The knowledge and control of this *prana* is really what is meant by *pranayama.* This opens to us the door to almost unlimited power. Suppose, for instance, a man understood the *prana* perfectly, and could control it, what power of earth would not be his? He would be able to move the sun and stars out of their places, to control everything in the universe, from atoms to the biggest suns, because he would control *prana*. This is the end and aim of *pranayama.* When the *yogi* becomes perfect, there will be nothing in nature that is not under his control. If he orders the Gods or the souls of the departed to come, they will come at his bidding. All the forces of nature will obey him as slaves.

When the ignorant see the powers of the *yogi*, they call them miracles. The question is raised in the ***Vedas***, **"What is that,**

knowing which, we shall know everything?" In the ***VEDAS***, just as the whole universe has been generalised into that One Absolute Existence – and he who has grasped that Existence has grasped the whole universe, so, too, all forces have been generalised into this *prana* – and he who has grasped the *prana* has grasped all the forces of the universe, mental or physical. He who has controlled the *prana* has controlled his own mind, and all the minds that exist. He who has controlled the *prana* has controlled his body and all the bodies that exist, because the *prana* is the generalised manifestation of force.

CONTROLLING *PRANA*

How to control the *prana* is the one idea of *pranayama*. All the training and exercises in this regard are for that one end. Each man must begin where he stands, must learn how to control the things that are nearest to him. This body is very near to us, nearer than anything in the external universe and this mind is nearest of all. The *prana* which is working this mind and body is the nearest to us of all the *prana* in the universe. This little wave of *prana*, which represents our own energies, mental and physical, is nearer to us than all the waves of the infinite ocean of *prana*. **[SEE DIAGRAM NO. 4]**

If we can succeed in controlling that little wave, then we can hope to control the whole *prana*. The *yogi* who has accomplished this gains perfection. No longer is he under any power. He becomes almost almighty, almost all-knowing. We see sects in every country that have attempted this control of *prana*. In many countries, there are **mind-healers, faith healers, spiritualists, Christian Scientists, hypnotists,** etc., and if we examine their different healing modalities, we shall find behind each this control of the *prana*. The *prana* is the vital force in every being.[4]

Thought – The Highest Action Of *Prana*

Thought is the finest and highest action of *prana*. Thought, as we conceive it, is not all; there is also what we call instinct or unconscious thinking, the lowest plane of action. If a mosquito stings us, our hand will strike it automatically, instinctively. This is one expression of thought. All reflex actions of the body belong to this plane of thought. There is again the other plane of thought, the conscious. "I reason, I judge, I see the pros and cons of certain things" – yet that is not all. We know that reason is limited. Reason can go only to a certain extent and beyond that it cannot reach.

The mind can exist on a still higher plane, the super conscious, where is goes beyond the limits of reason, and comes face to face with facts which no instinct or reason can ever know. All manipulations of the subtle forces of the body, the different manifestations of *prana*, if trained, give a push to the mind, helping it rise up to the super conscious, which is the plane of cause.[5]

The Universe Is Composed Of Vibrations

The actions of *prana* are most subtle. This very ether, in the finer state of vibration, will represent the mind, and there it will be one unbroken mass. If you can simply get to that subtle vibration, you will see, feel, and know that the whole universe is composed of subtle vibrations. Sometimes certain drugs have the power to induce us to that condition. Many of you may remember the celebrated experiment of **Sir Humphrey Davy** [developer of laughing gas]. When the laughing gas overpowered him during the lecture, he remained motionless, stupefied, and after that, he said that **the whole universe was made up of ideas**. For the time being, the gross vibration had ceased and only the subtle vibrations, which he called ideas, were present for him. He could only see the subtle vibrations around him; everything had

The Flow Of *Prana*

***Prana* (vital force) flows from . . .**

- Above downwards
- More important organs to less important organs
- Inside out
- Centre to periphery

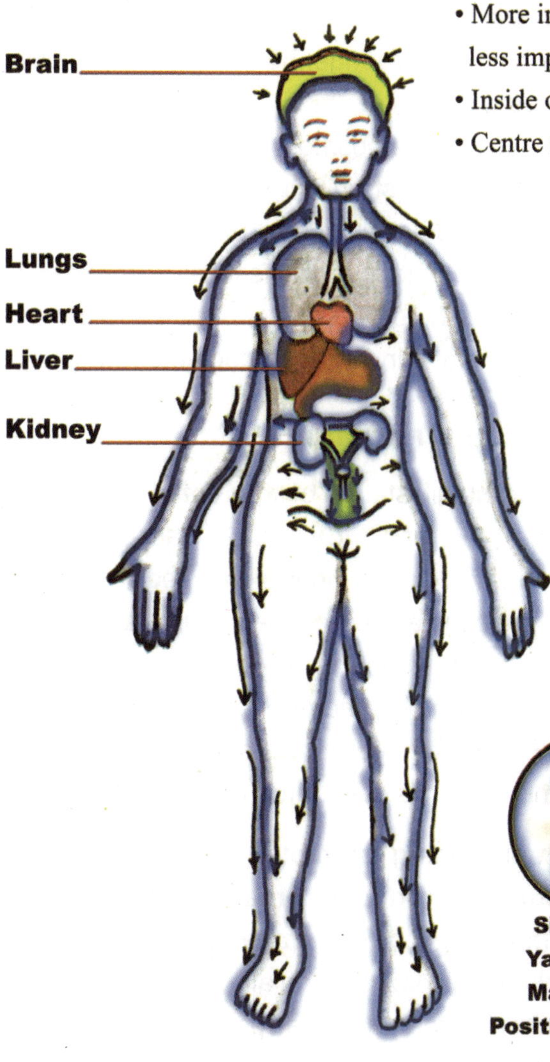

Siva	**Sakti**
Yang	**Yin**
Male	**Female**
Positive	**Negative**

Human Values And Health ~ Diagram No. 4

Source: Spirituality And Health, Author

become thought; the whole universe was an ocean of thought; he and everyone else had become little whirlpools of thought.

Thus, even in the universe of thought we find unity, and at last, when we get to the Self, we know that the Self can only be One. Beyond the vibrations of matter in its gross and subtle aspects, beyond motion, there is but One. Even in manifested motion there is only unity. These facts can no longer be denied. Modern physics also has demonstrated that the sum total of the energies in the universe permeates the whole cosmos. It has also been proven that this sum total of energy exists in two forms or states. One form is a quiet state where it is potential, toned down and restive. Energy then moves into an active state and manifests as all these various forces; again it returns to the quiet state and the cycle continues. Thus, it goes on evolving and involving through eternity.[6]

The Manifestation Of *Prana*

The most obvious manifestation of this *prana* in the human body is the motion of the lungs. If that stops, as a rule, all the other manifestations of force in the body will immediately stop. But there are persons who can train themselves in such a manner that the body will live on, even when this motion has stopped. There are some persons who can bury themselves for days and yet live without breathing. *Pranayama* really means controlling the motion of the lungs, and this motion is associated with the breath.

It is not breath producing the motion of the lungs; on the contrary, the motion is producing breath. This motion draws the air in by a pumping action. The *prana* moves the lungs and the movement of the lungs draws in the air. So, *pranayama* is not breathing, but controlling that muscular power which moves the lungs. That muscular power, which goes out through the nerves to the muscles and to the lungs, making them move in a certain manner, is the *prana* that needs to be controlled in the practice of *pranayama*. When the *prana* has become controlled, then we shall immediately find that all the other actions of the *prana* in the body will slowly come under control.

Prana And Healing

In *pranayama*, while drawing the breath in, you must fill your whole body with *prana*. In some English translations, *prana* is defined as breath, and you are inclined to ask, "How can the body be filled with breath?" The fault is in the translation. *Prana* is already in every part of the body to some degree, but when you are able to awaken and revitalise it you can control the whole body. All the sickness and misery felt in the body will be perfectly controlled and you will be able to inadvertently control another's body. **Everything is infectious in this world, good or bad.** If your body were in a certain state of tension, it will have the tendency to produce the same tension in others.

In the case of a man trying to heal through laying-on-of-hands, the concept is simply to transfer his own health to the other. This is a primitive sort of healing. Consciously or unconsciously, health can be transmitted. A very strong man, living with a weak man, will make him a little stronger, whether he knows it or not. When consciously done, it becomes quicker and better in its action. The first man, in such a case, has a little more control over the *prana*, and can arouse, for the time being, his *prana*, as it were, to a certain state of vibration, and transmit it to another person.

DISTANCE HEALING. Cases of *pranic* healing, as well as intense healing prayers from a distance are perfectly true. The *prana* can be transmitted over a great distance, but for every genuine case, there are hundreds of frauds. This process of healing is not as easy as it is thought to be. In the most ordinary cases of such healing, you will find that the healers simply take advantage of the naturally healthy state of the human body. An Allopath comes and treats cholera patients and gives his medicines. The Homeopath comes and gives his medicines and cures perhaps more than the Allopath does, because the Homeopath does not disturb his patients, but allows nature to deal with them. The faith healer brings the strength of his mind to bear and through faith rouses the dormant *prana* of the patient. New neuropeptides in the patient's brain are produced giving *prana sakti* to the patient.

Enlightened Beings And *Prana*

The man who has purified his *Hridayam* and controlled the *prana*, has the power of bringing *sakti* into a certain state of vibration, which can be conveyed to others, arousing in them a similar vibration. *Avatars*, as well as the great prophets and teachers of the world, such as Lord Jesus, Mohammed, Lord Krishna, Lord Rama, Guru Nanak, Zoroaster, Buddha, Shirdi Sai Baba and now *Bhagawan* Sri Sathya Sai Baba, can bring *prana* into such a high state of vibration, so great and powerful, that it can reach anyone at any moment. These great beings have the most profound control of *prana* and have tremendous power of will that enables them to bring *prana* to the highest state of motion, giving them the power to sway the whole world. All manifestations of power arise from this control.

Prana And Disease

Imbalances of *prana* within the body cause disease. The *pranayama* exercises balance the *prana sakti* in all the organs, keeping them healthy. Through *pranayama*, the feelings will become so subtle that the mind will feel that there is, for example, less *prana* in the toe or the finger than there should be and will possess the power to supply it. These are among the various functions of *pranayama*. When a man has concentrated his energies, he masters the *prana* that is in his body. When a man is meditating, he is also concentrating the *prana*.

It is often thought that faith directly heals a man. But faith alone does not cover all the ground. **There are diseases where the worst symptom is that the patient believes that he has a disease.** In this case, individuals are producing a different type of neuropeptide, which causes the disease they are worrying about to actually manifest. That tremendous belief or faith of the patient is itself one symptom of the disease, and usually indicates that he in fact will succumb to the disease. In such cases the principle that faith cures does not truly apply. It is by the *prana* that real curing comes.[7]

Prana And The Science Of *Yoga*

Wherever there is life, the storehouse of infinite energy is behind it. Starting as some fungus, this very minute form changes while all the time drawing from the infinite storehouse of energy. The form is changed slowly and steadily, until in the course of time, it becomes a plant, then an animal, then a man, and ultimately God. This transformation is attained through millions of eons, but what is time? An increase of speed, an increase of struggle, is able to bridge this gulf of time. The soul, by intensifying its action, attains perfection in this very life. All beings will at last attain that goal, we know. Why delay all these millions of eons, when it can be attained immediately in this body, this human form now? Why not get that infinite knowledge and infinite power now?

The ideal of the *yogi*, the whole science of *yoga*, is directed to teaching men how, by intensifying the power of assimilation, to shorten the time of reaching perfection, instead of slowly advancing from point to point and waiting until the whole human race has become perfect. All the great prophets, saints, and seers of the world—what did they do? In one span of life, they lived the whole life of humanity and traversed the whole length of time that it takes for ordinary humanity to come to perfection. In one life, they perfected themselves. They had no thought for anything else, never lived a moment for any other idea and thus, the way was shortened for them. This is what is meant by concentration, intensifying the power of assimilation and thereby shortening time. *Raja Yoga* is the science, which teaches us how to gain the power of concentration.

Pranayama And Spiritualism

Spiritualism is also a manifestation of *pranayama*. Assuming it is true that the departed spirits exist and we are unable to see them, then it is quite conceivable that there are hundreds and millions of spirits around us that we can neither see, feel, nor touch. **We may be continually passing and re-passing through their bodies and we do not see or feel one another.** In fact, studies in the U.S.A. have proved that departed souls do exist in this universe. It is a circle within a circle, universe within universe. We have five senses and we represent *prana* in a certain state of vibration. All beings in the same state of vibration will see another, but if there are beings who represent *prana* in a higher state of vibration, they will not be seen. We may increase the intensity of the light until we cannot see it at all, but there may be beings with eyes so powerful that they can see such light. Again, if its vibrations are very low, we do not see the light, but there are animals that may see it, such as cats and owls. Our range of vision is only on one plane of vibration of this *prana*. Take this atmosphere, for instance; it is piled up layer on layer, but the layers nearer to the earth are denser than those above, and as you go higher the atmosphere becomes finer and finer. Similarly, as you go deeper and deeper in the ocean, the pressure increases, and creatures that live at the bottom can never come up, or they will break into pieces.

An Ocean Of Vibrations

Think of the universe as an ocean of *akasa*, consisting of layer upon layer of varying degrees of vibrations under the action of *prana*; away from the centre the vibrations are less, nearer to it they become quicker and quicker. One order of vibration makes one plane. Suppose these varying degrees or ranges of vibrations are cut into planes, it then creates millions of miles of one set of vibrations that is nearer and nearer to the centre, and quickens in its vibration. Now suppose these sets of vibrations are further cut into planes creating still higher sets of vibrations, and so on. It is therefore probable that those who live on the plane of a certain state of vibration will have the power of recognising one another, but will not recognise those above or below them. Just as in the use of the telescope and microscope, we can increase the scope of our vision, similarly, we can by *yoga* bring ourselves to the state of vibration of another plane, and thus enable ourselves to see what is going on there.

Suppose your room is full of beings whom you do not see. They represent *prana* in a certain state of vibration, while we represent another. Suppose they represent a quick one, and we the opposite. *Prana* is the material of which they are composed as well as we. All are parts of the same ocean of *prana*; they differ only in their rate of vibration. All this bringing of the mind into a higher state of vibration is included in one word -- *yoga-samadhi* (union with the infinite, God). All these states of higher vibration and super conscious vibrations of the mind are grouped in that one word, *samadhi*, and the lower states of *samadhi* give us the visions of these beings. The highest grade of *samadhi* is when we see the Reality, when we see the material out of which the whole of these multiple grades of being is composed, and by that one lump of clay being known, we know all the clay of the universe.

Prana controlled by physical means is called physical science, and that part which tries to control the manifestations of the *prana* as mental force, by mental means, is called *Raja Yoga*.[8]

HATHA YOGA: PRANAYAMA AND *ASANA*

The control of *prana* through *yogic* breathing exercises in conjunction with *asana* (posture) plays a large role in the practice of *Hatha Yoga*. Over the last few decades, medical science has discovered what the sages of ancient Indian have known for centuries – intelligent manipulation of the vital life force *(prana)* can heal the body and promote long-term physical wellbeing. Details on specific breathing practices as related to the practice of *Hatha Yoga*, along with medical implications can be found later in this book.

Sri Sathya Sai Baba Says:

"*Pranayama* is the tapping of the cosmic energy – the *'Pranic'* life-giving force. Fire can be used to give warmth, but if not used properly it is one of the most destructive forces on earth. Likewise the *pranayama* exercise must be done under proper guidance by someone who is practising it."[9]

"Like metals purified over fire in the crucible, the slag of *karma* is removed by *pranayama* and the mind is freed from contamination. The mind and the body are both rendered pure. There are two types of breath control: with *mantra* (sacred words) and without it. Without *mantra*, it can at best transform only the body, but with *mantra* it also transforms the mind."[10]

---

1 *Bhagawan* Sri Sathya Sai Baba, **Summer Showers 2002,** Ch. 9.
2 *Bhagawan* Sri Sathya Sai Baba, **Discourses on the *Bhagavad Gita*,** Ch. 22.
3 *Bhagawan* Sri Sathya Sai Baba, **Summer Showers 2002,** Ch. 9.
4 Aurobindo, **The Life Divine.**
5 Author, **Spirituality and Health.**
6 Vivekananda, Swami, ***Raja Yoga.***
7 Hahnmanns, Dr. Samuel, **Organon of Homeopathy.**
8 Vivekananda, Swami, ***Raja Yoga.***
9 *Bhagawan* Sri Sathya Sai Baba, recorded in **Journey to God, III** by J. Jagadeesan.
10 *Bhagawan* Sri Sathya Sai Baba, Divine Discourse, 31/08/1983.

Nature has many mysteries in its makeup. Man is able to unravel only those that are cognisable through his five senses; he does not realise that there is a vast unknown beyond the purview of the five faulty instruments of perception that he has.

~ **SRI SATHYA SAI BABA**

chapter - 4

THE UNSEEN WORLDS

The basic component of the Unseen Worlds is the element *akasa* (ether or space). Its particles are composed of the finest individuated matter (the *Chidakasa* of the causal world) as well as the dense physical atoms from the *Bhutakasa*, the physical world. The plane in between these two has been called the "Astral World". The bulk of the Astral World exists in the *Chitthakasa* (the subtle mental world) and interpenetrates as a sphere into the physical world just as *akasa* permeates everything. So this Astral World is also everywhere in the physical world, vibrating at an unseen frequency.

Everything that exists, the Creator and the created, is energy, and energy vibrates according to its nature. The Astral World is no exception. It is simply a realm of experience with levels of vibration that are, as yet, beyond the capacity of scientific instruments to measure. It has, however, been well documented by human experience through the ages and recorded in the great spiritual texts of all the religions of the world. Sri Sathya Sai Baba uses the fine matter of this realm to communicate with His devotees around the world.

Sri Sathya Sai Baba says:

The subtle universe, which is so indescribably huge when compared to the physical universe, is itself only a microscopic part of a much, much vaster aspect of the universe, which can be described as the causal universe. It is known as the causal universe because it is out of this finest aspect that the gross and subtle worlds arise. All of these three worlds, the physical, the subtle (or mental/emotional), and the causal are so enormously big, the scriptures have declared that they cannot possibly be understood by the human mind or depicted in words. They are beyond imagination and beyond the ability of the mind to grasp. And yet beyond all these, transcending the gross, the subtle and the causal, is the Divine Principle, the ultimate cause of all.[1]

Subplanes Of The Subtle Mental World

The confinement of the soul in the physical body does not allow the ordinary person to have a glimpse of these worlds beyond the physical. Sages and seers have documented a number of sub-planes for the Astral World. **[See Diagram No. 5]** Here everything shines. It has transparency and is therefore called astral, meaning light or starry. The scenery is similar to that on earth, as there is replication of physical objects. Due to transparency, every object is visible inside out. The forms change their outlines quickly since they are flexible and are almost instantly affected by the impact of thoughts.

A number of beings live in the Astral World. There are human and animal spirits who have lost their physical bodies as well as natural elementals or nature spirits. These spirits belong to each of the five elements – ether, fire, air, water and earth. The divine energies work through these elemental beings. Sages and adepts who have mastered the arts of walking on hot coals or water and levitating, etc. have simply learned to commune and manipulate these nature spirits. Agriculturalists who know how to work with the nature spirits invariably have large, healthy crops at the harvest time. The truth of this has been documented over many decades of experience in the well known community of

The Astral World

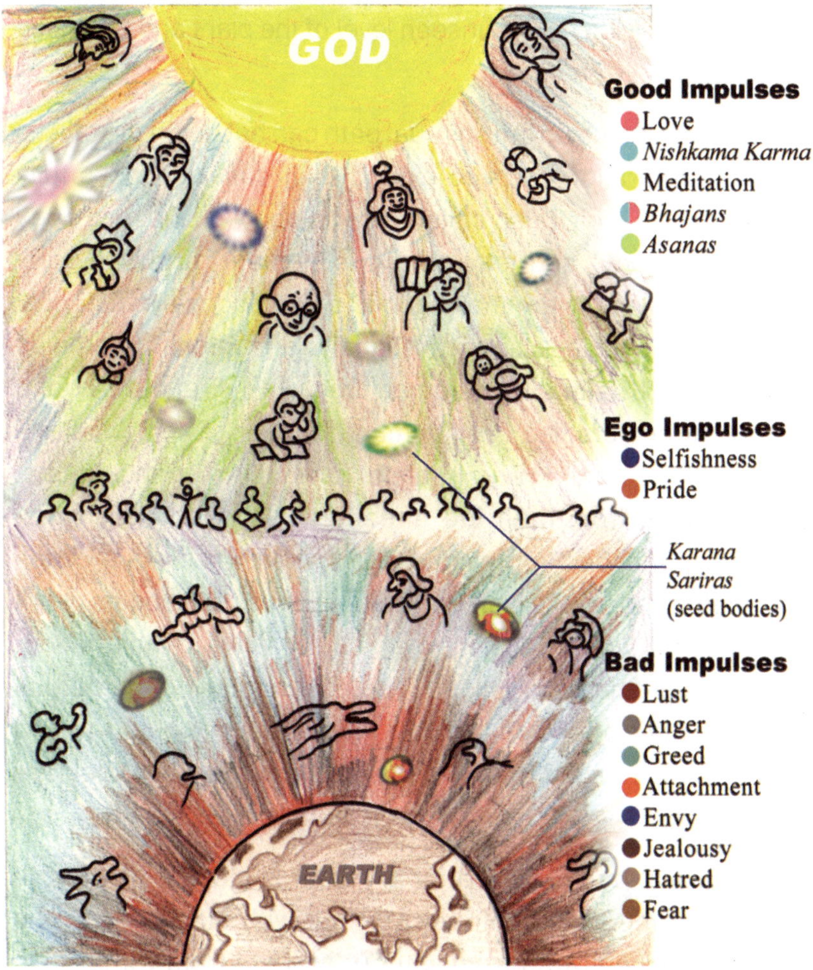

Human Values And Health ~ Diagram No. 5

Source: Divine Discourses of *Bhagawan* Sri Sathya Sai Baba, *Vedantic Method And Virtuous Children*, Author

Findhorn in Scotland. The ***Puranas*** as well, are full of tales of *rishis* and *mahatmas* who can work "miracles" due to their affinity with these beings. Many Education in Human Values classes have experimented by sending love to growing plants. It reaches the nature spirits living on the unseen level of the plant and produces the same positive result.

Those who take up the spiritual path can be taught the mystic practices that allow them to extend their consciousness fully into the astral body (also called etheric body, bioplasmic body and subtle body) and leave the confinement of the physical body. Because they are moving in finer vibrations of existence, they may become clairvoyant and clairaudient. Examples include Lord Krishna, Mohammed, Jesus, St. Francis, Buddha as well as healers like Hahnneman (founder of homeopathy), Mei-ling (teacher of *Pranic* healing), and Bhag Singh Lambha. Some people from birth are already developed in this area, due to experiences in previous incarnations. There are cases of people who, while asleep, have their astral bodies work in the astral world. Most human souls, while reincarnating, pass through the Astral World. The astral bodies of numerous animals linger after death. Their mental energy gets trapped due to the confusion and fear they experience when they are slaughtered.

The astral body of an ordinary man is cloudy, loose and not well formed. The colours are dull with little variety. His activity is accelerated from without and not from within. The shocks of the physical world are meant to stimulate the astral activity. The etheric material comprising the astral body may change for good or evil. When a man begins to be moved by his will or even divine will, rather than by desire, it shows a significant advancement in consciousness and there is a corresponding transformation in his astral body.

The Astral Planes

The ***Adi Guru Grant Sahab*** and the ***Holy Quran*** detail the varied experiences on the different planes of the Astral World. Each one represents a level of consciousness. "Like" attracts "like" and these planes are created when souls of similar vibrations come together. Everything is, as Sai Baba tells us, simply a matter of reaction, reflection and resound.

FIRST: This lowest astral sub-plane consists of the spirits of rough people such as murderers, ruffians, criminals, drunkards and others. They have dissatisfied desires, hatred and many longings. The spirits easily possess people on earth who have similar cravings and desires. They undergo tortures to fulfill their thirst, which they can never satisfy since they no longer have physical bodies. They are made to learn the lesson of nature's laws, such as *karma* (cause and effect), which they could have learned in earthly life.

SECOND, THIRD, FOURTH: The spirits on the second sub-plane are entangled due to their earthly interests. The following two sub-planes are the same; the souls that are held there are still susceptible to earthly stimuli, but they have progressed further along the path of wakefulness.

FIFTH: This sub-plane is radiant and luminous, justifying the name "astral" (meaning "starry"). This plane represents the so-called Heaven. Here the desires of human beings are realised as in the example of the so-called *Houris* (beautiful women) of the Muslim concept. As promised on earth, these cravings are enjoyed by the power of imaginative creations. An important feature of this plane is that communities are developed in the astral matter and religious faith is formulated, based on this very power of imaginative creations.

SIXTH: This sub-plane is also the so-called Heaven. It is like the fifth, but its vibration is much finer. The inhabitants on this plane are the saints, Sufis and self-realised souls whose mental energies work for good on the earth.

SEVENTH: The spirits of highly intelligent people occupy this sub-plane. According to Baba some students live for centuries in astral libraries. Those who were investigating any problems before death continue their investigations. They and others, such as politicians, scientists, etc. are still held to lower life as they cling to their earthly pursuits.[2,3]

Life And Death On The Astral Planes

After leaving the physical body at death, one enters the Astral World *(Chitthakasa)*. The exceptions are those who immediately take physical birth again or those elevated souls who, having gained knowledge of the *Atma*, are able to transcend all the *Akasic* realms to merge into the Supreme Consciousness.

As the bonds of one astral plane dissolve, the soul awakens on the next higher plane. The astral shell (also called *Karana Sarira*) is then disintegrated just like the physical corpse made of the gross elements. The released etheric material mixes up with the astral matter of that world.

Prayer and thought waves from near and dear ones on earth produces vibrations which affect the astral matter. When directed towards the departed souls, they strike the astral body, hastening its disintegration and helping the soul in its transition to higher planes. The departed souls are very much assisted by these loving and peaceful thoughts to break their fetters.[4]

Sages and saints of *Vedic* times possessed this occult knowledge, which explains the practice of multiple ceremonies, rites and rituals performed by them for the benefit of the dead. This is also the basis of the instructions given by the third Sikh *Guru*, Amar Das, at the time of his demise, beautifully recorded by Bhai Sunder, in the ***Holy Guru Granth Sahab***. In fact, every religion possesses very specific rituals around death and dying to support the soul to let go and reach the higher planes of existence.

In 1984, there was a very sorrowful incident in Bangalore in which 364 persons died due to liquor that was poisonous. The next day during the *Dasera puja,* I was sitting in the Poornachandra Hall, of Prasanthi Nilayam at Puttaparthi. In His discourse that day, *Swami* spoke on the Astral World and the *Karana Sarira* (causal body). *Swami* said, "Those who die in pubs due to drinking poisonous liquor have their *Karana Sariras* float in air around the pubs."[5] Similarly, there are those people, who die either in accidents or by committing suicide, whose wishes could not be fulfilled during their lifetime. The *Karana Sariras* of such people also float in the air at the lower level of the Astral World. Our prayers for the world, particularly, *Loka Samastha Sukino Bhavanthu* (may all the beings in all the worlds be happy), rise up through the ethers, giving welcome relief to these trapped souls.

Athi Rudha Maha Yajna was held during August 2006 in the Divine Presence of *Bhagawan* Sri Sathya Sai Baba in Puttaparthi. Such a *yajna* is the highest form of worship to Lord Siva, who is the very source of the whole manifested creation. The sole purpose of this *yajna* was to foster peace and wellbeing of all the beings - in the seen and unseen worlds - throughout the entire universe.

Attachment To The Living

Sri Sathya Sai Baba tells us that the thoughts of all human beings vibrate in their nervous systems and form energy patterns in the atmosphere around them. Vibrations coming from a man having feelings of hatred, envy, jealousy, lust, anger, greed, etc., reproduce certain vibrations in his nervous system and limbic system (*Hridayam*) which attract from the Astral World, astral bodies of like-minded dead persons who want to fulfill desires that were unmet on earth. Their astral bodies cling to the nervous systems of such a person, aggravating his troubles and negative emotions.

The energies of these dissatisfied *Karana Sariras* come in forms like lizards and snakes that cling to the spinal column of the back or form a cap on the top of the head. They are not visible to the naked eye, but can sometimes be viewed clairvoyantly by evolved souls, *avatars*, sages, *pranic* healers or during certain states of deep meditation. They drain the vital energy from the physical body through the nervous system, making a person weak and causing changes in behaviour. Those astral bodies enjoy adding to the evil qualities already present in these negative human minds. The invisible *Karana Sariras* get their desired acts done through the unfortunate persons to whom they have clung. Family members or friends of such unfortunate individuals observe the changed behaviour and often believe that these affected persons are mentally or physically ill. In some cases, they are taken to mental hospitals without anyone understanding the root cause. **When a man engages in these negative thought forms he comes under direct influence of these disembodied astral souls.**

Before 1950, Sai Baba Himself used to publicly treat individuals disturbed by these negative forces. Later this was not necessary. *Swami* has said that His Divine aura now extends way beyond Prasanthi Nilayam. When any affected person reaches the area, the evil spirits instantly flee due to His energy.

Staying Free Of Astral Bodies

In order to escape from the onslaught of these possessing spirits, a person must not fall a prey to negative attitudes and base emotions. The most effective method is to become involved in *satwic* activities such as the taking of pure food, attending *satsang,* doing *namasmarana* and singing *bhajans.* Even prior to these *satwic* activities, he must seek to change his nature by adopting the practice of Human Values. This will strengthen his will power, self-confidence and faith in God. One may also undertake *yoga* and make sincere efforts to clean their *Hridayam* by doing *nishkam karma* (activity with no attachments to the fruit thereof) and by avoiding hatred, envy, jealousy, lust, anger, and greed. *Satwic* activities will form a strong and positive magnetic field around the body which acts as protection against such evil *Linga Sariras* (subtle bodies) floating in the Astral World.[6]

Second-hand objects, particularly houses, can be inhabited by thought forms or restless spirits attracted by their prior owners. This is one reason why traditional cultures have maintained the practice of blessing new homes through rituals and ceremonies. Group *bhajans* are particularly effective in cleansing the atmosphere of any lingering spirits. As for any personal exorcisms, these should not be attempted by the uninitiated, as they can make innocent minds vulnerable to forces beyond their control. It is best to pray to God and keep up continuous *namasmarana* and *bhajan.*

Sai Baba And The Unseen

Throughout His life, Sri Sathya Sai Baba has been witnessed communicating with beings who are invisible to the people around Him. Some, Baba says, are unsettled *Karana Sariras*, others are life forms from the celestial realms. Baba, through His Grace, has given a few rare devotees the opportunity to see these beings for themselves with their physical eyes. Here are a few examples:

- It was shortly before dawn when an old devotee, Smt. Gali Sharada Devi (Peddabottu), who had climbed the hill above the *ashram* for morning prayers, witnessed celestial women, radiating extraordinary beauty and light, rising up above the Prasanthi *Mandir*. She guessed they were returning to their heavenly abode after entertaining Baba with music and dance. (***Tapovanam***)

- Baba was observed by one Raja Reddy in the *mandir* receiving homage from several celestial beings of brilliant illumination. Seven flames of light whom Baba afterwards confirmed were the *saptharishis* (seven sacred sages who are birthless and deathless) burned bright about Him. Sai Baba told the devotee, who had watched this through a crack in the door, that He had granted the devotee this vision and in fact protected him. Without this divine protection, Baba said, the devotee would not have been able to handle the refined vibration and light without being reduced to ashes. (***Tapovanam***)[7]

- In the early 1970's, Sathya Sai Baba paid an unexpected call on an old devotee. When she expressed her concern that there was no food in the house to serve Baba and His entourage, Baba consoled her by saying that He had brought much food along with Him in the car. This was news to His travelling companions, although one of them quickly followed Baba's orders and headed towards their parked car. When he arrived at the car, the shocked devotee was handed a huge basket of food by two angels. He reported this to Baba who replied, "they are always with me, only you just can't see them." (**My Baba And I**) [8]

We can't see these beings, Sai Baba declares, because "they are above the senses. Man is below the senses."[9] World scriptures are filled with stories involving heavenly and supra-sensual beings.

Astral Doctor

I myself, along with a number of other physicians from the U.K., had a personal experience of Baba's "astral travels" during a medical camp held at my hospital in Bhopal in 1987. While we doctors were gathered to discuss the discharge procedure of the patients, the night watchman of the hospital arrived and informed us, "The big doctor, whose photos are hanging on the wall, came every night at 2 a.m. to do His rounds. Only last night, I asked him if I should call the other doctors. He said, 'No, they are all tired - let them take rest.'" I stared at the man in shock, pointed to a photo of *Swami* and asked, "Do you mean the man in this photo has been taking rounds in this hospital?" "Yes, Madam," he responded. "I have talked to him many times. He comes from your residence and goes back to your residence."

I dismissed the fellow, suspecting that he had been taking drinks in the night. Imagine my great surprise when I was contacted one month later by one of the senior doctors of the camp. The whole group had just had an interview with *Swami* in Ooty. Not only did *Swami* know every detail of the medical camp, but He also reprimanded the doctors for sending home the men *seva dals*. "Why did you remove them when male eye patients were operated on and had their eyes covered?" *Swami* asked. "I had to go at night and help the eye patients to the toilet."

After one of the doctors returned to Bhopal and told me the story of the interview, we immediately went to the village to speak with some of the patients. This experience was confirmed by all the male patients operated upon during the camp. "Doctor-ji," they said, "some lady nurse with soft hands used to come and help us."

Guardians In The Unseen Worlds

The existence of the various worlds, which Baba has referred to in His discourses, has also been reported and documented through studies undertaken in the U.S.A., the U.K., and other countries, involving people under hypnosis, as well as those who have undergone a near death experience.

In these studies, people have described seeing a brilliant white light and beings of light within. Those who go through near death experiences give a uniform accounting of the light and the light beings. They have seen brilliant, dazzling, shimmering, white light coming from above, beyond the ceiling, and even beyond the sky. The light has been described as brighter than the sun, but it does not hurt the eyes. It comes from what appear to be Divine beings. The eyes of these beings are extraordinarily loving and kind, and their hands, when touched or held, feel warm and real. They are called *devas* and angels.

Some of these light beings appear as pure white light and may or may not have recognisable forms. Accounts have also been given that these beings of light are sometimes deceased loved ones seen through the eternal spiritual light. These loved ones can look very real. They are often young and healthy, although they may have been old, sick or crippled when they died.

As an example, I was staying in Baba's guest house in Brindavan with my eldest son, Anand. On April 30th, 1995 at about 10:30 in the morning, I was resting on the college green, when my genetic mother quietly appeared beside me. The following dialogue took place between us:

MOTHER: "How is Anand now?"

MYSELF: "Better, *Biji* (mother). Where have you come from?"

> **MOTHER:** "I saw you when I was passing through so I came to see you and Anand. (Pause.) Do not leave Sai Baba, He is God Himself. Stay here until Anand becomes alright."

She then left. Her appearance was that of a healthy woman and for some reason I took it all quite naturally. I thought it was because I loved my mother that I had a vision of her. The next day, Mr. Bhutia, the director of *Swami's ashram*, came to tell me that he had received a phone call from my brother in Delhi. My mother had died the day before – at 10:30 a.m. I realised then that she had come to me in her astral body. My mother's visit left me feeling so comfortable and confident that she was well, that I did not go to Delhi for her death rites.

Often a chosen God form or one with whom the person has a cultural affinity appears, like Rama, Krishna, Shiva, Parvathi, Guru Nanak, Mohammed, Buddha, Mother Mary, Jesus, the Angel Gabriel or St. Francis of Assisi. Many devotees have seen *Swami* Himself. There is of course the well-documented case of Walter Cowan, whose body lay dead in Chennai for three days before Baba brought it back to life. During that time *Swami* and other light beings reviewed the life of Walter's soul. Baba Himself has often publicly referred to Cowan's experience.

Universality Of Light

The word for world, or realm of existence, in Sanskrit is *loka*. Baba uses this to refer to any one of the fourteen visible and invisible worlds inhabited by living beings who take a variety of forms. At His behest, *bhajan* or prayer sessions in the Sai Organisation throughout the world conclude with the Sanskrit prayer, *Loka Samastha Sukhino Bhavanthu* (may all the beings in all the worlds be happy).

Experiences of worlds of light and dark beyond the physical planes are common to all of the world's religions.

- Buddhism teaches that after death, souls move into the *Bardo*, which reflects stages of consciousness through which the soul must progress before reaching the Clear Light. Through meditation, these realms can be explored before dying, preparing the soul for a good journey in the afterlife.
- Islam teaches of a barrier that separates the living from the dead. To safely reach heaven, a soul is escorted by the Archangel Gabriel through seven different levels of existence.
- Christians talk of Heaven and Hell; however, in the last book of the ***The Holy Bible,*** "Revelations", there are descriptions of many different realms through which a soul must pass before they reach the "pearly gates" of Heaven.
- Jewish religion includes a practice called *shiv'ah*, where the family of the departed one sits in prayer for seven days to ensure that the soul passes along to Heaven and does not get caught in an in-between state on the ladder that moves through the unseen realms.
- Ancient Egyptians made elaborate preparations for life beyond the body. After death, the soul was said to inhabit a world that was almost a mirror of the physical world, where they would need all the physical effects of their earthly life, including food, clothes, etc. There the soul would undergo some sort of moral judgment of their life on earth.

All these can be viewed as different vibrational levels of consciousness. Therefore, it is important that we practise human values, uplifting our vibration to reach the Divine planes of existence and eventually merge in the Pure Light *(Atma Jyothi)*, which is our true nature. All *sadhana*, Sai Baba tells us, culminates at the moment of death, when one's consciousness departs the body and is immediately drawn towards the *akasic* level represented by their final thoughts. It is only great souls, He says, who can leave the physical form with their contemplation fully on the Divine. We can prepare ourselves for this moment through daily devotions and the committed practice of Human Values.

The Silver Cord *(Sutra Atma)*

Uniformly throughout all cultures, the Cosmic Divinity appears or is experienced as pure Light and Love. Although the form of God as light is universal, representing the *Atmic* Light, it is called by a multitude of names.

All are One, and in His divine discourses Sri Sathya Sai Baba has frequently referred to the *Sutra Atma* which unites us all. **[See Diagram No. 6]** Although invisible to all but clairvoyant seers and sages (and Baba Himself, of course), it is a silver thread or cord of light that connects all beings to one another and to God. Those who have experienced it in meditation or during near-death experiences have described what appears to be billions of cords coming out from the Divine Source and going to all beings in all *lokas* all over creation. For those who have the inner eye to see, God reveals that throughout the whole of creation there is only One. That is why Baba says, "each one of you is a spark from the same Divine. Believe in unity. I am in all."

The Subconscious Mind – Window To The Astral World

The conscious mind is the thinking, reasoning and problem solving part of our mind. It is the normal state of awareness that deals with our day-to-day functioning. In the average person the conscious mind is constantly taking in signals through the five senses from the physical sensory world *(bhutakasa)* around us; it is cluttered with thoughts. In this state, it is impossible to get in

Sutra Atma

Every soul is connected with God and one another . . .

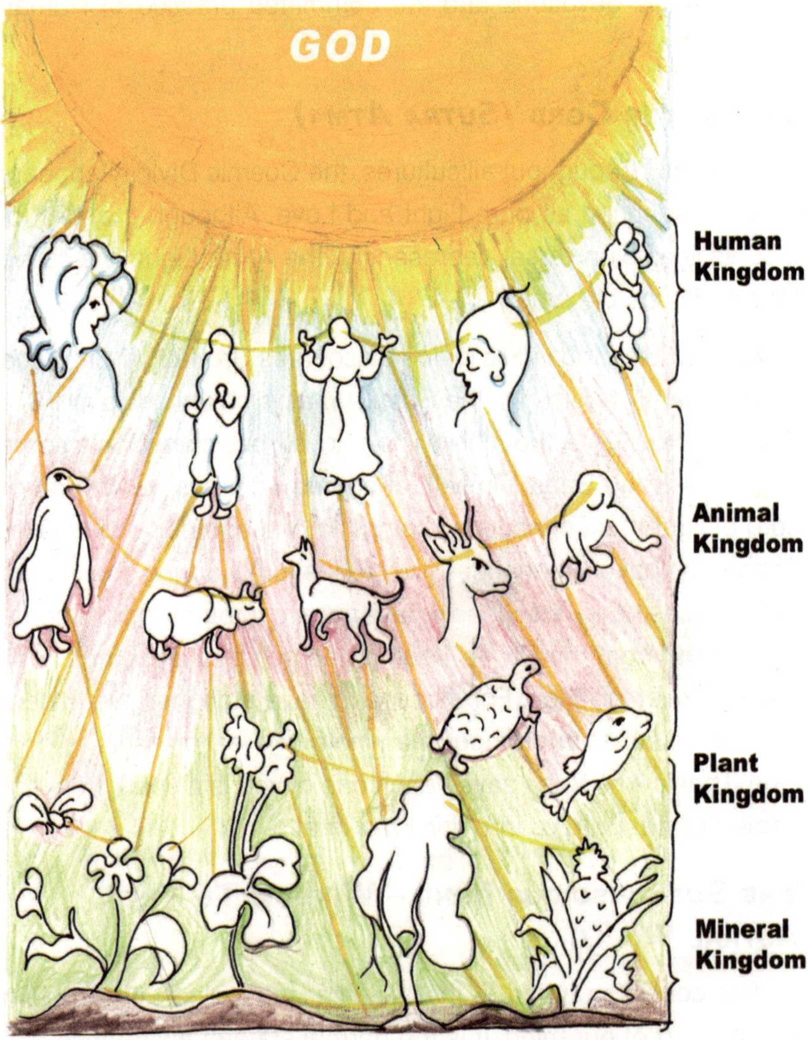

Human Values And Health ~ Diagram No. 6

Source: Divine Discourses of *Bhagawan* Sri Sathya Sai Baba

touch with the deeper sensitivity and wisdom available through the subconscious mind, which functions on the more subtle vibrational levels of *chitthakasa* and *chidakasa*.

Intense prayer, concentration, contemplation, meditation and ritual are methods of accessing the subconscious mind. They activate the limbic system of the brain. At the centre of the limbic system is the thalamus, where the sensory nerves form a sort of crossroads. The information received at the thalamus level is then distributed to the subconscious mind and the cerebrum. During meditation the thalamus actually blocks the sensory information from filtering into the subconscious. Spiritual *sadhana* creates soothing vibrations, which relax the thoughts and set aside the constantly chattering conscious mind. When the conscious mind is calm and quiet, it becomes easy to turn inward towards the *antakarna* (inner senses). In this state the consciousness can experience the more subtle vibrations of the unseen worlds, as well as deep inner wisdom. Frontal lobe, parietal lobe and limbic system – all open to receive enlightenment from *Paramatma*.

Storehouse Of Experience

The subconscious mind is also the universal repository of inner wisdom into which we all can tap. It is not restricted by time or space. According to sages like *Maharishi* Aurobindo, the subconscious mind is the **Archetypal sheath** around our soul; this is the **storehouse of every experience we have ever had since the beginning of time.** Sri Sathya Sai Baba confirms this.

We use the defense mechanism of **repression** to hold back many of our earlier memories. If we consciously remembered everything that has ever happened to us in this and other lives, without the benefit of repression, we would not be able to focus and function properly in our daily lives. The emotions generated by all those memories, especially the traumatic ones, would overwhelm us and could even lead to mental disorders.

If this repression should weaken due to physical injury, an emotional shock or even chronic stress, **memories can emerge** from the subconscious to the conscious mind, bringing with it associations of emotional, mental and physical problems.

The subconscious mind, which is situated within the ethers of the brain and surrounds the *Atma* or *Purusha*, is more than just a memory bank. Through meditation, prayer, etc., we can gain knowledge of the **sources** of emotional, mental and physical difficulties and conflicts. As a bridge to the Cosmic Mind, it can provide **solutions** for problems, promote healing and lead to Union with God, *Yoga*.

Past *Karmas*, Present Experiences

The information stored within the subconscious mind impacts every part of life. Positive and negative relationships with people, fascinations, likes and dislikes, gifts and talents, occupational choices, spouse, and friends, dreams, as well as physical, psychological and personality problems are created by the *vasanas* (impulses), that have their roots in past lives. They differ from *karma* in the sense that they are not actions but propensities that impel the choices and actions we make in our lives.

Our every experience has its roots in the *karmas* (actions) of past lives. Physical indicators such as beauty, athletic ability, musculoskeletal design, psychosomatic diseases and autoimmune disorders, even the predisposition for accidents, have their origins in the past. All of this is stored in the subconscious mind. **The subconscious mind has been programmed by the past. It is constantly sending out vibrations which attract like energies from the astral**

planes, and like experiences in daily life. It is our duty to reprogramme it with a life lived with Human Values. We thereby become conscious creators, not unaware victims.

Sri Sathya Sai Baba says:

The mind spins a cocoon for the *jivi* (individual soul) to be imprisoned in. *Karma,* which is the activity of *maya* (ignorance, illusion), encloses the individual in its grip; it is the husk that makes the paddy seed grow and yield more paddy plants and more grains of paddy. Remove the husk and there is no more sprouting. The husk, *karma,* makes the *jivi* sprout and undergo the penance of *vasanas* (going through the pleasure and pain produced by the impressions unconsciously left on the mind by past good or bad actions) and *samskaras* (performance of purificatory rites and sacred ceremonies). You reward and punish yourself as the result of your own activities; you are here because you wished to come here; you gravitate to the level to which your deeds drag or lift you. You make your own future by your thoughts and desires and deeds.[10] The Law of *Karma* is based on action and result, performance and consequence.[11]

A Continuous Journey

Sathya Sai Baba teaches that one has to live a life that is as good, loving, productive and ideal as possible. This may be thought of as "**Less Luggage – More Comfort.**"

Life thus becomes a soul journey, a spiritual journey through different planes of experience. Each life becomes a station along the way at which certain tasks are to be performed and certain lessons are to be learned. When, for whatever reason, we fail to do what we have planned, we carry that task or lesson on to the next life. In this way our baggage becomes heavier. At some point in the journey, it becomes necessary to resolve to lighten the load and venture toward the goal, which is *Moksha*, liberation of the cycle of death and rebirth.

Sri Sathya Sai Baba tells us that "past is past"; we have to bear the consequences of it. The future is uncertain; don't bother about it. So live in the present – the present is a present, a gift from God. Purify the *Hridayam* by following **Human Values** so that you may carry less baggage in the future Spiritual Journey.

Sri Sathya Sai Baba says:

> *You are on a pilgrimage to the Beyond, so you cannot long dwell in this Beneath. Some time or other, sooner or later, this birth or the next, you have to realise that this is but a dream you took to be true; you have to pack up and march. This is **Asat** (untruth); go towards the **Sat** (truth). This is **Tamas** (darkness); proceed towards the **Jyothi** (light). This is the realm of Death; proceed towards the realm where Immortality reigns.*[12]

---

1 *Bhagawan* Sri Sathya Sai Baba, **Discourses on the *Bhagawad Gita***, Ch.2.

2 Aurobindo, **The Life Divine.**

3 Lamba, Bhag Singh, **God Realisation.**

4 Aurobindo, **The Life Divine.**

5 *Bhagawan* Sri Sathya Sai Baba, Divine Discourse, ***Dasara*** *1984.*

6 Author, **Spirituality and Health.**

7 Sastry, Jandhyala Venkateswara, ***Tapovanam,*** 8th edition, 2005.

8 Hislop, Dr. John, **My Baba and I.**

9 *Bhagawan* Sri Sathya Sai Baba, **Conversations With *Bhagawan* Sri Sathya Sai Baba,** recorded by Dr. John Hislop.

10 *Bhagawan* Sri Sathya Sai Baba, Divine Discourse, 17/07/1962.

11 *Bhagawan* Sri Sathya Sai Baba, ***Sathya Sai Amrita Varshini.***

12 *Bhagawan* Sri Sathya Sai Baba, **Sathya Sai Speaks, Vol. 4.**

chapter - 5

THE HUMAN BODY, MIND AND DIVINITY

Creation

Sri Sathya Sai Baba says:

> *There was no one to know who I am until I created the World at My pleasure with one word! Immediately, mountains rose up; oceans, seas, lands and watersheds, sun, moon and the desert sands sprang out of nowhere. To prove my existence, came all forms of beings, men, beasts and birds – flying, speaking, hearing. All powers were bestowed upon them under My orders. The first place was granted to mankind and My knowledge was planted in man's mind.*[1]

It is only when the process of creation is understood in terms of the close relationship between the *Brahman* (Supreme) and Man can *Brahma-Vidya* (the Divine knowledge of the Supreme) be attained. *Brahman* represents the Infinite. From this Infinite, *Akasa* (ether or sound) emerged. From Ether came Air, from Air, Fire, from Fire, Water and from Water, the Earth. From the Earth came the herbal plants, from the plants, food, from food, *Purusha* (the spark of God present in all beings, dim in animals and plants, but very prominent in man). When the advent of Man through this process is understood, it will be clear that Man came from the Infinite. It is his duty to return there and sanctify his life.[2]

Humanness is a marvellous thing. It is boundless. It is significant. The term **Man** does not refer only to the physical body. A human being is a composite of Body, Mind and *Atma*. To perform actions with the body, to understand them through the mind and to have the *Atma* as witness to both, these three constitute human existence.

- Action (Body)
- Awareness (Mind)
- Realisation (*Atma*)

The three manifest the inner meaning of human life. "As a man thinks, so he becomes."[3]

The Human Body: *Ayurveda*, Allopathy, Homeopathy

The ***Gayathri Mantra*** is the universal prayer considered to be the core of the ***Vedas***:

Aum Bhur Bhuvah Suvah,
Tat Savitur Varenyam,
Bargo Devasya Dhimahi,
Dhiyo Yo Nah Prachodayat

Sri Sathya Sai Baba says:

In the ***Gayathri Mantra,*** *Aum Bhur Bhuvah Suvah* is the first line:

- *Bhur* refers to **matter** that is body
- *Bhuvah* refers to the *prana sakti* (**vital life force)** which animates the body
- *Suvah* refers to the *prajna sakti* (**integrated awareness**), which acts through radiation

Hence, man is made up of awareness, the vital force and the material substance. The doctors should not consider only the body (matter), but should take into consideration the *prana* and *prajna sakti. Prajna sakti* is the radiation energy that promotes wisdom. Vibration is the expression of the vital force (*prana*). **In every action, there is a vibration, which is in between the consciousness and the physical body.** We should see that the mind is not influenced by any external force, but by the internal source, which is *prajna* or integrated awareness.

These three basic elements in human being should be taken into account in the treatment of diseases and the promotion of health. This is the basis of the ancient system of *Ayurveda* (the Science of Longevity). One whose heart is filled with compassion, whose words spell truth, and who works for the welfare of others, will never suffer from difficulties or diseases even in the *Kali* age. In this wide world, everyone aspires for long life, prosperity and health.

Among the four ***Vedas***, the ***Atharva Veda*** is the one that has given the science relating to longevity, known as *Ayurveda. Ayurveda* transcends time and space and is valid for all places, at all times. It relates to the spirit, mind and body. The Allopathic system came much later. It is based on objective, external approach, while *Ayurveda* is subjective. Both have to be coordinated for better results. Since *Ayurveda* is subjective, it is more efficacious than the Allopathic system. It has a superior artistic sense. Doctors have to realise the distinction between subjective and objective approaches. The Allopathic has an external outlook, while the *Ayurvedic* doctor has an inner view. The object is a reflection of the subject.

Without realising this relationship between *Ayurveda* and Allopathy, doctors are wasting their time in arguments. *Ayurveda* affirms that purity of mind is more essential for one's health, while Allopathic doctors do not consider the mind as important. They give importance to the eradication of disease caused by germs and consider this as the only method to cure. This does not take into account the role of the mind and spirit in the eradication of disease. Allopathy is based on external knowledge and experimentation, while *Ayurveda* is based on inner knowledge and experience. There is a gulf of difference between the subjective and objective approaches in course of time. Allopathy resorts to the use of antibiotics to deal with various diseases. The antibiotics act powerfully and yield quick results in curing a disease, but in the process of curing a disease, they can give rise to adverse side-effects.[4]

Homeopathy

Homeopathic remedies represent the finest vibration of medicine. While making homeopathic Mother Tincture (the concentrated extract of the plant, used as a base for all formulations), the basic extracts of the plants are the same as *Ayurveda*, but they are further diluted and triturated (ground), leaving only the refined essence of the plant. When it is diluted above six times, it is called homeopathy.

Homeopathic medicine is absorbed through taste buds, going directly to the nervous system, thereby changing the vibration of *prana sakti* and bringing healing to the organs. The change in *prana sakti* affects the thoughts and emotions of a person as well. That is why a homeopathic practioner will always look into a patient's mental and emotional symptoms, in addition to the physical.

Homeopathy doesn't kill the bacteria. What it does is, it improves and strengthens the body's own immune system to fight off diseases. Many chronic diseases nowadays are being cured by homeopathy.

Integrated treatments are gaining more credibility and hence wider usage. In chronic cases, homeopathy and *Ayurveda* work well in tandem with allopathy to affect a cure. Allopathy is of course the king of pathies for emergency cases. In sub chronic cases, *Ayurveda* is the most effective, while homeopathy in conjunction with mental changes is best with persistent or recurring pathologies.

"Saipathy"

I have named all *Swami's* Divine Discourses on the medical aspect of the human body as **"Saipathy"**, which is a new perception of *Swami's* lectures on body, mind and soul. I find the application of these teachings in my day to day medical practice to be the best "pathy". It removes body tension and promotes healing from the inside out. By applying Saipathy, our brain produces a variety of healing neuropeptides which soothe the body and mind. The dose is always Divinely regulated, timed and administered; there is no danger of side effects or addiction. There is only health and nothing else.

The time is fast approaching when Saipathy, which teaches how to recite *Aum*, prayers, *bhajans*, *japa*, meditation, *yoga* and the practice of Human Values will be the pathy of choice. All pathies may fail, but Saipathy will never fail. It is from Saipathy that all my books have been compiled. With this Divine inspiration, it is my prayer that doctors of all pathies may join together to keep this abode of the Lord, the human body, healthy and happy.

Ayurveda: In Harmony With Nature

Sri Sathya Sai Baba says:

Allopathic doctors experiment only with matter. They do not take the inner consciousness (Self) into account. In spite of the prodigious technological developments in the world, man is not able to enjoy peace. Peace cannot be achieved by knowledge of the physical. Peace should come from the inner feeling or the spirit within. It is only when the body, the mind and spirit are in harmony that peace will prevail. Medical science should recognise the role of the mind in causing sickness. Good health confers mental peace. Mental worry impairs physical health. *Ayurveda*, therefore, lays emphasis on mental peace and aims at the elimination of the root cause of disease. There are three basic factors, which are responsible for health or disease in the human body according to *Ayurveda*. They are *vata* (vital air), *pitta* (bile) and *sleshma* (phlegm – also called *kapha*).

Vata accounts for 36 diseases, *pitta* accounts for 98, and *kapha* for 96 diseases. These three factors are essential for the human body, but they should be in proper balance without exceeding their respective limits. When they are in balance, there will be no disease. Moderation is the golden rule for good health.

Doctors have not made the human body. It is a gift of God. **The human heart beats 103,000 times a day. The blood circulation in the body is computed to cover 168,000 miles per day. Man breathes 21,600 times and consumes 438 cubic feet of air every day**. These are based on Divine Will and are regarded as Laws of Nature. God is the preceptor of *Prakriti* (nature). The body is unclean in many ways and is subject to various diseases. But, in such an inherently unattractive abode dwells the most valuable Divinity. Therefore, man should always act in harmony with Nature, which is a reflection of Divinity.

Hurry, Worry And Curry

What is the cause of heart ailments? Many doctors say that they are due to smoking, consumption of fatty foods, overeating, and other excessive habits. The relationship between food and habits should be properly understood. We should see that proper balance is maintained between the physical body and inner feelings (spirit). Modern man is continuously in a hurry. Hurry causes worry, which affects the physical health.

Worry also causes high blood pressure and hurry causes diabetes. They are like twins, one acting on the heart inside, and the other externally on the blood. Everyone should know how to control these causes.

Curry means fatty foods. Many doctors have made investigations in this field but the results have not been made widely known. Heart diseases are found more rampant among non-vegetarians, while vegetarians are not prone to heart ailments to the same extent. This is because in non-vegetarian food there is a higher percentage of fat, which increases the cholesterol in the blood.

Some people do not do any physical exercises and lead a sedentary life. My advice to office-workers and students is that it is good for them to commute by cycle or walk at least 5 or 6 kilometers a day. This cycling exercise is very useful not only for maintaining health, but also for reducing the money spent on automobiles. Another advantage is the avoidance of accidents. Moreover, it serves to reduce atmospheric pollution caused by the release of harmful fumes. The carbon dioxide smoke from motor vehicles and factories is already polluting the air in the cities and is affecting the ozone layer above the earth.[5]

The Divine In Human Form

Oh! Shining Spirits of the Divine in Human Form! God has put many types of power within your reach: The power of your body's muscles, the power of skilled hands, the power of intelligence, the power of influential position, the power of scientific knowledge, the power to command any situation, and the power which God gives you to merge in Him. Everything comes from God; everything is God. God created the human race as one vast living entity; all people are one people; all life is one life.[6]

Your highly evolved human body is a tool with which you may view the Infinite and proclaim God's true power and divine capabilities in the world. With your living example, the mysteries of God will become more evident to all humanity. You became human to shine with God's brilliance in the world. You wear a body, which will one day die, to show all that you never die. Your body walks in the troubled world to give forth the message that you are infinite bliss.[7]

This body is like a traveler's overnight rest-house. It is like a hotel for the *Atma*. As such, it is a temporary resting place. Like a watchman for the hotel, the mind is a watchman for the body. Life force or *Atma* is the traveler on a holy journey. There is no lasting connection between the traveler, the watchman and the hotel. The relationship is only temporary and fleeting. You are not permanently attached to your mind. Nor do you own the body. We should not waste this divine human life. This body is lifeless and negative in nature. It's not alive. When there is a divine positive [God] living within the negative body it can be put to good use. Just as we put clothes on the body, the body is the dress of the Divine Spirit.[8]

Humanness And Divinity Are Same

Humanness is not separate from Divinity. Both are one. So, when you develop a broad vision, you experience the feeling of the oneness of the individual, the Universe, and God. This is called the Divine Universal Form. How do you recognise this? Not by perceiving the myriad diversities among objects, but by recognising their underlying unity and the recognition of the Divine in each of them.

This means that human beings are not to be seen as so many innumerable separate entities. The *Chaitanya* (consciousness) that is in each of them is one and the same universal consciousness. It is all pervading. Judging himself by the limitations of his body, man considers himself a weak and powerless being. Once he is conscious of his Divinity, he will realise his boundless potentialities. Knowing these facts man must discipline his mind.

Although the thoughts of the mind, the actions of the body, and the role of the *Atma* as the witness appear to be different, they are all integrally interrelated. The differences are in form, but the bliss that is experienced is One. Hence, the ***Upanishads*** have declared the truth of the One in many.

Manava And Mind

The meaning of the term *Manava* (Man) has to be properly understood. It means *Atma* (the Self). It is from the *Atma* that the five basic elements have emerged. Man has brought under his control these five elements. Thereby, he has become their master. Failing to comprehend the basic nature of human existence, man today has become a slave of his senses.

The *Vedanta* has declared that one can know everything if he knows his own reality. To discover who you are, you have to rid yourself of the external vision. All the experiences based on sense perceptions are external impressions. These are merely reflections of internal responses. To regard these as real and permanent and to ignore the Divine, who is permanent, causes a man to waste his life. Hence, man has to utilise the mind to realise his Divinity.[9]

The Nature Of Mind

Sri Sathya Sai Baba says:

The mind is an adroit substance. Its actions are strange. It has no form of its own. It assumes the form of the object in which it is present. The mind is responsible for happiness and sorrow, good and bad and positive and negative qualities. Hence it is the foremost duty of a human being to recognize the nature of the mind. The mind is like the water that flows through a canal. Just like water, the mind also assumes the forms of the objects it contemplates upon.[10]

The mind does not have any powers. The only power is *Atma Sakti,* the power of the *Atma*. Actually, the mind does not exist. There is no mind. The moon is lit by the sun. What we see is the reflected light of the sun. What we take to be the mind is the reflected light of the *Atma* shining on the *Hridayam.*[11]

The mind operates with four aspects, which Sai Baba has referred to as *Antahchathushtaya*, or the Internal Four *Indriyas* (senses or organs). They are:

Chart No. 7 ~ The Levels Of Mind

Level	Consciousness	Activity	Site
MANAS	Waking, observing mind	Grasps the object with the senses; desiring	Head
CHITTHA	Subconscious, storehouse of memories from many births	Understanding the object; feeling and relating	Navel
AHAMKARA	Ego, 'I'-ness, personal self, place of "mine"	Changes the decision for or against by attachment; personalizes, claims	Heart
BUDDHI	Intellect; higher mind	Examines arguments for and against; intuitive, discriminating	Tongue
SOURCE: Discourses and writings of *Bhagawan* Sri Sathya Sai Baba			

The Levels Of The Mind

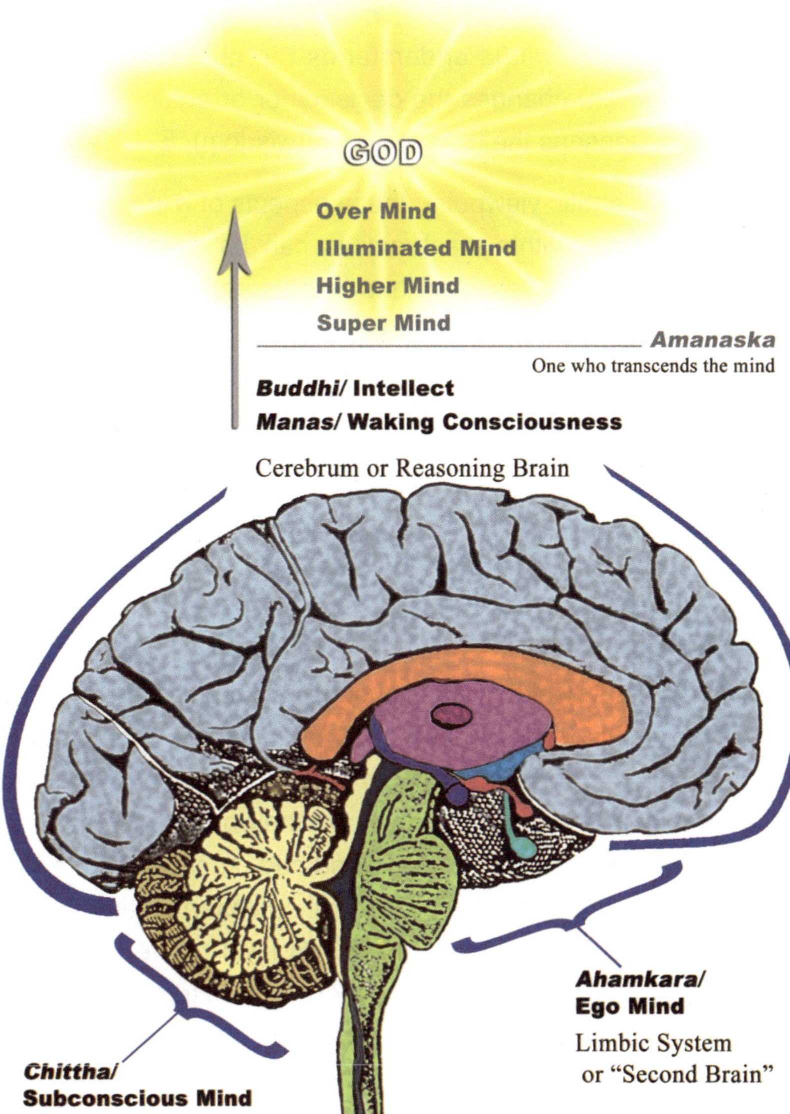

NOTE: Inner view along longitudinal fissure.

Human Values And Health ~ Diagram No. 8

Source: Bhagawan Sri Sathya Sai Baba, **Summer Showers 1993**, Divine Discourse, 19/12/1985

Sri Sathya Sai Baba says:

"*Manas* grasps the object, *Buddhi* examines arguments for and against, *Chittha* understands the object by means of these; *Ahamkara* changes the decision for or against – and, by attachment, loosens the hold of *Jnana* (wisdom)."[12]

From a scientific viewpoint, these aspects of mind also relate to certain areas within the brain as can be seen in **Diagram No. 8.** The following analysis has been compiled from various discourses of Sri Sathya Sai Baba.

1. Waking Consciousness *(Manas)*

This is the part of the mind that deliberates, desires and feels. The *manas* identifies itself with the body. At this level the intellect allows itself to be subservient and controlled by the sense organs.

2. Subconscious Mind *(Chittha)*

It works below waking consciousness and could also be called memory. This level carries out all the circulation, respiration, digestion, and repair work in the body. The autonomic nervous system of the body is responsible for the working of this level. It is also called habit-mind. Good and bad practices and talents of previous births, known in Sanskrit as ***vasanas*** (tendencies, impulses, talents), are stored at this level of the mind. This explains why some people are born with extraordinary skills as singers, painters, dancers, and poets or with phobias such as heights or public speaking. Their experiences from previous births are carried in this level. Purification of this portion of the mind is essential for realisation of the Self.

3. Ego Mind *(Ahamkara)*

The brain's limbic system gets sensations from outside itself through the five sensory organs (*Jnanendriyas*) and the five working organs (*Karmendriyas*). In addition, it receives messages from the higher brain centres, through thoughts, emotions, behaviour and actions.The ego mind, upon consulting the intellect *(Buddhi)*, gets illumination from the infinite mind. The cerebrum of the human brain is more highly developed than that of other animals because it has the qualities of the Higher Mind.

Generally, all people suffer from an incurable disease. It may be in a lesser degree in some while more severe in others. The difference is only in the severity but all are suffering from this. It cannot be cured even by expert medical treatment of experienced doctors. **This disease is Ego**. There are four types: vanity of clan, vanity of wealth, vanity of youth and vanity of scholarship. Though there are other types, they can all be grouped under these.

Where is the need to be egoistic for an ordinary mortal? When you consider your position in comparison to the entire world you are just an infinitesimal speck. If you think you are so big inflated with Ego, it is only sheer ignorance. If one identifies himself with Divinity, there will be no room for Ego. All are Divine in this world and you are also one of several billion people. When you realise this truth, where is the scope for ego?

4. Intellect *(Buddhi)*

The *Buddhi* or intellect is the light of intelligence in man, with the powers of reason, steadiness and discrimination. However it too often comes under the sway of the Ego or 'I'-sense, which is fundamental for to the human being. The *Manas* should be subordinate to the *Buddhi* but usually it serves the senses, which are but its servants. The intellect functions at four different levels:

a) SUPER MIND

The Super Mind is related to the subtle body (*Sukshma Sarira*). In the subtle body, the senses, the mind, the intellect, the will, the ego and the physical body are absent and only consciousness is present (*Chethana*). One has to proceed further to the causal body (*Karana Sarira*), which contains the power to control the body, the senses and the mind.

An internal enquiry has to be made to understand the super mind; it calls for turning the external vision inward. When this is done, the realization comes that the physical body is inert. The mind *(Manas)* is a reflecting mirror. The *Buddhi* (intellect), *Chit* (will), *Ahamkara* (ego), are aspects of the mind. All these are subject to change. But, they are also based on something that is unchanging. The first conclusion to be drawn from the internal enquiry is that there is an unchanging Divine entity in man.

b) HIGHER MIND

An individual experiences a feeling of delight on waking from the deep sleep state. It is the absence of mind in the deep sleep state which is the cause for such delight. This is attributed to the higher mind and is associated with the causal body.

c) ILLUMINATED MIND

The relationship between cause and effect accounts for all the happenings in the world. The Divine is the cause and the Cosmos is the effect. This is the *Mahakarana* (pure consciousness) which is responsible for all that happens in the universe.

d) OVER MIND

To experience the Cosmic Principle we need a Divine form. This is the Super-Divine Self. It is called *Purushatva*. The *Purushatva* is in fact the Over Mind, the Divine aspect. At present, all man's endeavours and enquiries are limited to exploring the physical, the vital and the mental. The journey ends there. Man has proceeded only up to the mind. The mind is needed for understanding the variety of physical objects and phenomena in the world. But as long as he confines himself to the powers of the mind he remains a human being. But, to rise to a higher level, he has to become *Amanaska* – one who transcends the mind.

FOUR TYPES OF INTELLECT *(BUDDHI)*. In addition to the four levels, Sri Sathya Sai Baba tells us that individuals manifest four different types of intellect:

1. ***SWARTHA BUDDHI***: always interested in his own welfare and fulfillment of his own desires.
2. ***SWARTHA PARARTHA BUDDHI:*** equally interested in his own welfare as well as that of others.
3. ***PARARTHA BUDDHI:*** does not desire anything for himself. Surrendering himself to God, he craves for His love alone. He believes that God is the indweller of all beings and desires for the welfare of the entire world *(Loka Samastha Sukhino Bhavanthu)*.
4. ***NISWARTHA BUDDHI:*** has no sense of I and mine. The feeling of 'I' (body) is ego and the feeling of 'mine' is attachment. The root cause of all sorrow and suffering of man is this feeling of 'I' and 'mine'; by giving these up man can purify his *Hridayam*. A pure *Hridayam* is the greatest achievement of man.[13,14]

Mind's Role In Health And Disease

Sri Sathya Sai Baba points out:

The causes of the maladies affecting people today are many – impure air, polluted water, adulterated foodstuffs are a few, but not all of them. Even minds are polluted. These mental ailments are the cause of man's degradation. Most diseases are caused by aberrations of the mind. **Ninety percent of the diseases are psychological.** Constant thinking about one's health is also the cause of many diseases. A heart specialist, who was constantly examining heart patients, was worried about his own heart. Ultimately he died of a heart attack. Another doctor, who specialised in treating digestive disorders, ultimately died of gastric troubles by worrying about his own digestion.

The mind has thus a vital role in one's health or illness. That was why the sages declared, "The mind is the cause of men's bondage or liberation." When the mind is directed towards sacred things, everything in a man's life becomes sacred. In such a state, all that you think, see or hear becomes pure and sacred. The *Hridayam* is like a Lock with the mind as the Key. Turn the key towards God; you develop detachment. Turn the mind towards the world; you get attachment. Our minds should not be immersed in mundane concerns. Deem everything in the world as Divine.[15]

The Thoughts

As will be said many times in this book:

> **Thoughts are things with airy wings, they go faster than a dove, they bring you back whatever you had in your *Hridayam* – hate or love.**

All thought processes are actually vibrations of energy. They produce a neuropeptide change which affects the nervous system, hormonal system and hence all the organs all the body. So it is thoughts that promote health or cause "dis-ease" in all the areas of human life.

Sri Sathya Sai Baba says:

Though the body is mortal, thoughts are immortal. The power of thought vibration runs around the world. As heat waves, electrical waves and light waves radiate, the mental waves too radiate. Thought vibrations are the cause of man's joy or sorrow, health or disease, woe and weal, birth and death. Man's life becomes meaningful if he conducts himself fully aware of the power of his thought vibrations.[16]

Thoughts lead to *karma* (action and reaction) and create feelings, which contribute to character. Character makes a man deserving to be termed "Human". So, one must develop character by having sacred thoughts and doing good deeds. For this, the primary requisite is control of mind. Which is the source of thoughts? The term for thought in Sanskrit is *sankalpa,* which means will or resolve. This *sankalpa* arises from *Hridayam,* the seat of God (*Sam*). *Sam*, is synonymous with *Sat*. ***Sat* is changeless Truth.** When thoughts are good and based on the Divine Truth, the state of man will be good. Similarly, *sampathi* (possessions) does not mean worldly or physical comforts. It comprises of *sat vichar* and *sat sankalpa* (good inquiry and good thoughts). Such good thoughts are based on the changeless Truth and this will come only from merits acquired in previous lives. This human birth itself is attained after innumerable lives of lower species. This being so, why should you venture to commit sinful deeds?[17]

Thoughts, *Karma* And Disease

Many people voice concern over why babies are born with birth defects or mental illness, or why young children suffer from cruel accidents, disease or abuse. What sort of negative thoughts could they have had? Sathya Sai Baba tells us that each human being is born with a necklace of *karma*. It is unseen, but nevertheless there. It has been created by the results – good and bad – of all our thoughts, words and deeds in our previous lives.

Sai Baba tells us, "In previous births, such people (with physical and mental handicaps) would have been completely amoral, with no standards of right or wrong, of good and bad. Their moral codes would have been very low and they would have engaged in acts of moral degeneracy and decadence. Such people will be reborn with physical and mental afflictions and will suffer in this way for past deeds."

In regards to pious souls, or sincere devotees who undergo great illness or stress, Sathya Sai Baba says, "Sometimes God sends them troubles to test the strength of their devotion. If the devotees realise that the main objective of man is not to be reborn again and again, and if they are striving towards this objective, they will be beset with untold miseries and sufferings as a means of burning away all the *karmas* of past births. This is all according to the judgment and Grace of God."

Sri Sathya Sai Baba continues:

Every action has an equal and opposite reaction, resound and reflection. It is only this, which is the basis for *Karmic* Law. You reap what you sow either in the same birth or in a succeeding birth. When you die, you carry with you not your worldly passions, assets, name and fame, but only your deeds and misdeeds into the other world. When you are born into this world you are born only with the garland of deeds around your neck.

When you talk of *karma* in the context of birth and re-birth you must know that the term *karma* does not mean only action. When there is an action, there is always a reaction. So *karma* refers to the chain of action and reaction. **When I talk of reaction I do not mean the result of action. What I mean is <u>your reaction</u> to the result, the response or the manner in which you receive the fruit of action...** you feel happy and elated when the result is good; you feel unhappy and dejected when the result is bad. These emotional responses set off further desires and impulses, which inflate or deflate the ego. This in turn leads to more action. Action results in reaction, and thus a never-ending chain of action-reaction is produced.[18]

Your own bad thoughts and actions are the cause of your misery. As you sow, so shall you reap. The seed determines the fruit. When man cherishes bad thoughts, bad results haunt him. When he has good thoughts, the results are also good.[19]

From now on at least, develop good thoughts, do good actions and redeem your lives. You have to start with the Path of Action (Work) and end with the Path of Wisdom. In between, there is the Path of Worship. This is the path you have to follow today. For this, have the firm conviction that God is omnipresent. When you have this conviction you will not indulge in falsehood or practise deception; you will not abuse others or cause harm to them; you will acquire all virtues. [20]

Discipline The Mind

Sri Sathya Sai Baba asserts that:

To develop one's moral and mental strength, one should practise *sadhana* for disciplining the mind. For this purpose, one has to promote eleven kinds of purity (*Satwa*) as listed below:

- **FIRST - PURITY OF PLACE:** It is necessary to fill the room in which one resides or studies with a *satwic* atmosphere. The pictures or other objects one sees should fill a person with peace and pure thoughts. Objects which arouse agitation and bad thoughts should have no place. The room should be clean and free from anything that is impure.

- **SECOND - FAMILY HARMONY:** In the family with which you live, there should be mutual understanding, cooperation, and a sense of harmony. There should be no discord in the family that will create a bad atmosphere. A harmonious atmosphere will give a person true peace of mind.

- **THIRD - *SATWIC* FOOD:** All food should be *Satwic.* This means that none of the edible items should be excessively sour, bitter or hot. One should eschew *rajasic* (aggressive) food like fish or meat. Even good *satwic* food should not be taken in excess. Some people consume so much *satwic* food that although it's *satwic*, when one sits for the meal with a light stomach and gets up from it with a weighty stomach, it becomes *tamasic* (dull).

- **FOURTH - PURE FLUIDS:** These should also be *satwic.* One should not drink whatever water is available; it should be pure water. Alcoholic spirits should be avoided.

- **FIFTH - *SATWIC* THOUGHTS AND FEELINGS:** These are of great importance. Especially students tend to neglect this factor. Only if one's thoughts and feelings are pure can one get the full benefit of a clean room, a good family, and pure God.

- **SIXTH - *SATWIC* VISION:** If one wants to develop *satwic* feelings and thoughts, the vision must be pure. All creation *(srishti)* is based upon sight *(drishti).* It is only when one has wrong vision that one has wrong thoughts. One must look upon every elderly woman as one's mother and all women who are younger as one's sisters. When one is filled with such pure thoughts, one will have pure feelings. Because you are students, you have to be told of this. Imagine how offended you will feel if someone looks at your mother or sister with an evil eye. Realising this, you have to entertain pure feelings towards other women. You should not commit the sort of offences which you will not tolerate in others.

- **SEVENTH - *Satwic* Study:** Whatever books you read or whatever you write should be pure. This is the *sadhana* relating to study *(sahitya satwica)*. If you read or write that which is not pure, it warps your mind. A good book makes a good mind. Any book you may study about physics or chemistry or other subjects does not affect your character. But books which are literary and are not good literature, do affect it. If improper books are prescribed for study, treat them as mere textbooks and do not attach any high value to them as guides for life.
- **EIGHTH - *Satwic* Service**: With regard to service, you have to decide what is *satwic* and what is *rajasic*. One goes and cleans streets, builds roads in villages, or digs wells, and does it all as a service to the community. But the kind of service which one does should give real happiness to the people. In the name of 'social work' if one goes to the hospital and approaches a patient unsympathetically, then it is not real service. Any person whom you wish to serve, you should regard as an embodiment of the Divine. Going to help the destitute and the neglected person, consider them Divine. Narayana has two forms: one is Lakshmi-Narayana, the other is Daridra-Narayana. Lakshmi-Narayana is full of wealth. He is able to help any number of people and will be able to get many persons to serve him. But for Daridra-Narayana (God of Poverty) there is nobody to serve him. It is to such persons that we should do *satwic* service.

- **NINTH - *Sadhana*: It is 'spiritual discipline'.** It must be *satwic*. Some people do *Hatha Yoga*. Some strive to develop the *Kundalini Sakti*. Some invoke evil spirits to do harm to others. These forms of *sadhana* are not *sadhana* at all. The individual is *Chit* (consciousness); God is *Sat* (the Eternal Absolute). When *Sat* and *Chit* combine one has *Ananda*; this is the meaning of *Sat-Chit-Ananda* (Divine bliss). Only the *sadhana* that is undertaken to realise *Sat-Chit-Ananda* is true *sadhana*. Where is this *Sat*? This *Sat*, the Divine, is in everybody. So, you must be prepared to serve everybody, regard everyone as the Divine. You may have normal relationship with your kith and kin and there is nothing wrong in this. But, you must perform *sadhana* in the spirit that the One pervades the many. In this process, you must cultivate the feeling of love. There is no higher *sadhana* than the cultivation of love.

- **TENTH - *Good Work*: Your occupation or profession** – what is the kind of work you should take up? It should be work which can benefit the nation, the community. The nation enables you to earn a living. You must see what you can give to the nation in return. You must ask yourself: "What is the service, what is the help I can do for the community?" You must see that there is no untruth in any work you do, no unfairness, no fraud, and no evil motive. These are the pure things which you have to observe in your life. If you engage yourselves in right action, you will not be bound by the consequences of *karma*. It is because of your past *karma* that you have the present life. By your present *karma*, you can ensure freedom from birth. Through love you develop faith; through faith and earnestness, you acquire knowledge; through knowledge, you develop *sadhana*, and through *sadhana*, you achieve the goal. So, for practising *sadhana*, you require wisdom, and for acquiring wisdom, you require *sraddha* (earnestness and faith), and for *sraddha* you must cultivate Love. So, Love is the means, and for this, you must acquire control of the senses. If gradually you reduce your desires, you will be able to bring the senses under control. Different branches of knowledge are like rivers, but spiritual knowledge is the ocean. Even as the rivers merge in the ocean, all types of knowledge merge in spiritual knowledge.

- **ELEVENTH - *SATSANG*: The company should be good.** You must bear in mind the company you keep. Kabir said, "I salute the bad and also the good." Kabir was asked: "We can understand your offering salutation to the good but what is the point in offering salutation to the bad?" He replied, "When I salute the bad I am saluting them saying, please remove yourself from my presence. I salute the good, saying please come to me!" Therefore, you must avoid the company of the bad and cultivate the company of the good. Association with the good is pure *yoga*. I desire that you should pursue this kind of *yoga* and confer happiness on all people with whom you are associated. Furthermore, you should strive to get rid of all your bad thoughts, give up all your bad traits, discharge your obligations to your parents, render disinterested service to the community, and thereby, redeem your lives and earn the grace of God. This is my blessing for all of you.[21]

PURITY IN SPEECH

Ek Do Jibha Lakh Howe, Lakh Howe Lakh Bees
Lakh Lakh Gara Akhiya Ed Nam Jagadish

If God gives me one or two tongues, or from
two to 20 *lakhs*, even every tongue of mine
shall chant the name of God!

~ ***Guru Nanak***

Sri Sathya Sai Baba says:

By pure actions, the mind also gets purified. But mere purity of mind alone is not enough; the mind has to develop concentration. For cultivation of concentration, *bhakti* (devotion) is of great value. *Bhakti* means getting rid of separation from *Bhagawan* (God). There must be the realisation that the Divine is omnipresent and that you cannot separate yourself from God.

To remember the omnipresent Divine, to chant His glories and adore Him, you need the **tongue** or the power of speech. This sacred instrument should not be misused in any way for speaking ill of others or causing unhappiness to them.

As enjoined in the ***Bhagavad Gita,*** one should avoid unpleasant speech and use only words that are true, comforting and good. Harshness in speech should be avoided. Only when the tongue is used in this way can it become pure and sacred. When the speech is sanctified, life itself becomes sanctified.

There is no *dharma* higher than Truth. "Truth alone triumphs." God is hailed as the Protector of Truth, the Propagator of Truth, the Embodiment of Truth. "Truth is God", goes the saying. This is the first purity of man. Purity in speech is the second purity that has to be ensured. Keep a strict watch over what you say. If the foot slips, you may suffer a fall and sustain a temporary injury. But a slip of the tongue may cause lasting harm.

Never go about criticising others. With plenty of faults in yourself, you have no right to point out the faults in others. It is a grievous sin to indulge in such fault-finding. He alone is wise who is conscious of his defects. The one who is looking out for the faults in others will acquire those faults himself, by a process of reflex action.[22]

The *Sadhana* Of Peace

Sri Sathya Sai Baba says:

We aspire for peace and comfort all the time, but where can we find it? Is it to be found in the material world around us? Experience shows that peace and happiness acquired from external objects is not enduring. It is like a mirage, which cannot quench the thirst of the deluded animal that runs towards it. The real source of peace is within every individual and it is this inner peace that can confer real joy.

Such a peace can be attained only through achieving equal-mindedness on all occasions. **Whether one is subjected to pleasure or pain, praise or blame, gain or loss, one should not be affected by criticism arising out of ill will, envy or hatred.** Reacting to such criticism in a like manner will destroy one's peace of mind. We should **ignore baseless criticisms motivated by ill will or jealousy.** We should be true to our own good nature and maintain our equanimity.

What every *sadhaka* needs to secure and should strive for is peace *(santi)*. It is the fragrant flower which is born out of pure love. It is the fragrance which is derived as a result of one's good deeds." If you lose this noble and fragrant quality of peace, then you will lose everything in life. Right from ancient times, in this country, there have been *rishis* and sages who have striven to proclaim the greatness of this *santi* (peace). They were criticised, ridiculed and derided, and were subjected to untold ordeals, but they never lost hold of this peace of theirs.

You must be like the sandalwood tree which transmits its fragrance even to the axe that is used to cut it. When an incense-stick is lighted, it burns itself away, but it radiates its perfume all around." In the same manner, a true *sadhaka*, a true devotee, should see to it that he keeps his peace intact under all circumstances. He should radiate happiness all round. This is the primary *sadhana*. Through this *sadhana*, try to get peace. Peace cannot be obtained in the world outside. Our kith and kin, our material possession or name or fame will not give us peace. **Peace is something which swells from within you. It is not something which is gathered from outside**. We desire peace, but we keep doing things, that far from giving peace, cause anxiety and worry. Trifles are known to upset one's peace of mind. The true *sadhaka* should remain unaffected by what others say about him.

Three-Fold *Santi* Of Body, Mind And Soul

The word *santi* is pronounced three times at the end of every prayer, ritual or offering. What is the meaning behind this? The first *santi* refers to the body, while the second and third refer to the mind and soul respectively.

- **Body:** "May we have peace for the body." It means that the body should not get heated by feelings of jealousy, hatred, attachments, and the like. Whatever news you receive about any event, you should receive it with calmness and serenity.
- **Mind:** "May we have peace for the mind." You should not get worked up when someone says something about you which is not true. You must simply dismiss it as something that does not concern you. If you get angry or irritated, you are losing your peace of mind. You should say to yourself: "Why should I lose my peace of mind just because someone says something about me which is not true?" You must resolve to stick to your truth and be true to your own nature.
- **Soul:** "May we have peace for the soul." This peace has to be realised through love.

This world has to be brought back onto the proper track, and it is **Love** and **Peace** alone which can achieve this. Fill your thoughts, actions, and emotions with love, truth and peace. There may be people who hate us, but love them too. Develop forbearance, patience, peace and love and carry on your work. This is your true *sadhana*.[23]

Harmony In Thought, Word And Deed *(Trikarna Shuddhi)*

The gross portion of the food nourishes the body, the subtle portion nourishes the mind, and the most subtle portion nourishes the power of speech. Thus, all the three constituents – mind, speech and body – are therefore sustained by food. All these three combine to make the full personality of man. Harmony in these three, thought, word and deed makes one a *Mahatma* (great soul). Disparity in these three makes a man *Duratma* (a wicked person.)

In the latter, the current of *Sathya* (truth) is absent and it will not shine. When there is harmony, the current of truth will not fail. You have a main switch in a house which controls all the other switches. If it is put off, the lights will go off.

In the body the main switch is the *Hridayam*. **When one has love in the *Hridayam* all one's thoughts, words and actions will shine brightly with love.** Therefore, you should fill the *Hridayam* with love, and share with others. When you fill the tank of *Hridayam* with truth and righteousness, all limbs of the body and sense organs functioning as taps will flow with the same truth and righteousness. Love is selfless and self is loveless. Love gives and forgives: self gets and forgets. When love is underlying your activity everything will be perfect.[24]

---

1 *Bhagawan* Sri Sathya Sai Baba, recorded in **Loving God,** by N. Kasturi, P 372.
2 *Bhagawan* Sri Sathya Sai Baba, Divine Discourse, 31/05/1991.
3 *Bhagawan* Sri Sathya Sai Baba, Divine Discourse, 20/05/1993.
4 *Bhagawan* Sri Sathya Sai Baba, Divine Discourse, 06/02/1993.
5 *Bhagawan* Sri Sathya Sai Baba, Divine Discourse, 06/02/1993.
6 *Bhagawan* Sri Sathya Sai Baba, Divine Discourse, 25/12/1977.
7 *Bhagawan* Sri Sathya Sai Baba, Divine Discourse, 25/12/1976.
8 *Bhagawan* Sri Sathya Sai Baba, Divine Discourse, 25/12/1979.
9 *Bhagawan* Sri Sathya Sai Baba, Divine Discourse, 20/05/1993.
10 *Bhagawan* Sri Sathya Sai Baba, **The Mind and Its Mysteries**, Dasara Discourses 1976.
11 *Bhagawan* Sri Sathya Sai Baba, recorded in **Conversations with Bhagawan Sri Sathya Sai Baba**, by Dr. John Hislop.
12 *Bhagawan* Sri Sathya Sai Baba, ***Sandheha Nivari***, P. 48.
13 *Bhagawan* Sri Sathya Sai Baba, Divine Discourse, 19/12/1985.
14 *Bhagawan* Sri Sathya Sai Baba, **Summer Showers In Brindavan**, 1993.
15 *Bhagawan* Sri Sathya Sai Baba, Divine Discourse, 09/07/1998.
16 *Bhagawan* Sri Sathya Sai Baba, **Summer Showers In Brindavan**, 1993.
17 *Bhagawan* Sri Sathya Sai Baba, Divine Discourse, 09/07/1998.
18 *Bhagawan* Sri Sathya Sai Baba, **Sathya Sai *Amrita Varshini***, P. 36-47.
19 *Bhagawan* Sri Sathya Sai Baba, ***Sanathana Sarathi,*** Aug. 1995.
20 *Bhagawan* Sri Sathya Sai Baba, ***Sanathana Sarathi,*** Mar. 1995.
21 *Bhagawan* Sri Sathya Sai Baba, Divine Discourse, 19/12/1985.
22 *Bhagawan* Sri Sathya Sai Baba, Divine Discourse, 19/01/1989.
23 *Bhagawan* Sri Sathya Sai Baba, Divine Discourse, 09/12/1990.
24 *Bhagawan* Sri Sathya Sai Baba, Divine Discourse, 01/04/1998.

chapter - 6

ATMA: THE INNER MOTIVATOR

Sri Sathya Sai Baba expresses the following ideas:

> *The body is made up of five elements and is bound to perish sooner or later but the Indweller has neither birth nor death. The Indweller has no attachment whatsoever and is the eternal witness. Truly speaking, the Indweller who is in the form of the* ***Atma****, is verily God Himself.* (Telugu Poem)[1]

The *Atma* is present everywhere and is in everything; it is unaffected; it is omnipresent like *akasa*; but it is even beyond the *akasa*, so it is referred to as *Param* or beyond. The *Atma* is unaffected and untouched by anything; it is beyond everything and devoid of agitation or activity. You should not doubt whether it is unlimited or not. It is beyond the three limitations of Space, Time and Causation. *Atma* is everything; there is nothing which is not *Atma*. *Atma* is all. So it has not limitation of *Vasthu* (thingness), of name and form. *Atma* is full and free; knowing this is the fullest, highest wisdom.

A doubt may be raised here: If the *Atma* is immanent in everything, like the *akasa*, is it not subject to transformations or change? No – existing, emanating, growing, changing, declining, dying – these are the six transformations or *Vikaras*, but the *Atma* is the Universal, Eternal Witness cognising *akasa* and other elements and hence it has no modifications at all. It is changeless. *Atma* is one; it subsumes all, and by knowing It, all is known.[2]

Atma Is The Inner Motivator

For every living being engaged in pilgrimage in the *Karma Kshetra* (literally "field of action", where all activities are considered as *sadhana*), the mind, the tongue, the ears, the eyes, the nose, the hands and the feet are the *Karanamula* (instruments). They are provided for our daily use. Therefore, to achieve success in this physical world, it is essential to have these three, namely:

- ***Karanamula*** or ***Karanas*** (instruments or tools)
- ***Kartha*** (doer or agent)
- ***Karanam*** (cause or purpose)

The one who uses the instruments is the *Kartha* (doer). The desire, which propels him to act, is the *Karanam* (cause). Man's primary aim should be to recognise the unity underlying these three factors. In common parlance, we say that the eyes see, the ears hear and the mouth speaks. But if this were to be true, why is it that after a man's death, these very instruments, though intact, cannot discharge their functions? Obviously, there is an invisible Divine power in the body, which imparts life and energy to all these organs; and when that power leaves the body, it cannot function.

In ordinary terminology, this power is called *prana* (life force). Where does this *prana* come from, where does it go, and at whose guidance? These are the questions raised by the ***Kenoupanishad***, which has undertaken to investigate whether this Divine energy, which animates the several instruments in the body, is inherent in *prana*, or whether it belongs to a power superior to *prana*. In this connection, let us consider an illustration. We see that the earth is illumined by moonlight. The moon itself shines because of the sun's light reflected on it. But where does the sun get its light?

It is Divine power that lends its luster to the sun. The hydrogen and helium contained in the sun have originated from that Divine power which the ***Upanishads*** designate as the *Brahma Tathwa* (the Principle of the Supreme Absolute Reality).

It is due to the effulgence of *Brahman* (Supreme Absolute Reality) that the world shines and **there is no effulgence in the universe, which can illuminate *Brahman*.** It is the light of *Brahman* that enables the eyes to see all things except *Brahman*. The mind is able to function because of the light of *Brahman*, but it cannot grasp or describe *Brahman*. This is why the ***Upanishads*** have proclaimed the truth that *Brahman* is beyond the reach of the mind and speech.

Inner And Outer Vision

Although such a unique Divine power resides in him, man is unable to recognise it. Why? It is due to man developing only *Baharya-drishti* (outward vision) in his daily life and not putting forth any effort to cultivate and experience the *Anthar-drishti* (inner vision).

> **The divine power is the life of our life, the mind of our mind, the eye of our eye, the ear of our ear, and the speech of our speech, because it is the motivating, coordinating and illuminating principle underlying all such body organs.**

We can easily grasp this truth by understanding that just as an automobile's headlights, horn, and engine, etc. depend on the battery's current for their respective functions such as giving light, sound, and propulsion, all the body's organs are animated or motivated by the Divine *Atmic* power, enabling them to discharge their respective functions. **As soon as the purpose and time for which man is born are over, his body loses its power and vitality and becomes lifeless.**

THE SEEN AND THE SEER

Let us now consider the *karanas* and *Atma* from the standpoint of ***drisya*** (seen) and ***drashta*** (seer). All objects seen by the eyes are the "seen" and the eyes themselves are the "seer". When the eyes are open but do not see the objects present before them due to the mind wandering somewhere, the eyes become the "seen" and the mind becomes the "seer". When the *Buddhi* (intellect) observes the wanderings of the mind, *Buddhi* becomes the "seer" and the mind, the "seen". In the state of *samadhi* (absorption in the *Atma*), *Atma* is the "seer" and *Buddhi*, "the seen"[3].

There is nothing that can see the *Atma*. Hence it is always the "seer" and never the "seen". **The *Atma* is the Universal Seer.** This seer is the cause of all delusion in this world; the seer creates silver in the mother of pearl; the varied scenes of the dream-world are the creations of the seer. So too, for the multiplicity of things experienced during the waking stage, the *Atma*, who is the seer, is the instrument.[4]

Thus we notice that the mind and other senses are *drisya* (the seen) and therefore are termed *karanas* (tools, instruments), which are put to work by the *drashta* (the seer, i.e., *Atma*). In the absence of the *drashta*, all the tools will be useless no matter how valuable they might be. For example, a machine worth billions of rupees is installed. If there is no current to operate it, it will turn out to be useless. Likewise, in the absence of the *Atmic* power, which enables all the organs to function, the body becomes a worthless mass of flesh and bones. Therefore, it is the foremost duty of man to realise the *Atma* (Self), which imparts value to an otherwise valueless body, and also to regulate the activities of all these *karanas* in the right manner so as to achieve the fulfillment of the purpose of human life.[5]

Atma And *Jiva*

What is the *jiva*? According to Sathya Sai Baba it is "the embodied soul, the individual soul in a state of non-realisation of its identity with *Brahman*. It is the self-deluded, bound spirit, unaware of its own true nature. It is subjected to sensations of pain and pleasure, birth and death."[6] It is sometimes called *jivatma*, because it is the spark of God, *Atma*, that is unaware of itself, "the wave that emerges from the sea," says Sai Baba. In the brain the embodied *Paramatma* is called *"Purusha"*.

Sri Sathya Sai Baba continues:

- *Deha* (body) + *Atma* = *Dehatma* (Body + Spirit)
- *Jiva* + *Atma* = *Jivatma* (Spark of Life + Spirit)
- *Param* (supreme) + *Atma* = *Paramatma* (Supreme Spirit)

Although *Deha* (the body), *Jiva* (the individual), and *Param* (the Supreme) are different terms, *Atma* (spirit) is common and is equally present in all the three.

When I begin My discourse with the words, *Divyatma-swarupulara* (Embodiments of Divine *Atma*), I intend to convey that the same Divine Spirit is in every one of you. **Just as the ocean, the wave and the foam contain the same water, the spirit that is present in the body, in the individual being and in the Supreme, is one and the same.**

To experience this spiritual oneness, your way of life should be holy. This can be accomplished only by entertaining sacred thoughts, which lead to good conduct. **The Divine can be experienced by human beings only as you deem yourself Divine.** Live with this firm conviction. Do not give room to any bad thoughts. The body is a temple of the Divine and no evil thoughts should be allowed to enter it. Man should strive to reach the sublime, regardless of difficulties and troubles.[7]

A ***Jivanmuktha*** (liberated soul) is established firmly in the knowledge of the *Atma*. He has achieved it by dwelling on the world and contemplating its failings and faults. By this means, he has developed an insight into the nature of pleasure and pain and has equanimity in both. He knows that wealth, worldly joy and pleasure are all worthless and even poisonous. He takes praise and blame and even blows with a calm assurance, unaffected by both honour and dishonour. Of course, the *Jivanmuktha* reached this stage only after long years of systematic discipline and unflagging zeal when distress and doubt assailed him. Defeat only made him more rigorous in self-examination and more earnest about following prescribed discipline. The *Jivanmuktha* has no trace of "will to live"; he is ever ready to drop into the lap of death.[8]

The *Atma* And The *Vasanas*

Of all the forces that propel the human being, the *vasanas* are one of the greatest. They are inherited impulses that influence behaviour, talents, likes and dislikes, character and life choices. The literal meaning of the word "*vasana*" is "scar", and a *vasana* is figuratively just that – a scar or groove created by repetitive thought patterns in the brain. These give shape to the *manomaya kosa* (mental and emotional sheath) that envelops the *Atma*. This "scar" represents tendencies and attachments, which we carry from birth to birth. *Vanasas* shape our character and destiny for good or ill and effect the actions we take. Good or *subha vasanas*, for example, give the *jiva* artistic and worldly talents, human values and a desire to pursue higher spiritual things. Maleficent *vasanas* can give the soul tendencies towards criminal behaviour, sensual pleasures and addictions.

There are four types of *vasanas*, says Sai Baba, and all others fall within these categories. They relate to:

1. **BODY** (i.e., health, beauty, vigour, physical and artistic skills, eating habits, addictions, choice of family, etc.)
2. **MIND** (i.e., scholarship, ego attachments [clan, wealth, youth], good and bad attitudes and outlooks to people and the world, mental abilities, etc.)
3. **WEALTH** (i.e., money – greedy, miserly, charitable, work and career, social status, lifestyle, etc.)
4. **SEX** (i.e., marriage, preferences in partners, attachments to children and friends)

Sri Sathya Sai Baba says:

It is certain that the features of the past life are carried to the next life. You can call them *vasanas* or *samskars* or the qualities of the past life. People with good *vasanas* will spend their time in a sacred way by participating in *satsang* (good company), *bhajan* (singing His glory), entertaining good thoughts and good deeds and good discussion. On the other hand, people with bad *vasanas* make their lifetime unholy by indulging in *duskarma* (misdeeds), entertaining bad thoughts and speaking falsehood. It is true that the body weakens, withers, dies and decays, but the *vasanas* don't die. They follow you to the next life.

A simple illustration will make this subject clearer to you. Suppose your hand was injured. You got it treated, and for some time you put a bandage also over and around the injured part. The hand was healed completely after some time. But in that part of your hand where the injury took place a scar or a mark is left, and it remains till now as well. Similarly, the body may die. But the *vasanas* remain as a spot in the next life.[9]

The impulses invade the realm of the *Hridayam* where they cause endless trouble. They remind you of pleasures, agitating the memory of past experiences and you start craving them again. The cravings make the senses and their leader, *manas* (the mind), engage in brisk activities; there is no escape for you from this. So you attempt to collect and enjoy the things that you crave. All this takes place in the twinkling of an eye, so to say.

The impulses operate so subtly and so powerfully that they are the cause of the objective happiness [or the lack of it]. If they are absent, the mind is pellucid and pure. If they are present, all purity is ruined; **they are obstacles in the path of Truth, of *Atma* and of Immorality.**[10]

Vasanas And Modern Neurology

A correspondence can be made between the *vasanas* and the neurological connections that appear in the human brain. Repetitive thoughts, experiences and behaviours very quickly form neural pathways. Any event with high emotional impact makes an instant impression, which is deepened as the memory of the experience is replayed over and again. When the same pathways are consistently followed, habits and belief systems develop which become difficult or even impossible to break.

This physiological process is identical to the way *vasanas* are formed in the subtle bodies of man. However, instead of pathways in the nervous system, patterns of energy are formed in the *Karana Sarira* (causal body) that is carried by the *jiva* (soul) from birth to birth. The *jiva*, entering a new body, impresses these thoughts upon the newly formed *annamaya kosa* (physical body), shaping its life and destiny.

The illustrations below show the proliferation of neurological pathways in the infant brain from birth to 15 months.

Diagram No. 9 - Neurological Pathways

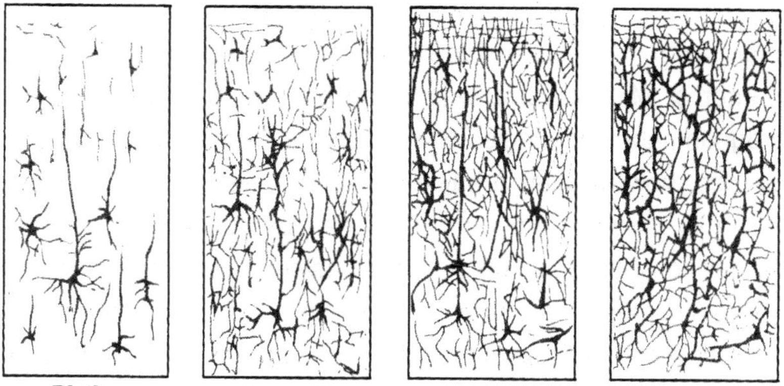

Birth **3 months** **6 months** **15 months**

Up through ages 6 or 7, new connections develop at an astounding rate. Hence the emphasis Sri Sathya Sai Baba places on filling young minds and hearts with Human Values.

Sri Sathya Sai Baba and *Vedanta* go a step further, reminding us that even before birth, while the child is still in the womb, the emotional events around the pregnant woman have a dramatic impact on the foetus in-utero. The womb is not an isolation chamber. In fact the developing foetus is even more vulnerable to subtle vibrations than children and adults. So if the parents and close relations follow Human Values, the child will be exposed to them while in-utero. Everyone around an expectant mother – extended family, friends – should be respectful of the developing human being within and help create a loving and peaceful environment. If strong value-based thought patterns are encouraged to form, the impact of the negative *vasanas* will be less profound. Eventually, like medicine that remains unused until past its expiry date, these scars simply lose their potency. This process of transformation is known in Sanskrit as *samskar* (refinement).

Story Of Abhimanyu

This story illustrates how a developing foetus could learn detailed information while still inside his mother's womb. Arjuna, the great warrior of ***Mahabharata***, was telling his wife Subhadra, who was pregnant, about strategies of war. Specifically he was relating, step by step, how to enter a battle formation called the "*chakra* view", if one is surrounded by so many enemies during a battle. During the telling of the tale, Subhadra fell asleep. However, the child in-utero, Abhimanyu was fervently listening and responding with great interest even from the womb with, "Hmm, hmm, hmm." Arjuna was deep in the story, unaware that his wife had fallen asleep and that his listening audience was his unborn child. At this point, Krishna interrupted. Arjuna had yet to explain how to get out of the formation safely. Being God, knowing the past, present and future, Krishna did not want Abhimanyu to have this information, knowing it was the young man's destiny to die inside the "*chakra* view". Sharply Krishna said, "Arjuna, stop! Your wife is sleeping, to whom are you telling this story?" Realising his wife was sleeping, Arjuna left off the tale before the end. Abhimanyu, therefore did not learn the full teaching. Later in life, after he had entered the "*chakra* view", he did not have the knowledge to exit it and therefore died.

As a gynaecologist I have done ultrasound testing of the baby in-utero at various intervals. This instrument is based on sound waves which bounce off the baby, showing great details of the developing body. Through ultrasound, every muscle, bone and organ of the baby gives off sounds that are not heard by the ears. Sound, words – and also thought – are therefore critical to the positive development of the foetus.

From The Unreal To The Truth

The *kosas* (sheaths) must be cleansed of these "scars", which obscure the light of the *Atma* in the same way as the clouds in the sky hide the light of the sun. The *vasanas* we bring with us into incarnation can lift us up or drag us down, so we must perform sincere self-enquiry and follow Human Values always. If we have good *vasanas* we will seek the feet of the *Guru* or God, and fervently pray to be raised up. For centuries this has been expressed in the Sanskrit prayer:

Asato Ma Sat Gamaya;
Thamaso Ma Jyotir Gamaya;
Mrityor Ma Amritam Gamaya.

(From the unreal, lead us to the truth;
From out of darkness lead us to the light;
From fear of death lead us to immortality.)

Sri Sathya Sai Baba says:

It is not that easy to change human nature. For instance, suppose you grow a crop of garlic by using the powder of aromatic camphor as the soil, a fragrant musk as the manure and scented rose water for irrigation, will the garlic produced, as a result of all your effort, give up its natural, pungent odour? So also, despite all his *sadhana* and *satsang,* the worldly *vasanas* accumulated in the course of his several past lives will not leave man so easily. Therefore, it is first necessary for man to understand the true nature of his own body.

What is this body? It is a repository of filth, urine, flesh, blood, and other such things. However, in this very body there shines the gem of the purest ray of serenity, namely the *Atma*. Gems do not grow like fruits on trees, but are to be found in dirt. Similarly, the body which is of the nature of *mrinmaya* (full of dirt), harbours in itself the *Atma*, which is of the nature of *chinmaya* (full of pure consciousness). The secret of man's success lies in this thorough understanding and unraveling of this principle of pure consciousness.[11]

How to destroy this ignorance and develop wisdom? That is the question! The answer is through meditation. The conquest of ignorance, ego, attachment and impulse brings about liberation for the *jiva*.[12]

MEDITATION: A TOOL TO REALISE THE *ATMA*

Sri Sathya Sai Baba says:

The *Atma* in its purity will be seen when the hindrances to clear vision are removed by spiritual practice, by *sadhana*. Real *sadhana* is not just sitting in meditation. **We meditate to rise above the source of thought into the realm of experience. It is experience that gives the possibility of transformation.**

Can anyone train another in meditation? Or claim to train? It may be possible to teach a person the posture, the pose, the position of the legs, feet or hands, neck, head or back, the style of breathing or its speed. But meditation is a function of the inner man; it involves deep subjective quiet, the emptying of the mind and filling oneself with the light that emerges from the divine spark within. This is a discipline that no textbook can teach and no class can communicate.

To enjoy the sweetness of Divine Love, you must attempt to get it directly. By means of meditation you can realise that I am the resident in all hearts, the urge, the motive, the guide, the goal. Yearn for that vision, that awareness, and make it your priceless possession.

The *Atma* is everywhere but for the purpose of sitting in meditation, the life principle or *jiva* can be considered as being 10 inches above the navel and at the centre of the chest, at the 9th, 10th and 11th vertebrae. If the spine is injured at this point, paralysis occurs. **[SEE DIAGRAM NO. 10]**

To sit straight is important. If the body is in a straight position, as if it were wound around a straight pole, the life force may rise up through the straight body and give the quality of intense concentration to the mind. Meditation for its proper practice should be at the same place, at the same time. In that way, it surely will be successful. If one is away from home in travel, in his mind he can go to the accustomed place no matter where he is. When away from *Swami*, by remembering Him doing this or that, the battery is recharged. That also is genuine meditation.[13]

The Posture Of Meditation

Human Values And Health ~ Diagram No. 10

Sri Sathya Sai Baba tells us that in meditation, three things come into play:

1. **Meditator**
2. **Chosen Form** or **Focus** of the practice (i.e., God form, light, breath, etc.)
3. **Process** of Meditation itself

Meditation, He says, falls into three stages:

1. **Concentration**: using discipline to focus the mind and intention beneath the senses and desires.
2. **Contemplation**: an in-between state, when focus deepens and the body is forgotten.
3. **Meditation**: above the senses, you are not aware that you are meditating. This cannot be forced, but happens naturally when contemplation is deep enough. "When all the senses and desires fall away, there is only God," says Baba.[14]

The *Atma Jyothi* (Light Of The Soul)

Sri Sathya Sai Baba continues:

To begin with, you must understand this most important principle, which is that you are not the body; you are the Indweller. When you understand that, you will no longer be bothered by body-consciousness. The body is temporary. God is eternal and permanent. Therefore it is said that the body is the temple of God and that the Indweller is God Himself.

This world is impermanent and full of sorrow; there is no use taking refuge in it. All the people you know will change. God is the only fixed entity. He is the lamp which does not get extinguished. Take shelter in Him. He is the supreme light, the *Paramjyothi*; He is the light of every soul, the *Jivanjyothi*; He is the unlimited and undiminishable light, the *Akandajyothi*; He is the one light, without second, the *Advaitajyothi*.[15]

Jyothi Meditation

Because God or *Atma* is so often equated with light, and the process of awakening, referred to as "illumination", Sri Sathya Sai Baba recommends *Jyothi* Meditation, or meditation on the light as one of the easiest and safest paths to realisation. "Light," He says, "is Formless, Eternal, Divine. It is the safe way and the sure way. What comes about in meditation is not the thinking of the light, but the forgetting of the body and thereby the direct experience that the body is not oneself. **To expand beyond self and see that your light is the light of the universe is liberation.** Liberation is not different from this."

JYOTHI MEDITATION

Sri Sathya Sai Baba explains:

- Have a lamp with an open flame, steady and straight, or a candle before you. Sit in the lotus posture or any other comfortable posture in front of the candle. Gaze straight ahead at the flame. Then take the candle flame, the *jyothi*, into your mid-brow at the place of the third eye.
- Look on the flame, steadily, for some time and closing your eyes, try to feel the flame inside you between your eyebrows.
- Let it slide down into the lotus of your heart, illuminating the path. When it enters the heart, imagine that the petals of the lotus open out, one by one, bathing every thought, feeling and emotion in the Light and so removing darkness from them. There is no space for darkness to hide. The Light of the flame becomes wider and brighter.
- Let it pervade your limbs; now those limbs can never more deal in dark, suspicious, wicked activities. They have become instruments of Light and Love.
- Let the Light reach the tongue; falsehood vanishes from it.

- Let it rise up to the eyes and the ears and destroy all the dark desires that infest them leading you into perverse sights and puerile conversation.
- Let your head be surcharged with Light and all wicked thoughts flee therefrom.
- Imagine that the Light is in you more and more intensely; let it shine all around you in ever widening circles,
- Taking in your loved ones, your kith and kin your friends and companions – nay, your enemies and rivals – strangers, all men and women, whoever they are,
- All living beings, animals, birds, trees, the earth, the entire world.
- Stay on that thrill, witnessing the Light everywhere.
- If you are adoring God in any form now, visualise that form in the all pervasive Light deep in your heart; recite the name.
- Draw the Light back inside the heart and come back to waking consciousness, the Light in the heart with you always."

"For Light is God. God is Light. When Light meets Light, it is all Light. When the individual meets the universal, all is universal." Sai Baba concludes, "By experiencing the oneness within yourself and all others, you are able to see and experience the oneness of all beings. Meditation on Light is real meditation." [16]

Sathya Sai Baba suggests that we practise this meditation daily, as a full cleansing for body, mind and spirit. "Since the light illumines all the senses every day, so deeply and so systematically," He tells us, "a time will come when you can no more relish dark and evil sights, yearn for dark and sinister tales, crave for low and harmful, deadening, toxic food and drinks, handle dirty, demeaning things, approach places of ill-fame and injury or frame evil designs against any one." [17]

Self-Enquiry

Sri Sathya Sai Baba consistently teaches the importance of self-enquiry, another form of meditation, as a way to purify the mind and *Hridayam* and ultimately discover the truth of the Self.

Sri Sathya Sai Baba tells us:

The greatest defect today is the absence of *Atmavichara*, the enquiry into the nature of the *Atma*. That is the cause of all this *Asanti* (lack of peace). Every spiritual aspirant should take up inner enquiry. In all your spiritual practices that you engage in, you should spend three-fourths of your time on self-enquiry; then you will get the full results.[18] There are four things in which every man must interest himself:

- Who am I?
- From where have I come?
- Whither am I going?
- How long shall I be there?

The four ***Vedas*** give the answers to these questions. All spiritual enquiry begins with these questions ... for the successful arrival at the correct answers, spiritual discipline is essential.[19]

Chart No. 11 ~ Who Am I?

Who Am I?			
Conscious	Acts	Who you think you are	Body
Conscience	Thinks	Who others think you are	Mind
Conscious-ness	Permanent beingness	Who you really are	*Atma*
SOURCE: *Bhagawan* Sri Sathya Sai Baba - *Divine Discourse, April 1991*			

You are not one person. You are three persons. The one you think you are; that is the body. The one others think you are; that is the mind. And the one you really are; that is the *Atma*. The body that you think you are is **conscious**. The mind that others think you are is **conscience**. The *Atma*, which you really are, is **consciousness**. Conscious (body) is full of ups and downs. It is like a water bubble. Conscience (mind) also changes. Consciousness *(Atma)* is permanent. So don't follow the body or mind. You are consciousness. You are God.[20]

Exercise 1: A Simple Self-Enquiry

Below is a simple exercise in self-enquiry to practise daily. It begins with a review of the day's events and concludes by offering love and gratitude to the Indweller.

Even if your house has only one door and one window, dust finds its way in, so you clean it every day. If you have a house with two doors and two windows you definitely must clean – the more entrances, the more dust and dirt finds its way inside. The body of a man has ten openings: ears (2), eyes (2), nose (2), mouth (1), anus (1), genital (1), skin (1). There is also the mid-brow, the third eye centre. Each can be thought of a door or window, which admits experience from the outside world. Can you imagine how much dirt enters into the *Hridayam* on a daily basis?

Every night lie down and witness your own mind and think how much dust you have accumulated today. Did you hurt anyone by thought, word or deed? Did you scold anyone? Did you do any theft? Were you rude to your boss, parents or children? Did you beat anyone, even a dog? Did you tell an untruth or were you just impatient or unkind?

Review whatever you have done the whole day, from morning to evening. Then say,

"God, I know you have given me a pure heart, with a seat only for You. Although I tried to keep it clean, I spoiled this beautiful single seat sofa that is meant only for you with bad *karmas*. I am cleaning it with loving thoughts, prayers and *namasmarana*. I am picturing your beautiful form resting blissfully. Please, Lord, give me strength and wisdom. Don't let me repeat again tomorrow the mistakes of today. Let me learn from this and proceed through life in a more loving way. You are the indweller in this house. Bless me that I may keep it clean."

With these kind words, now drift off to sleep, confident that the Lord who is before you, behind you, around and within you is also watching over you.

If you wish, you can then move on and offer thanks to all your body organs and gross sense organs.

Exercise 2: Thanking Your Body Organs

How amazing it is that when someone gives you a little pen or pencil you say, "thank you", or if you drop a hankie and someone leans over to pick it up, you say "thank you". How sad it is that our body organs work 24 hours for us keeping us alive, but we never thank them. At least once a day, when you go to bed, kindly thank each organ of your body, so that they all become happy children and they function well. Let them think, "oh, my Soul Mother has come to me, showing me so much gratitude, love and concern. Now I can relax, confident in her care."

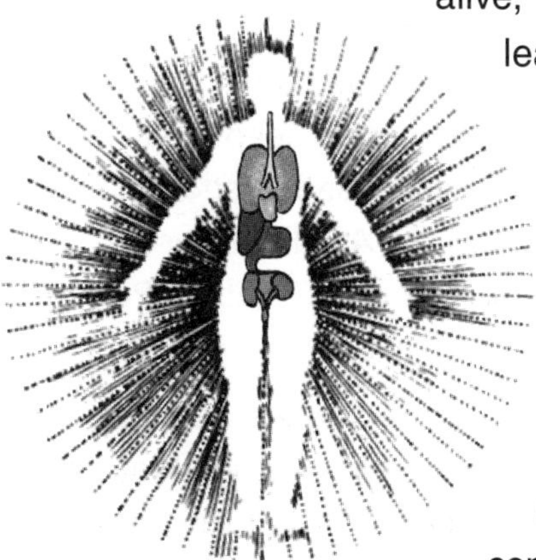

Thank Your Body Organs

- When you go to bed kindly remove your pillow. Lie straight, facing the sky, with both hands and feet relaxed, about 6 inches away from the body, hands also facing upwards. Take a few long deep breaths. Meditate on your **MID-BROW** where cosmic energy, soul or God lives. Now is the time to catch the cosmic energy from your own body and supply it to all your tired organs. So go on taking deep breathing, letting your mind settle at mid-brow. Chant the name of God in equal rhythm with the breath. Say *"Om Sai Ram"* or *"Allah Ho Akabar", "Vaye Guru", "Om Namo Narayana", "Om Namah Sivaya", "Om Mane Padme Om"* – whatever name of God or *mantra* most pleases you. Be sure to hold the picture of that God in mid-brow, or if you wish, just hold the image of **Pure Light**.
- Slowly, you will feel energy or light in your mid-brow. Your mind will be very happy with this connection. Now take your mind to your **BRAIN** and talk to the brain. "Oh, my brain! How wonderful you are! You are much bigger than any ten computers on earth. You receive all the impulses from the body, answer them and store them. What heavy work you are doing every day for me! You are helping me to realise the physical world. I am so thankful to you my brain. You must be very tired. I am now thanking you for all your tireless work for me." Go on taking deep breathing, letting your brain feel your gratitude, and finish by saying, "My dear brain, you are the seat of *Atma*. Because of you, I can feel God's love. It is only within you that My *Purusha* and I will become one."
- Go to your **EYES**. "Oh, my eyes! You are very Divine. Through you I see the whole universe. Please always try to see good. Go only to good places so that you catch

good energy and see the beauty of God's creation. I am so thankful to you. You work for me so heartily."

- Go on with deep breathing. Go to your **EARS**. "Oh, my dear ears! Without you, I cannot hear any voice or music. There are millions and millions of people on earth and you are the only organ that can recognise the voice and give me messages. Please kindly try to be in good company. Listen to the glory of God and hear kind speech. Listen to bhajan and sweet things. I am so thankful to you. Without you I would have been deaf, knowing nothing."
- Now go to your **MOUTH**. "Oh, my mouth! How much you work for me! Three to 4 times a day I take food. You chew it well and swallow it so that my stomach can digest it. What a divine work you are doing! Without food I could never survive. Always take in *satwic* food, pure, sweet water and abstain from smoking or taking in other substances that can destroy health. I am very thankful to you."
- "Oh, my **TONGUE**! Always talk sweetly and softly to everyone because God resides in everyone. If you hurt anyone, you are hurting God. A hurting word gives a wound deeper even than a sword. The damage done by a sword can be stitched, but the wound made by harsh words takes a very, very long time to heal. So thank you for speaking sweetly. Always sing the glory of God; always recite the *lilas* of God. Be careful. Don't do back-biting. God speaks through you and those who receive are also God."
- "Oh, my dear **NOSE**! How nice you are! You bring fresh air to my lungs, filtering insects and dust. You work hard breathing in and out 21,000 times in a day and you never stop. Even when I am sleeping you are working. Why should I not be grateful to you? You keep me alive by giving oxygen all the time. How happy I am with your efforts. I am very, very thankful to you."

- Now your whole head will be filled with Divine Light. From here now bring your mind down to the **HEART**. "Oh, my heart! You give me sensations that help me to experience emotions and feelings. You beat 72 to 80 times per minute round the clock. You filter and supply fresh blood to the body. Without you I cannot live. Thank you so much for looking after my body."
- Go to your **LUNGS**. "Oh, my lungs! You expand and contract 18 to 20 times per minute day and night. If you stop your work I will die. You bring *prana sakti* and oxygen from the atmosphere into my body. You expel bad gases and bring in good gases, purifying my blood, supplying the whole body with *prana sakti* and oxygen. I am very grateful to you."
- Go on taking soft deep breathing and go to your **STOMACH**. "Oh, my stomach! How thankful I am to you! I load you with food every 3 hours and you go on churning it and making it digestible. What a hard worker you are. You supply the liver and send roughage to the small and large intestines. I am thankful to you."
- "Oh, my dear **LIVER!** What a beautiful factory you are! You take all the energy of the food and manufacture many substances, circulating them as pure fluid into the blood stream and throughout the entire body. I am very thankful to you."
- "Oh, my **INTESTINES**! You digest the final matters and expel all the waste products through the anus. I know it is a dirty job. I am very thankful to you for keeping my body clean all the time from bad gases and wastes."
- "Oh, my dear **KIDNEYS**! You bring out all waste matter in the urine and keep my body free of toxins. You are maintaining water balance in my body, otherwise I would be swollen all over with water. You are the best diuretic

ever manufactured. The dose is correct, the action is always perfect, and there are no side effects. I am very thankful to you."

- Let this thankfulness settle into the centre of your body and then move your mind out to your **HANDS**. "Oh, my hands! You are Divine tools of God. Don't beat or hurt anyone. Everyone is God, so touch kindly and with love. Do your duty in this life with devotion and discipline. Give yourselves to good hard work, earning honest and good money, serving others with kindness and strength. God accepts only earning by hard work. I am thankful to you."
- "Oh, my **LEGS**! You are divine! Go to temples instead of pubs and parties. Take me only to good places to work with good people. Do the work of service with love and walk the straight path to God."
- Take deep breathing and now speak to your **WHOLE BODY**. "Oh, my body! I am very thankful you are here, but let me tell you that <u>you are useless unless I realise God in you</u>. Let me go always inside and purify my *antakarna* (inner senses) and mind, intellect and so I can realise the soul (*Atma*)."
- "Oh, my **MIND**! You are very unsteady. Please hold on to only good thoughts of God. This birth is given to me only to realise God. Don't be a mad monkey. Keep yourself always focused on the Lotus Feet of God."

And so now end, coming full circle, softly saying "Om Sai Ram, Om Sai Ram", or any other *mantra* you have chosen as you drift off to sleep.

Readers, you should practise this every day and experience the results yourself. This has been printed in my first book, **SPIRITUALITY AND HEALTH,** in a shorter version. I have been thanking my body for 20 years, and the effects are increased health, vitality and awareness. I have also become a happy-go-lucky person. Meditation upon the organs, offering them thanks, supplies additional *prana sakti* to your body and mind, thus keeping them healthy for their work here on earth. There are other benefits as well:

1. It will promote sleep.
2. It will increase your intelligence.
3. It will improve your memory.
4. It will clean the stress out from your organs, especially the brain, the five senses and the *antakarna,* purifying the *Hridayam* so that you can realise God.
5. It will encourage the actual experience that you are not the body, but only dwelling in it.

Purify The *Hridayam* Through Friendship With God

Sri Sathya Sai Baba tells us:

Hridayam (spiritual heart) is the son of the *Atma*. From *Hridayam* the Mind is born. So, the Mind is the grandson of the *Atma*. And from the Mind, Speech originates. So speech is the Great Grandson of the *Atma*. In short, one's *Hridayam*, Mind and Speech belong to the divine family and have received a share in the Divine prosperity. Therefore, *Hridayam*, Mind and Speech should be in constant communion with God. One should develop Friendship with God and be a recipient of His love. One undertakes many spiritual pursuits to obtain this love. In fact, one need not undertake any spiritual practices. It is enough to remember the relationship between oneself and God.

God is the only permanent friend in this world. As long as you are in His company, you will be happy and He is also happy. But when there is separation from His devotee, though God may not express it, He feels sad. Why is the individual going along the wrong path? Why is he forgetting the truth? Why is he distancing himself from Divinity? Why is he losing his purity? Thinking so,

God feels sad. He does so for the devotee's sake, not for His sake. Whatever God says or does is for your own good.

All your troubles are of your own making. God always gives you everything good. But you do not receive it. What is it that you need to do to make God happy? **You should go close to God and worship Him with a sense of surrender.** This is for your own sake. God does not ask for anything. A child sits on the lap of his mother for its own satisfaction. When the child goes near the mother, she showers her love. When you want to be close to God, you do not need to go through sacred texts or undertake great spiritual practices. Rituals and reading of holy texts are only worldly actions. They are meant to give only external satisfaction, but one has to make efforts to experience the inner satisfaction.

Think Of God And Go Nearer To Him

Sri Sathya Sai Baba insists that:

Think of God, then go closer to God and love Him wholeheartedly. Such nearness and dearness to God will ultimately make you one with God. This is what *Vedanta* has declared: the Knower of God becomes God. The food eaten gets digested and its essence is supplied to all parts of the body. This means that the food partaken becomes one with the body. **Similarly, one has to offer oneself completely to God.** Only then one can become one with Him. All thoughts should become Divine. *Jiva* is *Nara* (man) and God is *Narayana*. Both should become one. *Nara* means *Atmic* Principle. So, one is human only in form, but the nature is Divine. It is only the *Atma* that moves about from top to toe. Whatever is thought, said or done is only due to the presence of the *Atma*. That is why Krishna has said, "you are the eternal sparks of Myself". You are the reflection of God.

The relation between a devotee and God is only *Hridayam* to *Hridayam* and love to love. Nothing is greater than the Divine power. Once you have Divine Grace what harm can the *Navagrahas* (nine planets, i.e., your fate) do to you? So, work for God's grace and surrender to Him completely. There lies the true bliss.

Surrender With Pure *Hridayam*

> *The purpose of the spiritual pursuits lies in the unification of man with God. One has to unify one's senses, life principles, and speech, and offer himself to God.*

There is no need to search for God elsewhere. He dwells in one's *Hridayam*. That is why He is called *Hridayavasi* (Indweller of the Heart). If someone asks you, "Where do you come from?" You may say that you are coming from a hotel or someplace. You come from *Hridayam*. It is this *Hridayam* that is your dwelling place. Then where is the question of coming and going?

All actions are aimed at the purification of *Hridayam*. Purity alone is not enough to experience Divinity. With purity of *Hridayam* one should offer oneself to God. You will not offer a faded flower to God. Likewise the *Hridayam*, which may be compared to a flower, should be fresh and devoid of impurities before it is offered to God. There is an ocean of difference between *Archana* (worship) and *Arpitham* (total surrender). It is not *Archana*, but *Arpitham* that is the most essential. The aim of worship and rituals is to understand the principle of unity. You start with one name and one form and ultimately realise that everything is one. [21]

Atma Vidya

Sri Sathya Sai Baba says *Atma Vidya* (science of the Self) is "the real education and the only knowledge which can make one know all that he has to know."

"You are the *Atma*," He says, "the Supreme Master. You have the potential to realise this through the discriminating power of the *Buddhi*. Once you recognise this truth, you will also understand human nature, which is a combination of Human Values like truth, righteousness, peace, love and non-violence. You will then be rid of your animal qualities. Then you will realise the cause of diseases and the method of curing them."[22]

In a letter to His students, Sri Sathya Sai Baba asks them to recite the following:

> **I am not the body –**
> **a mass of flesh, bones and blood.**
> **I am not the mind –**
> **a bundle of wasteful desires, manifest and unmanifest.**
> **I am not the feeling –**
> **of infatuation that obstructs the way to liberation;**
> **I am that Eternal *Paramatma*,**
> **who is aware of the power that I AM.**[23]

---

1 *Bhagawan* Sri Sathya Sai Baba, Divine Discourse, 13/07/2003.
2 *Bhagawan* Sri Sathya Sai Baba, ***Jnana Vahini***, reprint 1998.
3 *Bhagawan* Sri Sathya Sai Baba, Divine Discourse, 25/05/1991.
4 *Bhagawan* Sri Sathya Sai Baba, ***Jnana Vahini***, reprint 1998.
5 *Bhagawan* Sri Sathya Sai Baba, Divine Discourse, 25/05/1991.
6 *Bhagawan* Sri Sathya Sai Baba, **Sathya Sai Speaks, Vol. 1**, P. 232.
7 *Bhagawan* Sri Sathya Sai Baba, Divine Discourse, 26/06/1994.
8 *Bhagawan* Sri Sathya Sai Baba, ***Jnana Vahini***, reprint 1998.
9 *Bhagawan* Sri Sathya Sai Baba, recorded in ***Sathyopanishad***, Vol. 1 by Anil Kumar Kamaraju.
10 *Bhagawan* Sri Sathya Sai Baba, ***Dhyana Vahini.***
11 *Bhagawan* Sri Sathya Sai Baba, Divine Discourse, 25/05/1991.
12 *Bhagawan* Sri Sathya Sai Baba, ***Dhyana Vahini.***
13 *Bhagawan* Sri Sathya Sai Baba, recorded in **Conversations With *Bhagawan* Sri Sathya Sai Baba,** by Dr. John Hislop.
14 *Bhagawan* Sri Sathya Sai Baba, recorded in **Conversations With *Bhagawan* Sri Sathya Sai Baba,** by Dr. John Hislop.
15 *Bhagawan* Sri Sathya Sai Baba, **Discourses On the *Bhagavad Gita***, Ch. 18, 1984.
16 *Bhagawan* Sri Sathya Sai Baba, recorded in **Conversations With *Bhagawan* Sri Sathya Sai Baba,** by Dr. John Hislop.
17 *Bhagawan* Sri Sathya Sai Baba, **Light of Love**.
18 *Bhagawan* Sri Sathya Sai Baba, **Discourses On the *Bhagavad Gita***, 1984.
19 *Bhagawan* Sri Sathya Sai Baba, **Teachings of *Bhagawan* Sri Sathya Sai Baba**, 1974.
20 *Bhagawan* Sri Sathya Sai Baba, Divine Discourse, 04/1991.
21 *Bhagawan* Sri Sathya Sai Baba, Divine Discourse, 11/10/1998.
22 *Bhagawan* Sri Sathya Sai Baba, ***Sanathana Sarathi***, Mar. 1994.
23 *Bhagawan* Sri Sathya Sai Baba, ***Prema Dhara***, Vol 1.

In these five sheaths are encased three types of bodies: physical, subtle and causal. Divinity is there in all the sheaths of the body. It is Constant Integrated Awareness in different forms – in speech, action and feelings.

~ **Sri Sathya Sai Baba**

chapter - 7

THE HUMAN INSTRUMENT: *KOSAS*, BODIES AND *CHAKRAS*

THE *PANCHAKOSAS* (FIVE SHEATHS)

Sri Sathya Sai Baba says:

Kosa means sheath, a case, a cover. A sword is put into a scabbard. Money is kept in a treasury or *kosa*. You must realise that the thing kept in the case is the real 'I'. To see one's own Truth, one has to remove the five cases. [1]

Man is enveloped by five sheaths called *Kosas* in Sanskrit. These can be thought of as various bodies interpenetrating each other in a successively more subtle way, each one finer than the previous one, the last being beyond the aspects of mind, where only the veil of ignorance remains to hide the *Atma*.[2] **[SEE DIAGRAM NO. 13]**

Sri Sathya Sai Baba tells us that each sheath has a relationship to one of the five human values, although the value of love permeates all *panchakosas*.

Chart No. 12 ~ The Five *Kosas*

Kosa	Properties	Human Value	Level of Consciousness
ANNAMAYA	gross, material, food component	*Dharma*	Body
PRANAMAYA	vital air, breath, life force	*Prema*	Vital force, nervous system
MANOMAYA	mental, emotional, will, ego	*Santi*	Mental
VIJNANAMAYA	rational, discriminatory, intellectual	*Sathya*	*Chittha* – intellect, all-pervading
ANANDAMAYA	blissful, equanimous	*Ahimsa*	Pure Divine Self, *Purusha*
SOURCE: 3, 4			

1. *Annamaya* (gross, material, food component)

> *The body grew in the womb of the mother with the help of* ***Anna*** *or food taken by the mother. After birth, the body grows and is sustained by food. After death, the body becomes part of the earth which produces food. So it is called* ***Annamaya****. ~ Sai Baba*[5]

This is the physical body, also known as ***Sthul Sarira***; it constitutes 25 principles and is called the wakeful state:

a. Five *Panchmahabuthas* (gross elements: ether, air, fire, water, earth) +
b. Five *Karmendriyas* (gross or working organs: vocal organs, hands, legs, genitals, excretory organs [bladder, anus]) +
c. Five *Jnanendriyas* (sense organs: ear, skin, eye, tongue, nose) +
d. Five *Pranas* (vital airs) +

The *Panchakosas* & Three *Sariras*

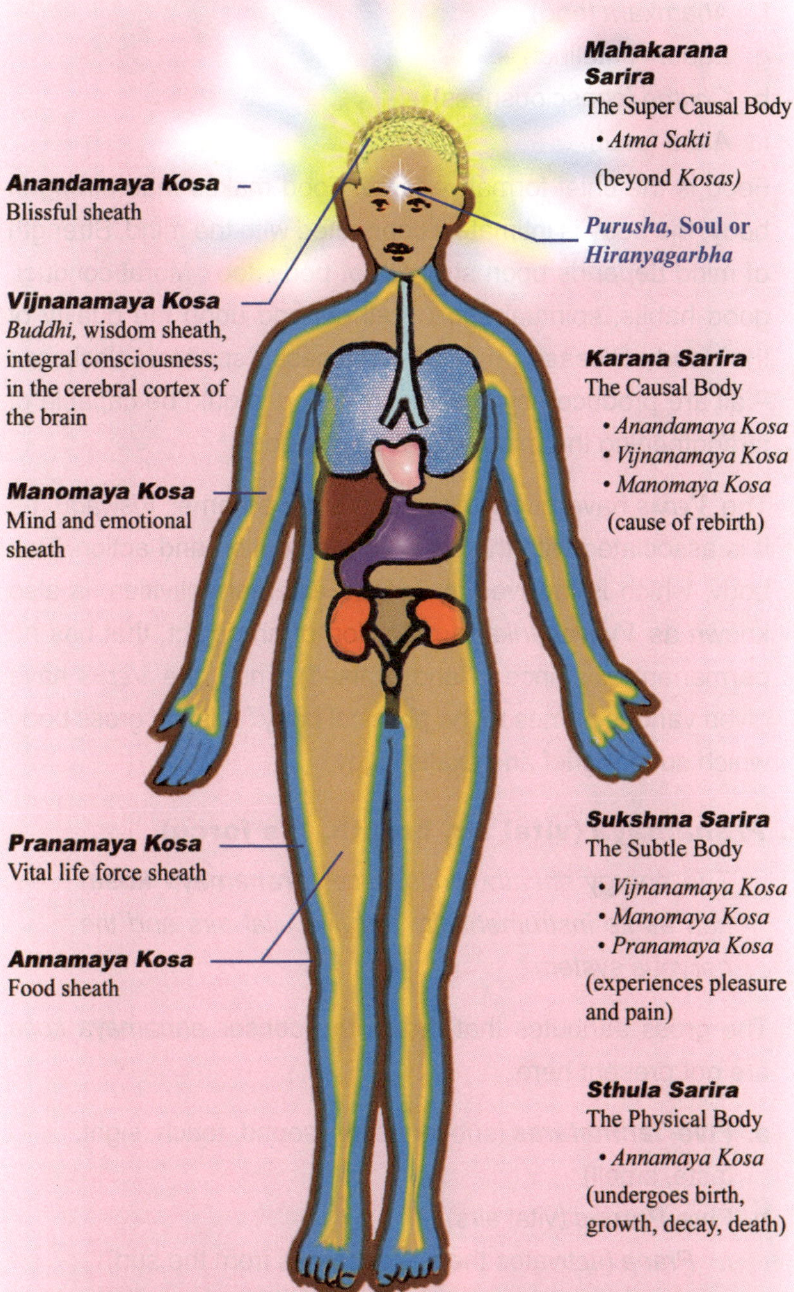

Human Values And Health ~ Diagram No. 13

Source: Divine Discourses of *Bhagawan* Sri Sathya Sai Baba

e. *Manas* (mind) +
f. *Ahamkara* (ego) +
g. *Buddhi* (intellect) +
h. *Chittha* (consciousness) +
i. *Atma* (soul)

Food is the chief formative force. Food makes man strong in body; the body is intimately connected with the mind. Strength of mind depends upon strength of body, too. Moral conduct, good habits, spiritual effort – all depend upon the quality of the food. Disease, mental weakness, spiritual slackness – all are produced by faulty food. Food should be capable of strengthening the mind as well as the body.[6]

The ***VEDAS*** have given this gross body a name, *Viswadu*, as it is associated with the sense of perception and action. This body, which is involved in various external activities, is also known as *Vyavaharika* (a reflection of an object, that has no permanent existence in and of itself). Thus, the ***VEDAS*** have given various names to the physical body.[7] It is the gross body which suffers grief and exalts in joy.[8]

2. *Pranamaya* (vital air, breath, life force)

*The energy sheath or life force (**pranamaya kosa**) has as its instrumentality the five vital airs and the nervous system.*[9]

The gross attributes that define the denser *annamaya kosa* are not present here.

a. Five *Tanmataras* (subtlenesses: sound, touch, sight, taste, smell)

b. Five *Pranas* (vital airs)

i. *Prana* (activates the head, comes from the sun)
ii. *Apana* (activates the lower parts of the body, comes from the earth)

iii. *Vyana* (activates the right side of the body, comes from air)
iv. *Udana* (activates the left side of the body, comes from fire)
v. *Samana* (activates the central part of the body, comes from space)

c. **Five *Upa-pranas*** ('sons' of vital airs)
i. *Naga* (belching)
ii. *Kurma* (blinking of the eyelids)
iii. *Gridhra* (sneezing)
iv. *Devadatta* (yawning)
v. *Dhananjaya* (causes body to grow fat)[10]

The life force (*pranamaya*) is subtle and separate and different from the physical body. It is activated by air (*vayu*) and is saturated with it. It pervades and includes the entire physical body (*annamaya*). You can say that the *pranamaya* is the soul power of the *annamaya* for it makes it function from head to foot. The physical body cannot survive without the life force (*prana*). It is the motive force. By contemplating that the life force (*pranamaya*) is the soul (*Atma*) of the physical body (*annamaya*), the notion that the physical body is the Self will disappear. You rise from gross to the subtle. The *prana* is like the molten metal in the crucible. By effort, *pranamaya* can be experienced. *Prana* appears in the form of breath.[11]

3. *Manomaya* (mental, emotional, volitional)

The mind is called a ***karana****, an instrument. The senses are instruments used to contact nature and gather information about objects. The mind is the overall instrument which controls and directs the senses. The mind is very unsteady. The mind is stirred by the objects of the outer world and the impression they make on the* *inner senses. The mind is either disgusted or drawn towards the objects. This disturbs equanimity.*[12]

Manomaya Kosa is made up of:

a. Manas (mind) +
b. Buddhi (intellect) +
c. Chittha (consciousness) +
d. Ahamkara (ego) +
e. Atma (Soul)

Sri Sathya Sai Baba says:

The mind is called ***Abhayendriyas*** (place where there are no senses) and there are neither *Jnanendriyas* (the sensory organs) nor *Karmendriyas* (the working organs). The mind is nothing but a bundle of thoughts. Good thoughts positively charge the nervous system, while bad thoughts discharge its vitality. Primarily, all health of the body is contingent upon one's thoughts and actions.[13]

Thoughts, which come and go like passing clouds, have no effect on the human brain. However, thoughts which repeatedly get stirred up and stay, form definite grooves in the brain, producing various types of neuropeptides that lead to different types of behaviour, resulting in good and bad actions (*karmas*).

Thoughts are the things with airy wings – they go faster than a dove – they bring you back whatever is held in your *Hridayam*: hate or love.

Desires too, create good and bad thought forms. That is why we must pay careful attention when we entertain negative thoughts, as they can have disastrous consequences.

Sri Sathya Sai Baba continues:

A person who has a strong will is able to send forth positive thoughts that hit the mark like a bullet. An evil thought sent to an innocent or just person, boomerangs in an intensified force, striking the person who had projected it. The best way is to **love all and serve all with love** – then health will be attained. Man should purify his thoughts first, words next, and deeds last. These three are called the ***Trikarna Shuddi*** and are known as the triple purity.[14]

The Self manifests as intellect in this body which when organised by spiritual practices, becomes etherically well defined. However, it does not become an exact replica of the physical body, as does the astral body. It becomes egg-shaped and can assume any form and extend to any size, even to a size that would cover the whole universe. It is not visible to astral sight, but is seen by those whose mental sight has been opened and the physical consciousness appears as a dream. When the mental sight is opened, the astral consciousness appears as the manifested world multiplied a hundred-fold. Thus, there is great expansion in consciousness.[15]

Sri Sathya Sai Baba says:

The Mental Body becomes conscious of everything without any of the organs of the five senses. No words are spoken on this plane, but thoughts are conveyed with pictures or thought forms by means of vibrations. The mental body can only be developed by the exercise of mind through *Sathyam* (truth), *Shraddha* (faith in God), *Ritam* (following cosmic laws or rhythms), and *Maha Tathwa* (accepting that you are God). **[See Diagram No. 14]** This replaces the coarser particles with finer and finer vibrations until it becomes a perfect vehicle for the working of consciousness. Mental consciousness can only be acquired when He Himself (GOD) shows the path to the spiritual student, who learns through mystic practices to work in the mental body with as much ease as in the physical body. It is much easier to work in the astral body by going out of the mental body first, rather than by directly coming out of the physical body into the astral body. In the latter case, one is likely to be deceived, confused and even terrified. Nevertheless, regarding consciousness with its vehicle of the mental body, one can be in heaven perfectly liberated though not free from the cycle of birth and death.[16]

4. *Vijnanamaya* (integral consciousness; rational, discriminatory, intellectual)

> *Human life is extremely precious. Of the five sheaths, man has in large measure the* ***Vijnanamaya Kosa*** *(integral awareness). This awareness is not present in other beings. For this reason man is regarded as supreme among all living beings. He has qualities and capacities not present in other creatures. Man alone has the capacity to recognise the past, the present and the future and to take note of changes occurring over time.* [17]

The Soul *(Atma)* in the body is located at the level of mid-brow of the brain and is surrounded by *Buddhi* or *Vijnanamaya Kosa*. *Buddhi* (the intellectual body) is also known as the higher mental body and it acquires light from the soul. A man who has achieved this level becomes a sage. He does everything for the benefit of humanity and attains liberation after death.[18]

The *Buddhi* has some other names. One of them is *Antaryami* (the Indweller). Man is guided by the voice of this Indweller in the conduct of his life. When problems arise, man waits for

Buddhi Bird

Human Values And Health ~ Diagram No. 14
Source: Author

the directives of the Inner Voice. If this Inner Voice does not give him satisfactory answers he will be in a quandary. When he gets satisfactory guidance from the Inner Voice, he will be able to come to terms with the external world. The Inner Voice is the voice of the conscience. Another name attributed is *Vijnana* (confirmed knowledge). It helps to decide the truth relating to external objects.

Occasionally, *Ahamkara* (the Ego) tends to envelop the *Buddhi*. The Ego is extremely subtle. It enters into all one's actions. It is the identification with the body that promotes the sense of *Ahamkara* (literally meaning, "I-am-the-doer"). This is why man is unable to transcend the ego and comprehend the *Atma*. Hence, efforts must be made to throw off the cover imposed by the ego on the *Buddhi*. If the *Buddhi* is kept totally pure and untainted it will be possible to transmit to the body the full power of the *Atma*. Hence, man has to strive to keep the *Buddhi* pure and holy.

The *Buddhi* is not to be regarded as an ordinary aspect of the mind. It could be described as an image of the *Atma*, a reaction and an echo of the *Atma*. Only after understanding the true nature of the *Buddhi* will the students be able to know whether they are guided by intelligence or mental delusions. [19]

5. *Anandamaya* (blissful, equanimous)

The fifth and innermost sheath is the ecstatic, the blissful ***Anandamaya****, the causal body. The* ***Ananda*** *(bliss) we get when hunger is appeased by a meal is short lived.* ***Brahmananda*** *(the bliss of God), however, is different, for it is native to man, his very source and sustenance. The purpose of human striving, through stage after stage of spiritual progress is to attain that Supreme Bliss (****Ananda****) that is immanent in every thing in creation. For* ***Ananda*** *is* ***Brahman****, the Universal Absolute. Everything is* ***Sat*** *(being),* ***Chit*** *(awareness) and* ***Ananda*** *(bliss), that is to say, Divine.*[20]

Bliss is one's rightful nature; it does not come and go. Bliss is not something that comes to one; it is one's real nature, and it is permanent. When senses are transcended, above the senses there is the state of Bliss as the universal body or God which is light. That state, when fully realised as natural, always remains. Then the world is bliss, always bliss. Think God, eat God, drink God, breathe God, live God.[21]

From The Unreal To The Real

By constant contemplation of the sheaths or *kosas*, the *sadhaka* (spiritual aspirant) attains discrimination to recede from the outer to the inner –the more real. Thus, step by step, he abandons one *kosa* after another and he is able to dissolve away all of them to achieve the knowledge of his unity with *Brahman* (God).[22]

The Three *Sariras* (Bodies)

These interpenetrating sheaths overlap and work in harmony, making up the three subtle bodies of the human instrument, called ***Sariras***. The literal meaning of *Sarira* is "that which wears out or wastes away". If we inquire deeply into this we can see that these bodies are only instruments, bound to change and meant to be used until we discover who we truly are, the *Atma*.

As Sathya Sai Baba tells us, "You are not limited by these containers, one within the other, one finer than the other … even the bliss sheath is a limitation, a phase, a characteristic. The 'I' has no such bounds or bondage. The *Guru* who can make you recognise this 'I' is your own mind. If you turn it towards intelligence and *Ananda*, you are on the right path; if you turn it towards the vital and material, you slide down the path of perdition." [23]

Chart No. 15 ~ The Three *Sariras* (Bodies)

***Sarira* (Body)**		***Kosas***
STHULA SARIRA	Gross Body	*Annamaya*
SUKSHMA SARIRA	Subtle Body	*Pranaymaya, Manoyama, Vijnanamaya*
KARANA SARIRA	Causal Body (Seed Body)	*Manoyama, Vijnanamaya, Anandamaya*
MAHAKARANA SARIRA	Super Causal Body	Beyond all the *kosas*, the supreme consciousness, the cosmic thought
SOURCE: 4, 6		

1. *Sthula Sarira*

The physical body is sustained by food and hence is called the Sthula Sarira (the Gross Body).

2. *Sukshma Sarira*

Next comes the *Sukshma Sarira* (the Subtle Body) which is comprised of three sheaths:

a. *Pranamaya Kosa* (Life Force)
b. *Manomaya Kosa* (Mind)
c. *Vijnanamaya Kosa* (Integral Consciousness)

The subtle body is the basis for the pleasures and pains experienced by man and all his experiences are based on it. It is constituted of seventeen elements: five *Jnanendriyas* (sense organs), five *Tanmataras* (subtlenesses), five *Pranas* (vital airs), the *Manas* (mind) and the *Buddhi* (intellect). It is also known as the Dream State and is called *Taijasa* (The Effulgent One).[24]

The Etheric Body

As *prana* is the life force that flows along the nerves, the Etheric Body is the vehicle of *prana* for the working of the ego on the physical plane. The subtle etheric body interpenetrates the physical body and projects around it for a distance of approximately three inches. It is composed of four grades of ether and is rarer than the ether above the atmosphere in the physical plane through which radio waves are reflected back. It is so subtle that it is almost like a vacuum around the body. As mentioned, *prana* is the life force and in addition is an electric action. Therefore, the current is proof of the existence of ether, which is present everywhere on the physical plane. Electrocardiograms of heart functions and electroencephalograms of brain waves substantiate that muscle reflexes are electrical in nature.

Death is the result of separation of the etheric body (*pranic* body) from the physical body. In some abnormal cases, a partial division of the two bodies can occur while living. This division produces a great strain on the nervous system leading to many physiological and psychological diseases, thereby making the life process less than peaceful. The etheric body is also called the etheric double, as it is an exact copy of the physical body. Apparitions can occur when the etheric body and its counterpart the physical body are separated by death. It is said that the etheric body, after separation, hovers around the physical body like a cloud for 36 hours, because it is troubled by the separation, as the two have been lifelong companions. Reference to old Hindu wisdom reveals that the chief reason people choose cremation as the mode to dispose of the dead body is to afford release to the mind still working within the etheric body.[25]

This subtle body is a part of the physical body as well as the *pranic* body. It gives life to the physical body through the cosmic *nadis* (subtle channel or stream). There are 72,000 cosmic *nadis* in the physical body, of which three are very important. They are the ***Sushumna nadi, Ida nadi, and Pingala nadi***. These *nadis* distribute *prana* to the whole body. *Prana* flows along the nerves and the cosmic *nadi* and provides the *prana sakti* (vital force) to the three bodies. [26] These are discussed in more detail below in the section on "*Chakras*".

Sri Sathya Sai Baba says:

Almost every human being has the awareness of only his physical body. When God's grace comes to him and he is well advanced on the spiritual path, he becomes aware of all his subtle bodies (*Sukshma Sarira*). Out of *crores* (tens of millions) of devotees perhaps only one can perceive his real self and out of those there is one who can perceive the subtle bodies. Consequently, that one is then liberated because he is taught by the mystic practice, the art of coming out from the imprisonment of the physical body and enjoying the consciousness in his other bodies. While living on Earth, he comes back into the physical body by willing it. [This entire book is geared to give readers a greater understanding of the *Sukshma Sarira* (subtle body).]

3. *Karana Sarira*

This is also called the Causal Body and is made up of three sheaths:

a. *Manomaya Kosa* (Mind)
b. *Vijayanmaya Kosa* (Integral Consciousness)
c. *Anandamaya Kosa* (Bliss)

Anandamaya Kosa is the last fine veiling between the *Atma, (Sat-Chit-Ananda, Hirayanagarbha, Purusha, Sai Tathwa)* or spark from *Paramatma* (God-himself). This is situated behind the mid-brow at the level of limbic system, which is the seat of the Divine Light, the *Atma*. Baba says of the *Atma*, "It is a single-seated sofa and only God can sit in it."

Sri Sathya Sai Baba continues:

When *Hridayam*, the spiritual heart, is free from hatred, jealousy, envy, anger, lust, greed and ego, the divine light is visible. Purity of *Hridayam* is very necessary in order to enjoy the bliss of *Atma*. The soul is still imprisoned in five *kosas*, but when the *Guru's* grace is showered upon the individual he is liberated. ***Mohakshaya***, liberation, occurs when the individual soul merges with the universal soul and enjoys permanent bliss. Here is *chittha* or consciousness, which is in association with *Janntha* (the Knower). The knowing principle is called *Prajna* (deep sleep) or *Turiya.*

Transcending all these is the Pure Divine Self – the Supreme *Purusha*. This is the source of all power. It is the embodiment of the Infinite Will. This is the power that protects the Cosmos. The ancient sages strove to explore the nature of the *Anandamaya Kosa*. They sought to discover how they could experience Bliss.[27]

The following are the steps to use in approaching the blissful state:

- Receive pure food from all the sensory organs.
- Purity of the place where you live.
- Regular study of religious books.
- Company of good people.
- Regular prayers.
- Regular practice of human values.
- Regular *yoga* exercise of *Pranayama*, *Asana, Yama* and *Niyama*.
- Regular *Namasmarana* with love, *Kirtan, Nagarsankirtan.*
- Devotional *Bhakti* called *Bhava Bhakti*
- Regular Meditation.
- Selfless service to society.
- Regular purification of thoughts, words and deeds.
- Faith in self and God.
- Adopt a self-realised *Guru* – without a proper *Guru*, you cannot follow the divine path.
- Speak sweetly and softly.

The Astral Body

This is also called the Emotional body, Mental body, or *Manomaya Kosa.* The astral body is a body of light that surrounds and interpenetrates the *Sthula Sarira* and *Sukshma Sarira*. It projects about three to nine inches beyond the physical body and three inches beyond the etheric body. These bodies together have been called the Bioplasmic Body. **[See Diagram No. 1, Page 43]**

The astral body of an ordinary man is loose and not well formed. The colours are dull and there is little play of colours; the body is cloudy. His activity is accelerated from outside and not from within. The traumas of the physical world are meant to stimulate the astral activity. The materials comprising the astral body may change for good or evil. When a man begins to be moved by his intellect other than by desire, it shows a significant advancement towards astral consciousness.

Normally, man in his physical body can perceive only physical objects on the physical plane and is unaware of his astral body and the astral plane. However, those who are on the spiritual path begin to perceive their astral body by means of their *Guru*'s grace. The astral body is then developed perfectly by the working of the divine force from within the man and forms a replica of the physical body. With appropriate training, an aspirant can be shown how to slip out of his physical body and into the astral body. This then becomes his instrument of consciousness, allowing him to function on the astral plane. In this manner, he is liberated from the imprisonment of the physical body. He then transcends space and time and instantly can go anywhere in this universe.

The astral body moves faster than thoughts. In a spiritually under-developed man, the astral body remains near the physical body during sleep, while in a spiritually developed person it can go anywhere and do some useful work on the astral plane. However, the man to whom it belongs may be unaware of its whereabouts, until the links between the physical and the astral bodies are fully developed and strengthened by mystic practice. This practice connects the *chakras* or energy centres of the two bodies. When accomplished, one is continuously awake, as he is constantly conscious. Since the physical brain is connected with the astral body, he can actually will to see and reach any place at any time. This is the attribute of **Omnipresence**. When further developed, one can even materialise in any place or multiple places. The ***Avatars*** like Lord Krishna, Guru Nanak, Jesus Christ, Mohammed Sahib, Buddha, Zoroaster, Shirdi Sai Baba and other elevated human beings had this ability. Sri Sathya Sai Baba, who is Pure Consciousness, embodies all these abilities.

When the astral sight is opened, one becomes a clairvoyant and can see from all parts of the body, front, back and top, as the physical eyes are not involved. This sight is called *Shive Netri* or the Third Eye. When one is dreaming and then awakens, one realises that what was believed as real, was only a dream. Similarly, when the astral sight is opened, the physical life of man appears to him as if it were a dream.

The astral world is several times vaster than the physical world because there are no physical bodies, but rather layers of different types of vibrations. When a person is highly advanced spiritually, fully conscious on the astral plane and free from the entrapment of the physical body, he becomes an **Adept** or master and is then able to relieve those who are in need of spiritual support. An Adept knows how to work in the astral body and is able to see anything inside or outside himself since his vision can penetrate through any solid matter. He can read a closed book or the thoughts of another and is both able to perceive and produce all etheric vibrations. He controls super-physical forces and can set up etheric currents and pressure. By producing sympathetic vibrations on the astral plane, there is no limit to a man's achievements. Ultimately, the forces of gravity can be overcome or even reversed, and then one even can fly in the air or walk over water by setting up electromagnetic forces with his will.[28]

Ethics Of Enlightenment

These types of trans-physical powers are what is called in Sanskrit, ***siddhis,*** benefits won through intense ascetic practice. As with all *siddhis,* individuals must question why they want to obtain this power and under what authority they will use it. *Siddhic* powers, such as clairvoyant vision or the ability to travel in the astral world, come only from the Divine. As such, they must be used only for the promotion of Human Values – that is, with full ethics and *dharma*, to offer love, healing or comfort to someone in need – never for personal gain or adventure. When the powers of the ***Siddhas*** (great beings) are used in an egocentric way, they can only inhibit an individual's spiritual growth in the long term and even do great harm to others. Sathya Sai Baba does not support the pursuit of such powers. Rather He advises His devotees to follow the path of Human Values in daily life, with the end of loving all, serving all and seeing all as ONE. Once this Oneness is realised, all types of *siddhic* powers become superfluous.

However, for some individuals who are actively involved in exploring their inner vehicles and the higher vibrational realms of consciousness, mystic experiences, clairvoyant vision and *siddhic* powers may be an unsought after bi-product of *sadhana.* It is for this reason that the practice of Human Values on a daily basis is so important, particularly for spiritual aspirants.

Human values – seeing good, doing good, being good – help one store good memories in the cortex, so that only the good impulses can come back from the higher centres, birth after birth.

Thought impulses and ideas called **intuitions** can come from the **Infinite Mind (GOD)** to the cerebrum. When various emotions such as anger, hatred, jealousy, envy, fear, love, compassion, devotion, gentleness or tolerance arise, they produce different colors of the aura, the *pranic* body, the astral body and the mental body of a person. As one practises human values more and more in daily life, the person's health improves at all levels. The effects of good and bad thoughts can be seen upon the face of a person, making him either beautiful or ugly. Bad thoughts attract negative *pranic* or astral bodies from the astral world and make the body sick. Some psychological diseases could also result, such as bi-polar functioning, suicidal and homicidal tendencies, as well as schizophrenic ideation. Conversely, good thoughts attract positive *pranic* bodies from the astral world, helping the body to do good work and move it towards total health. Therefore, the adoption of Human Values in daily life is important in order to be healthy and useful to society.

The Seven *Chakras* And Nerve Plexus

Three ethers of varying densities form the etheric body. These make up the vital body, or *pranamaya kosa.* They interpenetrate and act as a life giver to the gross physical body. The life process depends on the seven energy centres in the gross physical body called **nerve plexus.** These correspond to energy centres in the etheric body called ***chakras*** (literally meaning "wheels"). The *chakras* in the etheric body are the true absorbers of energy from the sun and the atmosphere, and supply the life force to the nerve plexus in the physical body in the way that background music provides the mood for a film. Automatically, the etheric body and ultimately the physical body are refined by the seven *chakras*.

The ***kundalini sakti*** sleeps at the base of the spinal column in the sacral region. The main ***chakras*** or seven energy centres run parallel to the spinal column and connected by a vast system of *nadis*, channels that conduct energy throughout the *pranamaya kosa*. **[See Diagram No. 16]**

The main *nadis* are:

- ***Sushumna:*** Large central *nadi*, situated in the spine. The *ida* and *pingala* intertwine it.
- ***Ida:*** Starts from the left nostril, then moves to the crown of the head and then down to the base of the spine. As lunar energy flows through it, this is also called *Chandra-nadi.* Its colour is white.
- ***Pingala:*** Starts from the right nostril, then moves to the crown of the head and then down to the base of the spine. As solar energy flows through it is also called *Surya-nadi.* Its colour is red.

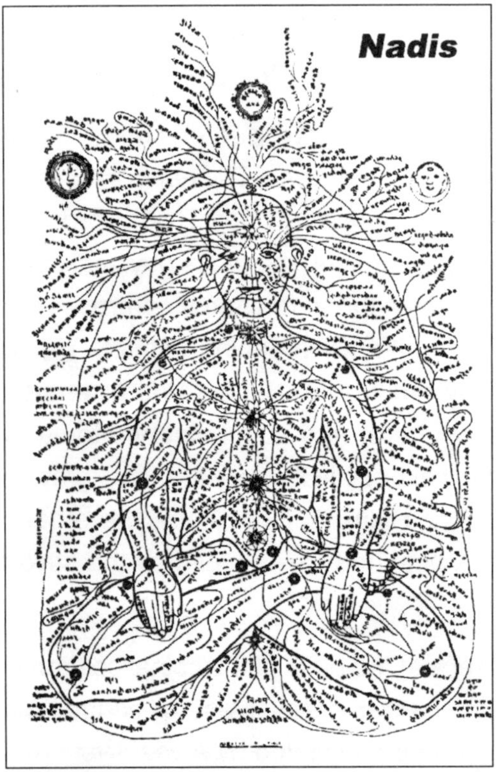

All *yogic* exercises charge and balance the *prana sakti* in the *chakras* and bring health to the body. *Pranic* healers claim to heal patients by touching the *chakras* in addition to healing from a distance. Acupuncture and acupressure too, charge and balance cosmic energy through cosmic points on the skin. They, however, do not work with the seven main *chakras*, but through the extended system of *nadis* that run throughout the body, called "meridians" in Traditional Chinese Medicine.

The *Chakras*

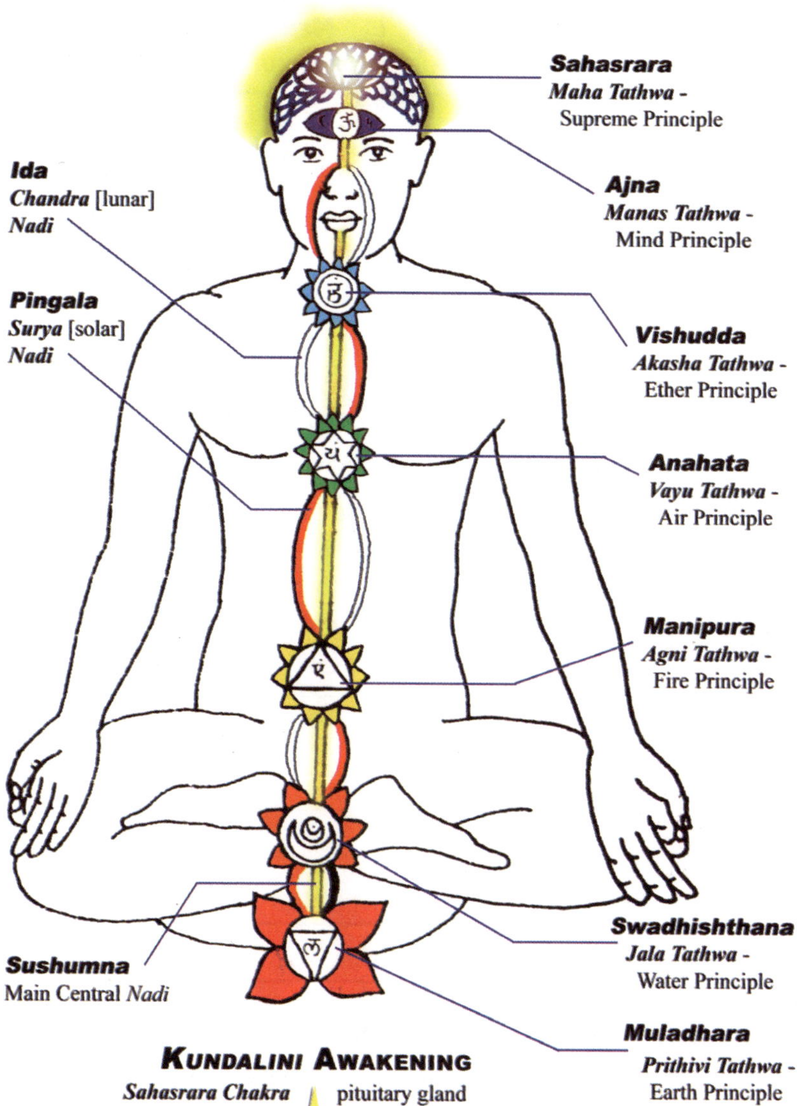

Kundalini Awakening

Sahasrara Chakra	pituitary gland
Ajna Chakra	pineal body
Vishudda Chakra	thyroid, parathyroid glands
Anahata Chakra	thymus gland
Manipura Chakra	pancreas gland
Svadhishthana Chakra	suprarenal gland
Muladhara Chakra	sex glands

Human Values And Health ~ Diagram No. 16

Chart No. 17 ~ The *Chakras*

Chakra	Location	Nerve Plexus	Endocrine Organ
MULADHARA	Base of the spine	Coccygeal plexus	Sex glands (ovaries & testes)
SWADHISTHANA	Pelvis	Pelvic plexus	Adrenals & suprarenal glands
MANIPURA	Navel	Solar plexus	Pancreas
ANAHATA	Heart	Cardiac plexus	Thymus
VISHUDDA	Throat	Cervical plexus	Thyroid and parathyroid
AJNA	Third eye (between the brows)		Pineal
SAHASRARA	Crown of the head		Pituitary
SOURCE: Author			

The First *Chakra: Muladhara*

This is the root *chakra* and is situated at the base of the spine in the area of the coccyx. It energises the sex organs in the physical body. In addition, it brings general vitality by balancing the quality of blood and other fluids in the body. It energises the musculature, the hormonal system, the skeletal system, and brings beauty to the whole body. *Yogis* meditate on this *chakra* to awaken the sleeping power of the ***Kundalini***, which can create a long and healthy life and awaken them to self-realisation. Meditating on this *chakra* can cure sterility, infertility, and some of the blood-related diseases. When heat and cold are felt intensely, concentrate on this *chakra* while taking a deep breath. They both can be regulated with this technique. During pregnancy, the growth of the embryo and its proper birth are also controlled by this *chakra*. Emotionally, imbalances in this *chakra*, usually correspond to issues relating to family, physical health, money, housing and survival. It corresponds to the element of earth and the colour, red.

The Second *Chakra: Swadhishthana*

This *chakra* is located at the sacral plexus and energises the adrenal glands and sex glands. All the pelvic organs get the *prana sakti* from this *chakra* and the lower limbs are kept alive by this *chakra*. The *kundalini sakti* is usually asleep here. When it is awakened by intense meditation and regular practice of Human Values it charges all the other six *chakras*. Heat is generated because of concentrated *prana sakti* following the *kundalini's* trip up the *shusumna* to meet the *Ajna chakra*. This is possible only when any of the *yoga* paths are regularly practised. The pelvic organs: bladder, rectum and sex organs are energised by this *chakra*. Life issues corresponding to *Swadhisthana* would be sexuality, emotional wellbeing, children, self-worth, response to change. It corresponds to the element of water and the colour, orange.

The Third *Chakra: Manipura*

This *chakra* is located at the back of the navel and is called *nabhi* (navel) *chakra* by *Vedanta*. This *chakra* serves as a pumping station and sends *prana sakti* to almost all the organs of the body, but the abdominal organs like kidneys, adrenal glands, small intestine, large intestine, pancreas, liver and stomach get more *pranic* energy than the rest from this *chakra*. By regulating the digestive and excretory systems, this *chakra* increases the vitality of the body. Life issues here relate to worldly work, metabolism, interaction with society and community, authority figures, self-confidence and will. The element governing this *chakra* is fire and its colour is yellow.

The Fourth *Chakra: Anahata*

This *chakra*, the cardiac plexus or heart *chakra*, is named the *anahata chakra* because the ***Aum*** or *anahata* sound is heard in meditation. It is very sensitive to thoughts and emotions; and if you have violent emotional impulses, the heart and lungs will be affected, which will lead to disease. If you experience serene emotional impulses, the heart and lungs also will be affected by a healthy calmness. The fourth *chakra*, at the level of the thymus gland, is the meeting place of the centrifugal and centripetal *prana* (cosmic energy). Here they are revitalised, boosting the immune system, providing health and vitality for both the physical and *pranic* bodies.

Most people are under the impression that emotions are experienced at heart level; hence the term "heartfelt" and the value cultures have continually placed on the heart as the seat of love. Physiologically, emotional changes are brought first to the heart before being felt throughout the rest of the body. But, it is just the physical heart that is in the chest, whereas, the spiritual heart (*Hridayam*) is in the brain at the level of limbic system. Emotions and thoughts start as a reaction to signals received through the senses which must go to the brain for cognition and processing. This information is then routed by the limbic system, which uses the nervous and endocrine systems as well as the *nadi* channels to send sensations to the plexus and *chakras* throughout the gross and subtle bodies. We feel emotion throughout our body. The heart, being the most significant organ of the body, responds more definitively and immediately to emotional sensation. The heart beats faster in order to supply more blood to the emotionally upset organs of the body.

Life issues in *anahata* relate to love and marriage as well as higher vibrations of love, such as compassion, generosity, empathy and social consciousness as well as self-love and the ability to receive life. The element of this *chakra* is air and the colour is green.

The Fifth *Chakra: Vishuddha*

This *chakra*, the cervical plexus, is in the area of the thyroid gland and is opened in those who are singers and orators. That is why they have sweet and melodious voices. Those who speak sweetly and softly are spiritually highly developed souls; they are helped in their development by this *chakra*. When you sing devotional songs with *Bhakti*, it opens all the *chakras* of the physical body and light is visible at the level of the mid-brow. A sage will emanate brilliant ***auras*** from the Physical, Vital and Astral bodies. *Udana Vayu,* the vital air found in this *chakra*, is white in colour, and helps in mastication, and swallowing of food materials. This *chakra* energises the thyroid gland, parathyroid gland, and the lymph system of the body, keeping it healthy and young. Life issues in this *chakra* relate to vibration, communication with the inner realms as well as with other people, personal expression, creativity and receptivity to the ideas of others. The element relating to this *chakra* is sound, and *Bhutakasa*, the lowest vibration of ether. The colour is sky blue.

The Sixth *Chakra: Ajna*

This *chakra* is situated at mid-brow. When meditating on this *chakra*, *yogis* see effulgent light and their *Ishtadeva* (chosen form of God), or realised *Guru*. Without the help of God or a realised *Guru*, it is not possible to see the effulgent light of the *Atma* (soul). The *Atma, Hirayanagarbha, Purusha* or *Sai Tathwa* are different names given to the Soul that resides within the human brain and *Hridayam* and has a golden white light. **The sole purpose of human birth is to attain self-realisation.** The sixth *chakra* energises the pineal gland as well as the pituitary gland, which is the master endocrine gland that controls all the other endocrine glands of the body. *Pranic* healers charge this *chakra* and free the body from all types of disease. The sixth *chakra*, in turn, charges all the other *chakras* of the body. Life issues in this *chakra* correspond to the thinking process, intuition, imagination, ability to vision and plan and connect with the deeper levels of the self. The element corresponding to *Ajna* is *Chitthakasa* or light. The colour is indigo or violet.

The Seventh *Chakra: Sahasrara*

The crown *chakra* is situated at the top of the head in the brain. In meditation, *yogis* can see thousands of shining petals in this *chakra* and that is why it is named the *Sahasrara Chakra*. It illumines the entire brain and energises the pituitary gland as well as all the body organs, providing complete physical, mental, and emotional health to the body. If the nervous system is not purified by dedicated practice of Human Values, the illumination of this *chakra* may cause psychological imbalances. The *prana sakti* from Omnipresent God flows like a waterfall from this *chakra* to the whole body. When this *chakra* is open, a brilliant aura glows around the person, reflecting his spiritual communion. Life issues in this centre relate to spirituality, ability to perceive or believe in a cosmic consciousness, and feelings of unity with all life. The element relating to this *chakra* is *Chidakasa*, the highest vibration of ether or thought. The colour is pure white.

It should be noted that while being a doorway to cosmic consciousness as well as a plexus of energy, technically *Sahasrara* is not part of the main system and is not connected to the other six *chakras* through the *sushumana*.[29]

Sri Sathya Sai Baba says:

"These are the wheels in the spiritual body. Whatever qualities are described for the universe, they are present in this body itself."

Bodies Are Many, God Is One

Bodies may be multifarious like light bulbs, but the energy that makes them shine is one. When this truth is realised, you have the awareness of the Cosmic Divine. Though the thoughts of the mind, the actions of the body, and the role of the *Atma* as Witness appear disparate, they are all integrally interrelated. The differences are in form, but the bliss that is experienced is one. Hence the ***Upanishads*** declared the truth of the One in the Many.[30]

---

1 *Bhagawan* Sri Sathya Sai Baba, ***Prasnottara Vahini,*** Ch. 7.
2 *Bhagawan* Sri Sathya Sai Baba, **Discourses on the *Bhagavad Gita,*** Ch 17.
3 *Bhagawan* Sri Sathya Sai Baba, Divine Discourse, 19/10/1970.
4 *Bhagawan* Sri Sathya Sai Baba, Divine Discourse, 20/05/1993.
5 *Bhagawan* Sri Sathya Sai Baba, ***Prasnottara Vahini,*** Ch. 7.
6 *Bhagawan* Sri Sathya Sai Baba, ***Geeta Vahini***, Ch. 26.
7 *Bhagawan* Sri Sathya Sai Baba, source unknown.
8 *Bhagawan* Sri Sathya Sai Baba, ***Prasnottara Vahini,*** Ch. 7.
9 *Bhagawan* Sri Sathya Sai Baba, **Sathya Sai Speaks,** Vol. 7.
10 *Bhagawan* Sri Sathya Sai Baba, ***Prasnottara Vahini,*** Ch. 7.
11 *Bhagawan* Sri Sathya Sai Baba, ***Upanishad Vahini,*** Ch. 11.
12 *Bhagawan* Sri Sathya Sai Baba, **Voice of the *Avatar,*** Ch. 1.
13 *Bhagawan* Sri Sathya Sai Baba, source unknown.
14 *Bhagawan* Sri Sathya Sai Baba, source unknown.
15 Medical Research Group, **Mysteries of Healing,** Theosophical Research Centre, London.
16 *Bhagawan* Sri Sathya Sai Baba, source unknown.
17 *Bhagawan* Sri Sathya Sai Baba, Divine Discourse, 15/04/1995.
18 *Bhagawan* Sri Sathya Sai Baba, source unknown.
19 *Bhagawan* Sri Sathya Sai Baba, **Sathya Sai Speaks,** Vol. 23, Ch 16.
20 *Bhagawan* Sri Sathya Sai Baba, ***Sanathana Sarathi,*** January 1984.
21 *Bhagawan* Sri Sathya Sai Baba, recorded in **Conversations With *Bhagawan* Sri Sathya Sai Baba**, Ch. 18.
22 *Bhagawan* Sri Sathya Sai Baba, **Voice of the *Avatar,*** Ch. 2.
23 *Bhagawan* Sri Sathya Sai Baba, Divine Discourse, 26/10/1972,

24 *Bhagawan* Sri Sathya Sai Baba, source unknown.
25 Medical Research Group, **Mysteries of Healing,** Theosophical Research Centre, London.
26 Gopikrishna, **The Secret of *Kundalini Yoga*.**
27 *Bhagawan* Sri Sathya Sai Baba, Divine Discourse, 20/05/1993.
28 Medical Research Group, **The *Chakra*,** Theosophical Research Centre, London.
29 Medical Research Group, **The *Chakra*,** Theosophical Research Centre, London.
30 *Bhagawan* Sri Sathya Sai Baba, Divine Discourse, 20/05/1993.

Nanak Nam Jahaz Hai
Chadre So Uttare Par
Jo Shradha Kar Savnde
Guru Paran Uttaran Har

(*Namasmarana* [remembrance of the name of God] is a ship, which if you board, will take you across the sea of *samsara*. The *Guru* takes those who recite the name with emotion safely.)

~ **Guru Nanak**

chapter - 8

THE HUMAN BRAIN

Three thousand years ago, more or less, inscribed above the portals of the Temple of Apollo at Delphi were these words, "*Gnothi Seauton*". When translated from the original Greek to modern English, the phrase means, **"Know Thyself"**. That we may know ourselves better than before, let us consider today the human brain, its functions, limitations and capabilities. No one can reveal in fullness and perfection the mysterious and marvellous instrument that is the human brain. So intricate a subject can never be fully understood, except by the Infinite Mind (God), who has planned and created the most amazing organ in the human body. However, we may comprehend in small measure the mechanisms of the brain, and by careful study, come to some degree of understanding of this wonderful organ, and also the disastrous effects brought on by its misuse.

Basic Structure Of The Brain

No one can deny that God the Almighty has taken extraordinary pains in designing and fashioning the head of the human body in order to protect its extremely delicate occupant from harm. The brain is a rare masterpiece of Divine craftsmanship, virtually a sealed book to the doctors. Layer after layer of protective coverings, some tough and some of downy softness, interpose between the rough skull and the body of its delicate tenant. God has beautifully designed these layers to protect the most vital organ of the body from blows, knocks, strokes, heat, cold, radiation, light, fatal injuries and even negative energies. These layers are **[See Diagram No. 18]**:

1. **THE PERIOSTIC** (outside the skull): this includes the hair, scalp and muscles. The scalp is a thick, durable covering, forming the base and groundwork whence springs that luxurious adornment, the human hair. The scalp is thicker than the skin of any other portion of the body. A dense scalp protects the brain from accidental injuries and prevents a rapid influx of ideas from the astral world.

2. **THE BONY CRANIUM** (commonly called the skull): At the skull's base there are many openings for the transmission of nerves, blood vessels, muscles, etc. The skullcap proper is very strong and capable of resisting heavy blows. The various bones of the skull are laced together by what are called the sutures, in such a way as to oppose the fracture of any bone by force acting in a single direction. In many instances, the splintered fragments of a fractured skull will vigorously resist all encroachments from without.

3. **THE SUB-OSSEOUS:** The tough membranes lying beneath the skull and over the cerebral mass provide additional protection and cushioning for the brain.

Apart from this triple line of defense, the cerebrospinal fluid fills every cavity, nook and corner of the brain to act as a shock absorber of incredible potency for protection from the forces of jerking and jolting. The blood supply to the brain is so skillfully handled and ample that its shortage is very unlikely. In fact, **one sixth of the body blood is supplied to the brain**. In addition, there are ingenious devices in the sensory organs, directly

The Anatomy Of The Human Brain

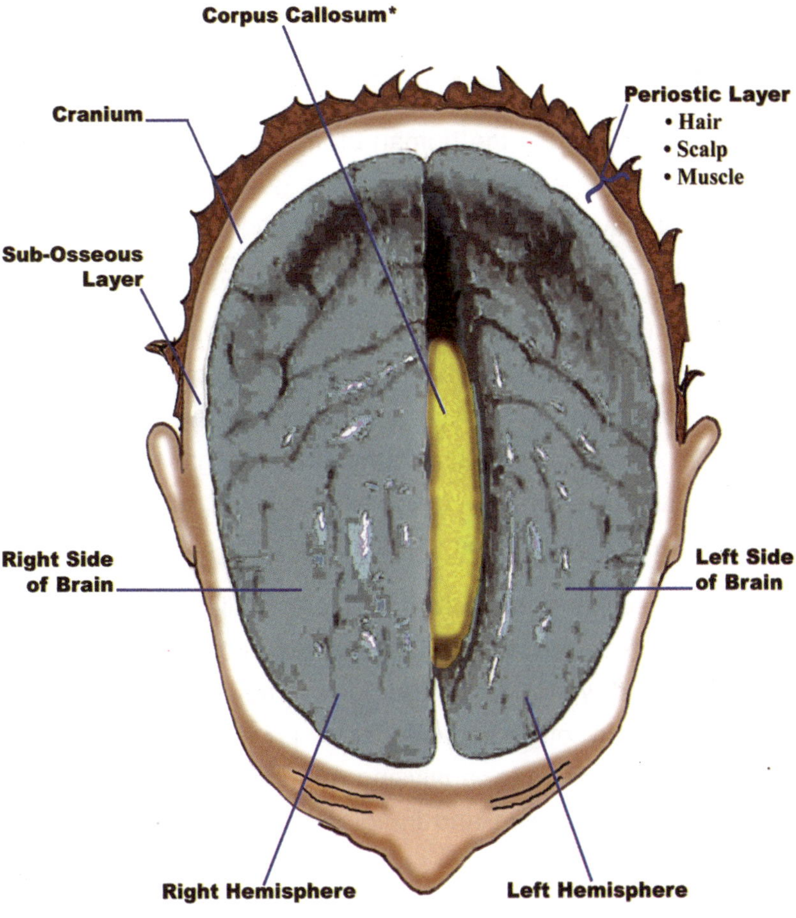

** The Corpus Callosum is the main connecting link between the left and right hemispheres.*

Human Values And Health ~ Diagram No. 18

linked to the brain, which prevent harm or pollution from coming in through them. There is no other organ of the body, including the precious heart and the priceless eyes, so well enclosed and protected against a rough environment and the possibility of injury.[1]

The Uniqueness Of The Human Brain

What distinguishes the human brain from other brains is the relative size of the cerebral cortex, the quarter of an inch thick covering of gray matter on the lobes and two hemispheres of the cerebrum.

The human cerebral cortex is further distinguished by its great quantity of foldings and refoldings (the *gyri*, *sulci* and ridges), all of which increase the surface area of the cortex. This allows a maximum amount of what is commonly called "gray matter" to be packed within the confines of the skull. Only in human beings is the cerebral cortex so large in relation to body size.

Most scientists agree that the unique abilities of the human brain are directly attributable to the cerebral cortex. The powers of speech and written language, for example, reside there and separate us from other animals. These powers go hand in hand with thinking, observing, analysing and integrating experiences to solve problems, plan and imagine what may happen in the future.

The human brain has three sections **[See Diagram No. 19]**:

1. **THE REPTILIAN:** The first is made up largely of structures at the very top of the spinal cord, including portions from which the brain stems. Because it resembles in some ways the total brain of reptiles, this part of our brain is called Reptilian. Like the entire brain of a lizard or snake it is mainly devoted to life support such as the regulation of breathing, heartbeat and

The Sections Of The Human Brain

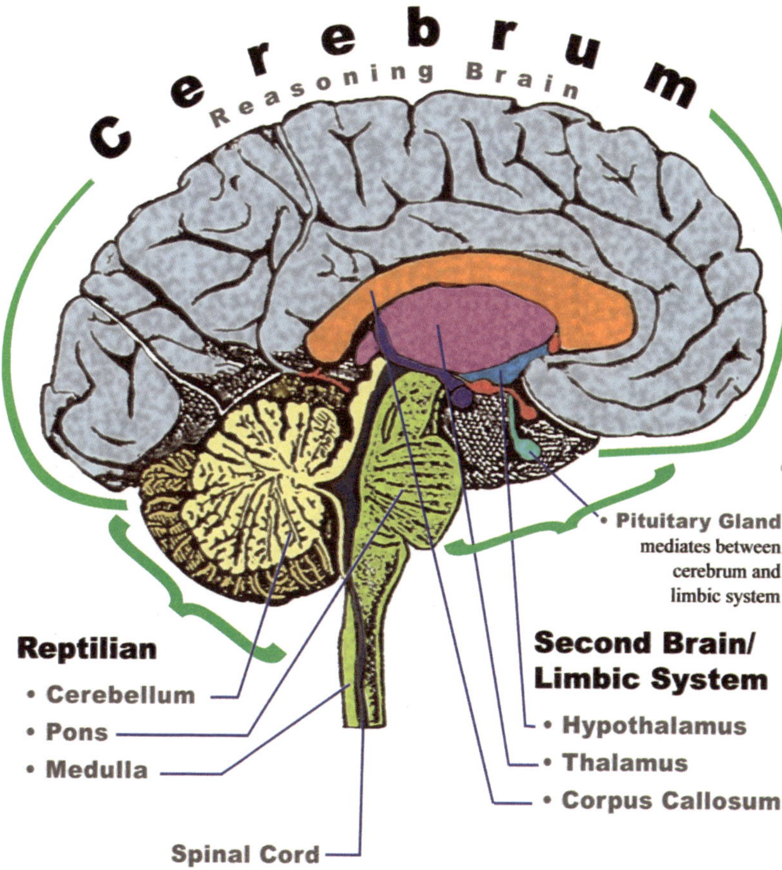

NOTE: Side view along longitudinal fissure.

Human Values And Health ~ Diagram No. 19

muscular movements, and to basic drives such as eating, mating and self-protection.

2. **"SECOND BRAIN" AND LIMBIC SYSTEM (MAMMALIAN BRAIN):** This adds to the dimension of emotional response which is not well-developed in reptiles. The core of the second brain is the Limbic System. This is the collective name for several interconnected structures near the brain's core. The limbic system is a borderland between the "lower" or "animal" parts of the brain and the highest, uniquely human brain areas associated with the cerebral cortex.

3. **THE CEREBRUM OR REASONING BRAIN:** This third section of the brain is composed of the outer bulges of the cerebrum and the overlying cerebral cortex. The surface of the cerebrum, called the cerebral cortex, is covered with gray tissue containing billions of neurons. This is the "gray matter" that has come to be a colloquialism for intelligence, although a person with more gray matter is not necessarily smarter than someone with less. Beneath the gray matter and throughout the nervous system is the tissue called white matter. The whitish colour comes from the myelin sheaths that are attached to the axons of neurons in these areas. In addition to gray and white matter, the brain has a great many other kinds of tissues including the "red matter" of blood and blood vessels.

The Human Brain Is Divided Into Two

Our brain has two hemispheres, the right and the left. They share our thinking and the control of our body. The left half of the brain controls the right side of the body and the right half of the brain controls the left side.

The most commonly accepted theory as to why the brain is divided in the middle tells us that each half can provide a backup if the other is damaged. There are no doubt other reasons only the Divine Designer can elucidate. This duplication is common in other internal organs, such as the lungs and kidneys, and of course in eyes, ears, limbs and so on. When injury to the brain occurs at birth, a healthy hemisphere can often take over wholly or substantially the function of the damaged one.

Although our brains are divided in half, the two halves are not identical. For that matter most persons have faces that are not quite symmetrical, and one foot that is usually a bit larger than the other. The asymmetries in the brain's halves are a clue to the different specialties of each hemisphere.

The **left side** of the brain's specialties are spoken and written language, logic, number skills and scientific concepts. Work that might involve primarily the left brain includes writing, book-keeping, selling and laboratory jobs.

The **right side** of the brain excels in recognising patterns and shapes and how they relate to one another. It is probably instrumental in remembering faces. It is the half of the brain that seems to contribute most to insight and imagination, and that appreciates the arts and understands humour. The work of an architect would draw heavily on the right hemisphere, as that of a musician or gardener would. Although it does not initiate speech, the right hemisphere apparently has a role in creating and perceiving the emotional nuances of speech. Subsequent research has shown the role of the right hemisphere in perceiving spatial relationships and in many kinds of creativity. In fact, so much attention has been given to so-called "right-brain thinking" in recent years, that some people believe that the right hemisphere, not the left, is the dominant one. Probably the middle ground is closest to the truth: both hemispheres working together are important.[2]

The Different Lobes Of The Brain

The **Frontal** lobes are just behind and above the eyes, six percent of which includes the motor cortex at the rear of each lobe, and serve as a control centre for the body movements. The left frontal lobe plays a key role in speech. The prefrontal (nearest the front) part of the lobes seems to have much to do with the interaction of thought, emotions and behaviour. **[See Diagram No. 20]**

The **Temporal** lobes, named for their location at the temples, are involved in hearing and memory. If one temporal lobe is damaged, hearing is not lost, since nerves from both ears go to each temporal lobe. Through links with the limbic system, the temporal lobes seem to affect how we experience fear, anger, lust and jealousy.

The **Parietal** Lobes (from Latin *paries*, "wall") are named after the bones that form the back top half and sides of the skull. These lobes are to the rear of the frontal lobes. The front-most portion of the parietal lobe is the **Somatosensory Cortex**. It is directly across a groove from the motor cortex, the rear-most portion of the frontal lobes. The somatosensory cortex is a receiving area for sensations.

The **Occipital Lobes**, beneath the occipital bone that forms most of the lower back and base of the skull, are the smaller lobes, but no less important than the others. Among other functions, they are centres for vision.

How The Lobes Work Together

About 12 years after the Frenchman, **Paul Broca,** identified a piece of the left frontal lobe as the centre for producing speech, a German neurologist, **Karl Wernicke**, discovered an area on the left temporal lobe not far from Broca's area, that was a centre for understanding speech. The interdependence of lobe functions

The Lobes Of The Human Brain

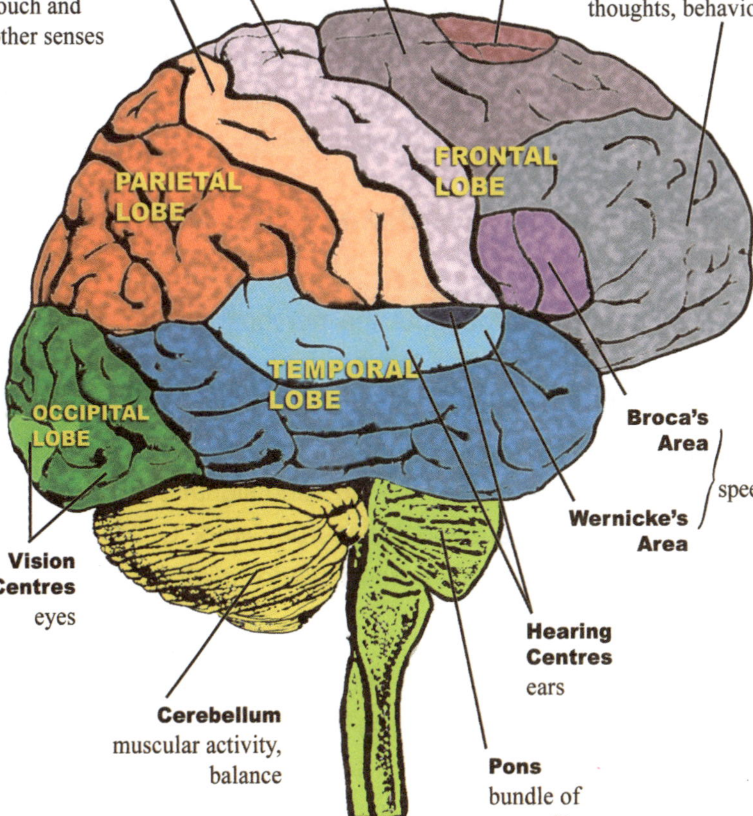

LATERAL VIEW

While the four lobes have specialised functions, they also work interdependently.

is beautifully demonstrated by the shared work of **Broca's** and **Wernicke's areas** in enabling us to repeat aloud a word that we have just heard spoken.

From the ears the sensation of a heard word travels by neurons to the auditory (or hearing) cortex on the temporal lobe. The word is not understood until it passes through Wernicke's area, also on the temporal lobe, where it is processed so that we recognise it in auditory form. Then it goes to Broca's area on the frontal lobe, which sends instructions to the motor cortex, at the rear of the frontal lobe, to drive the muscles of your lips, tongue and larynx to utter the word. What an incredible design is the brain!

The Networks In The Brain Cells And Their Workings

In the brain and throughout the nervous system, there are two main classes of cells: the neurons, or nerve cells **[See Diagram No. 21]**, and all the rest, which are described simply as non-neuronal cells. Roughly speaking, neurons are the brain's excitable cells, the ones that "fire" to send signals, while the rest are non-excitable and support the neurons' work. Collectively, the bulk of support cells is called *neuroglia* (or *glial*) from Latin and Greek words for "nerve glue".

The neurons' main job is communication – sending and receiving information. Each neuron has hundreds to thousands of connections with other cells, and some neurons in the cerebrum may have a great many more links. More than 100 billion neurons in the brain work together in ever-changing relationships, to form an enlightened machine that gives us cognitive functions way beyond any other life form on earth.

In addition to neurons and *neuroglia* cells, the brain has several other kinds of cells that serve brain tissue such as those making

Neurons In The Human Brain

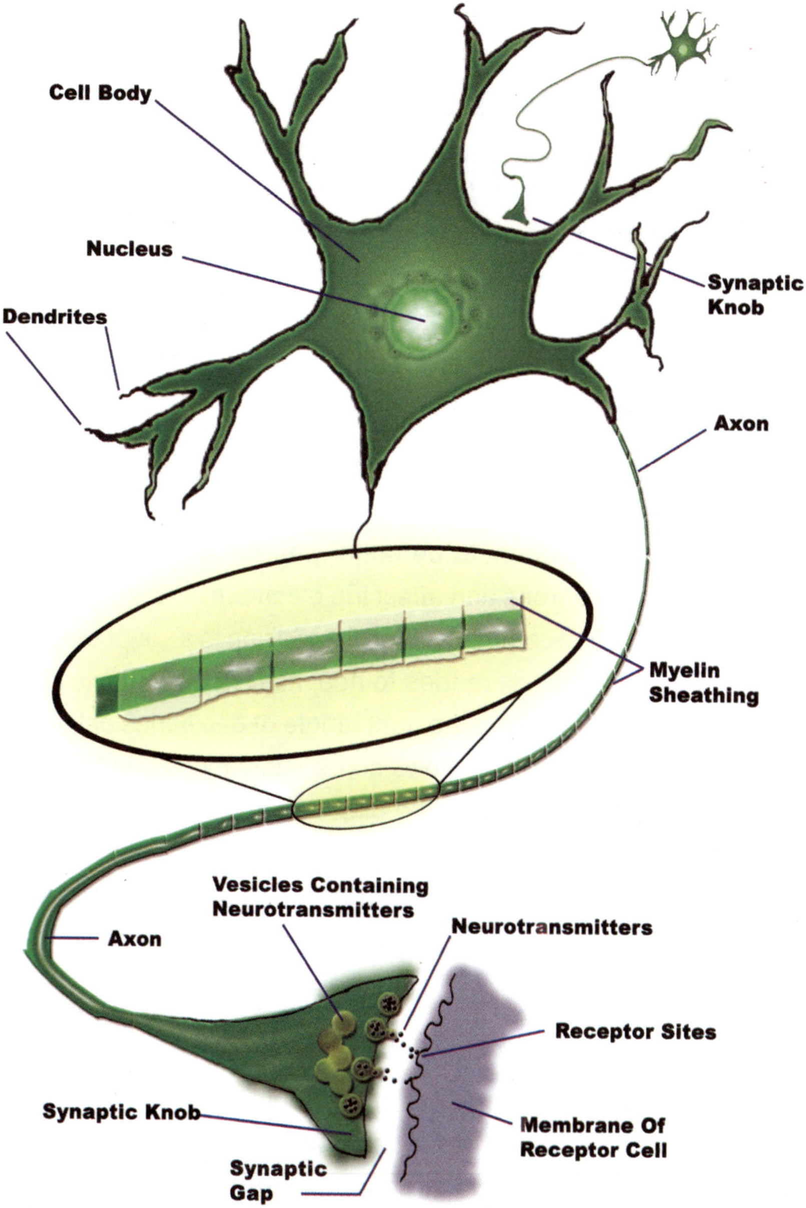

Human Values And Health ~ Diagram No. 21

up the blood vessels: capillaries, arteries and veins. Special cells line the canals and cavities that hold the brain's cerebrospinal fluid, acting as a shock absorbers to protect the brain.

The "Nerve Glue"

The neurons are the key units in the brain's amazing ability to process information and they have received the lion's share of attention from the scientists. However, the neurons are outnumbered, five or ten to one, by the **glial cells** of the surrounding "nerve glue". During the development of the brain before birth, certain glial cells aid neurons in their migration to their ultimate places in the nervous system, acting almost as ladders or scaffolds for the neurons.

Glial cells are in two major forms, the star-shaped **astrocytes** and the **oligodendrocytes**. Recent research suggests that these cells, long thought to be rather passive and inert, interact constantly with neurons and affect the electrochemical processes that underlie neural communication. In addition to a suspected role in how injured brain tissue tries to heal itself, the astrocytes may also play a part in forming the tight tangle of capillaries called the blood-brain barrier, which allows some substances into the brain and keeps others out. As for the oligodendrocytes, they form the myelin sheath that wraps around the main protruding tentacle (called an **axon**) of a neuron covering and seem to facilitate the transmission of signals by the neuron, although not all neurons have it.

How The Nerve Cells Communicate

Everything we do and all we know depends on the transfer of signals from nerve cell to nerve cell. Underlying this extraordinary phenomenon is the unique structure of neurons and their ability to make certain chemical and electrical events happen. A neuron has one big tentacle, its **axon**, and many smaller ones, its

dendrities. The axon is responsible for sending signals which are received by the dendrites of other neurons. For a signal to pass between an axon and a dendrite, these two structures must be very, very close – but not quite touching. The place where they almost touch is called a **synapse**, or **synaptic gap**, and it is no wider than a few billionths of an inch.

A message, traveling as an electrical impulse, moves down an axon toward the synapse. There it stimulates the production of molecules, called **neurotransmitters**, from the end of the axon into the synapse. A neurotransmitter diffuses across the narrow space between the two cells and affects the dendrite of the receiving neuron. This causes a change in the electric charge of the receiving neuron with the resultant transmission of an electrical impulse that may excite or inhibit future impulse transmission.

The scientists have proved that the brain produces more than 100 neurotransmitters. These are sometimes called **neuropeptides**, which is an error. Neuropeptides consist of short chains of amino acids, with some functioning as neurotransmitters and some functioning as hormones. The characteristics of both vary according to the quality of the thought waves that generate them. This is how thought waves move through the *akasa* (element of space), influencing the inner and outer environments of man.

The emotions generated by the limbic system cause distinctive vibrations in the neuropeptides which then cause a complimentary firing action in the neurotransmitters. The practices of meditation, prayer and a life of Human Values, particularly love, produce soft, smooth electrical impulses that soothe the brain, with comforting neurotransmitter activity that promotes healthy brain function. These soothing neuropeptides send health-giving electrical impulses to the brain and then on to the organs of the body. The negative emotions of hate, jealousy, anger, fear, fight or flight, etc. produce stress neuropeptides that release the more aggressive electrical impulses that cause disease.

The Nervous System And Endocrine System

Some of the most complicated body processes of respiration, digestion, circulation, growth, reproduction and repair are more or less involuntary. These functions are under the control of two different systems that work in concert: the nervous system and the endocrine system.

The nervous system (specifically the autonomic nervous system) sends short messages, as brief as a few thousandth's of a second, by electrical impulses, to produce rapid responses. These signals travel through nerve cells as rapidly as 650 feet (200 metres) per second.

The endocrine system sends most messages relatively slowly by means of hormones to produce more long lasting effects. Hormonal messages travel through the bloodstream and may take several hours or days. Certain cells have receptors for one or more hormones. A receptor is like a lock and only the right hormones have the key to a particular kind of cell. When it links with a cell, the hormone then alters such cellular functions as protein production, storage or release of glucose (the carbohydrate fuel used for many body activities) and production of other hormones.

How Does The Endocrine System Work?

The endocrine system is a collection of ductless glands throughout the body that secrete hormones directly into the bloodstream. The word **hormone** means to "set in motion", and these secretions carry signals that stimulate actions in the body. The primary glands include the pituitary, pineal, thyroid, thymus,

The Endocrine System

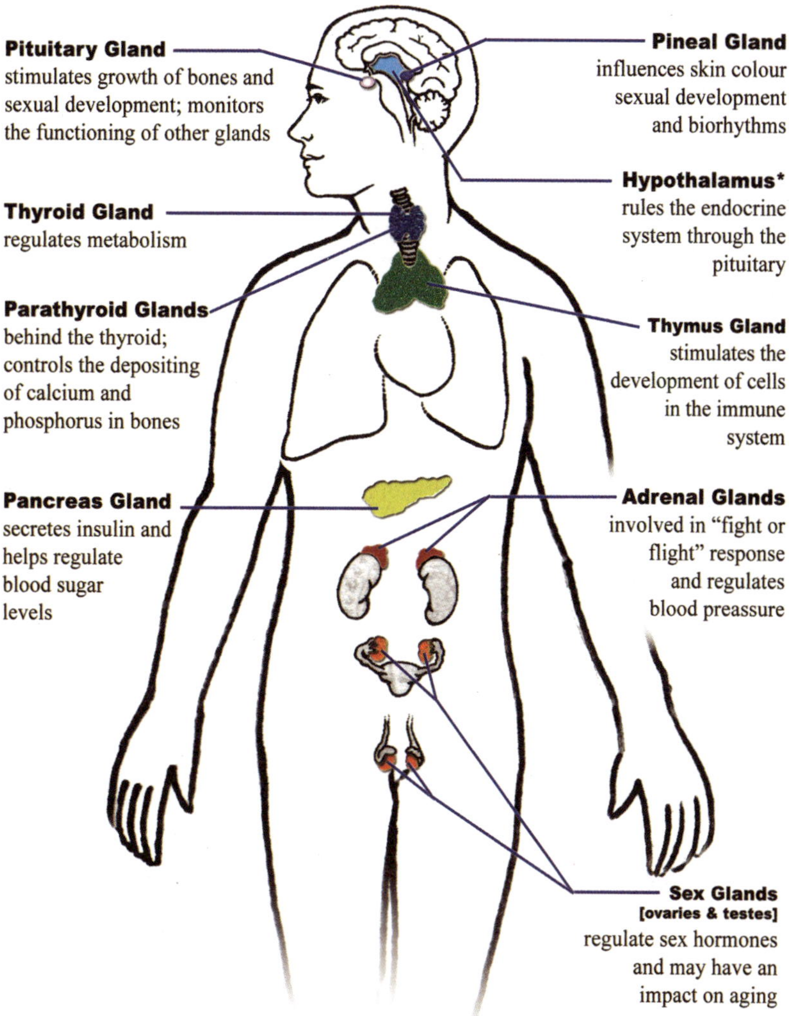

* The Hypothalamus weighs only about a gram, but it controls the release of hormones for the entire endocrine system. The brain produces 20 of the more than 200 hormones in the human body.

Human Values And Health ~ Diagram No. 22

adrenals, pancreas, ovaries or testes and many other smaller glands. Their job is to control the internal environment, not only of each cell and organ but also of the entire body. **[See Diagram No. 22]**

The **hypothalamus** is the main command centre of the endocrine system and directs operations through the **pituitary**, a pea-sized gland situated under the hypothalamus. The operation of the other glands are dependent upon the orders of the pituitary. For instance, when the hypothalamus discovers the need to raise the level of thyroid hormone in the blood, it releases a hormone to the pituitary that instructs the pituitary to send thyroid-stimulating hormone by way of the bloodstream to the thyroid gland. When the thyroid receives the chemical message it releases the thyroid hormone, thyroxin. The end result of all this is that metabolic processes are speeded up.

On a spiritual level, the glands of the endocrine system correspond to the *chakras* in our subtle bodies. These organs are a bridge which allows our physical health to have a direct impact on our mental and spiritual wellness and vice versa. *Chakras* transmit the *prana sakti* to the body organs, connecting the physical body, through the etheric body with the greater elemental *akasa*. In this way the physical body draws subtle energy from food, all the *panchamahabhutas* and the cosmos. Positive loving energy brings wellness; negative thoughts bring disease.

Can You Feel Hormones Being Released?

You cannot feel the release of a hormone any more than you can feel a message traveling in your nerve cells. But sometimes you can be very aware that a hormone has been released. When you blush either with love, embarrassment or pleasure, you are feeling the effects of released hormones.

When you are in a dangerous situation, such as a big snake coming in your path, your hypothalamus signals a release of adrenaline into your system. Adrenaline, the fastest hormonal message, acts immediately to prepare your body for "fight or flight." Your heart beats more strongly, your breathing deepens, perspiration increases to cool your body, your pupils dilate to sharpen your vision, and your face turns pale as blood vessels at the surface of the skin contract, perhaps to reduce bleeding in the event of an injury. From this we can see how our mental and emotional reactions to outer events create a direct chemical reaction in the body.

Daily Care Of The Brain

At the time of birth the head comes out first, protected by a marvellous fluidic cushion, the uterine membrane. During pregnancy this is full of liquid to ensure safety for this extremely delicate organ. But with these extraordinary precautions taken by God before our eyes, how do most of us behave with this sovereign part of our mortal frame? Does it take priority in our daily tasks and command more attention than other parts of the body? The answer, in all probability, is "no". It almost certainly does not even figure in our daily thoughts at all. To enhance our beauty, charm, or strength, do we not pay more attention to the face, figure and limbs than to what goes on inside our head? Are not beauty salons, health clubs, plastic surgery clinics, swimming pools, golf courses, tennis courts, and so on, everywhere a testimony to our bodily attachment? Does the care of the brain figure anywhere in these numerous establishments for body care?[3] Generally not, although the last decades have definitely seen an upsurge in mind-body therapies. Whether we acknowledge it or not, the brain is the master organ, responsible for all the inner and outer beauty we experience in our lives.

The Brain Is The Divine House Of The Soul

"Man is not a mere creature of flesh and blood," Sai Baba tells us, "He is the embodiment of the Spirit. Concentrating all the time on the physical body as the only reality, time is wasted on external observances. The body should be regarded as a temple of God. To consider it otherwise is a sign of foolishness."[4]

The brain is the most precious and tender organ in the human body. But who is the Master of the master organ? We must consider that beyond physiology the human brain is the seat of the *Atma*; it's the temple of God. Knowing this, how can we continue to expose this exquisite instrument to blistering heat and biting cold, to jolts, jerks and knocks, to dizzy speed and giddy sports for amusement, to grinding labour and killing work for gain or fame, and to sleepless nights and hectic days in our quest for earthly pleasures? We give less respect to the care of the brain than we do to the other organs and parts of the body such as the heart, lungs, stomach, arms and legs. The Divine Self is eternal, but on a physical level the brain's resources are not unlimited, and there must be a border beyond which it is not safe to strain our brain.

Good And Bad Emotions And Thoughts

Apart from all these physical excesses, we make this invaluable organ a helpless tool for our selfish desires, subjecting it to tension and distraction in pursuit of our worldly dreams. We indulge in ceaseless worry and anxiety as the fruit of acute rivalry and competition, and send it into "fight or flight" mode by fostering what Sai Baba calls the **six enemies of man** (lust, anger, pride, envy, attachment, greed). On top of these, we expose it needlessly to rapid change of emotions – excitement, shock, terror, revulsion, passion and more by our infatuation with television, news media, novels, films, and now, the current time drain of the modern world, surfing the Internet. The brain is repeatedly subjected to angry outbursts and emotional storms that can leave even a tough body sick and exhausted.

As Sai Baba says, "The most common source of illness amongst people today is tension. What is the cause of tension? It is indulgence in excess of various kinds. Men must learn to moderate the hectic pace of living. Hurry causes worry and worry causes disease."[5]

Above all, many people still indulge in intoxicants like drugs, alcohol and tobacco, which Sai Baba tells us are sure poisons for the brain and body. "Three-fourths of the human body is ruined because of smoking; one-fourth is ruined due to drinking. Because of alcohol people lose their intelligence and memory, and become nervous. They are damaged 100% by smoking and drinking."[6]

Modern culture is undoing the handiwork that God took millions of years to refine. There is a simple reason for this: even at this present height of culture, mankind is still a stranger to his own brain.

The Care And Feeding Of The Brain

Our ceaseless activity of thought and endless play of emotions, from the tender to the violent, make an ever-present process of repair an essential requirement of our brain. The amount of bio-energy used in this continuous work of renewal and restoration depends on the extent of the wear and tear. Everything we take in through any one of the *Pancha Jnanendriyas* (five sense organs) and the *Pancha Karamendriyas* (five working organs) must be processed through the nervous system and brain. A simple life lived in beautiful surroundings that are free of pollutants goes a long way towards creating mental health. Regular exercise, which flushes toxins and waste material from the cells and moderate eating of *satwic* food also play critical roles.

"Since body and mind are strongly interdependent," Sai Baba tells us, "one cannot afford to neglect eating pure, nutritious food. As is the food so is the mind, as is the mind so is the thought, as is the thought so is the act. Food determines alertness and sloth, worry and calm and the brightness and dullness of the mind. The type of food you consume determines the degree of concentration you can command; its quality and quantity decide how much your self control is lessened or heightened."[7]

Sound too can be healing and plays an extremely important role in our brain's wellbeing. Whether we are in the womb or even in a coma, sound reaches our brain and our bodies through skin, bones and ears. Every person listens in different ways. When rhythm, melody and harmony are organised in beautiful forms, the body, mind, spirit and emotions are brought together in harmony.[8]

Sai Baba has defined devotion as that **"which enables the unmanifest Divine principle to manifest itself when the inner vision of the devotee is pure"**. Devotion is a cosmic healer. When care of the senses is balanced with generous doses of devotion in the form of prayer, mediation, *bhajan*, *niskama karma*, (desireless action) and practical Human Values like kindness, patience, compassion, purity, love, forgiveness, forbearance, etc., the brain is actually soothed and cell restoration is promoted. "Devotion and morality are as important for physical health as they are for mental health," says Sai Baba, "They free the mind from agitation; they feed it with joy and contentment; they quiet the nervous system and help even bodily processes." For this reason, at every stage of the mental or cultural progress, Human Values must be taught to improve the intellect, the character, the health and ultimately the way of the life of all humanity. It is the lack of the practice of Human Values that has caused the rise in discontent and consequently physical and mental diseases in the masses.

Sleep: The Brain's Restorative

It is vital to remember that the object under discussion, the brain, is the receiver of cosmic energy in every human being. But from all that is happening in modern lifestyles, it is clear that people are not truly conscious of the Saviour they carry in their heads. How many of us understand that every time we fall asleep at night, we entrust ourselves into the hand of the Divine Mother, God, who looks into every nook and corner of our reclining figure and with a soft touch makes order where a jumble has been caused by our hectic daily activities?

About sleep Sai Baba says, "Feel that you are born with the dawn of every new day; that you nestle in the lap of death when your eyes close in sleep. What happens in deep sleep? The body, senses, the mind, the intelligence, all are negated, and there is not a trace of awareness of the world. If you let go [the mind and its attachments], there will be no accumulation of the consequence of acts from day to day; the accounts of every day will be closed with the little 'death' at the end of the day ..."[9]

When we awake in the morning, refreshed and calmed, cured of a mental fever or a bodily ailment by a restful sleep, how many of us send thanks to God for this priceless boon? Sai Baba tells us that, "without sleep man as well as other beings cannot live. Of all the joys that the world provides, sleep is the most rewarding. All the rest are arid and dry, trivial and wasteful."[10]

The Universal Mind And Man's Mind

There is in existence a Divine Plan with Cosmic Laws propelling the evolution of Humankind. Some believers disregard this idea, believing God to be a figurehead who lets His creatures manage their affairs as they like. It is hard to imagine for a dry intellect that every quantum leap of an atomic particle, every descent of a raindrop, and every fall of a leaf happens by Divine command, yet all religions say it is so. We are encompassed by an intelligence that is beyond the widest flight of human thought. Unless we are active spiritual aspirants, we seldom consider, when face to face with a wonder of creation like the human brain, that the intelligence behind it surpasses our understanding.

The Inner Light

Consciousness expands through inner awareness, not outer sensual perception. The cerebral cortex of the brain must be illuminated from within by the *Atma*. In this way, the human being can perceive the otherwise invisible planes of creation to which our mind and spirit belong. Inner light has been a common feature of all genuine mystical experiences everywhere. Inner light can only be experienced when new neurological pathways in the brain have been stimulated. This marks a kind of shift in consciousness that creates transformation. The health and efficiency of the brain is important, as it is the home of the *Atma*, the sole director of humanity's destiny.

The Divine ideal will be realised and humanity will be transformed as more and more people put into practice the Human Values that have been restored to us by Sri Sathya Sai Baba. Practice of these Human Values literally opens up new neurological pathways and transforms human brain matter. Baba is bringing the Golden Age when love, intuition and reason, the scientists and the sages will walk hand in hand.

The Brain Is The True Beauty Parlour

According Sri Sathya Sai Baba's teachings, the face shines when the character is fine. The brain is the great assistant in cleansing the *Hridayam* (spiritual heart) within the limbic system. Unlike outer beauty programmes which require little energy output but cost much, this inner beauty programme is free of cost but takes much effort. The benefits are that you will always look young, energetic and full of life.

Sri Sathya Sai Baba says:

"When you go on an excursion, you will take a mirror, a comb and a handkerchief. These are necessary to help you to maintain facial cleanliness and a neat appearance. If you want to correct the disturbed beauty of your heart, you have certain aids. Whether your hair is disturbed or not is shown to you by the mirror. Whether your *heart* is disturbed or not is shown to you by your **devotion**, which acts as the mirror. This mirror must be pure. When the mirror is clean, you will be able to see if your heart and mind are pure or if they have become covered by impurities.

When you recognise that your heart is disturbed you have to correct it, and for this purpose you need a comb, namely, the comb of **wisdom**. Wisdom clarifies the heart and returns it to a state of order and beauty. Then just as you keep a cloth to clean off the dirt that has come on your face, you have to remove the dirt that has entered your mind with the cloth of **detachment**. With the help of detachment you can wipe off all the dirt that has accumulated in the mind. Just as you take these three things, the mirror, the comb and the handkerchief wherever you go in your journey in the world, so also, in your journey of life, you will have to take devotion, wisdom and detachment to keep your heart and mind pure. [11]

"Physical charm is but a flash that disappears in a moment – but Divine beauty is eternal, full, free. Pursuing paltry physical beauty leads man astray; it is as calamitous as the pursuit of trivial joy."[12]

PERSONAL BEAUTY-*SADHANA*

So put the lipstick of *namsmarana* and *namasankirtan* on your lips. Powder your face with the Human Values of kindness, patience, love, compassion and forgiveness. Let your ears be decorated with the earrings of God's *bhajans* and *lilas*, and your eyelids glow with the image of your *ishtadevata* (chosen God). Let the *bindi* between your brows be bright from a consciousness focused on your Lord and your Love. For the hands, wear the bangles of charity and selfless service to humanity. The feet are beautiful when they walk on the path of *dharma*, and anklets jingle pleasantly when good people get together in *satsang*. Let the hair on your scalp shine with the oil of truth and curl with the name of God.

Let your brain make these efforts to achieve long-lasting beauty, for these are the adornments that bring peace and health. "The brain is the true beauty parlour."

---

1 Grey and Wright, **Anatomy and Physiology of the Brain**.
2 Grey and Wright, **Anatomy and Physiology of the Brain**.
3 Gopikrishna, **Wonders of the Brain**.
4 *Bhagawan* Sri Sathya Sai Baba, **Baba, the Breath of Sai.**
5 *Bhagawan* Sri Sathya Sai Baba, **Baba, the Breath of Sai.**
6 *Bhagawan* Sri Sathya Sai Baba, Divine Discourse, 27/08/1994.
7 *Bhagawan* Sri Sathya Sai Baba, Divine Discourse, 21/09/1979.
8 The Mozart Effect.com (website).
9 *Bhagawan* Sri Sathya Sai Baba, **Baba, the Breath of Sai.**
10 *Bhagawan* Sri Sathya Sai Baba, **Baba, the Breath of Sai.**
11 *Bhagawan* Sri Sathya Sai Baba, **Discourses on the *Bhagavad Gita*,** Ch. 30.
12 *Bhagawan* Sri Sathya Sai Baba, **Sathya Sai Speaks,** Vol. 18, Ch. 26.

chapter - 9

THE *HRIDAYAM* AND LIMBIC SYSTEM

THE BORDERLAND

If there is any one control centre for the emotions in man, it is the Limbic System, the collective name (from Latin *limbus*, meaning "border") for several interconnected structures that lie near the brain's core. **[SEE DIAGRAM NO. 23]** The limbic system includes the **corpus callosum, thalamus, hypothalamus, amygdala, hippocampus, olfactory lobe, right frontal lobe, right inferior temporal lobe,** along with the **pineal** and **pituitary glands**. The hypothalamus, amygdala, hippocampus are primitive organs that have evolved from our earlier primitive bodies, but their influence upon the human mind is considerable. Enveloping the top of the brain stem, they form a borderland between the "lower" or "animal" parts of the brain (mainly involved with instincts, drives, and automatic regulation of body processes) and the highest, uniquely human brain areas, associated with the cerebral cortex, which permit advanced reasoning and planning. This strategic spot is a kind of crossroads where visceral feelings, cognition, and memory meet. Here, the limbic system helps shape the basic motivations and emotions of our lives.

The survival advantage of the limbic system is clear; it gives animals the aggressiveness they need to find food, the fear that allows them to evade predators and other dangerous situations and the connective longing they need to mate and care for their young. But in human beings, the primal feelings produced by limbic activities are linked with higher connective functions from the neo-cortex resulting in richer, more varied emotional experiences.

Limbic System: The "Heart" Of The Brain

The human limbic system interweaves emotional impulses with higher thoughts and perceptions to produce a broad, flexible repertoire of highly complex emotional stages such as delight, love, compassion, devotion, suspicion, shame, disgust, frustration, envy, surprise, sexual attraction and more. These emotions, although built on primal emotions, are found to some extent in animals also, but in humans they are much more developed.

Studies are going on in U.S.A. and U.K. on spiritual aspirants and meditators by neurophysicans under SPECT Scanning (single photon emission computer tomography) which show that **the limbic system is integral to religious and spiritual experiences.** Electrical stimulation of the limbic system in human subjects produced dream like hallucination, out of body sensation, *déjà vu* and illusions – all of which have been reported during spiritual states induced by meditation, intense prayers, group singing, and even dancing and distance running. Researchers have discovered "inner light" that correlates with experiences of seers and sages since the beginning of recorded time. On the other hand, when nerve input into the limbic system is blocked, visual hallucinations may also result.

Because of its involvement in visual and spiritual experiences, some scientists have referred to the limbic system as the "transmitter to God". It is in this context, as a perceiver and transmitter of subtle emotional awareness, that it becomes

The Limbic System *(Hridayam)*

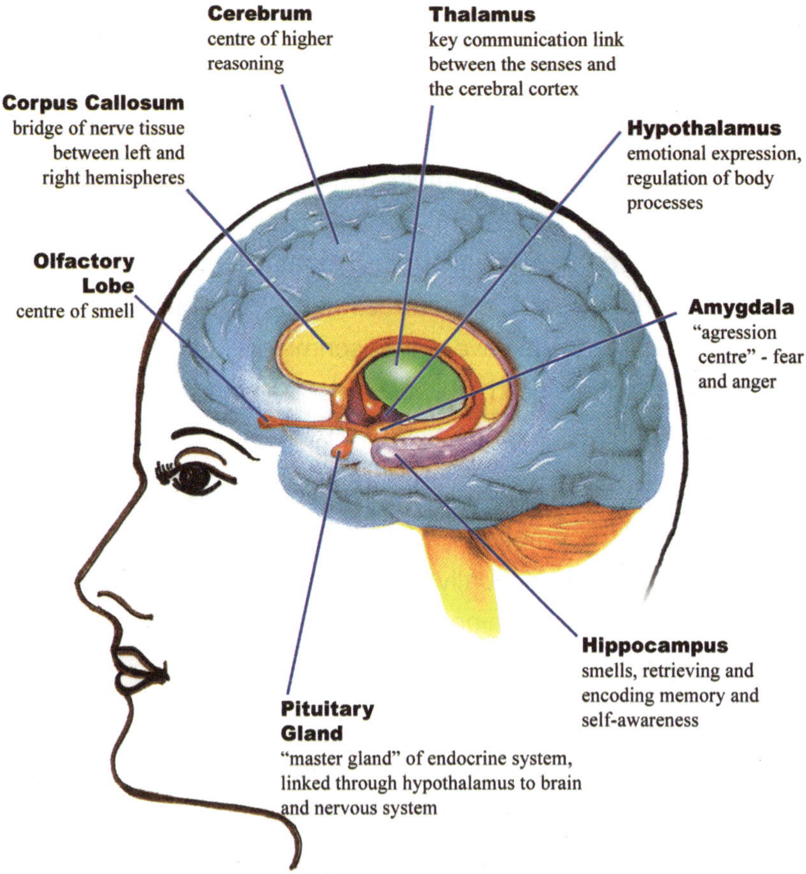

The Limbic System acts as a bridge between the subconscious mind, the ego mind and the higher mind, which communicates with God. Because of this, some scientists have called it the "Transmitter to God". This is the physical manifestation of the ***Hridayam*** in the human brain.

Human Values And Health ~ Diagram No. 23

significant to spiritual aspirants. Whatever is its relationship to the spiritual, however, before it learns to submit activity, the limbic system's most fundamental purpose is to generate and modulate primal emotions such as fear, aggressiveness and rage, possessed by most animals with a central nervous system.

The structure of the limbic system is ancient in evolutionary terms. What separates our limbic system from those of animals and our earlier ancestors are the many subtle expressions of emotion that we have developed. Empathy, humour, humility, reverence, pride, regret, embarrassment, covetousness – as well as the ability to deceive and discriminate right from wrong – all are the products of a highly developed limbic system, whose function is combined with the rest of the brain.

Poetry, song and folklore have long portrayed the heart as the province of the emotions, while making rational thought the business of the brain. Actually, emotions have not one cause or source but several, beginning with the internal or external events that provoke them.

Although emotions often involve a quicker heartbeat and other "**heartfelt**" effects, the heart, as the central organ of the body, is just one part of a complex story. Each conscious emotion is the result of a jumble of signals travelling back and forth on nerve and brain pathways.

The Limbic System Controls Our Behaviour

When functioning normally, the limbic area seems to act as a switchboard where emotional power is imparted to ideas, and reason curbs drives and emotions. In this complex interaction, the energising force can be either an idea, a memory, a sensation or any kind of stimulus, external or internal. One way of looking at what happens is to imagine that the limbic system proposes and the cortex, the thinking part of the brain, disposes; but the cortex can also propose, or originate an emotion, in which case the emotion is routed back by the limbic system to the cortex for review and moderation by reason and experience, if necessary. **In providing a place where reason and emotion can mix, the limbic area seems to help keep our behaviour within certain limits:** neither too coldly rational, nor too hotly emotional. What takes place in the limbic area may keep us from quitting a job after some slight criticism from a boss, for example; and conversely it may give us the courage of conviction and faith when we must take a stand for what we believe.

Limbic System And Man's Spiritual Heart

The Limbic System is the area of the physical brain that Sri Sathya Sai Baba refers to as the *Hridayam* (spiritual heart). But whereas the limbic system exists in the *Bhutakasa* – the gross level of *akasa* comprised of the *panchamahabhutas* (five elements) in their material forms of ether, air, fire, water and earth – the *Hridayam* is its correspondence in the *Chitthakasa* (mental world). The *Hridayam* is infinite and does not exist on the gross physical plane of matter, although it interpenetrates it. *Hridayam* might be said to be the limbic system at a higher frequency of vibration, where the *panchamahabhutas* are experienced in their subtle form as sound, touch, form, taste and smell.

As we infuse Human Values into the sounds we make and hear, the things we see, touch, taste and smell, we purify our *Hridayam,* which exists on this mental level of the *akasa*. It is the mental and emotional projections of the *Chitthakasa* that must be refined by the active practice of Human Values in thought, word and deed. This initiates a cleansing process, which allows the light of the *Chidakasa* (causal world, place of the cogniser of

Atma) and eventually the *Atma* to manifest in the human being. Sai Baba likens it to a lantern, where the glass must be cleansed of soot and dirt before the light can be seen. The glass might be considered the *Hridayam* and the flame the light of the *Atma*. The cleansing or purifying process is Human Values. A purified *Hridayam* allows soothing, *Atmic* vibrations into the limbic system, which in turn relays positive signals through the nervous system, endocrine system and other systems to the organs of the body. The organs feel safe and well. They function as God intended. This manifests as physical health. This is why the practice of Human Values can make such an impact on our physical as well as emotional wellbeing.

Why It's Important To Purify The *Hridayam*

This sensitive region is like a TV antenna, which receives information from the subtle, unseen worlds. For any number of reasons, the limbic system of some highly intelligent people may be open from birth. If they are full of anger, hatred, greed, jealously, pride, selfishness, ego, etc. they catch similar negative vibrations from the unseen, leading them to behave like demons.

Alexander the Great was filled with greed. He repeatedly invaded India, carrying away Her gold, jewels and ancient treasures, but like everyone, he died empty-handed. Adolf Hitler was greedy for power and jealous of the ruling classes. He calculated the massacre of six million people before taking his own life. Terrorism, mass murder, social oppression and war are brought about by people who have developed their minds, but not purified their *Hridayams*.

When the limbic system (*Hridayam*) is purified by adopting Human Values likes *sathya, dharma, santi, prema* and *ahimsa,* it can receive similar pure vibrations from the subtle, unseen worlds. Britain will never produce another Shakespeare; his mind was so immersed in love, he could write dramas like "Romeo & Juliet" and "Antony and Cleopatra", which made him immortal. Turkey will never produce another Jalalluddin Rumi, whose love for God poured forth as countless *rubiyans* (love songs for God), which even today are sung around the world. India will not produce another Mirabai, who was so immersed in devotion to God that even though she was a princess, she sang out her love for Krishna door to door. Bulle Shah was soaked in love and wrote the immortal love stories, "Heer Ranjhe" and "Soni Mahival."

There are other saints and sages throughout the ages like Guru Nanak, the ten Sikh *Gurus*, Mohammed, Kabir, Rabia, St. Francis of Assisi, St. Terese of Liseux, John the Baptist, Meister Ekhard, Valmiki, the author of *Ramayana*, Mahatma Gandhi and modern mystics like Eckhart Tolle and others who show us what is possible when the limbic system is cleansed through truth, right conduct, peace, non-violence – and love. What we are actually able to witness through the lives of these individuals is the evolution of the brain and mind from man to human, to philosopher-poets, to *mahatmas,* to Sufis, saints and sages, until the consciousness eventually merges into Absolute Mind.

Great scientists like Thomas Edison, Louis Pasteur and Leonardo Da Vinci were also motivated by energy which flowed from the Cosmic Mind into their open limbic systems. Founders of alternative healing systems, like Dr. Samuel Hahnnman (developer of Homeopathy), Mei Ling (*pranic* healing) and Edward Bach (flower remedies) have experienced this vital cosmic intelligence flowing into their astral bodies, limbic systems and *chakras* and then being distributed throughout the organs of their bodies. Even *ayurveda* was developed in such an intuitive way, through meditation, by Sage Barathwaja and other ancient seers and sages of India.

The cosmic intelligence can only enlighten from within through a limbic system that is ready to receive. In all these cases, new neurological pathways are established and the brain matter itself actually develops, leading these individuals to a higher state of evolution than the common man.

Faith Is The First Step

Sri Sathya Sai Baba says:

Human virtues cannot be acquired from others. They have to be cultivated by each person and the resulting joy has to be personally experienced. Today, the world sorely needs Human Values. Attempts are being made to promote these values in the field. But they cannot be promoted through materialistic, worldly or scientific means. Without developing devotion to God, no human quality can grow. Therefore, the first requisite is **faith in God**.

Doubts are raised whether God exists or not. Those who affirm that God exists and those who deny Him are equally incompetent to say something about God, as they know nothing about His Nature. To assert the existence of that which does not exist is ignorance. To deny the existence of that which does exist is folly. God is omnipresent. There is no need to search for Him anywhere. Everything that we see is manifestation of God. Wherever we are, there is God. There can be no greater folly than to deny the existence of God when the whole cosmos bears witness to His handiwork. **Everything in creation must be viewed as a manifestation of God.** Only with this basic faith can one develop one's personality.[1]

If we take this one step further, remembering that every person we come across and every experience we undergo are only a reaction, reflection and resound of what is within us, we can see that the more we are able to manifest our inner Divinity through a purified *Hridayam* and limbic system, the more we can experience a state of Total Health, which is the birthright of every human being – God's divine design.

It is important to note that this is a process, not an instant panacea. Our *Hridayam* has been a repository of every experience we have ever had – in this life and all our previous lives. These experiences have created tendencies, desires and habits, which are called *vasanas*. Through our actions we have created *karma* (results of our good and bad thoughts, words and actions) that also must be balanced.

We can add impact to our own concentrated efforts if we work with a *Guru* or spiritual master. When in the presence, either physically or at thought level, of elevated beings who live at God consciousness, our own consciousness is automatically raised up and purified. The awakened Divine within them calls out to the sleeping Divine within us. That Divine is, after all, only ONE. To reach these beings, however, our own efforts are necessary. But as Sathya Sai Baba says, "when your efforts come together with My Grace there is transformation. Bird flies with two wings. One wing is your effort, the other wing is My Grace."

Cultivating Your *Hridayam*

Sathya Sai Baba tells us:

God dwells in *Hridayam*. *Hridayam* is the centre of love and peace. Only sacred qualities should emerge out of *Hridayam*. But instead animal qualities like anger, hatred and jealousy emerge; then you are a beast, not a human being. Such a *Hridayam* is a dwelling place for animals, not God. If you conduct yourself with peace, love, and compassion, you are God.

God is all brilliance, full of effulgence, and beyond the darkness of ignorance. God is not far off in a distant land, but is present in the human body. The saints had the vision of God, who is *Chinmaya* (full of effulgence), in the body, which is *Mrinmaya* (made of clay). So, we should not underrate the human body and use it for bad acts and worldly pleasures. The body is the temple of God. This body may be compared to an iron chest. Just as the precious jewels are kept in the iron chest, so also God is present in the human body. So, the body has to be maintained and made proper use of for the sake of the precious jewel, the *Atma*. You get jewels only from the earth. Similarly, you have to search for the jewel of the *Atma* only in the body, which is made of clay.[2]

Regard the *Hridayam* as a vast field, the Mind as a plough, the *gunas* (qualities) as the bullocks, and the use of the intelligence (*viveka*) as a whip. With these aids, cultivate the field of your *Hridayam*. What are the crops that must be grown in it? *Sathya*, *Dharma*, *Santi* and *Prema* are the crops, *Bhakti* is the rain, meditation is the manure. *Brahmananda* (divine bliss) also is the crop. This is your task today. Cultivate the *Hridayam* to raise a harvest of truth, righteousness, peace and love. These crops are to be raised in one's *Hridayam* and should be shared with others. Our life is like a block of ice, which melts away at every moment. Before it spends itself, devote it to the service of others. The Human Values should be regarded as a basic requirement for every human being. In spreading the message of these values to the world, you should all cooperate with each other and act in harmony. Whatever may be the experience in everyday life, the basic inner Truth should not be forgotten. "The Reality is one though it may be called by different names."

What is Truth? It is not in these bombs and missiles hovering over us that are the menace. Our bad qualities are the more serious problem for us. The reason for this is if bombs are used, they will make an end of humanity and nothing will remain. The bad qualities in man are devastating the lives of people all the time. This calamity is worse than the other. If we want to eliminate bad qualities like hatred, envy, pride and ostentation, we have to employ the five Human Values of *Sathya* (Truth), *Dharma* (Duty), *Santi* (Peace), *Prema* (Love) and *Ahimsa* (Non-Violence), as these are the cleansing instruments. [3]

The Message Of The Watch

W (Words) - The first letter **'W'** in the word watch reminds us of the *Sadhana* of watching the Words. One should not revel in idle gossip or spread slander and scandal, thereby, wounding others while polluting oneself. Examine the word before the tongue pronounces it. Is it true? Will it hurt? Is it necessary? Warn the tongue against uttering falsehood or indulging in outbursts of vilification and the like. Adhere to Truth, ***Sathya***, at all costs. It is the basic Human Value.

A (Actions) - The second letter **'A'** reminds us of the additional *Sadhana* of watching the Action. Be vigilant that every activity aligns your moral progress with the welfare of society – that is to say, follows the moral code, *Dharma. Dharma* also means innate nature. Fire has to spread warmth and light and also to burn. These are its *Dharma*. Sugar without the sweetness is but paltry powder. A rose without fragrance might as well be a plastic substitute. Man's *Dharma* is to love and serve fellowman, practising truth without causing injury to others. 'A' teaches us to manifest *Dharma* in every action of ours. *Dharma* is another great human value.

T (Thoughts) - The third letter **'T'** indicates that we must watch our Thoughts. While adhering to the earlier two, one trains the mind not to react vehemently or vengefully when one is blamed or extolled. Why should one worry if the blame has no basis? Thoughts must reinforce the innate peace and tranquility, which are one's heritage. They should not create anxiety or anger, arrogance or envy, which are alien to the Divine Core of human beings. Thoughts, when watched and warned, promote *Santi*, another precious human value. *Santi* is the jewel worn by the sages. It resides in a *Hridayam* that is free from pride and greed.

C (Character) - The fourth letter, **'C',** teaches one to watch the Character. The *sadhaka* (aspirant) has to direct himself to the acquisition of the three values already mentioned, through steady vigilance. Man is the very embodiment of love; so, his character finds expression through character saturated with love. A life without love is really a living death. Every thought, word, and deed must emanate from love. Love must bind the community as one; it must strengthen the feeling of brotherhood and satisfy the craving for expansion. Love must reach out to all mankind and to God. Does love motivate him for every action? These are the tests.

H (Heart) - The fifth letter **'H'** instructs us to watch the *Hridayam* and the feelings it originates. It reminds us of the human value of *Ahimsa* (Non-violence). Heart does not mean the fist-size physical equipment we have to purify and pump blood. It is the centre of emotion, good and bad. It has to be watched, so that good emotions alone are manifested. It must expand to include all living beings to feel kinship with all creation. "My reality is the reality of All" – this truth is ever springing forth. Then, the idea of violence can never find place in the heart. The sense of unity cannot produce competition and confrontation. The fifth human value, *Ahimsa*, is promoted by the *Sadhana* indicated by the letter H.

The word 'watch' thus advises you to watch yourself. A hundred eyes will be watching every word and deed of yours to discover whether you have mastered the Human Values and whether you are practising them. Most importantly, **God, the Universal Watcher, is witnessing and weighing your every thought, word and deed**. God examines and judges and you are able to acquire self-satisfaction through sincerity and serenity. Prove your humanness by the practice of the values, which are the unique qualities of man.[4]

The *Atma* Is Eternal Witness

For everything, conscience is the witness. If you do not follow the conscience, everything becomes unsacred. **The *Atma* is the eternal witness and that is conscience.** The *Atma* is everything. It is in every individual and every creature. It has no form. It is attributeless, eternal, ancient, unsullied and immortal. Who can understand such an *Atmic* principle? You speak of truth and consider whatever you see and hear as truth, but all this is limited to the senses. But the *Atma* is beyond the senses. Then how to know this *Atmic* Principle? You do not need to search for this elsewhere. Turn your vision inward.

The ***Vedas*** said: "*Pashyannapi Na Pashyathi Mudho*" (he is a fool who sees, yet does not see). All that you see is Divine but you mistake it for Nature. The one with *Atmic* vision will see the entire Nature as Divine. But, if you have the worldly view, you can only see the world. *Viswam Vishnumayam*, (Vishnu [God] pervades the entire universe). Names and forms may vary, but the *Atma* is uniform in all. To understand this unity, you have to turn your vision inward. There is no separate path to know God, other than knowing one's own Self.[5]

Removing Bad Qualities

Sri Sathya Sai Baba says:

Let us investigate what comes in the way of experiencing the *Atmic* principle. Ego and attachment stand as obstacles in our path. Only when you give up ego and attachment, you will have purity of *Hridayam*, which in turn will lead you to the experience of Supreme Wisdom. The more you develop attachment, the more restless you become. Ego is much more dangerous. It has become an incurable disease in human beings. So, you have to keep ego and attachment under control and engage yourself in the quest of *Atmic* bliss.

The Six Virtues

1. *Visvasam* (faith or confidence)
2. *Sahasam* (daring or determination)
3. *Dhairyam* (patience)
4. *Buddhi* (intelligence)
5. *Sakti* (energy)
6. *Parakramam* (valour)

When a man has these six qualities, the Divine will stand by him in all his endeavours. In any age or at any place or in any circumstance, these six good qualities are essential. No worry will haunt any man who has these six virtues. These six qualities cannot be acquired by education. Nor can they be imparted by any preceptor. Nor can they be inherited from one's parents. These qualities are secured only by Self-confidence (*Atma - Visvasam*).

Faith has become rare nowadays. Self-confidence is totally absent. How can one have faith in God without confidence in himself? And how can such a person hope for God's grace? Hence, every man must cultivate firm faith.

Faith is thus essential for every activity in life. The ancient sages accomplished many great things by their faith. Their achievements are cherished by people today even after thousand of years. Unfortunately, because of the influence of *Kali* in the present age, faith is declining from moment to moment. People change their beliefs constantly; such changes are mental aberrations. They do not pertain to the Spirit (which dwells in the *Hridayam*).

The Six Enemies

The Creator has endowed man with numerous qualities. In addition to the six virtues, man has six vices:

1. *Kama* (Desire)
2. *Krodha* (Anger)
3. *Lobha* (Greed)
4. *Moha* (Fascination or Attachment)
5. *Mada* (Pride or Ego)
6. *Mathsarya* (Envy or Jealousy)

These are known as the six enemies of man. They are a part of creation. The mind is the master of these vices. Man tries to train the mind to overcome these vices. But this is not easy for all. The reason is that being unaware of how to control the mind man becomes an easy prey to its vagaries. Everyone should strive to find out how to use the mind in any situation, at any time and in any circumstance. Men today are dominated by three evil qualities: anger, hatred, and envy. These three qualities poison the mind of man. Consequently, every action of man gets poisoned. Every word he utters is venomous. All actions done by the prompting of the mind become false. All sensory actions are equally polluted.

The Power Of Love

To transform these evil thoughts and actions into good ones, it is necessary to infuse love into all thoughts and actions. When the mind is filled with love, all actions get suffused with love. Today man is totally unaware of what is meant by love. Man equates desire with love. He imagines that whatever he yearns for is prompted by love. This is not true love (*Prema*). *Prema* is totally free from desire. It is utterly selfless. It seeks no return. It is all-encompassing. It makes no distinction between friend and foe. Forgetting this concept of universal, selfless love, and filling himself with selfish love, man fancies that he is filled with love. This is mundane attachment. It is quite apart from the love that flows from the Spirit inside. Spiritual Love is boundless. It is free from the feeling of hatred. It is capable of expressing itself in universal terms. It is vital to fill the mind with love and expel the six enemies residing in it. Every part of the body should be filled with Divine Love. That is the way to Divinise man.

Divine Love Is Natural To Man

Many people imagine that to Divinise man and make him a godly being is a superhuman exercise. This is not so. **Divine Love is within reach of man, because it is natural to man.** He is entitled to possess it. Divine Love should not be considered as something transcendental or alien to man. But men tend to degrade this love by giving it different forms and names that lessen its value. The defect lies in the perversion of love and is not inherent in it. Convert anger into love. Turn hatred into love. To affect this change what is needed is to change the *Hridayam* by filling it with love. **When the *Hridayam* is filled with love, the whole world becomes loveable**. The mind is restless and fickle. All troubles that afflict man stem from the mind. The thoughts arising from the mind are the cause of human birth.[6]

You are my own Self. The sweetness of love coming out of life is the great and unique principle that is at the source of everything. You can put this love in any field of activity by practising Human Values at every step of your life. This practice will bring about unity in thought, word and deed. This integration will lead to the spontaneous release of the Divine energy of love from within, purifying your thoughts, words and deeds even further. Verily **love** is the under-current that flows through all Values. The practice of these values will bring inner harmony between the five elements within you – earth, water, fire, air and space. They are present in every cell of your body. When you enjoy them within limits of the five Human Values, there is perfect joy in you and harmony outside.[7]

Man Is The Cosmic Being

Man has no need to seek anything outside of himself. He has the universe within him, in his *Hridayam*. He is potentially the Cosmic Being. He has in him the magnetic power of attraction. It is derived from the Divine. Every atom has this Divine power. Man thinks that what is perceived by the senses is real and what is beyond human perception is unreal. This is wrong. **It is the unseen that contains everything.** When you see a man, you consider his physical features as the only reality about him. But you can have no conception of his powers and talents, which are not externally visible. He has compassion, love, the spirit of sacrifice, sublime thoughts, none of which are apparent to you. For that reason, can you say that they do not exist? Likewise, the secret of a man's actions may not be apparent. A flower, for instance, has fragrance, which has no visible form. The form of fragrance is to be found in the form of the flower. Without the flower there is no fragrance. It is said that love (*Prema*) has no form. But love has a form. The mother who loves her child, expresses the form of love. So, love God in any form - Father, Mother, Brother, Beloved or Friend - and come closer to the proximity of God.[8]

God Is In Your *Hridayam*

Sri Sathya Sai Baba echoes the Vedas:

If you follow the dictum, *Sathyam Vada*; *Dharmam Chara* (Speak the truth; practise righteousness), then you are bound always to have success. Truth is common to all countries and all times. If you follow truth, which is God, you will invariably do only righteous work. Divine Love will flow to such persons. This will ensure your doing sacred work. **There cannot be love without *Dharma* and *Dharma* without love**. God is in your *Hridayam*. Wherever you go and whatever you do is known to God, even if you think none has noticed it. People start worrying about petty temporary things, which are passing clouds, and sometimes falter in faith and devotion. This is not correct. You should never give up devotion. Your good work will beget God's grace without fail. Sin or merit comes only from one's own deeds, not from outside.

You should say to yourself, "I am not man, I am Divine. I am not body, I am *Atma*." The body is like a dustbin of all foul matter and flesh and bones. You are awareness or *Chaithanya*. The instruments are negative and work through positive Divinity. Tread along the Divine path so that you can get peace. Let us experience peace. Let us experience peace and share it with others. Only then we will be liberated and the world will be happy.[9]

Love Is The Greatest Healer

The limbic system has both nuclei for Hate and Love close by. Love has been scientifically proved the greatest healer for the brain. Pure Love heals all types of mental, emotional and physical diseases. Of all the many motivating forces in life, there are fundamentally only love and hate, and all others are derivatives from these two. Those motivating forces that spring from love are creative, constructive, healing and life giving. Those which arise from hate are mutually destructive, hurtful and death dealing.

Some of the sub-values of love as enumerated in the Sri Sathya Sai Education in Human Values Programme are: kindness, helping, compassion, humility, gentleness, sacrifice, generosity, friendship and loyalty. It is through the dedicated, daily practice of the innate values which make us healthy and human, that we are able to grow in our Divinity.

---

1 *Bhagawan* Sri Sathya Sai Baba, Divine Discourse, November 1993.

2 *Bhagawan* Sri Sathya Sai Baba, Divine Discourse, 25/09/1998.

3 *Bhagawan* Sri Sathya Sai Baba, Divine Discourse, March 1996.

4 *Bhagawan* Sri Sathya Sai Baba, Divine Discourse, March 1996.

5 *Bhagawan* Sri Sathya Sai Baba, Divine Discourse, 25/09/1998.

6 *Bhagawan* Sri Sathya Sai Baba, Divine Discourse, 25/12/1997.

7 *Bhagawan* Sri Sathya Sai Baba, "I Am God, You Are God", pamphlet from *Chaitanya Jyothi* Museum.

8 *Bhagawan* Sri Sathya Sai Baba, Divine Discourse, 25/12/1997.

9 *Bhagawan* Sri Sathya Sai Baba, Divine Discourse, 18/04/1998.

*In the beginning was **Hiranyagarbha**.*

The seed of elemental existence,

The only Lord of all that was born.

He upheld the heaven and earth together

To what God other than Him,

Could we dedicate our life?

~ ***Atharva Veda***

chapter - 10

HIRANYAGARBHA: THE CREATOR WITHIN YOU

In the beginning of the present order of things, in some far-off period, in some distant point of time, the whole universe existed in a state of *paramanu* (*anu* = atom, *param* = beyond, thus "before or beyond the atom"), invisible, subtle and unmanifested. That which we know now as the earth, the sun, the moon and the stars was then, in the beginning of the *Kalpa* (age), but formless matter in its most elemental and attenuated condition – *akasa* (ether), no doubt. Our ancient Aryan philosophers called it *asat* (non-being). We involuntarily exclaim with our glorious *Rishis*, "Before, O, child! This was a mere state of *asat*, one only, without second. From that non-being proceeds the state of being."

There is nothing, therefore, inappropriate in the name which the ancients gave this ether-spirit – the *Hiranyagarbha*: the womb of light.

First in the beginning was this *Hiranyagarbha*, one only without the second. The next step towards evolution was the generation of heat. The atoms of ether came closer together and united in different proportions and formed molecules. Thus the various elements were first evolved out of the homogeneous atoms of ether.[1]

Thus states the *Vedic* theory of creation, which is in full congruence with modern science. Why is this significant for us in our daily lives as human beings? Because, if we understand that we are the very form of God, holding the attributes of God, then it must follow that we also have God's full creative potential. We are creating our lives every moment with every thought, word and deed, but are we doing it consciously or unconsciously? The "Existent One" created the universe through an act of conscious creation – and, according to the *Bible*, "saw that it was good". When we consciously choose to infiltrate the practice of Human Values into every area of our lives, we too are becoming the conscious creators of a good and positive destiny.

Sri Sathya Sai Baba says:

You have it in your power to make your days on earth a path of flowers. The key to all knowledge of the universe lies within you. In the Creation, the first place was granted to mankind, and My knowledge was placed in your mind. When you access the website of infinite Divine knowledge within, the purpose of your life will be fulfilled.

You determine the nature of your actions, thoughts and desires. Sow a seed of good thought, reap a fruit of good action. Go straight along the path of *karma* (action) and *dharma* (virtue) towards the Supreme Reality. I am God; you are also God. I know I am God; when will you realise that you are also God?[2]

The Cosmic Person

The ***Upanishads*** have revealed three forms in which the transcendental *Brahma Tathwa* (Supreme Principle) manifests Itself. The three forms are: *Virat, Hiranyagarbha* and *Avyakrita*. These three forms are related to the gross, the subtle and the causal forms of the human body. They are also related to the three states of consciousness: Waking, dream and deep sleep.

Chart No. 24 ~ The Cosmic Person

Cosmic Form	Attributes	Body	State
VIRAT **Gross**	• "The Cosmic Person" • Entire cosmos, animate & inanimate • Manifests in many forms, under many names • Five basic elements	*Sthula Sarira*	Waking
HIRANYA-GARBHA **Subtle**	• "The Golden Womb" or "The Golden Embryo" • The first manifestation of God: entire creation emerged from here • Form of a golden egg • Source of all knowledge	*Sukshma Sarira*	Dream
AVYAKRITA **Causal**	• Formless • Control over everything • Engaged in all activities relating to creation, but no form	*Karana Sarira*	Deep Sleep
SOURCE: *Bhagawan* Sri Sathya Sai Baba, Divine Discourse, 31/05/1991.			

Virat - Gross

The *Virat* form is the gross physical form assumed by the *Atma* in the waking state for leading a long life in the world. He manifests himself in many forms under many names. The entire cosmos, consisting of animate and inanimate objects, is the form of *Virat*, permeating the five basic elements. The *Virat Purusha* (the Cosmic Person) is manifest in every creature from an ant to the Absolute, demonstrating thereby that the cosmos is a manifestation of the Divine. He is called *"Virat"* (totality of created objects) because of his cosmic manifestation and His immanence in everything in creation that is perceivable.

HIRANYAGARBHA – SUBTLE

The second form is called, *Hiranyagarbha.* He is the source of all kinds of knowledge – ethical, spiritual, physical, scientific and social. He may be described as *Jnanabhaskara* (the Sun of knowledge). When the Sun rises, he assumes a golden hue. By his golden rays, he turns the whole of nature golden. The entire creation emerged from *Hiranyagarbha* at the beginning. *Hiranyagarbha* is in the form of an oval-shaped golden egg. From *Hiranyagarbha*, the first to emerge was the mouth. Sound started from the mouth. Then came the nose, from which arose air. Then came the eyes, from which emanated fire. The ears came thereafter. The ten directions arose from the ears.

Hiranyagarbha is the primary source of the origin of man. *Hiranyagarbha* is the prime source of all living beings. It is *Hiranyagarbha* who endowed all these beings with the power to discriminate between the eternal and the ephemeral, between what should be sought and what should be renounced, between what ought to be and what ought not to be done.

What is the Supreme Knowledge that man needs to make his life sacred and meaningful and what is the path he should pursue to lead a purposeful life? *Hiranyagarbha* offered to man the knowledge he needed for this purpose. This is the primary activity of *Hiranyagarbha*.

Hiranyagarbha has two other names: *Suthratmaka* is one [also known as *Sutra Atma*]. It means the one who functions like a string through all *Atmas*, even as a string runs through a necklace of gems. This means that he is present in all beings like the string that keeps together the gems in a necklace. This string is called *Brahma-Sutra* (the string of Brahman). The principle of *Hiranyagarbha* indicates how the Divine unites all human beings equally like the string of a necklace. *Hiranyagarbha* thus demonstrates a division-less universe.

Hiranyagarbha And Dreams

The other name for *Hiranyagarbha* is *Prana* (vital life force). *Hiranyagarbha* assumes a subtle form in the dream state of a human being. He is the entity who is awake in the dream and sleeping states. In the waking state, the *Virataswarupa* (cosmic form on the physical plane) creates the visible cosmos. In the dream state, *Hiranyagarbha* creates the figures in the dreams. All objects in this state have no physical basis. **All that is perceived in dreams are the creations of *Hiranyagarbha*.** *Hiranyagarbha* in his subtle form creates everything in the dream state.

On account of attachment, fear and hatred, man forgets his true nature. This fact can be witnessed in the dream state. You have a dream in which you are travelling by a train. You pass a number of stations in the dream. You see many passengers and you spend your time in talking and joking. Wherefrom did the train come in the dream state? It is a creation of your mind. Likewise the stations you passed by and the passengers you moved with are all creations of the mind. All that was experienced in the dream are products of the mind. Nor is that all. You created even yourself in the dream. This is the activity of *Hiranyagarbha*.

Avyakrita - Formless

The third one is *Avyakrita*. He is one who has no form of any kind. He is present in the *Karana Sarira* (causal body), without any form, and enjoys the *Sushupti* state of man (the deep sleep state). Though he has no form, he has control over everything. Without limbs or organs, he performs all actions. He travels long distances. Without eyes, he sees everything. Without ears, he hears everything. He is thus engaged in all activities relating to creation, but has no form.

This *Avyakrita* has two other names: *Antaratma* and *Iswarathwam*. *Antaratma* means one who impels from within all activities (*Antaravani* or inner voice). Every impulse arises from *Antaratma*. All the sounds uttered by man come from the *Antaratma*. The *Antaratma* is the basic source of all sounds.

Easwara is the third name for *Avyakrita*; though he is the possessor of all forms of wealth, he is the entity who judges good and bad actions and metes out punishment or reward according to deserts. He presides over actions. Hence, he decides on good and bad actions and metes out justice. As *Easwara* is the Lord of all wealth, he gives to each man what he deserves according to his good and bad actions.

All Powers Are Present In Man

Virat, Hiranyagarbha and *Avyakrita* are not entities existing in some separate place. When you examine carefully, you will find that every human being is an incarnation of *Virat*, of *Hiranyagarbha* and *Avyakrita*. This profound truth is not realised by men because of their narrow outlook.

- Human Body x Infinity = *Virat*
- Mind x Infinity = *Hiranyagarbha*
- Life x Infinity = *Avyakrita*

These three forms are related to the gross, the subtle and the causal bodies of man. All the three bodies are in the human being. *Hiranyagarbha* is not in some distant place. He is installed in the mind. The *Virat-Purusha* (Cosmic Person) is in the human form. The five basic elements (representing the faculties of sound, sight, smell, taste and touch) are in the human body, as well as in the cosmos.[3]

The Gold In Man

Sri Sathya Sai Baba declares:

Thus, there is the principle of *Hiranyagarbha* within every individual. *Hiranya* means gold. When gold is mixed with other metals such as copper, silver, brass and alloys, it loses its effulgence, value and identity. At this juncture it is impossible to ascertain whether it is gold, silver, brass or copper. Similarly, man's *Hridayam* (spiritual heart) is losing its brilliance, value and identity because of its association with *Vishaya Vasanas* (attachment to sense objects). Consequently, it is impossible to ascertain whether one is a human being, an animal, a devil or a demon. There is no love at all in human beings today. Life devoid of love is a devil's life. Can a man be called a human being, if he has qualities of devils, demons and beasts?

Hiranyagarbha Is The Principle Of Love

Past is past, the future is uncertain, only the present is in our hands. It is the foremost duty of man to live in the present and share his joy with his fellow beings. Truly speaking, the human being is the most fortunate one among all the living beings. Compared to the entire cosmos, man is very small like an atom, yet he is able to comprehend the magnitude and vastness of the creation, which is very startling indeed. He attains immortality by understanding the unity between the microcosm and macrocosm. Whosoever reaps the harvest of love in the field of his *Hridayam* is a true Christian, a true Sikh, a true Hindu and true Muslim. In fact he is the true human being on earth. Man cannot exist without love. This principle of love is *Hiranyagarbha*.

This *Hiranyagarbha* is situated on the right side of the human body and the physical heart is on the left. *Hiranyagarbha*, located on the right side of the human body, is always right [correct]. It is immortal, eternal and all encompassing. It is present not only in human beings, but also in birds, beasts, and all other living beings. The ***VEDAS*** declare, "*Easwara Sarvabhuthanam,*" (God is present in all the beings). "*Isavasyam Idam Jagat,*" (God pervades the entire cosmos). It is love that originates out of this *Hiranya* (gold). [4]

HIRANYAGARBHA AND THE *LINGAM*

Each year on the holy festival of *Maha Sivaratri*, a night dedicated to the Siva principle, Sathya Sai Baba manifests a *lingam.* It is an egg-shaped object, created within His own body, which emerges through His mouth. Sai Baba says, "The *lingam* that emerges from the Universal Absolute (*Brahman*) is the cosmos, conceived first as an idea, formed later as a will and finally adopted as a wish. It is the symbol of the emergence of the five primordial elements. The *lingam* is the essence of all attributes and names. It is the formless with Form, nameless with Name, the primal emergent of the Divine.[5]

"The *lingam*," Sai Baba continues, "is in every one of you … through attachment and consequent suffering the individual learns the need for and the efficacy of the *lingam*, or God, who is his innermost core." [6]

Sri Sathya Sai Baba asserts:

Everybody's *Hridayam* is on the right side of the body. **The principle of *Hiranyagarbha* is spread all over the body. It assumes a form when I will it.** It is changeless. You cannot see such manifestation anywhere else in the world. It is possible only in Divinity. [7]

God is sometimes called the *Hiranyagarbha*. The golden *lingams* emerge from *Hiranyagarbha* itself. Don't conclude that only *Swami* is *Hiranyagarbha*. All of you are manifestations of *Hiranyagarbha*. You are also eternal and self-effulgent. Hold this truth firmly in your heart. Keep this awareness firm.

There is gold in every man. Iron and various other metals are also present in him. The ***VEDAS*** declare, *Raso Vai Saha* (God pervades the body in the form of essence). What is the significance of *Lingodbhava* (emergence of the *lingam*)? God is known as *Hiranyagarbha* (one having a golden womb). The golden essence present in His womb undergoes a vigorous churning process and assumes the shape of a *lingam*. *Lingam* means a symbol or a sign. It has no distinctive features like eyes, face, etc. It has neither feet nor head. It can be placed in any manner. It symbolizes the formless Divinity. [8]

What is the meaning of the term *lingam*? It is the symbol of divinity, as it has neither beginning nor end. Divinity is immanent in the *Hridayam* of every man. *Hridayam* means that which is suffused with compassion. So, Divinity is the embodiment of compassion.[9]

REACTION, REFLECTION AND RESOUND

The three principles of reaction, resound and reflection originated from *Hiranyagarbha*. Unable to recognise his true identity, man is wasting his life in the pursuit of temporary, fleeting, transient and ephemeral pleasures. Gold loses its value, effulgence and identity when it is mixed with different metals such as silver, copper, and brass. So also, *Hridayam*, which can be compared to gold, loses its value, brilliance, and identity because of its association with the metals of worldly desires. This is the present plight of the world. Man is behaving like a demon, devil and beast because he has forgotten his divine nature. **Divine**

love originates from *Hiranyagarbha*. This Divine love lives by giving and forgiving, whereas selfish love lives by getting and forgetting. Such Divine love is essential for man. [10]

Are You Creating Good Or Evil?

Hiranyagarbha lives in each human being as full creative potential. When you look around, are you happy with the world that has been created? Whatever has become of the beautiful resources God has given, is fully the reaction, reflection and resound of the collective thoughts of man. If we see bad in others, it is simply a reflection of our own negative qualities. Conversely, the good we see in others is an indication of our own progress towards the light.

Sri Sathya Sai Baba says:

Man is leading a life of a demon unaware of the path of truth, righteousness, peace and love. God has not created creatures such as devils and evil spirits. These are the creations of man. It is just a reflection of the evil qualities within man such as hatred, anger, jealousy, etc. The anger in you is manifesting in the form of a demon. Its power is increasing in proportion to the intensity of anger in you. The evil qualities of man are the real demons troubling him today.

No one else is responsible for the good and bad in an individual. Each one is responsible for his own good and bad. Who is good, who is bad? First eliminate the bad in you. Be in the company of good. It is a sin to point a finger at others when there is mountain of evil within you. Man today is not making an attempt to recognise the innumerable faults in himself, instead he is magnifying the minutest faults in others. In fact, he is searching for mistakes in others with a thousand eyes. This is the sad state of man today. Man is losing his true identity because he has allowed the evil qualities to enter his *Hridayam*. People today are more interested in finding faults, rather than the good in others. He is a true human being who sees only good in others. Unfortunately, today no one is sowing the seeds of love in their *Hridayam*. Then how do you expect the harvest of love?

Follow The *Hridayam*, Not The Head

All negative thoughts are the products of the head. Science and technology are associated with the head. Today technology has become 'tricknology' because you are traversing along with a negative path. What is the use of having intelligence in the absence of positive qualities? Man today has acquired all forms of knowledge, yet he does not know himself. In spite of having acquired various forms of knowledge, a mean-minded person cannot give up his evil qualities. All this worldly knowledge bolsters excessive argumentation, but not total awareness. **After all, one has to die in spite of acquiring all the worldly knowledge; so study that which makes you immortal**. Today the acquisition of the worldly knowledge is on the rise, whereas noble qualities in the *Hridayam* are on the decline.

What is the use of ten acres of barren land? A small piece of fertile land is better than ten acres of barren land. **Develop at least one noble quality, which emerges from the *Hridayam* instead of ten from the head**. All the thoughts that emerge out of the head are useless. Most of the activities of the scientists are based on the head rather than on the *Hridayam*. So your studies also should be under certain limits. Only then you can retain your intelligence and memory power.

The feelings that emerge out of the *Hridayam* are immortal and nectarous. But are you making use of at least one of them? It is enough if you can develop peace. How do you expect to experience peace if you do not cultivate love in the field of your *Hridayam*? Instead of cultivating love, you are cultivating the evil qualities of jealousy and hatred. If some one criticises you, do not take it to the *Hridayam*. Consider it as for your own good. It is the worst of the sins to search for mistakes in others. In the first instance, correct your mistakes and accept the good in others.

Serve Your Fellow Beings

Serve your fellow beings. Taking this path amounts to devotion. Devotion does not mean performing worship and offering flowers to God. Worship amounts to good action alone. One should have good thoughts within. One will not be redeemed if one undertakes good actions with bad intentions. There should be unity in thought, word and deed. "The proper study of mankind is man." This is true humanness. Sage Vyasa declared: "*Paropakara Punyaya Papaya Parapidanam,*" which means "Help Ever, Hurt Never." If possible try to help others. Never hurt anyone. Love even your enemies. Never use harsh words and hurt the feelings of others. If you hurt someone today, you will have to suffer ten times more in the future.

Tread The Inner Path

Vedanta declares: "Know Thyself." A person who follows *Pravritti Marga* (outward path) is interested in collecting information about others and their whereabouts. He keeps asking others, "Who are you?" "Where do you come from?" A person who treads along *Nivritti Marga* (inward path) looks within and enquires, "Who am I?" "Where do I come from?" *Nivritti Marga* is positive and *Pravritti Marga* is negative in nature. How can you expect positive results when your *Hridayam* is full of negative feelings? **The external is the reflection of the internal.** You will reap what you sow. Love, Peace, Compassion, which originate from the *Hridayam*, are positive in nature and generate positive feelings.

Never blame God for your difficulties. Good or bad you are bound to face the consequences of your actions. But if you have God's grace, even bad will be turned into good. So develop faith in God more and more. Do not give scope for bad feelings and bad thoughts: Do not criticise anyone. Slander is the worst of the sins.

Control The Five Senses And Experience Bliss

Ultimately you will realise that mastering the senses is essential for acquiring knowledge of the Self. The five senses are the gift of God. Make proper use of them. Only then can you realise the Self. What is the use of going through sacred texts and undertaking spiritual practices without proper utilisation of the five senses? You should have control over the five senses and put them on the right path, as a result of which you will be experiencing bliss; the human being is born in bliss, sustained in bliss and ultimately merges in it. **Bliss can be experienced by controlling the five senses. This is the true *sadhana*.** Mere chanting of the Lord's name will not suffice.

First and foremost the senses have to be controlled; otherwise you are mixing the metals of worldly desires into your *Hridayam*. As a result, *Hridayam* becomes polluted and loses its true identity, i.e. bliss. Ancients have said that bliss lies in visualising and experiencing your true form, that is, the Principle of *Atma*. Proper utilisation of the senses will lead to the knowledge of *Atma*. Sage Patanjali said, "*Yoga chitta vrithhi nirodhana,*" (the control of senses is true *Yoga*). No *sadhana* is greater than this. All the spiritual practices such as *japa* (chanting of the Lord's name) and *tapas* (penance) will be of no avail if it is not possible for a human being to control the senses. Here control does not mean total cessation. Discharge your duties. But whatever you do, do it with a feeling that it is to please God (*Serva Karma Bhagavath*

Preethyartham). Once you develop this feeling all your senses will naturally be controlled.

The Universe Is Within You

Truly speaking the whole world is contained within you. The body may undergo change, but the Divine principle remains the same. Love never undergoes any change. It always remains as love. The quality of sugar is sweetness. It does not change whether it is added to coffee, tea, water or rice pudding. That which remains changeless is referred to as *Sat* (being). This *Sat* is within you. Love is its sweetness. We have to turn this love towards God, not towards objects of the senses.[11] The process of creation is subtle and cannot be perceived by any of the senses.[12]

What is Creation? Creation means the expression of the Will of God. It is called nature. Everything that has emerged from nature must necessarily have the quality of nature. Man is born to express the quality of nature. **Creation refers to manifestation of thoughts.**[13]

---

1 Vidyalankar, Pandit Satyakam, **The Holy *Vedas*,** Clarion Books, reprint 1998.

2 *Bhagawan* Sri Sathya Sai Baba, "I Am God, You Are God", pamphlet from *Chaitanya Jyothi* Museum.

3 *Bhagawan* Sri Sathya Sai Baba, Divine Discourse, 31/05/1991.

4 *Bhagawan* Sri Sathya Sai Baba, Divine Discourse, 14/02/1999.

5 Kasturi, N., ***Sathyam Sivam Sundaram*,** Part IV.

6 *Bhagawan* Sri Sathya Sai Baba, **Sathya Sai Speaks**, Vol. 6, Ch. 3.

7 *Bhagawan* Sri Sathya Sai Baba, Divine Discourse, 15/02/1999.

8 *Bhagawan* Sri Sathya Sai Baba, Divine Discourse, 13/03/2002.

9 *Bhagawan* Sri Sathya Sai Baba, Divine Discourse, 12/03/2002

10 *Bhagawan* Sri Sathya Sai Baba, Divine Discourse, 15/02/1999.

11 *Bhagawan* Sri Sathya Sai Baba, Divine Discourse, 15/02/1999.

12 *Bhagawan* Sri Sathya Sai Baba, ***Sanathana Sarathi*,** Nov-Dec 1995.

13 *Bhagawan* Sri Sathya Sai Baba, Divine Discourse, 17/02/1996.

chapter - 11

THE *YOGA* PATH OF SELF-REALISATION

The literal meaning of *Yoga* is union of *jiva* with *Purusha* in the human brain. According to Sri Sathya Sai Baba, *jiva* lives in the spine at the level of the 9th, 10th and 11th, vertebrae. *Purusha* (the spark of *Paramatma* in the human body), lives at the level of the mid-brow between the pineal and pituitary bodies. **[See Cover Diagram, Page VII]** It is called *Purusha* or *Atma* in the ***Vedas***, *Neotis* by the Greeks, *Sai Tathwa* by Sufi saints, and many other names in different traditions. To achieve this union we may take the path that most suits us, be it *Jnana, Karma, Bhakti, Raja* or *Hatha Yogas*. This union is called self-realisation, or *Atmajnana* (highest wisdom of the *Atma*). Sai Baba says, "He who knows the *Atma* has learned the knowledge of everything, because the *Atma* is omnipresent."[1]

When we speak about self-realisation, we are face to face with the most profound, constantly repeated phenomenon of religious experience. Again quoting Sai Baba, "A word used by realised souls to describe their experience of God is *Jyothiswarupa* (embodiment of light) meaning 'whose nature is splendourous glory or effulgence, who is illumination itself'. Ten million suns cannot equal the splendour." He continues, "You can see without eyes, hear without ears, speak without tongue, smell without nose, touch without body, walk without legs; yes, even experience without the mind. For you are the Pure Essence Itself; you are the Supreme Self."[2]

"The knowledge of the immortal Self allows you to overcome all suffering and misery; it bestows on you all happiness. You will be ever blissful," *Swami* tells us.[3]

The real cause for this extraordinary state of mental absorption, which in some can be attended by insensibility to the external world or even a cataleptic condition of the body, is still largely unknown by the scientific community. Indeed, understanding is elusive even for those on the spiritual path. Sai Baba says, "When fire burns, its light can be discerned from a distance; but those who are far cannot hope to feel its warmth. So too, it is not easy to describe the splendour of realisation for persons who are far from acquiring it; only those who have actually neared it and felt it and are immersed in it can experience the warmth and the joy emanating from the passing away of illusion."[4]

The views expressed by many able writers on mysticism, as also the testimonies made by sages, saints and mystics themselves, make it clear that in the genuine mystical trance the subject loses, wholly or partially, the awareness of the sensual world. The subject experiences a state of lucidity and self-expansion in which the soul identifies its oneness with God or a Divine Eminence.

Explorers On The Frontiers Of Consciousness

Most seekers after Self-Realisation or God-Realisation have no clear-cut idea of the final goal to which the discipline they are undertaking will lead. They are following a yearning that is indescribable. Nor are they aware that the *samadhi* brought about by *Yoga*, or the ecstatic trance of the Christian mystics, or the *Satori* among the *Zen*, or the state of absorption of the *Sufis,* or the union of *Sakti* with *Siva* of the *Tantrics*, signify, when genuine, the same experience.

The accounts of the saints and sages are so varied. Their experiences are diverse in character – a combination of exaltation and depression, ecstasy and agony, hope and despair, light and darkness. They are explorers on the frontiers of consciousness. Ironically it is their experience of the oneness that is goal of all religious practices, that has fostered the many religions of the world. As Sai Baba says, "Paths are many, goal is one."

The mystical experience is so influenced by the state of health, age, mental disposition and environment of the subject that, in its external features, the phenomenon is not different from the other psychological states of human beings. If mystical ecstasy were only a spirit-to-spirit encounter of formless Divinity, the bodily or mental state of the mystic would not be allowed to colour the experience. But this is not the case. Divine ecstasy is a psychosomatic phenomenon, which can be investigated if approached in the right way.

It is important to understand that the mystical experience involves the whole human being on the physical, psychological and spiritual levels. It is the limbic system – that borderland between the lower "animal" section of the brain and the cerebral cortex – which is the bridge between all these levels. This experience of mystical communion has been misunderstood due to specialists in these various areas of study refusing to collectively take into account all the three perspectives.

Atmajnana - Physical Perspective

Physically considered, communion or *samadhi* is a trance, the depth and time of which can vary. The subject may slide into it gradually from a period of absorption in, or contemplation of his *ishtadevatha* (chosen form of God), which has filled the field of consciousness. It may come on suddenly with the appearance of the *Guru*, or even some word or symbol suggesting a divine idea, immediately moving the subject into an entranced condition. One writer on the physical effects of the mystical experience further suggests that: "During the union, breathing and circulation are depressed. The body is more or less cold or rigid, remaining in the exact position which it occupied at the oncoming of the ecstasy, however difficult and unnatural this pose may be. Sometimes communion is so deep that there is complete anesthesia."

Sri Sathya Sai Baba abides in a state of full God consciousness, beyond the collective experience of Self-Realisation. In *Vedic* parlance, it would be pure *Sat-Chit-Ananda* (being, awareness, bliss), which is simply His nature as *Avatar*. Since birth, Baba has continually transformed His physical body to manifest the Divine Energy. Over the years, devotees have experienced extraordinary physical healings in His presence, jolts of *sakti* and flashes of light. They have seen His glowing aura, and even witnessed Him becoming immobile, immersed in *Sat-Chit-Ananda*, functioning on other planes as no other being can, with full omnipresence, omnipotence and omniscience.

There are also inexperienced seekers who read about the spiritual experience and begin a *yogic* practice without proper guidance of a *Guru* or teacher. The *Kundalini Sakti* in the spine is awakened and this new intense energy can cause the individual's nervous system to simply crack, resulting in mental illness or even insanity.

When knowing how intimately the body and mind are inter-connected, it is not difficult to believe that a mental state, indicating the union with God and filled with unutterable bliss, can be the experience of not only the Soul but also the physical brain. However brief it may be, the transcendental flight of the Soul is reflected in the cerebral matter in some way. The brain itself may even cause a mystical reaction, brought on by intense concentration, constant worship, prayer, extreme longing for Divine vision, or consuming love of God. Even intense, meditative physical activity, like distance running or dancing can trigger a transcendental state. If one is disciplined in *sadhana* (spiritual effort) over long periods of time, new vibrations enter the brain, initiating a process of transformation in the physical matter that is conducive to spiritual experiences. What we're talking about is **communion of the soul with God**, as well as a revolution (or evolution) brought about in the fabric of the brain.[5]

The Human Brain Is A Big Pharmacy

The brain produces many psychochemicals that can lead to divine ecstasy, mental disease or transformation in the human personality and behaviour. Distressing, depressive, or painful mental conditions in an individual can be caused by chemicals released due to a physical disorder of the brain, specifically, the area of the limbic system. Intensely blissful, elevating, and rapturous transport of mystical ecstasy can also be the result of chemicals released due to some physiological, psychological or spiritual event in the endocrine or limbic systems. These conditions could be triggered by an illness, a blow to the head, an extreme emotion or an outside chemical stimulant. In mankind's search for communion with the Divine, many indigenous cultures have developed plant-based hallucinogenic drugs that promote mystical experience. Modern pharmaceutical companies have stepped up to the plate in the last century.

However, as far as medical research is concerned, it is proved that the human brain is the best pharmacy ever devised. It produces diuretics, painkillers, tranquilizers, sleeping pills, antibiotics and bliss inducing endorphins, much more than can ever be manufactured by any drug company – and with much greater refinement. The dosage is always perfect, delivered on time with minimal side effects. And directions for use are given by the Soul.

Atmajnana - Psychological Perspective

The energy generated by spiritual exploration is not to be dealt with lightly or irreverently. On the psychological level, if a human being has not properly cleansed his limbic system with Human Values and pure loving thoughts, he can, unwittingly, attract negative forces from the astral planes which will cling to his mind.

Then there are those individuals who have a desire for magical powers or control over others, which causes them to seek communion with energy forms that are not of the highest order. Working from fear and hate rather than love, they have little respect or understanding of the forces they are dealing with. The thought forms that can attach to this type of person have been called devils and demons. "Like" attracts "like" and they are a reflection of the individual's outwardly projected evil qualities. Sathya Sai Baba says, "All are figments of one's own imagination. God or the devil, good and bad, are denizens of one's own heart. Where God is, there the devil cannot be. It is like the game of 'musical chairs'; only one person can occupy one chair. Seat God forever in your heart after ridding it of other occupants. Let the inert body be activated by Divine Consciousness."

To souls who have surrendered to the Divine, God never fails to communicate high things. When we develop a loving, emotional relationship with God, He will literally reach out to us in the form we have chosen – mother, father, child, sister or brother, friend, lover or spouse. For the devotee who yearns for God as the Beloved, the divine energy can touch them on all levels, physically, spiritually and mentally, as a feminine or masculine presence according to their desires.

It is important to note that the nervous system must be prepared for such ecstatic communion with cosmic forces. Human being is in essence divine, and when *Atma,* living inside the limbic system, meets *Paramatma*, the light can break down the nervous system in the unprepared brain and lead to mental illness. But when the *Hridayam*, which infuses the limbic system, has been purified by prayers, *niskama karma,* compassion, love, forgiveness and Human Values, the brain is ready and open to receive God. This union in the purified brain actually evolves the neurological pathways, allowing for the small self to realise the Self. Worldly wisdom also comes, which can be offered in service to society, evolving the whole human race.

Atmajnana - Spiritual Perspective

Yoga and other spiritual disciplines are designed to create a state of preparedness of the aspirant's brain that makes the ecstasy beneficent and Divine in one case, or maleficent and diabolical in the other. As they make their way along the spiritual path, the same individual can have both types at different times, corresponding to the condition of the brain and mind.

On the path of *yoga*, even pure-minded souls can suffer from diseases. Guru Nanak, Kabirji, Mirabai, Aurobindo, Ramakrishna Paramahamsa, Shankaracharya, Mohammed, St. Francis and St. Clare of Assisi, St. Teresa, St. John of the Cross, and the *Sufi* poets Jami, Jalalludin Rumi, Sultan Bahu, Omar Khyam and Bulle Shah suffered from poor physical health. Their mystical activities reacted upon their bodies in a definite and special way, producing in several cases, a particular kind of illness or physical disability. These maladies are accompanied by pains and functional disturbances where no organic cause could be discovered, unless that cause were the immense strain which an exalted spirit put upon a body adapted to a very different form of life.

Some physical manifestations were the direct result of extreme devotion, as in the case of St. Francis of Assisi who received the *stigmata* (the wounds of Christ) in his hands and feet. Other saintly souls take on the physical *karma* of devotees who have surrendered to them, protecting the disciple from illnesses or accidents that might have proved fatal. *Bhagawan* Sri Sathya Sai Baba has done this on many occasions – currently, and in His previous *avatar* as Sai Baba of Shirdi.

The different *Gurus, rasuls,* saints and sages have had union with God, or as in the case of full *avatars* like Sathya Sai Baba or Sri Krishna, God Consciousness has taken human form. It is the state of wakefulness of these beings that has produced the various religious paths. All these Holy Ones, like Rama, Krishna, Buddha, Mohammed, Zoroaster, Guru Nanak, Sai Baba of Shirdi and Jesus led souls to the same truths through paths appropriate to their place and time. Today, the Supreme Lord, Sri Sathya Sai Baba, is making a different kind of union, creating a *sanathana dharma* (eternal path) joining all religions together and taking all on the inward path to the One God.

The Divine Laws Are Common To All Religions

The basic features of consecrated religious life have always been the same. They can be summed up as follows:

1. Unwavering belief in a higher power
2. Truthfulness (*sathya*)
3. Fellow feeling, brotherhood
4. Purity of heart by adopting Human Values
5. Compassion and a passionate desire for self-conquest
6. Service to humanity (*santi*)

7. Help Ever - Hurt Never *(dharma and ahimsa)*
8. Love All-Serve All with love *(prema)*
9. God is omnipotent, omniscient and omnipresent
10. God is One, experienced as Effulgent Light

Wherever we look, a mosaic of these traits is found to be a common characteristic of the enlightened mind in any part of the earth. How could God who is omnipotent, omniscient and omnipresent be brushed aside in the search for knowledge in recent times? The responsibility of this rather strange behaviour is shared both by religion and science – the former because of its rigid fundamentalism and the latter for over-emphasis on the intellect!

Sri Sathya Sai Baba says:

He is in you, and it is God that has prompted you to project Him into the outer world as this idol or that image, to listen to your outpouring and give you peace. Without the inspiration, solace and joy that He confers from within, you will be raving mad, as one who has lost his moorings and is tossed about, rudderless on a stormy sea. Hold on to Him in the heart, hear Him whisper in the silent words of counsel and consolation. Hold conversation with Him, guide your footsteps as He directs, and reach the goal, safe and soon. The picture before which you sit, the flowers which you place on it, the hymns you recite, the vows you impose on yourselves and the vigils you go through, are activities that cleanse and remove obstacles in the way of your becoming aware of the God within.[6]

The Cosmic Mind And Human Mind

Sri Aurobindo writes, "We can no more divide the mind into conscious and unconscious parts. The mind has a cosmic dimension in which our individual minds are like drops of water in an ocean, or extremely slender beams of light radiating from a gigantic sun. Our mind knows all about us for it is the intelligence *(buddhi)* within us, while we know only as much as we are permitted, according to the capacity of the brain. How it has been assumed that each individual mind is restricted to one particular body, in two divisions, the upper and the lower, is a riddle.

How then can it be supposed that mind, subtler than all of them, can stay in isolated units, clinging to the highly porous mortal frame of each living creature, without intermingling with the surrounding fields? The position remains unaffected whether the mind is considered to be a chance product of organic activity or as a self-existing constituent of the Universe. It also remains unaffected whether it is held to be incorporeal, etheric or organic in its composition."[7]

HEREDITY NEEDS TRANSFORMATION

Our constitution or heredity needs correction, i.e, transformation. *Vedanta* teaches that our mind is a bundle of desires. These desires are carried over from previous births as patterns of thought, habit and emotion that infuse our DNA and RNA, impelling our actions and shaping our destiny. They are called *vasanas*. An entire chapter is given on this subject in my earlier book, ***VEDANTIC* METHOD AND VIRTUOUS CHILDREN**. The DNA and RNA can be changed and the *vasanas* reprogrammed by cleansing the limbic system. Success in this takes great effort – and a *Guru*. Sathya Sai Baba writes: "The *Atma* principle is beyond the reach of even the most profound *pundit* who has learned the *Sastras;* it can be understood only by direct experience. That is why it is said that even a person who has had the vision has to approach the *Guru*. Without guidance from such a teacher the *Atma* cannot be grasped."[8]

On the search for self-realisation, it is the blessed *jivas* who get a true *Guru* as guide through the inner landscape. How many thirsty souls have followed one path after another, some genuine, others fraudulent, in search of God and truth? Sathya Sai Baba, whose name is Truth Itself, is now offering the safe path of practical Human Values to those who are ready to be free from negative qualities, turn towards love and achieve union of the self with the Self.

This experience of *yoga* (union with the Divine) is only a reflection of our own *Hridayam* purified through the Human Values. The methods prescribed by Sai Baba through the teaching and application of **Educare** and **Education in Human Values (EHV)** now in place in His numerous institutions and internationally throughout the Sri Sathya Sai Organisation, have proved effective in this process. EHV training guides children and adults to refine their character through *sathya, dharma, santi, prema* and *ahimsa*, to practise unity of thought, word and action, and thereby experience the truth of the Divinity latent in all human beings. Baba tells us that realisation of the *Atma* is the birthright of humanity.

Gopikrishna writes: "We have still to grasp the colossal mystery surrounding our existence. Just as by constant attention to and study of the **external world** we were able to make the amazing progress in the knowledge of matter, of which the fruits are before our eyes, in the same manner by constant attention to and study of the **inner world** we can make progress in the knowledge of the spirit of which, too, the rich harvest will be no less commensurate with the effort made."[9]

The human perceives *Prakriti* (nature) through the *Pancha Jnanendriyas* (Five Sense Organs) and the *Pancha Karamendriyas* (Five Working Organs). He has sensual experiences, develops body-consciousness, habits and attachments. He stores these sense memories in the brain, believing this to be the truth. When he or she begins to cleanse the senses through Human Values, the impermanence of sense objects becomes clear. They no longer thrill, and with God's grace, the little self begins to actively practise one of the *yogic* paths. The outward gaze turns inward, the limbic system is gradually cleansed and the *vasanas* wiped out as sensual memories and desires are replaced with an experience of cosmic truth. The self sees though the eyes of the soul, discovering at last that inner and outer perceptions are simply reflections of the same pure consciousness.

Sri Sathya Sai Baba says:

> *This nature is but an infinitesimal fraction of this glory; yet you feel content with the pleasure it gives, the knowledge you gather about it, the wonder it reveals. The reflection of* ***Siva*** *(God) in the mirror of nature is* ***jiva*** *(individual consciousness). Self-realisation is the moment you see your own beauty and are so filled with it that you forget all else, you are free from all bonds. Know that you are all the beauty, all the glory, all the power, all the magnitude of the universse.*

---

1 *Bhagawan* Sri Sathya Sai Baba, ***Jnana Vahini.***

2 *Bhagawan* Sri Sathya Sai Baba, ***Jnana Vahini.***

3 *Bhagawan* Sri Sathya Sai Baba, Discourses on the Bhagavad Gita.

4 *Bhagawan* Sri Sathya Sai Baba, ***Jnana Vahini.***

5 Gopikrishna, **Wonders of the Brain**.

6 *Bhagawan* Sri Sathya Sai Baba, recorded in **My Baba and I**, by Dr. John Hislop.

7 Aurobindo, **The Life Divine.**

8 *Bhagawan* Sri Sathya Sai Baba, ***Jnana Vahini.***

9 Gopikrishna, **Wonders of the Brain**.

chapter - 12

YOGA AND ITS MEDICAL APPLICATIONS

The pure soul, cleansed through the control of breath and meditation soon attains salvation and becomes one with God through ***yogic samadhi****.*

~ ***Atharva Veda***

Sri Sathya Sai Baba stresses the fact that eight limbs of Yoga have been prescribed by Sage Patanjali in his ***Yoga Sutras*** for man to enjoy health and happiness. These eight are *Yama, Niyama, Asana, Pranayama, Prathyahara, Dharana, Dhyana,* and *Samadhi*, which are detailed below. The text states explicitly that *Yoga* is not just for the ochre clad monks, renunciates in the forest and mountain climates. Modern investigations show that in today's machine age, it is the ordinary man who actually needs *yoga* the most. Man struggles the whole day to feed and foster his family; this effort makes him restless and robs him of his sleep. He then resorts to artificial means to induce sleep and give rest to the body, like sleeping pills or intoxicating drinks. These artificial inducements have disastrous side effects and when combined with the lack of rest, cause heart disease, high blood pressure, etc. The researchers have hence concluded that *yoga* is ideally suited for all these problems. Modern man needs to create a life of balance, which is what *yoga* offers.

The Misfortune Of India

Sri Sathya Sai Baba says:

The sacred texts have been born in India, but due to the rise of blind beliefs that are consequences of modern education and civilisation, Indians show scant interest or belief in these works of brilliance. It is the misfortune of Indians that today these sacred texts are much more fostered and believed abroad, because these people are quick to realise their importance. Now people have investigated and understood that due to lack of rest, the body weakens. This causes the breathing process to speed up. This in turn spoils the lungs. As the blood circulation also speeds up, a stage arrives when high blood pressure sets in. Medicine cannot cure it completely and hence *yoga* is prescribed. This has been a finding supported by researchers at the **International University in America** and some others at the **University of Hawaii**. Some of these researchers even reversed their views on *yoga* after seeing the positive results of their studies.

Yoga For Health And Happiness

It is shown that the bliss and vitality enjoyed after two hours of sleep can be achieved by just twelve minutes of *yoga*. Though man can adjust without food, he cannot do the same without sleep and rest. Lack of sleep is a common problem in many countries, including India. This extracts a heavy toll on one's health. To achieve the four goals of life, *Dharma*, *Artha*, *Kama* and *Moksha,* a healthy mind and body is essential.[1]

There is an increase in the number of people suffering from physical ailments and mental maladies all over the world. Experiments were conducted on prisoners in a jail in Mexico to find out the exact cause for the rapid rise in mental patients amongst the inmates. They concluded after thorough investigation that the problem was caused not by food, but by tension and worry. The professors made the prisoners undergo *yogic* practices to rid them of mental tension. In a short time the patients became normal. They not only made a total recovery, but gained great happiness due to the practice of *yoga*. Additional investigations showed *yoga* induced addicts to give up their habits of drugs, smoking and drinking. So many lakhs of people have begun to practise *yoga* abroad that it has become a global event.[2]

Importance Of Discipline

Yoga prescribes some major disciplines as pre-requisites for deriving its benefits, notably with respect to diet. The food taken is to be both *Mita* and *Hita*, i.e. both limited and nutritious. Since food and water are only "medicines" to cure the ailment of hunger and thirst, they must be taken in that spirit—**taste should not be the yardstick to eat food,** for it is only to protect the body that one eats, after all. Foreigners have realised this and have found that by reducing *chilis*, salt, tamarind, etc. from their diet and by limited eating, they can stay healthy. Sage Patanjali states that excess food weakens the nerves, causing blood pressure problems. Man becomes prone to excitement easily.

Lack of health among men also causes agitation and restlessness in society. In Germany, research conducted on monkeys showed that when the primates practised sitting silently for three to four hours daily, they soon became very intelligent, developed their memory, became highly enthusiastic, and in some cases even more than man. A similar experiment on a student considered a dullard and roguish, showed that with the help of *yoga*, in just a few months, the boy has become one of the most intelligent and well-behaved boys. Being encouraged, even the boy's 70-year-old father began to practise *yoga*. Soon his body was functioning with the vitality of a 50-year-old man.[3]

Human Values In *Vedanta* And *Astanga Yoga*

Sri Sathya Sai Baba has suggested:

How are human qualities to be promoted in society? Society is made up of individuals. None can be an island to himself; living amidst fellow human beings, man has to sow the seeds of love, rear the plants of harmony, and offer the fruits of peace to society. Thereby his humanness is manifested. In *Astanga Yoga* (the Eight-Fold *Yoga*) **[See Chart No. 25]** the disciplines are:

1. *Yama* (Ethical Disciplines)

Yama figures as the first among the different disciplines. These are five Human Values to be cultivated, in the language of *Vedanta:*

a. ***AHIMSA*** (non-violence): This does not mean, as is commonly understood, not causing harm to others. It really means that one should not cause harm to anyone in thought as well as word and deed. This is the most important human quality. Only when this has been developed one will be qualified to practise and experience Truth.

b. ***SATHYA*** (truth): This does not mean merely telling the facts as one sees or knows them. Truth is that which does not change with time. It must be spoken with complete purity of mind, speech and body.

c. ***ASTHEYA*** (non-stealing): This means refraining from stealing what belongs to others. Even the thought of taking another's property should not arise in the mind, nor should one tell others to commit theft. This is the third human value.

d. ***BRAHMACHARYA*** (celibacy): Observance of this means that whatever one thinks, says, or does should be filled with thoughts of *Brahman*. Thus, to be ever immersed in this consciousness is *Brahmacharya*. When the thoughts, which are the prelude to action, are centered on God, they are unlikely to go astray. *Aham* (the Ego) arises from the *Atma*. Thoughts are produced by the ego and give rise to speech. Hence, all actions are based on the *Atma*. All thoughts, desires and speech emanate from the *Atma*. When all these are sanctified by dedication to God, the consciousness *Aham Brahmasmi* ("I am *Brahman*") ensues. That *Brahman* is *Prajna* (constant integrated awareness).

e. ***APARIGRAHA*** (non-acquisitiveness): It is usually interpreted as not accepting another's property as gift or gratuity. This however is not the correct meaning. It really means performing actions without expecting any reward, without any acquisitive motives, and in a complete selfless spirit. Today, because all actions are done out of self-interest and desire for acquiring wealth, they lack true human quality. Even worship, religious ceremonies, pilgrimages and the like are done with some kind of expectations and not in a spirit of disinterested devotion. People today are totally immersed in self-interest. By multiplying desires without limit they become demonic. They are not content with having what they need for essential purposes. They wish to accumulate enormously for the future. They are filled with worries and discontent. Thereby they forfeit their happiness here and in the hereafter. Birds and beasts are content to live on what they can get. Man alone is afflicted with insatiable desires. Birds and animals have no desires to hoard or to exploit others. But man is a prey to these vices. He forgets his natural human qualities and behaves worse than animals. When these tendencies are given up, the inherent Divinity in man will manifest itself.[4]

Chart No. 25 ~ *Astanga Yoga*

Limb	Practices
YAMA **Ethical Disciplines**	1. *Ahimsa* - non-violence
	2. *Sathya* - truth
	3. *Astheya* - non-stealing
	4. *Bramacharya* - celibacy
	5. *Aparigraha* - non-aquisitiveness
NIYAMA **Rules of Conduct**	1. *Saucha* - purity
	2. *Santosha* - contentment
	3. *Tapas* - austerity or penance
	4. *Swadhyaya* - self-enquiry
	5. *Iswar Pranidhana* - dedicating one's actions to God
ASANA **Posture**	The complete *yoga asana* posture flow
PRANAYAMA **Control of Breath**	1. *Puraka* - inhalation
	2. *Kumbhaka* – retention, holding
	3. *Rechaka* - exhalation
PRATYAHARA **Turning inwards, away from the senses**	1. *Sakara* - worship of God with form
	2. *Nirakara* - worship of formless God
	3. *Atmanabhava* - realising the bliss of the *Atma*

*Communion with the Divine is True **Yoga**. All other **yogic** practices are merely physical exercises.*

~ **Sri Sathya Sai Baba**

LIMB	**PRACTICES**
DHARANA **One-pointed concentration**	1. *Ksipta* - mind is scattered, desiring objects of the world
	2. *Viksipta* – mind is agitated and distracted, attached to the fruits
	3. *Mudha* – foolish, dull, stupid
	4. *Ekagra* – mental faculties concentrated on a single object
	5. *Niruddha* – *manas* (mind), *buddhi* (intellect), and *ahamkara* (ego) are all restrained and offered to the Lord
DHYANA **Meditation**	1. Concentration
	2. Contemplation
	3. Meditation
SAMADHI **Oneness with God, equal-mindedness**	"When the senses fall away and there is only God." ~ ***BABA***
SOURCE: Divine Discourses of *Bhagawan* Sri Sathya Sai Baba	

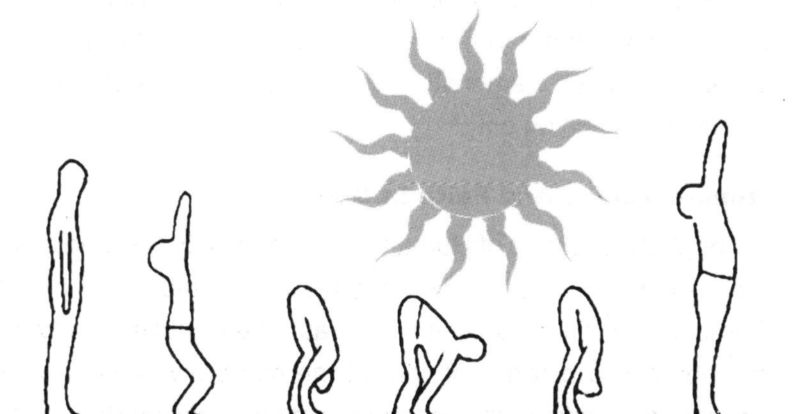

2. *Niyama* (Rules Of Conduct)

Niyamas are codes of conduct that help an individual to develop personal discipline and discrimination and cultivate Human Values.

According to *Maharishi* Patanjali, the five Niyamas are:

a. *Saucha* (purity)
b. *Santosha* (contentment)
c. *Tapas* (austerity or penance)
d. *Swadhyaya* (self-enquiry)
e. *Iswar Pranidhana* (dedicating one's actions to the Lord)[5]

Sri Sathya Sai Baba stresses the importance of developing one's personality and character:

Human values cannot be promoted merely by repeating the words *Sathya, Dharma, Santi, Prema* and *Ahimsa*. The ***VEDAS*** declare: *"Sathyam Vada, Dharmam Chara"* (Speak the Truth, adhere to *Dharma*, the right conduct). In practising *Dharma*, there should be no *marma* (secret Desires). Actions performed with such secret motives result in bondage. Truth and right conduct should be adhered to with pure intentions. Both of them are rooted in the eternal. A righteous life leads to peace. Love is to be experienced in the depths of peace. Love should find expression in non-violence. Where love prevails, there is no room for doing harm or violence to others. All these basic values are to be demonstrated in actions and must not be limited to preaching only.[6]

Human Values And Faith In God

Through the practice of Human Values and all types of *yogas*, the aspirant is able to have a glimpse into their own Soul. Perhaps it first makes itself known as a new subtle energy in the heart or a pinprick of light at the mid-brow. Slowly, with continued practice, this communication is expanded. The awareness increases, the light gets brighter strengthening the faith that – yes, God is there, and is the *Atmajyothi,* the effulgent light of the Soul.

Sri Sathya Sai Baba says:

Human virtues cannot be acquired from others. They cannot be nourished by the mere study of books, nor can they be acquired ready-made from teachers. They have to be cultivated by each person and the resulting joy has to be personally experienced. Today, the world sorely needs Human Values. Attempts are being made to promote these values in the field. But they cannot be promoted through materialistic, worldly or scientific means. Without developing devotion to God, no human quality can grow. Therefore, the first requisite is **faith in God**. Doubts are raised whether God exists or not. Those who affirm that God exists and those who deny Him are equally incompetent to say something about God, as they know nothing about His Nature. To assert of the existence of that which does not exist is ignorance. To deny the existence of that which does exist is folly. God is omnipresent. There is no need to search for Him anywhere. Wherever we are, there is God. There can be no greater folly than to deny the existence of God when the whole cosmos bears witness to His handiwork. **Everything in creation must be viewed as a manifestation of God.** Only with this basic faith can one develop one's personality.

Angarpanam

Yoga prescribes a process called ***Angarpanam*** as the method to achieve Divine thoughts. *Angarpanam* means to offer one's limbs and organs to the Lord. It does not mean to cut them off and place them at the Lord's feet. It means to use these limbs and organs only in actions that will please God. This is where the importance of discrimination is stressed in *yoga*. When such *Angarpanam* is done real bliss results. Bliss is related to the *Hridayam*. But when used in pursuit of sensual pleasures only, happiness results. This is called *santosha*, as it means *some-tosha* or limited happiness. This *santosha* is related to the head, the centre of responsibility. Hence, one must take care to think well, contemplate on the thought and then put it into action. This is the real EHV (Education in Human Values) – the values of **Head**, **Heart** and **Hands**; it is the unity of thought, word and deed.[7]

3. *Asana* (Posture)

The series of postures so often associated with *yoga* in the mind of the layman were evolved by the ancients of India and are designed to exercise every muscle, nerve, gland and organ in the body. Regular practice of *yoga asana* in conjunction with *pranayama* reduces fatigue, releases toxins, soothes the nervous system and helps to keep the body free from disease. The practice of *asana* is truly a meditation in motion. Through focused concentration an alignment is made between body, breath, senses, intellect and soul. This purifies the senses, limbic system and *Hridayam* and opens the channels to receive Divinity. The aim is not to perfect posture, but to perfect Presence. *Asana* in conjunction with *pranayama* calms body and mind, making the individual a better vehicle for the greater union with the Divine. The true *yogi* has united body, breath, mind and conscious awareness in the present moment, which leads to being in the Presence of God. This kind of integrated practice is one of the foundations of a long and balanced life and most definitely leads to Total Health. The practice of *Hatha Yoga*, which focuses on *asana*, has become a global phenomenon in the last decade; as such it is critical to find an experienced *Guru* to avoid injury and promote the practice of consciousness as well as exercise.

4. *Pranayama* (Control Of Breath)

The practice of regulation of the breath has such a positive influence over both physical and mental health and spiritual development that a large portion of this chapter is dedicated to the subject. Note that although there are several exceptions, the majority of breathing exercises are done only through the nose.

About *Pranayama*, Sri Sathya Sai Baba says:

Pranayama is the tapping of cosmic energy – the *pranic* life giving energy. There are two types: the one with *mantra* and the one without. Without *mantra*, it at best transforms the body, but with *mantra* it transforms the mind also. If practised with faith and feeling, *pranayama* will tame the agitations of the mind; otherwise it becomes mere physical exercise, improving physical health.[8]

This *yoga* consists of three parts; each is to be done one after the other. It starts with *Puraka*, then *Kumbhaka* and finishes with *Rechaka*.

- ***PURAKA*** is the inhalation of breath. One must note carefully the time taken for this process; the duration of time can be justified as per the capacity of the person. Care must be taken to see that gasping and such kinds of exhaustion do not occur during the process.
- ***KUMBHAKA*** consists of the breath that is taken in, which must be retained for the same duration as it has taken for the inhalation process.
- ***RECHAKA*** means exhalation of withholding breath. Once thus retained, it must be exhaled in the same time limit that it has taken for both the inhalation and retention.

While doing *Pranayama*, one must not concentrate or aim to hold the breath for as long as possible. One must instead, concentrate on assuring that all the three processes take the same amount of times. Otherwise, this process spoils the lungs. Practice under the direction of an inexperienced teacher can also prove to be dangerous.

Caution is advised to monitor the time factor during the *Pranayama*, taking into consideration the individual capacity. It should be performed with meticulous care, lest it damages the lungs and the brain. Breathing should also be without any strain or panting. As we have to keep the ingredients for cooking in proper proportion to ensure proper cooking, so also inhalation, retention and exhalation should be in proper proportion.[9]

Pranayama ~ Physiological Considerations

For the following analysis, I am in debt to my teachers at Lonavala *Yoga* Centre in Bhopal and the teachings of B. K. S. Iyengar.

ORGANS OF ELIMINATION. Starting with the organs of elimination, we find that the **Bowels** and the **Kidneys** are situated in the abdomen and the **Lungs** in the chest. In normal respiration the alternate rises and falls of the diaphragm and the alternate contraction and relaxation of the abdominal muscles give constant movement and gentle massage to the bowels and the kidneys. During the breathing technique of *Pranayama*, the movement and massage are much more accentuated. If there is any congestion, it is relieved by the pressure exerted through *Pranayama*. It tones up all the nerves and muscles, which control the functions of the bowels and the kidneys. Thus, the bowels and the kidneys derive benefit not only during the time that *Pranayama* is being practised, but also throughout the day. The nerves and muscles once toned up continue maintaining that tone for a considerably long time.

Consequently, the bowels and kidneys are rendered healthier due to *Pranayama* and carry out the function of elimination more effectively.

The same is the case with the Lungs. Healthy respiration depends upon strong respiratory muscles and good elasticity of the lungs. On the physical side, *Pranayama* is a method of strengthening these muscles and lungs. By fully expanding the chest several times a day and by stretching the lungs to the utmost, the organs are strengthened to efficiently perform their functions. What is true in the case of bowels and kidneys is true of the lungs. The training given to them for a short time prepares them for efficient work throughout the remainder of the day. Thus, *Pranayama* is a very valuable exercise for all the organs of elimination.

ORGANS OF DIGESTION AND ABSORPTION. The organs of digestion and absorption are not different as far as the effects of *Pranayama* on them are concerned. The Stomach, the Pancreas and the Liver, which play a very prominent part in the digestion of food and drink, are also exercised in *Pranayama*, as a result of the massage given to them by the diaphragm and the abdominal muscles. In a very large number of people who are dyspeptic and constipated, the liver becomes habitually congested and consequently faulty in function. For relieving this congestion *Pranayama* is an excellent exercise. An unhealthy pancreas gets very good stimulation and exercise with *Pranayama*. Many cases of gastric disorders have been effectively relieved through *Pranayama*. With a perfectly functioning digestive system, absorption is aided and the blood is enriched with the necessary nutritive elements. As discussed in the previous section, a liberal supply of oxygen in the circulating blood is of supreme importance for the health of the body. This supply is effectively improved by means of

Pranayama, as it is capable of improving the oxygen supply of the blood as no other exercise can do.

One might assume that through *Pranayama* greater quantities of oxygen get absorbed, but this is not the case, as will be explained. If *Pranayama* is done correctly, then every round of breath (inhale-hold/exhale-hold) should take at least one minute. During normal inspiration, an average person inhales about 7,000ml of air in one minute with approximately 16 to l8 rounds of breath. The same individual, during *Pranayama*, will inhale at the most 3,700ml of air in one minute with one round of breath. The total intake of air is far less with *Pranayama* and results in lesser amounts of oxygen absorbed. The degree of absorption of oxygen does not vary in proportion to the time of the breath that is retained. For this reason when the breath is held even for half a minute, the increase in the absorption of oxygen over the normal absorption is not considerable. Thus, it is not true that an individual absorbs larger quantities of oxygen during *Pranayama*.

Where then is the advantage of practising *Pranayama* for enriching the blood with oxygen? It is through *Pranayamic* exercises that you train the respiratory apparatus, which results in more efficient respiration throughout the day causing greater quantities of oxygen to be absorbed than ordinarily would be the case.

CIRCULATORY SYSTEM. With the efficient functioning of the organs of digestion, elimination and respiration, the quality of the blood remains satisfactory. Now this blood is to be distributed to the different tissues of the body. This is the duty of the circulatory system and especially of the heart. The changes of pressure that are produced around the heart during *Pranayama* have been carefully studied and, during the technique, conditions are much more favourable for this massage than with the Western type of deep breathing. The massage given to the heart makes it healthier, enhancing the performance of the Circulatory System. However, the matter does not end here. During one type of *Pranayama, Bastrika,* that features forceful exhalations of breath, the vibrations start and spread themselves to nearly every tissue in the human organism, such as the arteries, veins and capillaries. Thus, the entire circulatory system is exercised and massaged and is prepared for efficient functioning.

NERVOUS AND ENDOCRINE SYSTEMS. Next, we come to the Nervous and the Endocrine Systems. The rich quality of blood and its satisfactory distribution to all the nerves and glands ensure their health. During *Pranayama*, especially during *Bastrika*, the circulation of the blood becomes very rapid and the quality of the blood rendered is very rich. This richer and more liberal blood supply brought to the endocrine glands makes them healthier. The same is the case with the brain, spinal cord, and the cranial, spinal nerves, and sympathetic nerves.

A richer and more liberal blood supply is not the only advantage the nervous system gets from *Pranayama*. The nerves themselves are directly exercised. During inhalation, the diaphragm is contracted and lowered and the abdominal muscles are kept controlled and slightly contracted. The combined action of the diaphragm and the abdominal muscles pulls up the lower part of the spinal column. If *Jalandhara Bandha* (where the neck and throat are pressed firmly against the chest) is practised, the upper part of the spinal column is also pulled up. This pulling up of the vertebral column as a whole gives exercise to the sympathetic nervous system and to the roots of the spinal nerves. The entire nervous system is very exquisitely exercised by the practice of *Pranayama*. Thus the nervous and the endocrine systems, which are of supreme importance in human physiology, and also the respiratory, the circulatory and the digestive systems, upon which the health of the first two systems depends, are all simultaneously exercised in *Pranayama*.[10]

Pranayama ~ For Cleansing All Body Organs

Pranayama was used as a routine therapy by the ancient Indian *rishis* for chronic pulmonary pathology, chronic heart disease, skin diseases and mental diseases.

The function of the lungs is to provide the blood with enough oxygen to nourish all the cells of the body. This depends essentially on two factors: (1) Ventilation, and (2) Perfusion. All chronic pulmonary pathologies encroach upon one or the other of these factors.

VENTILATION. Healthy breathing depends on the elasticity of the respiratory muscles. In *Pranayama* the muscles of the chest are strengthened and stretched to the maximum and the lungs opened to their limit. They are thus better prepared to carry out their functions of breathing in nourishment in the form of oxygen, and breathing out waste materials and toxins in the form of carbon dioxide.

PERFUSION. Oxygen feeds the blood. Blood feeds and irrigates the tissues. The quantity and quality of nourishment the body receives depends on the efficiency of the respiratory system. Insufficient breathing reduces the absorption of oxygen into the blood, leading to undernourishment in the tissues. The tissues are also less irrigated, which allows more toxins to build up. Without this exchange, the body simply cannot function at peak performance. This eventually leads to a decline in health.

KRIYA YOGA. This is a simple psycho-physiological method by which human blood is decarbonized and recharged with oxygen. The atoms of extra oxygen are transmuted into the life current to rejuvenate the brain and spinal centres. In this practice, the yogi is effectively stopping the accumulation of venous blood, thereby preventing decay of tissues.

Role Of *Pranayama* In Pulmonary Pathology

1. It inflates all the alveoli of the lungs from the top to bottom.
2. It expectorates phlegm collected in the trachea, bronchi and alveoli, leading to a clearing out of air passages.
3. In asthmatic cases, it soothes the ragged breathing and creates a mental calmness. Continued practice can even heal completely.
4. In bronchitis, it exercises the expectoration from the bronchi leading to a complete cure.
5. It improves general circulation of the blood in the body, which accelerates the healing of any pulmonary pathology.

Basic Rules Of Practice

1. It should be done in a state of complete relaxation.
2. The stomach should be empty.
3. In the beginning it should be done under the guidance of a master. This is particularly advisable for people suffering from hypertension.
4. The air around the venue must be fresh.
5. Avoid places where the air is full of dust, petrol and strong or cold drafts.
6. Ideal timings are early morning or bedtime.
7. The ideal postures are *padmasana* (lotus pose) or cross-legged, seated comfortably in a straight chair or lying down on the back.

8. It is very important to keep the spine, neck and head in straight alignment from the base of the spine to the crown of the head.
9. Breath should be rhythmic and regular.
10. Breath is always through the nose, unless otherwise indicated. The small screen of hair inside the nostrils prevents impurities, dust, harmful gases and even minute insects from entering the body. There is a Hindu saying: **The nose is to breathe; the mouth is to eat and to speak only when necessary.**

Practice Of *Pranayama*

There is a mathematical relationship between man's respiratory rate and the variations in his states of consciousness. A person whose attention is wholly engrossed in following an argument under hot discussion or in attempting some delicate physical work automatically breathes very slowly, enhancing concentration. In the same way, the practice of *pranayama* enhances awareness and concentration of our inner realities, beginning with the physical body.

Fixing attention depends on slow and even breathing. Quick or ragged breath is an inevitable accompaniment of harmful emotional states like fear, anger, lust or jealousy. When you are compassionate, tolerant and feeling selfless love, your breath slows down, sending these soothing vibrations throughout the body and into the environment.

The restless monkey breaths at the rate of 32 times a minute, in contrast to 18 times on average for man. Animals like the elephant, tortoise, snake and others noted for long life, breathe at a much slower rate than man. The giant tortoise, who can attain ages of 300 years or more, breathes about 4 times per minute. *Yogis,* who breathe very slowly, know that the slower the breath rate, the longer the life.

THE COSMIC BREATH. The cosmic breath is the slowest of all. Manifested creation came into being through the out-breath of God with the *pranava* (first sound), AUM. It is said that as the Creator breathes in, He is drawing us back into Himself.

Pranayama is an excellent way to silence the mind and connect with the Infinite. Meditation on the mid-brow, *Ajnachakra* in the area of the third eye, while practising *pranayama*, draws down energy from the Cosmos through the *Hirdayam* to the limbic system in the brain. It is then distributed to all body organs and the mind through the system of *chakras* and *nadis* as well as the nervous and endocrine systems. In addition to its vast healing properties, *Pranayama* allows us to reach deeper states of inner awareness, attuning our small breath to the great, subtle Cosmic breath and thereby attaining *Samadhi*, true union with God.

THE COMPLETE *YOGIC* BREATH (3-PART BREATH). This combines the three types of breathing, from the abdomen, thorax and upper chest. The breath is drawn into the lower belly, then thorax, and then upper chest. It is exhaled in reverse, first releasing the air from the upper chest, then thorax, and then lower abdomen. The pattern is repeated, forming a flowing wave-like motion.

The lungs must be totally filled up, allowing the maximum quantity of oxygen and *prana sakti* to be drawn in. *Yogis* feel that such breathing ensures a long life, unflagging vitality and great power of resistance to diseases. In addition, it builds up the essential force a man needs for spiritual development.

SIMPLE RHYTHMIC BREATHING. Rest your hands gently on the knees. Inhale as in complete *yogic* breathing, mentally counting 6 heartbeats, then slowly exhale again through the nostrils, also to the count of 6.

A variation features a holding breath. Breathe in for 6, hold for 3, out for 6, hold for 3. (6:3:6:3) Repeat.

Once rhythmic breathing becomes automatic, we start to feel that each inhalation transmits vitality to the tiniest fibers of the body, rejuvenating the cells. Eventually, we shall feel that the whole body is breathing, with all the molecules moving harmoniously in the same direction.

ABDOMINAL BREATHING. The easiest method is to place the hand on the abdomen to feel its movement. During inhalation the abdomen should be allowed to expand a bit, and then sink back during exhalation.

This is an excellent internal massage of all the abdominal organs. It regulates the intestinal track, relieves constipation and stimulates digestion.

THORACIC BREATHING. Put the hand on either side of the lungs without pressing, inhale slowly, then exhale, like an accordion.

This purifies the blood, improves circulation and calms the heart. Angina patients can use this breathing at the onset of an attack. There will not be a second.

UPPER CHEST BREATHING. Put the hands of each side of the clavicle, touching it with the fingers. Contract the stomach slightly. Inhale slowly, as you push the clavicle upwards, exhaling while pressing it down. Repeat.

This thoroughly cleans and fortifies the upper portion of the lungs.

SIMPLE DEEP BREATHING WITH *SO-HAM*. Inhale as deeply and fully as your lungs permit, fixing your gaze within at the mid-brow. Sri Sathya Sai Baba advises: "In practice one says *'SO'* with every in-breath and *'HAM'* with every out-breath. Say it in your mind (mentally). It is intended to keep the mind fixed and quiet. After a while it becomes automatic. During the day, say *'SO-HAM'*. At night during sleep the sound naturally changes to *'AUM'*. It is not an Indian word or an American word. It is the sound of what the breath is saying. When the mind is without movement and the breath is perfectly in rhythm, spontaneous and natural, the sound of that breath (through the nostril) is *'SO-HAM'*."

TECHNIQUE TO PURIFY THE RESPIRATORY TRACK. This exercise is performed standing with the knees soft and the legs slightly apart. Inhale slowly through the nose, as in the Complete *Yogic* Breath while raising the arms overhead vertically. Hold the breath for a few seconds, then lean forward, allowing the arms to hang down loosely, while exhaling forcefully through the mouth. This will produce an "aaahhh" sound as the air is suddenly expelled from the lungs. Slowly straighten the body while again raising the arms above the head as you breathe in deeply through the nose. Exhale through the nose as you lower the arms. Relax for a moment, then repeat.

This enlivens the circulation, clears the lungs and sends a feeling of vitality and warmth throughout the body. This exercise is excellent at relieving depression. It strengthens the mind, helping it to resist outside influences.

VARIATION FOR BEDRIDDEN PATIENTS. Lying on the back, inhale deeply and slowly, as in the Complete *Yogic* Breath, while stretching the arms out behind the head.

Hold the breath for several seconds. Quickly bring the knees up to the chest, pressing them firmly against the abdomen while exhaling with the "aaahhh" sound through the mouth. After a few seconds, inhale slowly through the nose, again lifting the arms behind the head, while straightening out the legs. Exhale through the nose, while lowering the arms. Relax for a moment and then repeat.[11]

The effects of these practices can be profound. It is therefore advisable for anyone desiring a deeper experience of *pranayama* and *asana* to seek the guidance of a trained *yoga Guru*.

5. *Pratyahara* (Turning Inwards, Away From The Senses)

This is the practice of withdrawing the *Karmendriyas* and the *Jnanendriyas* from the external objective world and turning them towards the internal mental consciousness, the *Chit*. Becoming aware "that the external world is *Maya*-born and *Maya*-sustained will provide the motive force to withdraw the senses," says Sai Baba, which "frees the mind for uninterrupted meditation on the inner world." It is the sense organs and our attachment to the things they perceive that cause joy, sorrow and unsteadiness. Controlling them through the practice of *pratyahara* is imperative if one wants to attain a vision of the *Atma*. Sai Baba says, "You have to do some spiritual exercises. Constant practice and detachment are essential for gaining control over the senses. If you understand that all things are impermanent, you will be able to gain control over your senses and develop detachment ... the primary basis for all sacred action and for enjoying a worry-free life is control of the senses."[12]

6. *Dharana* (One-Pointed Concentration)

Sri Sathya Sai Baba says:

Even if students find *Pranayama* difficult, they can still do *Dharana*. It is the single-pointed concentration on some chosen object. It is not very difficult. If practised well, it easily leads us on to *Dhyana*. It is said that with the power of *yoga*, one can control anything, including the evil in any form, from entering the mind through the senses. Senses are like doors to a house through which only authorised personnel may enter. *Yoga* helps to strengthen this guard. This absolves us of animal qualities like ego, restlessness, fickleness, anger and jealousy. In the first place, **if one sees God in each form, then within three days one can feel the Divine feeling latent in oneself beginning to develop.** Otherwise, even thirty generations of *sadhana* will be of no use.[13]

7. *Dhyana* (Meditation)

In the popular understanding of the word, "meditation" refers to concentration upon an object and through that object, reaching the ultimate. But this is not the correct approach to meditation. If you examine the origin of the word, *Dhyana*, which means meditation, you will find that it refers to meditation on God and only God. Therefore, meditation and devotion are really the same; both are the process of concentrating on the Lord to the exclusion of everything else, thinking only of Him. Without such mediation or devotion it is impossible to realise the unlimited effulgence of the Lords and gain true spiritual knowledge. When you meditate, the effulgence enters the *Hridayam* in you. By constant chanting of the name of the Lord, devoting all your thoughts to *Narayana* (all-pervading Lord) you will be filled with the power of the Divine and experience ineffable bliss.[14]

The effects of meditation on health have now been well documented. Cardiologists in major hospitals in the U.S. are now recommending it in follow-up treatments for heart patients. The results for those who practise are consistently positive.

8. *Samadhi* (Oneness With God)

Sri Sathya Sai Baba asks:

What does *Samadhi* mean? Is it a state of trance? No. Is it a state of emotional utterance? No. Is it absorption in one's self? No. When people refer to a man in trance or in an unconscious state as one experiencing *Samadhi*, they are thoroughly mistaken. It may be a case of hysteria or of epilepsy. It may be the result of some strong emotion or one caused by excitement. The true meaning of *Samadhi* is the state of union with *Sat* (God).

Sama + Dhi (*Sama* = Equal, *Dhi* = Mind)

Equal mindedness is *Samadhi*. To treat alike pleasure and pain, heat and cold, darkness and light is true *Samadhi*. This is the quality of *Sat*. It has no pleasure or pain. It is all-pervading. The question is often asked: "Where is God?" The usual answer is that He is in *Vaikunta*, in *Swarga* (Heaven) or in *Kailasa*. Not at all. The Lord has nothing to do in these places. The Lord is in *Naraka* (Hell). As the denizens of Hell are perpetually suffering and calling out to God, the Lord remains there.

It is among those who seek peace that the Lord dwells. A hospital is needed to tend the sick. Where there is no ailment there is no need for a hospital. Likewise, the Divine doctor goes to those who are in pain and distress. *Vaidya Narayano Harih* (Narayana or Hari is the doctor). Therefore, where there is humanity there is the Divine.[15]

Yoga And Its Role In Healing Disease

The *yoga* path leads to a life of wholeness in body, mind and spirit. But what about its role in healing? Recently, several institutes in the international field have been established to diagnose diseases through *yoga*. It has been established beyond doubt that many "incurable" and chronic diseases can be either cured or managed through *yoga*.

The *yoga* treatment is perfectly scientific. It is an auto-treatment method. *Yoga* therapy includes nutritious food, restraint and a code of conduct to be followed by the patient – exactly the prescription Sri Sathya Sai Baba advises to all.

Sri Sathya Sai Baba says:

The human body is sacred. Man is a combination of body, mind and spirit. For proper function, each is dependent upon the other. The body depends on the mind and the mind should depend on the *Atma* or Spirit. Only by maintaining the proper interrelationship can the body be healthy. For preserving health, food, drink and rest are needed. Disease has become rampant today because of the neglect of the discipline regarding food, which should be balanced and limited according to the capacity of the system to digest and assimilate. There are two types of cells in the body, one that helps and the other that causes harm to the system. If one does not take proper food illness is caused.

For accomplishing any good task good health is necessary; the ancient sages realised the Divine by maintaining perfect health. The body is given to do righteous deeds. As the instrument for action it should be maintained in proper condition. By controlling food and avoiding excessive stress and strain, one can maintain good health.[16]

If we change our vision, we will experience peace. When people view the world with the vision of love, they will have peace. All diseases will be cured. Most diseases have their origin in the mind. Everything has a psychological basis. When a person feels that something is wrong with him, he develops an illness. A healthy mind is needed for a healthy body. But it is not enough to be physically healthy. Man needs God's Grace also. To acquire God's grace you have to cultivate the love of God. Love has become today a kind of show. Genuine love should emanate from the heart. "Start the day with love, spend the day with love, end the day with love, that is the way to God." If you develop love, disease will not come near you.

Moderation in food, moderation in talk and in desires and pursuits, contentment with what a little can be got by honest labour, eagerness to serve and to impart joy to all – these are the most powerful of all the tonics of health.[17]

Whatever happens is for your own good. Fill your *Hridayam* with this conviction. Consider everything as coming from God for your own good. God knows what is good for you just as a loving mother knows what a child needs. No one can expect to receive whatever he prays for because in his ignorance he may ask for what is not good for him. **A wise man will not seek anything from God, but leave everything to God.**[18]

1 *Bhagawan* Sri Sathya Sai Baba, Divine Discourse,

2 *Bhagawan* Sri Sathya Sai Baba, **Summer Showers In Brindavan**, 1993.

3 *Bhagawan* Sri Sathya Sai Baba, Divine Discourse, November 1993.

4 *Bhagawan* Sri Sathya Sai Baba, Divine Discourse, November 1993.

5 Patanjali, Maharishi, ***Astanga Yoga Sutras.***

6 *Bhagawan* Sri Sathya Sai Baba, Divine Discourse, November 1993.

7 *Bhagawan* Sri Sathya Sai Baba, Divine Discourse, November 1993.

8 *Bhagawan* Sri Sathya Sai Baba, ***Sanathana Sarathi,*** May 1965.

9 *Bhagawan* Sri Sathya Sai Baba, **Summer Showers In Brindavan**, 1993.

10 Lonavala Centre, Bhopal.

11 Author, "*Pranayama*, the Only Exercise for Chronic Pulmonary Pathology", paper delivered at Asian Homeopathic Conference, Bangkok, 1989.

12 *Bhagawan* Sri Sathya Sai Baba, **Discourses on the *Bhagavad Gita***, Ch. 17.

13 *Bhagawan* Sri Sathya Sai Baba, Divine Discourse, November 1993.

14 *Bhagawan* Sri Sathya Sai Baba, **Discourses on the *Bhagavad Gita***, Ch. 17.

15 *Bhagawan* Sri Sathya Sai Baba, Divine Discourse, 26/06/1994.

16 *Bhagawan* Sri Sathya Sai Baba, ***Sanathana Sarathi,*** December 1994.

17 *Bhagawan* Sri Sathya Sai Baba, ***Sadhana,* the Inward Path.**

18 *Bhagawan* Sri Sathya Sai Baba, Divine Discourse, 10/01/1993.

Neither charity, nor the performance of sacrifices, neither penance, nor the highest knowledge, nor any other thing can be equal to the power of control of the senses.

~ **Sri Sathya Sai Baba**

chapter - 13

PURITY OF THE SENSES

Every experience that is drawn through the senses has an effect on one's health.

~ SRI SATHYA SAI BABA

Sri Sathya Sai Baba remarks:

The five gross sense organs, the ear, the skin, the eye, the tongue and the nose, called the *Jnanendriyas* in Sanskrit, reach out to the sense objects through the subtle sense organs, called the *Tanmatras,* which comprise sound, touch, sight, taste and smell. The *Jnanendriyas* and the *Tanmatras* are inextricably related; without the subtle the gross does not function. For example, you may have eyes, but no sight; you may have ears, but no hearing; you may have a tongue, but no taste.

In the ***BHAGAVAD GITA*** Krishna told Arjuna, "The primary cause of your present grief is your attachment, and the basis for your attachment is ignorance. It is out of ignorance that you allow your sense organs to govern your actions. If you want to free yourself from attachment and sorrow then you must control your senses. You have to understand the nature of the sense organs."

THAT WHICH MEASURES

Krishna gave a new name to the sense organs. He called them *Matraha*, which means, "that which measures." For example, what is it that measures the bitterness or sweetness of food? It is the tongue which measures and determines the taste of food, deciding whether it is bitter or sweet. Or you might describe a person's face by saying that all his features are normal, but he has a long nose. What is it that measures the length of the nose? Your eyes. In the same way, your ears determine whether some music is melodious or not.

Whenever these sense organs come into contact with the objects of the senses they measure different qualities. For example, the sense of touch may measure such qualities as heat and cold as a result of which you experience joy or grief. By merely having senses you do not get joy or grief; it is only when the sense organs come into contact with the sense objects that you experience joy or grief.[1]

Sensory Perception – A Medical Perspective

From a medical perspective, sensory data enters the neural system in the form of billions of tiny bursts of electrochemical energy gathered by countless sensors in the skin, eyes, ears, mouth and nose. These neural impulses race along neural pathways, cascading like a line of falling dominoes, leaping synaptic gaps and triggering the release of chemical neurotransmitters as they carry their sensory messages toward the brain. Once inside the brain, sensory information is routed and re-routed to appropriate processing areas for sight, taste, touch, hearing and smell. **[See Diagram No. 26]**

The first level of sensory processing occurs in the primary receptive areas dedicated to each of the five sensory systems. These areas assemble the raw data into preliminary perceptions, which then travel to secondary receptive areas where they are further refined.

Sensory perceptions then move into what are called **association areas**, where more sophisticated processing occurs.

Senses In The Human Brain

NOSE & MOUTH
Olfactory System
Smell & Taste
Receptors send messages to the olfactory bulb, which connects to the amygdala-hippocampus complex.

MOUTH
Broca's Area
Speech

SKIN
Somotosensory Cortex
Touching, Hearing, Seeing
Processes raw data from the eyes, ears and body and the sensory association areas.

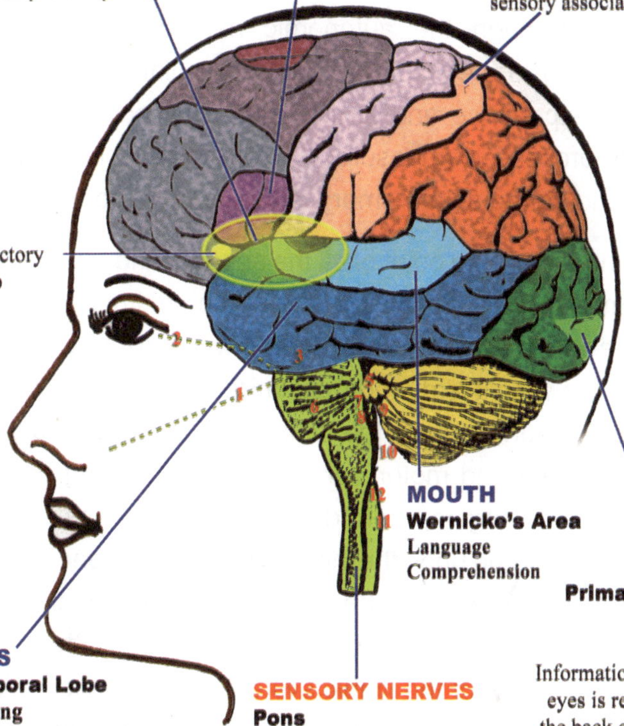

MOUTH
Wernicke's Area
Language Comprehension

EYES
Primary Visual Cortex
Seeing
Information from the eyes is registered at the back of the brain and sent forward for interpretation

EARS
Temporal Lobe
Hearing
All auditory processing takes place here. Changes in this area are linked to religious experience.

SENSORY NERVES
Pons
Cranial Nerves
1- Olfactory nerve: *smell*
2- Optic nerve: *sight*
3- Oculomotor: *eye movment*
4- Trochlear nerve: *eye movement (not shown)*
5- Trigeminal nerve: *face-sensory*
6- Abducens nerve: *eye movement*
7- Facial nerve: *face (motor)*
8- Vestibulocochlear nerve: *hearing & balance*
9- Glossopharyngeal nerve: *swallowing*
10- Vagus nerve: *gastrointestinal tract*
11- Accessory nerve: *shoulder muscles*
12- Hypoglossal nerve: *tongue (movement or motor)*

Human Values And Health ~ Diagram No. 26

Here information is associated or gathered together from various parts of the brain. At this highest level, information from a single sense is integrated with information from all the other senses. Memory and emotional centres are also tapped to create the multidimensional perceptions that form human consciousness. Nothing enters our consciousness whole. **There is no direct objective experience of reality.** The brain filters all sense experiences through the autonomic nervous system before moving it along to the limbic system, particularly the thalamus. The sense experience and all its various associations is then thoroughly processed (measured) by man's reasoning faculties (*Buddhi*) and stored as a memory in the cerebral cortex.

The central crossing point of all the sensory and motor nerves, the thalamus plays a significant role in the spiritual experience. When the awareness is focused deeply inward on the *Ajna Chakra* at the mid brow, as it is during meditation, slow *mantra* chanting or intense emotional prayer, the thalamus actually blocks signals from the sensory and motor nerves from proceeding on to the cerebral cortex. Imagine, no body sensations or sensual stimuli are allowed to intrude upon the inner awareness; so one becomes extraordinarily relaxed. The heartbeat slows automatically; the breath becomes deep and rhythmic, soothing all the organs. Thus the physiology of the limbic system, of which the thalamus is a central organ, has been divinely designed as a tool to lead the soul into *samadhi*. The light shines on the face of the person, and, with constant practice of this inner awareness, he or she can become a *yogi*.

Sensory Perceptions Are Only Reflections

So what we perceive as a real sensory experience is in actuality a collection of neural perceptions. Whether the experience is pleasurable or not is also a function of our perception.

Sri Sathya Sai Baba says:

Consider an example. A dog has found a hard bone. Once he has this bone, it becomes very dear to him and he does not want to share it with any other dog; so he takes it to some solitary place. There he looks at it, admires it and starts gnawing on it. Since it is an old bone, it is very hard. With all his enthusiasm and strength he goes on biting until he dislodges a tooth from his gums. Some blood spills out and oozes onto the bone. The dog is convinced that the blood has come out of that bone, and he immensely enjoys the taste of it. But the blood has not come out of the bone; it has come out of his own mouth. The dog does not realize the truth and he has become deluded after following the imaginations of his own mind.

The ignorant think that they are getting joy out of the sense-objects; but this limited joy that they experience does not come from outside themselves. **Ever present within their own hearts is the true joy, and it is this unchanging inner joy that gets superimposed on a particular object, making that object appear as if it is the source of joy.**

If the sense object truly gave joy, then that joy should be uniformly the same for all people. Yet you know that this is not the case. If a particular object gives joy and pleasure to some people, the same object may be objectionable to other people, giving displeasure to them. If the joy were really inherent in the object itself, it should be the same for everyone.

Taking Control Of The Senses

If the sense organs make their demands you should not listen to them. Instead, you should have your mind contact the intellect. Then, whatever the intellect decides, the mind will command and the sense organ will have to obey. This is the proper way to curb the senses.

You must be careful to your very last breath of your life not to yield to your sense organs. To gain the *Atma* you must control the outgoing senses. Once you gain full control of your senses you will easily be able to master *Bhakti Yoga, Karma Yoga, Jnana Yoga* and all other *yogas*.

When *Swami* is asking you to control the senses and control the mind, some of you might be wondering if you will be able to live at all and carry on your routine functions. *Swami* is not asking you to drive with your foot on the brake, but to use the brakes when necessary to control your car whenever there is some danger. It is when there is some danger, such as bad thoughts, bad feelings, bad seeing, bad hearing, bad taste and so on that you have to exercise control. Use all the senses in a proper and ethical way, appropriate to the time and the circumstance. It is in this context that the ***Bhagavad Gita*** has taught discipline by observing limits in all your activities.[2]

A Daily *Sadhana*

To control the senses, says Sri Sathya Sai Baba, is difficult at first. However, when we apply Human Values to our experience of sense objects, the senses are gradually controlled and purified in a natural way. This is a daily *sadhana*, which requires being present to each moment – and dedicated practice. Sri Sathya Sai Baba has given many ways to approach this with each of the five senses.

Although there are five *Jnanendriyas,* Sathya Sai Baba places the greatest emphasis on controlling two, the eyes and the tongue. When these two are properly restrained, the rest fall in line. Sai Baba tells us, "The Lord said, 'You silly man! Take note that I have provided natural means for closing the eyes and the mouth.' If you don't want to see anything undesirable, you can close your eyes with your eyelids. The mouth has lips which can seal the tongue."

It is our duty to learn to use our mind to control the gross sense organs in the physical body: eyes, tongue, ears, nose and skin, ensuring that what is filtered through them to the subtle sense organs (sight, taste, sound, smell and touch) is pure. It is in this way that the *Hridayam* also becomes pure, allowing the light of the *Atma* to shine through.

The Eyes (Sight): Vision Of Truth

Sri Sathya Sai Baba says:

The first requisite is *Samyagdarshana* (vision of truth). The implication of this statement is that, having been bestowed with the great gift of eyes, man should use them for seeing sacred objects and holy beings. But on the contrary, by using his eyes to look at unsacred objects and evil persons, man fills himself with bad thoughts and becomes a prey to evil tendencies. What one sees influences the feelings in the *Hridayam*. The state of the *Hridayam* determines the nature of one's thoughts. The thoughts influence one's speech and one's life. Hence, to lead a good life the first requisite is a pure vision. Man has to cultivate a pure and sacred outlook. As a result of looking at cruel, ugly and wicked scenes man leads an animal existence. The very first enquiry one should make is to ascertain what is pure, edifying, and Godly that he should see. **Whatever he sees leaves its imprint on man. Evil scenes give rise to evil thoughts; good scenes evoke good thoughts.** When sacred thoughts are implanted in the *Hridayam*, there will be no room for bad feelings or thoughts to grow in it.[3]

Sight ~ A Medical Perspective

According to medical science, vision has several functions. First, sight immediately sets off the initial, 'gut' response to an experience. This is called a 'reflex', the nervous system's automatic and involuntary reaction to a stimulus. Later, the higher mind can take over, enabling us to take a more thoughtful course of action. Here is a simple example: we see a cockroach. We become alarmed, and imagine that that it might crawl over us. Our first 'reflex' would be to stomp on it or run (fight or flight). However, by turning the situation over to the higher mind, we realize that we are much larger than the cockroach. In fact, it is more frightened of us than we are of it, hence there is no need for fear; we can simply chase it away. **What happens is a physical event. Our response is a reflection of our inner being.**

The other senses are easily activated by sight. If we see what looks like a delicious plate of food, before we know it, the nose is tingling to catch the scent, the mouth has begun to salivate and the hand is itching to reach out for the object, ensuring all these senses are satisfied.

Science asserts that sight is largely responsible for memory as well. The more we take in pure sights through our eyes, the more we are able to store good memories. This purifies our *Hridayam* enabling us to 1) become more discriminating and, 2) more readily see the good in each situation.

The Pure Vision Of Divine Love

No other sight can purify the sense of vision as effectively as the image of God. Sri Sathya Sai Baba, the *Kaliyuga Avatar,* is daily giving *darshan* (the sight of a holy being or God). Once you have looked upon the face of Pure Love, the memory of this sight becomes permanently impressed upon the *Hridayam*, initiating an on-going process of purification. He explained the process in this way to a group of students:

Sri Sathya Sai Baba said:

Right now, here in the *mandir* of Prasanthi Nilayam there are about a thousand people seated, listening to this discourse. This is the present situation which will last from one to two hours. Along with the devotees seated here there is also *Swami*. This experience is associated with a certain time, a certain activity; but the very same experience can be re-experienced when you go home. It will be there in your *Chitakasa* (ethers of the mind) … one thousand people, *Swami*, the *mandir* of Prasanthi Nilayam, and the discourse. In the external vision and in your experience in the waking state, you can see that all of you are now sitting in the hall of Prasanthi Nilayam. What happens when you start thinking of this back home? The answer is: *Swami* and Prasanthi Nilayam will be in your heart.[4]

The Door Swings Both Ways

The practice of pure vision does not only mean watching what you see. It is also necessary to be aware of how others see you. Eyes are considered to be the window of the soul. They can speak volumes, sending out love, jealously, hatred, approval, affection, disgust and a host of other emotions. Eyes are reflectors as well as receivers; whatever is in our heart is reflected out to be picked up by all who would see. We must take care not to harm anyone by casting an 'evil eye', but to use the eyes to transmit positive energy instead. If we cannot do that, we can at least lower the eyelids and keep 'silent'.

The Tongue: The Organ With Double Power

Sri Sathya Sai Baba tells us:

The main door leading to *Yoga* is control of the tongue; this must be exercised both in the area of taste and in the area of speech. ***Gita*** has declared that without control over the tongue it is impossible to follow the path of devotion and enter the mansion of *Yoga* which leads to God.

The tongue is endowed with a double power; it has both the power of speech and the power of taste. In the *GITA*, the Lord cautions you to be very careful in using your tongue; He praises the devotee who has attained complete control over the tongue, for such a one will soon develop a pure and steady heart and feel the constant presence of the Lord. To gain such control, devotees have been practising a number of special disciplines such as observing silence, controlling their diet or maintaining a complete fast.

If the tongue is properly controlled all other sense organs will come in line by themselves. Because man has not been able to gain control over the tongue he is afflicted by numerous doubts, emotional turmoils, contradictions and confusions. Control of the tongue refers not only to food, but also to speech.[5]

The tongue has been given to speak the truth, to expound on what is sacred and pure. The tongue has not been given to man to pamper the palate with delicious sweets. It is not given for talking as one likes; it is not to be used for causing displeasure to others. Nor is it to be used for indulging in falsehood. The tongue has been given to man to speak the truth, to be sweet to others, to praise the Divine and to enjoy the bliss derived from such sacred speech.[6]

The Power Of Speech (Tongue)

Speech is the cause of prosperity,
Speech secures friends and kinsmen,
Speech brings about bondage,
Speech can also lead to certain death. (Telugu Poem)

The power of speech gifted to humanity is very important and majestic. It gives him all the wealth. So we should talk sweetly and softly in an acceptable manner. Only such sweet talk will give us all the affluence and prosperity. Words can win many friends and relations and even kingdoms. We may have few relations, but with our sweet talk, we can develop good relationships with the entire world. Sacred talk will give us all the education and elevate us to exalted positions. But we should also know that words spoken with bad thoughts and bad feelings will not only lead us to bondage, but can also lead us to death. Both good and bad are present in the words we utter. For the one with sweet words the universe itself becomes a mansion. He will feel the bond of fraternity prevailing everywhere. So **words form the basis to make you feel humanity as one caste** and the universe as one mansion. Good words coupled with humility will take you to higher levels.

God is adored by you when you do *puja* calling Him as *Mridhu madhura bhashine*, (He who speaks softly and sweetly). This is a meaningful characterization of the Lord. Through soft and sweet speech we can transform even demonic persons into decent individuals. From words, honey drips; words are fragrant flowers; words enshrine *Vedic* wisdom; words can build a heaven or hell. Words can plunge you into prison or release you into freedom.[7]

Silence

You should not talk too much. The divine energy which is in you will get wasted in the process. By engaging in too much talk your memory power will get lost and weakness will develop in your body. Premature old age will be the final result. Besides that, you will get a bad name.

Many sages have described how the tongue always longs to enjoy good things and how everything will be easy once you gain control over it. Another word used for describing this control is silence. Silence does not merely refer to the restraint of the tongue. Not only should you exercise silence in speech, but you should also be silent in thoughts. Your mind should remain free of thoughts; that is true silence.[8]

In silence you discover your own truth. Close your eyes and sit in silence. Then out of the vibration comes, *"So Ham"*. *"So"* is the inhalation, and *"Ham"* is the exhalation. *"So"* means God, *"Ham"* means, I. **"I am God."**[9]

Power Of Taste

The tongue is important. Among the eight million four hundred thousand species of living beings, all except human beings live on food as provided by Mother Nature. The human tongue has 40,000 taste buds. 20,000 hot, 20,000 cold. These are mostly used by *Ayurvedic* physicians for diagnostic purposes.

Because of these taste buds, man alone strives to make such food more palatable, more attractive to the senses of sight, touch, taste and smell by boiling, frying, freezing, mixing, grinding and soaking. The consequence of this greed is ill health. Thus, greed is the cause of ill health and debility. One should realise that food materials, as offered by nature are really more beneficial. When heat is applied they lose the vitality, giving away their essential components, lessening their ability to confer strength and efficiency. The person ages faster and loses the sprightliness of youth; catering to the cravings of the tongue and swallowing heavy foods three or four times a day can only add to the heap. Regular and limited intakes alone enable a person to discharge one's duties.[10]

In addition, if you take food without discrimination, without trying to find out whether it is desirable or not, paying attention only to satisfying your hunger and indulging your taste buds, you will not be able to control your attachments and feelings. You would sink down into weakness. If anyone were to make adverse comments about you, criticizing or blaming you, you would start shrinking and feel that the entire world is against you. The single most important reason for this kind of weakness is the type of food you take in.[11]

Purity Of Food

Sri Sathya Sai Baba advises several means to ensure that our food is pure, which also purifies our tongue and our thoughts – "as is the food, so is the mind," He says.

1. Food should be *satwic*, neither too hot, too bitter, too salty, too sweet – or too abundant.
2. There should be purity of the vessels and utensils used in cooking. Neither food nor utensils should have come through improper means.
3. The thoughts and feelings of the person who cooks should be pure.
4. Prayer before taking any food – offering it fully to God is important. This consecrates the food, making it *prasadam*.
5. The environment where one is eating must be pure, clean and pleasant to all the senses.

The Cycle Of Talking And Eating

Actually the two functions of the tongue are closely related. Too much talk leads to unnatural hunger. When the talker feels more hunger he will, of course, take more food. On account of this excess food, feelings will arise which will express themselves in still more talk. In the process, controlling the sense becomes an almost impossible task. If you wish to acquire only good qualities, i.e., human qualities instead of animal qualities, then you will have to acquire control of the tongue in both the areas of food and speech. This is the royal road for human beings.

Sanctifying The Tongue

Especially in this *Kali* Age, the tongue can get easily sanctified by repeating the holy name, *Namasmaranam*. Instead of wasting your precious divine energy and your precious time in idle talk, let the tongue constantly sing the praises of God and repeat

His name. Sing the name of the Lord! That is the proper way to spend your life, saturating your very existence with the glory and holiness of His presence.[12]

The Ears (Sound): Hear No Evil

Sri Sathya Sai Baba says:

Through the process of listening, a dirt-laden heart will be transformed into a clean illumined heart, shining with genuine light. To the foul odours of sense pursuits, keenness to listen to the glories of God is a valuable disinfectant, besides being in itself so full of sweet fragrance. The listening will cleanse the heart through the prompting it gives for good work.[13]

Ears can hear a million voices and their half-inch oracle can catch any number of sounds. Ears are big doorways, yet they catch the finest vibration. Sound waves carry energy. What you hear can make your soul dance with joy or writhe in pain. Hence, along with sacred speech, Sai Baba advises **Sacred Listening.**

"Every little movement or incident results in sound;" He says, "only you may not be able to hear because the range of your ear is limited. The falling of an eyelid over the eye makes a sound; the dropping of dew on a petal makes a sound. Any little agitation disturbing the calm is bound to produce sound. The sound caused by the primal movement that resulted in the enveloping of *Brahman* by self-evolved *Maya* is the *Pranavashabda* (first sound) or AUM. The *Gayathri Mantra* is the elaboration of the *Pranava* and so it is now held so venerable that initiation into the spiritual life is achieved by its contemplation.

"The sound of a *mantra* is as valuable as its meaning. Even a poisonous cobra is quieted by music; sound has that allaying property. The child in the cradle stops wailing as soon as the lullaby is sung; it may not carry any meaning; it may be a nonsensical rhyme or a just a jingle, but it quiets, soothes the nerves and induces sleep."[14]

Physiologically, if you listen to bad things, the vibration depresses the brain and it actually hurts. Don't sit in a place where gossip, scandal or falsehood is being spoken. It will rob you of your peace. Don't allow your ears to listen to undesirable talk; hear only the Lord's stories, moral stories that will boost your spirit and strengthen your faith. Even if you are forced to hear wrong things – tell your brain not to store that information, that it is filth. The best action is to bring your feet into the game and simply walk away. What you can't hear will have no effect, but if you stay and listen and are not yet in full equanimity, you could get elevated when praised or sad when blamed or defamed.

Sathya Sai Baba says, "If someone says an untruth, such as 'Baba has no hair.' Why should I let this bother me? I have lots of hair. If someone says, 'Sai Baba has big curly hair, it's unattractive.' Why should I care? I like My hair. If someone blames you for something, think over it. If there is no truth in it, don't take it in. If someone praises you wrongly, just for the sake of flattery, don't take it in. This is truthful hearing – analyse and store only what is right."

Sri Sathya Sai Baba continues:

Falsehood pollutes the tongue of the speaker, the ear of the listener and the air which carries it from tongue to eardrum. There are beneficent and maleficent sounds and they produce corresponding echoes in the atmosphere. Words that emanate from faith in God and the humility it fosters will render the atmosphere pure, while those trumpeted by vanity and execrated by nihilism and atheism will contaminate it. Use only such sounds as will cleanse the air. Do not be harsh; never use expressions which sear and hurt, which are the evil progeny of hate and pride.[15]

Listening to *bhajans* gives immense joy to one and all. Community singing sets up vibrations, which cleanse the atmosphere. Guru Nanak started group singing *Prabhat Pheri* (*Nagarsankirtan*) and Community Lunch where poor and rich sit together to eat, showing equanimity.[16]

Bhajans, *Kirtan* and *Nagarsankirtan* will have a maximum influence on your *Hridayam*. They soothe the nervous system, refresh the brain and wash away the bad vibrations in the cortex. They suppress the ego, freeing your mind to flow onto higher levels.

"Sound," says Sai Baba, "is the very core of the ***Vedas***. Sound is associated with harmony and melody and hence, the *Veda* has to be heard and ecstasy derived therefrom. It is not to be analysed, commented upon and judged. This is the reason why *Veda* is called *Sruthi* – that which is heard."[17]

"The unmanifested," said Guru Nanak, "manifests Himself in sound, and from sound the whole creation flows forth."

Sound never dies. Astronauts and cosmonauts experienced music and chants, while flying high above the earth during their space missions. Now science is confirming that sounds float in the *akasa*. This includes all types of music – devotionals and pop music. In the not too distance future these sounds will be traced, accessed and recorded.

The Nose (Smell): Taking In The Breath Of God

Sri Sathya Sai Baba says:

God has given you a nose so that you can use it for smelling and for breathing, inhaling and exhaling. You must use the nose for the things which are specified for it and be happy with it. If instead of using the nose for breathing and smelling good things you use the nose to inhale snuff, then you are not using it in a way specified by God and you are disobeying the commands of the Lord.[18]

The nose of the average person breathes 21,600 breaths per day, drawing in oxygen and *prana sakti* from the atmosphere and exhaling carbon dioxide. At times of exertion or stress the breathing process will be very fast; at times of peace and quiet it will be slow. Some people have an average of more than 21,600 breaths per day. A practised *yogi* may breathe less than 15 breaths per minute and even as low as 6 or 7. The short lived monkey will breathe some 40 times per minute. The long life snake will breathe 3 or 4 times per minute.[19]

The best instrument in the body to collect more and more *prana sakti* from the atmosphere is the nose, so for optimum health and energy reserves, it is critical that the nose be kept free of any pollutants. For those new to *Pranayama*, Sai Baba advises a simple, regulated breathing process, practiced three times a day, so this *sakti* can be gathered from the atmosphere.

The Sense Of Smell

The sense of smell is well developed in animals. It tells them what to eat and what not to eat. "Human beings have lost their sense of discrimination," Sai Baba warns. "As soon as good food is in front of you, your eyes see, the nose smells, the mouth salivates and the hand goes forward. This is unity. God has given the nose to you to smell nice things. He has not given it to you to use snuff or exhale smoke. They are medications and prolonged use will produce a bad effect on your body."[20]

The nose can also diagnose certain diseases. If the left nostril is blocked there is too much alkaline in the body. If the right is blocked, there is more acid. *Yogis* of the past recognized the importance of acid/alkaline balance and would not step out of the house before examining their nose.

The sense of smell comes from the older, reptilian portion of the brain and can activate animal instincts and behaviour. If used indiscriminately, our nose can encourage the other senses to get out of control. However, if we use it to catch the aroma of incense or flower offerings or to inhale deeply the scent of the Lord, it can lead us to transcendence.

The Skin (Touch): The Largest Sensory Organ In The Body

The skin is the largest sensory organ, covering the whole body. The *Tanmatra* corresponding to it is touch. Touch is the most active and subtle sensation. Most of our tactile and spatial knowledge is perceived through the skin, which works in close partnership with the nervous system. Many sensory nerves open up into the skin, which makes it the perfect monitor for the body's thermostat. This is how we can feel whether or not something is soft or hard, cold or hot, rough or smooth. Many traditional medical practices, particularly acupuncture and acupressure, work with the skin's delicate system of nerve meridians to balance energy and activate the human body's natural healing properties.

The skin itself is not considered a vital organ, although all the other organs of the body are encased by it. It is vulnerable to stress and quick to reflect signs of 'dis-ease' in our emotional state or other body organs. Digestive problems in particular can refer to the skin in the form of rashes. This makes the condition of the skin a keen barometer for our Total Health. Skin reflects the inner beauty and purification of the *Hridayam* will add luster to the face. Whether you are dark or pale, the light of your *Hridayam* shines through the skin.

An Organ Of Excretion

The skin is an organ of excretion. Stress, fatigue, poor diet or illness can make it prey to acne, moles, rashes, warts, etc. In a healthy body, the pores regularly secrete waste materials from the sweat glands and billions upon billions of (epithelial) cells quietly die and fall off every day. These processes of elimination are natural to all ever-changing matter in the objective universe.

Sri Sathya Sai Baba says:

From every being and thing, constantly without intermission, millions of minute particles and millions of vibrations are issuing forth. Certain substances like camphor emanate so many particles that a lump disappears in a few days. The bodies of others affect us by their emanations and we too affect them in the same way. For good or bad, we are interacting in this manner, inescapably. Naturally the growth of the body is affected, as well as its health and strength, by the contact of company we develop. These emanations are intensified when dirt accumulates or sewage collects or drains are choked. Five types of baths are prescribed in the Hindu scriptures in order to maintain physical immunity from the emanations of others.

1. **MUD BATH:** Fine mud is applied over the body and kept on for sometime before being washed away.
2. **SUN BATH:** The rays of the sun are powerful disinfectants; they feed as well as freshen. (Body also manufactures Vitamin D from sunlight.)
3. **WATER BATH:** If the water is a flowing river, considered holy, and if the bath is taken after propitiatory hymns, etc. the bath will cleanse the body and at the same time elevate the spirit.
4. **AIR BATH:** The body is exposed to the cool breeze and its salutary effect.

5. **ASH BATH:** The body is given a coating of fine ash or *Vibhuti* revered as the mark of Siva. The ash guards the body from evil contacts and deleterious effects of the vibrations proceeding from others; it also sanctifies and purifies the vibrations of the individual wearing the ash, for it reminds him always of the inevitable end of all that one feels as one's own, except the Lord who is the very person himself.[21]

Satsang

These unseen, but very potent emanations are the key reason that *satsang* (good company) is one of the foundations of spiritual practice. Emotions from one person to another are transmitted through the skin. Most of the people are quick to sense whether someone is touching them with love or with malice. Touch is so important that we should exercise great caution in allowing someone to hug or touch us. The skin absorbs vital energy from other people. If a highly spiritual person is sitting by you, you will absorb their emanations through the skin as well as through the subtle bioplasmic body. This is one reason why people are so keen to be in close proximity to a holy person. It elevates consciousness and health. Conversely, if a negative person sits by your side, your own good energy and health may be dissipated out to that person, depending on the degree of your own wellbeing and inner alignment with Divine energy.

Sri Sathya Sai Baba says:

The company of the good is supremely important. Good company, by promoting good thoughts, leads to the highest achievements in life. Bad company, on the contrary, is like the shadow caused by the morning sun. At dawn, the shadow produced by the sun is long. As the morning progresses, the shadow gets shorter and shorter. Ultimately, it gets limited to one's feet. This is how the effects of bad company operate. At the beginning the gains seem to be large, but as time goes on, the gains vanish and the Human Values are destroyed.

The power of thoughts is immense. Thoughts survive unchanged at the death of a man. Therefore, everyone should foster noble thoughts. Bad thoughts should not be allowed to enter the mind. Bad company must be avoided as much as possible. For that reason, meditation is important. For *yogis* who wish to sacrifice, it is important to relinquish wealth. For devotees, singing a *bhajan* or reciting a devotional poem is important. For the sick, medicine is essential. The company of the sick will make you sick. The company of *yogis* will make you a *yogi*. Through *yoga* you realise the Divine; through *yoga* you control the mind.[22]

The Hands

Through the hands, the sense of touch finds expression. As Sathya Sai Baba teaches, "What is thought of in the head must be weighed by the heart and only then put into action by the hands." Thus when we reach out to touch the world, it is important to do so with discrimination as well as love. Sai Baba says, "The hands are the most important of the organs of action. They should always be used only for doing good – for carrying out one's duties with devotion and discipline."

Sense Control Leads To Immortality

Sri Sathya Sai Baba tells us:

The control of the senses is itself a form of sacrifice which leads to immortality. Sacrifice of wealth or possessions is no sacrifice at all. It is the sacrifice of the desires caused by the senses which is the highest sacrifice. Man has to make the right use of the senses for sacred purposes to realise his Divinity. The joy in being master of the senses is far greater than being their slave.

From today you must resolve to use your eyes properly to see only the good. Why use binoculars to see a distant object? If your vision is impaired, do not lament over it. Consider even blindness a blessing. If your hearing gets worse do not mourn over it. How much of the noise of the world is worth hearing at all? What is the use of listening to the cacophony of mutual abuse? Welcome the fact that you are saved from listening to such gossip. **Whatever your disabilities, look upon them as gifts from God. All things will turn out to be for your own good.** Ignore incidental troubles, which are like passing clouds. Think about God alone. There is nothing more vital than to acquire Divine Love. Love is God. Live in Love. The best way to love God is to love all, serve all; all are embodiments of God. Foster love. Adhere to Truth. Follow Righteousness. Achieve peace. This is the special benediction of *Swami* on this day for all. Wherever you may go, speak softly and sweetly. Thereby you will earn the esteem of society. [23]

The five elements are present not only throughout Creation, but all in the human body as *Angirasa* (energy in each cell of the body). You experience and derive benefit from them in the form of the five senses of sound, touch, sight, taste and smell. When you enjoy them within the limits of the five human values, there is perfect joy in you and harmony outside.[24]

---

1 *Bhagawan* Sri Sathya Sai Baba, **Discourses on the *Bhagavad Gita***, Ch. 17.
2 *Bhagawan* Sri Sathya Sai Baba, **Discourses on the *Bhagavad Gita***, Ch. 19.
3 *Bhagawan* Sri Sathya Sai Baba, Divine Discourse, 05/02/1998.
4 *Bhagawan* Sri Sathya Sai Baba, **Discourses on the *Bhagavad Gita***,, Ch. 3.
5 *Bhagawan* Sri Sathya Sai Baba, **Discourses on the *Bhagavad Gita***,, Ch. 7.
6 *Bhagawan* Sri Sathya Sai Baba, Divine Discourse, 05/02/1998.
7 *Bhagawan* Sri Sathya Sai Baba, Divine Discourse, 21/11/1981.
8 *Bhagawan* Sri Sathya Sai Baba, **Discourses on the *Bhagavad Gita***,, Ch. 7.
9 *Bhagawan* Sri Sathya Sai Baba, **Sathya Sai Newsletter, USA,** Spring 1995.
10 *Bhagawan* Sri Sathya Sai Baba, Divine Discourse, 21/11/1981.

11 *Bhagawan* Sri Sathya Sai Baba, **Discourses on the *Bhagavad Gita*,**, Ch. 7.

12 *Bhagawan* Sri Sathya Sai Baba, **Discourses on the *Bhagavad Gita*,**, Ch. 7.

13 *Bhagawan* Sri Sathya Sai Baba, ***Bhagavatha Vahini.***

14 *Bhagawan* Sri Sathya Sai Baba, **Sathya Sai Speaks,** Vol. 8, Ch. 48.

15 *Bhagawan* Sri Sathya Sai Baba, **Sathya Sai Speaks,** Vol. 7, Ch. 28.

16 *Bhagawan* Sri Sathya Sai Baba, **Discourses on the *Bhagavad Gita*,**, Ch. 3.

17 *Bhagawan* Sri Sathya Sai Baba, ***Vidya Vahini.***

18 *Bhagawan* Sri Sathya Sai Baba, **Discourses on the *Bhagavad Gita***, Ch. 17.

19 *Bhagawan* Sri Sathya Sai Baba, recorded in **Conversations With *Bhagawan* Sri Sathya Sai Baba** by Dr. John Hislop.

20 *Bhagawan* Sri Sathya Sai Baba, Divine Discourse, 21/11/1979.

21 *Bhagawan* Sri Sathya Sai Baba, **Sathya Sai Speaks,** Vol. 9, Ch. 26.

22 *Bhagawan* Sri Sathya Sai Baba, Divine Discourse, 10/01/1993.

23 *Bhagawan* Sri Sathya Sai Baba, Divine Discourse, 05/02/1998.

24 *Bhagawan* Sri Sathya Sai Baba, "I Am God, You Are God", pamphlet from *Chaitanya Jyothi* Museum.

It is easy to conquer anger through love, attachment through reasoning, falsehood through truth, bad through good and greed through charity.

~ **Sri Sathya Sai Baba**

chapter - 14

THE INNER ENEMIES AND THEIR TREATMENTS

Sri Sathya Sai Baba tells us:

The human *Hridayam* can be compared to the Ocean of Milk (*Ksheera Sagara*), but today it has become the Ocean of Salinity (*Kshara Sagara*). Lord Vishnu dwells in the Ocean of Milk, which means He resides in the *Hridayam*. But if we make our *Hridayam* *Kshara Sagara* then the whales and sharks (bad qualities) will enter. Human *Hridayam* should be pure, only then Lord Vishnu can reside in it.[1]

For human progress, mental strength and purity of *Hridayam* are essential. It is only the mental strength and purity of *Hridayam* that can turn the human into the Divine. Mind is the basis for the existence of mankind, and thoughts are responsible for the existence of Mind. Mind is only a bundle of thoughts and desires. Human behaviour, whether good or bad, is based on thoughts. Human life is the result of the thought processes.[2]

When the stone is cast in a well, a series of ripples start where the stone has fallen. From there the ripples go up to the edge of the well and cover the entire well. In the same manner, when the stone of thought is cast on the lake of the mind, the ripples start by filling all the senses and limbs in the body. **When the thought is a pure and sacred one, the ripples emanating in the mind**

fill all the senses and limbs in the body, from head to toe, with pure reactions.

This pure thought entering the eye purifies the vision. The same thought entering the ear makes it listen only to sacred sounds. Entering the mouth, this pure thought brings purity to the speech. Permeating the hands, the sacred thought induces them to engage themselves in sacred acts. The sacred ripples from the mind entering the feet induce them to go on pilgrimages. If the thoughts are impure, they travel in ripples to the senses and induce them to indulge in unholy acts. Hence, the well-known saying, "The mind is made up of thoughts and aberrations." It follows that people should not allow room for bad thoughts, bad associations or bad relationships.[3]

Arishadvarga (The Six Enemies)

The main thing about which all should be concerned today is how to get rid of the negative thoughts in their minds. The six cardinal enemies of man – the six basic vices – have found their abode in the *Hridayam* of human beings. There is no room in their hearts for love or kindness.[4]

The six evil qualities in man are called *Arishadvarga* in Sanskrit. Sathya Sai Baba outlines them as:

1. ***Kama*** (Desire): for riches, property, honour, status, fame, children, etc. Attachment to all things of the sensory world, this false, temporary, impure world.
2. ***Krodha*** (Anger): yearning to harm others and causing ruin to them.
3. ***Lobha*** (Greed): determination that no one else should partake of even a small fraction of what one has earned or what one has; also, that even in times of distress, one's possessions should not be diminished by use.

4. ***Moha*** **(**Fascination or Attachment): the delusion that some people are nearer to one than others and the desire to please them more than others, leading to exertions for earning and accumulating for their sake.
5. ***Mada*** **(**Ego or Pride): the swagger that develops when one feels that he has either scholarship or strength or riches or fame, more than others. When one has not got these, *mada* makes men move about without reverence for elders and consideration for others' feelings and craving only for one's own comfort and security. *Mada* is extreme egoism. Man is egoistic about family, wealth, youth and scholarship.
6. ***Mathsarya*** **(**Envy or Jealousy): when others are happy or happier than yourself, *mathsarya* makes one miserable; one cannot tolerate it.

There are other evils too. *Dambha* prompts people to do *yaga* and *yajna* (sacrifices) and to give away vast sums in charity in order to win the applause of the world. *Darpa* is the pride that haunts man when he is rich and happy. There is also *Eershya*, the desire that others should get the grief, misery and worry, which one is suffering from. *Asuya* means thinking always of doing evil to others, the willingness to put up with any trouble in order to satisfy this desire to harm others.

All these are called Inner Foes. So long as man is caught up in this net of delusion spread by these foes, the yearning for liberation will not dawn in his mind.[5] **[See Diagram No. 27]**

Kama (Desire)

Sri Sathya Sai Baba says:

> *The mind is a web of desires. Peace of mind is no desires and in that state there is no mind. Man is life with desire; life without desire is God.*[6]

You must learn how to keep your impulses under control and to master the senses that tend to drag you into wrong and vicious paths. When the desire for pleasure overcomes your reason and your innate goodness, you are left only with the shape and form of a human being; you have no right to be called human. If you aspire to earn the grace of the Lord you have to control your worldly desires. [7]

Desire for worldly objects produces pleasure and pain, whereas desire for God confers bliss and does not produce pain. **God works through you as desire.** There is a strong thrust of life force, the desire to live. If it goes into action in a favorable field it becomes love, otherwise it remains as desire. The force, the strength, the energy, the motivation in desire is God. Whether the desire is good or bad is related to time, place and person. In early years, a desire for worldly achievement might be good. In later years the same desire is bad.[8]

Animal qualities mean excessive desires. "I want this". "I want that." Mankind is bound by desires. For example, a young man has two legs and he is single. After some time he says, "I want to be married." Desires start; he gets married. Now he has four legs. So long has he had two legs he could walk wherever he wanted. But after marriage, he has four legs; he lost his independence. After some time, he says he wants a son. Desires continue; he has a son. Then there are six legs; he is now more and more bound with six legs. Later he says, "I want a daughter." Then there are eight legs. When he has eight legs, he becomes fearful. Because of fear, he wants to hide. As the number of legs goes on increasing, bondage increases. Where did he get the bondage? It was the result of desires. Therefore, control your desires. In *Vedantic* parlance, this is called detachment or renunciation.[9]

Impulses In The *Manomaya Kosa*

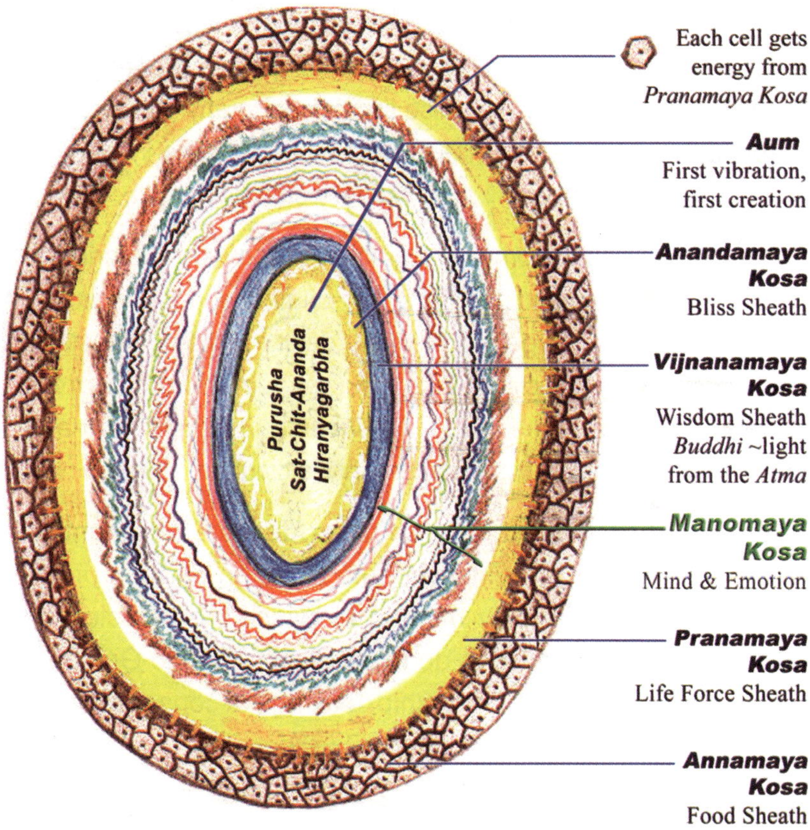

Bad Impulses	Good Impulses
Kama (lust)	***Prema*** (love)
Krodha (anger)	***Niskama Karma*** (desire-less action)
Moha (attachment)	***Bhajan*** (devotional singing)
Lobha (greed)	***Dhyana*** (meditation)
Mada (pride, ego)	**Compassion**
Matsarya (jealousy)	**Charity**
Ghrana (hatred)	**Equanimity**
Eershya (revenge)	
Dewsha (hatred)	
Bhaya (fear)	

NOTE: Bad impulses in the *Manomaya Kosa* can be purified by energizing good impulses, which allows more and more light from the *Purusha*, the embodied *Paramatma*, to shine through, leading to realisation of the Self.

Human Values And Health ~ Diagram No. 27

Source: Divine Discourses of *Bhagawan* Sri Sathya Sai Baba

TREATMENTS FOR DESIRE. To conquer desire you have to develop a sacrificing nature; you must be steeped in renunciation. Renunciation does not mean that you give up your family and go to the forest; nor does it require you to give up all your property and take up *Sanyasa*. Once you realise the defects in any object, once you recognise its transitory nature and worthlessness in helping you reach your goal, you will automatically stop desiring it.

When desire has become an ingrained part of you it is only by reversing the process and practising detachment and renunciation that you will be able to get rid of these deeply ingrained pests.[10] If desire comes, analyse it. If it is good for you and not harmful to others, go ahead. If not good, put it aside at once. If you are uncertain, do nothing until the uncertainly is clarified.[11]

Desires, when fulfilled, breed further desires; when unfulfilled, they lead to further installments of life on earth in order to calm the urge. The only method by which the delusion of desire can be destroyed is to dedicate all activities to God and engage in them in a spirit of worship, leaving the consequences to Him and ceasing to attach yourself to them.[12]

Ceiling on desires is a must for leading a peaceful and meaningful life. You must curb your desire to seek more and more wealth and turn your effort to realise the reality within. In pursuing this effort, you must not waste food, money, time, energy and knowledge as all these are forms of God.[13]

KRODHA (ANGER)

Sri Sathya Sai Baba says:

> *Anger is harmful; it makes you do things blindly. You will have to repent much for whatever you do in anger; when your anger cools down, you see things clearer and then it is too late to correct the wrong you have done.*[14]

There is no escape for anyone from the consequences of His actions. Death may come at anytime, in any place and in any form. No one can tell the time or manner of anyone's death. It is pre-ordained. There is no meaning in analysing the pros and cons of such happening. Even good devotees sometimes develop doubts and argue over trifles. A man's strength is considerably reduced by his anger. A man's life span is cut to pieces by the shears of envy, anger and hatred. Anger is the main cause of shortening a man's life; when a man gets angry his whole body trembles. His blood gets heated. It takes three months for the blood to get cool again. One moment of anger may consume the energy obtained from six months of eating. This is the way anger debilitates a person.[15] **[See Diagram No. 28]**

A man consumed by anger can never be free from misery. Anger carries with it a blazing fire. Anger is also described as *Krodhagni*, the fire of anger. As long as one is consumed by this fire, he cannot have happiness. To get free from misery, man has to get rid of anger. Anger is also the cause of depravity in man. It ruins him in various ways. It alienates him from his kith and kin. For the decline in human qualities today, pride and anger are primarily responsible.[16]

CONTROLLING ANGER. The easiest way to control anger is this: the moment you become aware that anger is rising within you, just laugh very loudly. Or go to the bathroom and have a cool bath. You can also take a glass of cool water and relax in a cool place. The moment anger comes it is most helpful to leave where you are and go to some other place. If with all these measures you still have not been able to control your anger, then stand in front of a mirror and examine your face; after seeing your appearance you will surely feel so much disgust that at once you will be able to control your anger. So these are a number of ways in which you will be able to deal with anger.

Inquire into the cause of this anger. Is it justified? Remember that if someone is going to be harmed in the process of your anger you will be committing a sin; and that cannot possibly be good for you. To undertake all these methods will be quite difficult for an ordinary person, but it is enough to remember not to let your tongue go into action immediately after you get angry and spill out a torrent of angry words. Take some time to think things over. In a number of ways anger weakens a person who is trying to do *sadhana*. If you make some effort to control anger when it arises, these efforts will act to strengthen your body and purify your mind.[17]

Anger is a great cause of ill-health, besides being dangerous for other reasons. It brings a long line of camp followers, each of whom adds its share to the final ruin. So you must conquer this passion when it arises in the mind by reminding yourself of the omnipresence of God, of God as the inner motivator of all, of His being the director of this Play called Life. Think of something else other than the circumstances that roused your anger, do some *Namasmarana*, lie down in bed, go on a long walk, drink some cold water – struggle with yourself until you win. Do not fight with others, fight with your own urges. Stop the enemy at the threshold, then the body's safety can be assured.[18]

Desire And Anger: The Twin Evils

Only when you can still your thoughts will you be able to overcome desires, and only after you have controlled your desires will you be able to control anger. Anger is born of desire. Desire arises from thoughts. Therefore, thoughts alone are responsible for both anger and desire. This fire of anger has the extraordinary capacity to destroy all the human qualities and to suppress the divine spark that is inside you, leaving only the demonic nature remaining. This fire of desire has no long-term aim. It will not

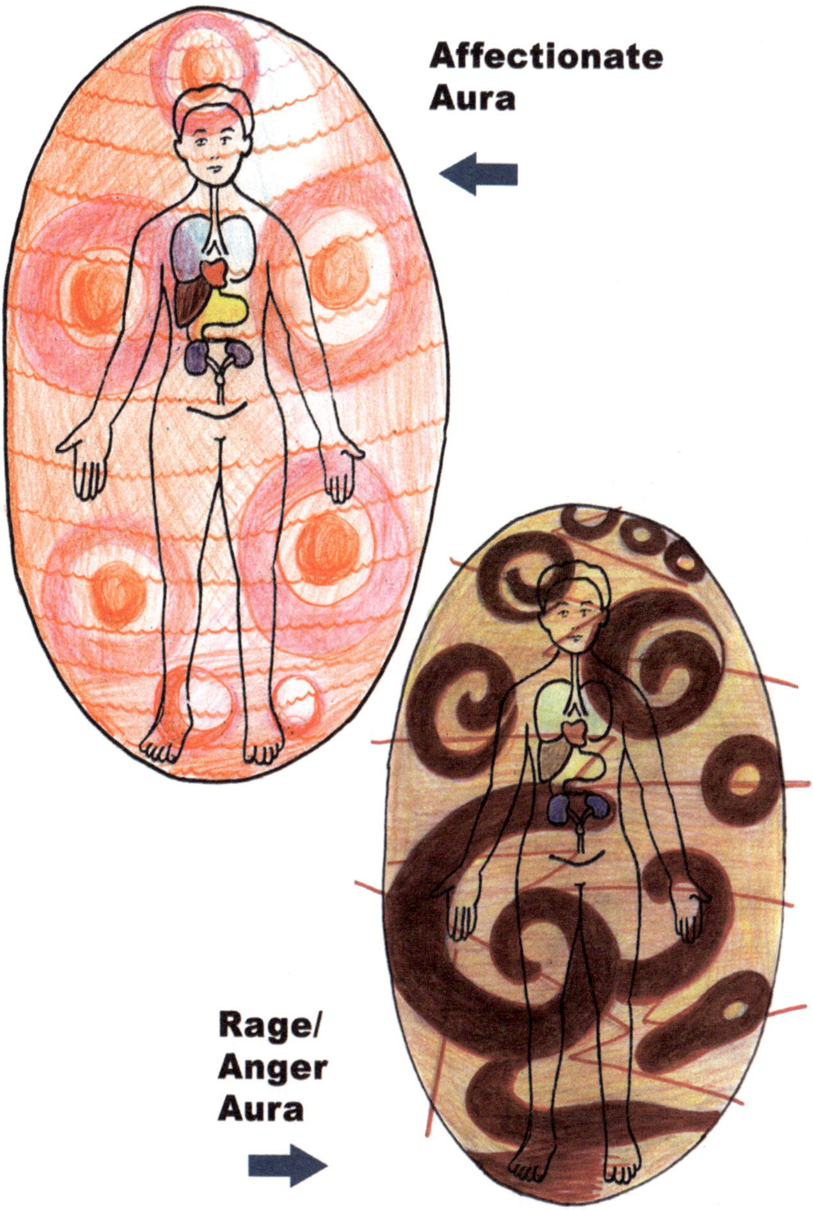

Human Values And Health ~ Diagram No. 28

be appeased once some goal is reached; on the contrary, it can never be satisfied.

TREATMENTS FOR THE CYCLE OF DESIRE AND ANGER. The Lord declared in the ***Gita***, "You can conquer anger through love, and you can conquer desire through renunciation and sacrifice." Where there is love there can be no anger. If you develop love, then there will be no room left in your heart for hatred or anger to take root. Love is always prepared to shower itself freely, to overlook defects and weaknesses in others. Love has this extraordinary quality; it lives by giving and forgiving.[19,20]

Lohba (Greed)

Sri Sathya Sai Baba says:

> *Greed yields only sorrow; contentment is best. There is no happiness greater than contentment.*[21]

No man filled with greed can achieve anything in this world. Excessive desires degrade a man. You cannot give up desires entirely. But there should be a limit to them. When they exceed the limits, a man goes astray. Desires are dreadfully dangerous. Today's enemy may become tomorrow's friend and vice versa. But desires are perpetual enemies. They haunt man ceaselessly. The ***Bhagavad Gita*** declares desire as the eternal enemy of man. Hence desire has to be kept under control.[22]

Avarice is nothing but insatiable desire and lack of self-discipline. It makes a man greedy. When the longing for material pleasures reaches its zenith, man thoughtlessly employs immoral means to achieve his ends.[23]

Evil thoughts cause ill-health. Anxiety, fear and tension also contribute their share. All these result from greed -- greed to have more things, for power, for fame. Greed results in sorrow and despair.[24]

Sri Sathya Sai Education in Human Values teaches that greed can be recognised by acquisitive behaviour, employing unfair or illegal means to acquire the objects of desire, miserliness or overspending, over indulgence in food and other material pleasures and constantly scheming to fulfill desires. It is greed that has led to over indulgence in the so-called technologically advanced nations of the world and severe poverty, disease and starvation in developing countries. This greed for MORE of everything – money, cars, houses, food, education, etc.— has put the Mother Earth in severe crisis as Her resources are taxed to the maximum. Sai Baba has said, "There is more than enough for everyone's need, but not enough for everyone's greed."

Sri Sathya Sai Baba offers treatments for greed:

TREATMENTS FOR GREED. For everything there is a limit; there is a range of healthy functioning. Do not encourage the multiplication of desires. It is best for you to be content with what you have. In the chapter on *Bhakti* Yoga in the ***Bhagavad Gita***, Krishna enumerated the 26 noble qualities of a devotee which endear him to the Lord. Of these, contentment stands out as one of the most important. It means not running after worldly enjoyments. Having enjoyed so many types of luxuries and so many sensual things in your life without having gained peace and fulfillment from them you should be content with whatever you have, regarding what you already have as being all you need.[25]

Contentment can only come from a spiritual outlook. The desire for worldly goods has to be given up. One should not distinguish between 'my work' and 'work for God'. All work should be worship. Whatever the reward, it is the gift of God. It is for our lasting good.[26]

Charity is a quality much greater than all the possessions associated with wealth. If there is no charity, wealth has no intrinsic value at all. Through sacrifice you will come to know that your real nature is charity. Charity does not mean that you have given some money to an individual or an organisation. The removal of all the evil thoughts that are within you is true charity. Charity will, in turn, confer purity upon you."[27]

Moha (Attachment)

According to *Vedanta* the most difficult attachments for human beings to break are:

1. Attachment to how others see us
2. Attachment to what we think and believe
3. Attachment to kith and kin
4. Attachment to the body and possessions

Sri Sathya Sai Baba says:

The Earth is a place where men come and stay for the night and when dawn breaks, one by one, they tramp their different ways. Kith and kin are the words we use for the attachment to the travellers cultivated during the short term of our acquaintance. If you think, you will know that the wife, the children, the possessions, the relatives are not yours for long, they are yours only for a short time. So why waste away, worrying over these impermanent things?

As a result of our attachment to the body and its organs we go on praising the beauty of the world. One gets attached to the sensory organs if one has attachment to the body. So long as man is attracted by outer Nature, he cannot escape the blows of joy and grief, of profit and loss, of happiness and misery.[28]

Do not cultivate too much attachment to things of the world, which appeal to carnal desires and sensual thirsts. A moment comes when you have to depart empty handed, leaving all that you have laboriously collected and proudly called your own.[29]

Sri Sathya Sai EHV points out some additional forms that attachment can take: addictions to substances, not letting go when necessary, nepotism or resorting to unrighteous actions to provide for loved ones. Mentally we can become attached to fanatical ideas or patterns of behaviour and become obsessed with objects or people.

Sri Sathya Sai Baba says:

> *The basic lesson is that man should not have any desires of any kind. Everything belongs to God.*

TREATMENTS FOR ATTACHMENT. Attachment to the body is a kind of disease that has to be treated by three kinds of remedies. One observes dietary restrictions while taking medicine. If diet control is not observed, the medicine alone will not cure. Diet control without medicine will be equally ineffective. Both diet control and medicine are equally necessary for curing the disease. With regard to the "disease" of attachment to the body, one has to abide by divine injunctions and practise love for the Divine to get rid of the ailment.[30]

Although Sai says 'Love everyone' do not develop too much attachment to them. Say 'hello, hello', 'good-bye, good-bye'. This is spirituality; it is discipline.[31]

Take the troubles that come to you as tests and opportunities to learn non-attachment. It is the hot summer that sends you to air-conditioning. Grief sends you to God.[32]

Mada (Pride, Ego, Arrogance)

Sri Sathya Sai Baba says

> *Considering oneself as different from others is ego.*

Ego (*Ahamkara*) is misinterpreted as arrogance, pride or carelessness. This is not the correct meaning. *Aham* means 'I', *akaram* means the 'form' or body – I am this body. Considering the body as the self is real ego. You have to destroy this feeling. When people behave in a proud or arrogant way it shows their animal nature, but does not mean ego.[33]

Egoism is the greatest factor in making people forget their basic Truth. Once egoism enters man, he slips from the ideal and precipitates himself from the top of the stairs in quick falls from step to step, down to the very bottom floor. Egoism breeds schisms, hatreds and attachments. Through attachment, affection and even envy and hatred, one plunges into activity and gets immersed in the world. This leads to embodiment in the physical frame and further egoism. In order to become free from the twin pulls of pleasure and pain, one must rid oneself of body-consciousness and keep clear of self-centered action.[34]

Whenever you act with body-consciousness, that is, when you identify yourself as the doer of an action, then that action cannot become *Karma Yoga*. Any action performed with the feeling of ego, the sense that 'I' did it or with the sense of attachment, that it is 'my' action, all such actions only bring sorrow.[35]

Egoism arises because of the ignorance which is inherent in man. If you were to take true cognisance of the vastness of the world you would not have egoism. It is only when you are oblivious to the greatness of the universe in relation to your minute size can you ever be filled which such a foolish notion.

TREATMENTS FOR EGO AND PRIDE. Perhaps you are proud of your body. But the body consists of only the five elements. One day or other it will have to perish. Only the indweller is permanent. Look to this indweller and you will not be deluded by pride and egoism. Turn towards the eternal; take shelter in the Lotus Feet of the Lord. Do not keep looking towards this body and feeling proud. This body is full of diseases; it undergoes many changes.

It is not even able to journey on this ocean of worldly existence and survive.[36]

Once the ego or body consciousness is surrendered, there is no bar to one's realisation. It is body consciousness that stands in the way and makes you forget God.[37]

Surrendering to the Lord is surrendering all thoughts and actions, not wishing for the fruits of the action, not doing action to gain its fruit, but doing the action because it is one's duty. The act is dedicated to the Lord and the results, therefore, are borne by the Lord. Actions done thus – fruits abandoned at the time of action – such action is free of *karma*. Since in this way the ego is not fed and cultivated – it disappears before long.[38]

When an action is performed without desire and without any feeling of egoism, then it may be called *Karma Yoga*. Remove your egoism. Drive it away. Remove your desire for the fruit. When you perform action with this attitude it becomes a *yajna*; it becomes work in the spirit of true sacrifice; it becomes *tapas* or penance and it becomes *yoga*.

The ego is most easily destroyed by devotion to God, by dwelling on the magnificence of the Lord and by humility and service to others as children of the Lord.[39]

MATHSARYA (ENVY AND JEALOUSY)

Sri Sathya Sai Baba says:

What is the root cause of discontent? **It is envy**. This has been the besetting vice of man from the beginning of time. Only when envy is eradicated from the human *Hridayam* will man have self-satisfaction. The contented man enjoys peace. How does envy arise? When one compares himself with those who are better off, or who hold higher offices, or score higher marks, or are more handsome, and suffers from a consciousness of his own inferiority, envy arises. Discontent over what he lacks gives birth to envy.[40]

It is the weakness of ordinary human beings to develop jealousy against people who excel them in terms of wealth, position, beauty, intelligence and such qualities. The moment jealousy enters into a person all the virtues which that person has cultivated over a long time will be destroyed. Jealousy is not just going to live harmlessly inside a person. It destroys all the great qualities and virtues which are in him. It is all pervasive in this *Kali* age. Jealousy is prevalent in all types of people, be they *yogis*, *bogis* or *rogis* (the sacred, the worldly or the sick). It is mostly on account of jealousy that people lose their peace of mind and waste their lives. It is only a mean type of satisfaction that through your jealousy and hatred you give trouble to others. But you are not giving trouble to others at all; you are only troubling yourself. In a number of ways, jealousy will create difficulties for the person who is infected with it.

TREATMENTS FOR ENVY AND JEALOUSY. In the very first place, everyone has to see to it that jealousy does not enter into him. You should enjoy the prosperity of others. You should enjoy the progress of others. You should enjoy the welfare of others. This is true virtue. This is what the ***Bhagavad Gita*** taught: desiring the welfare and good of others is a good quality and a very important quality which everyone should possess.

Jealousy is a vicious disease which must not be permitted to gain a foothold. You must feel that God will always bless you with His Grace, even if you are in a lesser position than you think you deserve. You won't be able to exterminate jealousy by merely reading scripture. But if you make a determined effort to transform your thoughts and develop selfless love, you can destroy this pest and offer all your bad thoughts at the Feet of the Lord.[41]

To get rid of this evil quality, one has to look at those who are worse off than himself. For instance, when you look at those who got lower marks than yourself, you can derive comfort from the fact that you have done better than many others. Likewise, when one views the state of those holding lower jobs he can feel satisfied with his own position. Thus, if envy has to be got rid of, this sort of comparison with those who are worse off has to be undertaken. In due course, one develops a sense of equal-mindedness both towards those who are better off and those who are worse off. Such equal-mindedness is a Divine quality. There is nothing wrong in aspiring for higher positions. But one should not feel envious about those who are already in such positions. It is a crime to entertain such feelings. [42]

Fear – The Great Illusion

> *It is said that a person charged with fear dies every step of the way, while a fearless person dies once.*
>
> ~ **Sri Sathya Sai Baba**

Although fear is not listed as one of the six inner enemies, it is one of the most devilish foes of man. It has been referred to by the acronym **F**alse **E**vidence **A**ppearing **R**eal. This is the truth of it.

Sri Sathya Sai Baba says:

Why is man afflicted today with fear and anxiety? Are we to search for the reasons outside us or do they lie within us? The reason lies in the false emphasis we have laid on things of the material world, ignoring things of the spirit. The body that man bears is essentially the receptacle of God. It is a temple where God is installed and where God is the Master.[43] **[See Diagram No. 29]**

Of all the great virtues, fearlessness occupies the place of primary importance. Unless you have fearlessness, you will never be able to live comfortably. Be it in the secular field in the battle of life in the world, or be it in your struggles in the realm of the spirit, you must never leave room for fear to creep in; it should find no place in your life. When a person is obsessed with fear he becomes extremely timid. He won't be able to accomplish even the smallest job. Once a man is full of fear he cannot shine in the world. Therefore the ***Bhagavad Gita*** has taught that one should become totally fearless. Fearlessness, *Abhaya*, cannot be considered as just absence of fear, which is called *Nirbhaya*. They are not the same. Both fear and absence of fear are associated with body consciousness. Absence of fear can sometimes be foolish, such as when the body is threatened with harm. But fearlessness, on the other hand, is beyond body consciousness. It can be experienced only when you recognise the truth of the one divinity without second, resident in full measure in every heart.

MANY FACES OF FEAR. Fear, this "False Evidence", can appear in many guises. There is the common daily variety that comes from anxiety or worry about the future. Living in the present moment is the key to managing this type of fear. If we execute each action that comes before us with love, concentration and integrity, offering the fruits to the Lord, we should have full confidence that God will certainly look after our future.

Life also brings us into situations that may be truly threatening, which activate the human "fight or flight" response. You may encounter people who are unkind to you, who hate you, who speak harsh words or hold jealous feelings towards you. There are also dangerous situations where your physical safety is threatened. Whatever face fear takes, the greatest remedies are **courage and love**.

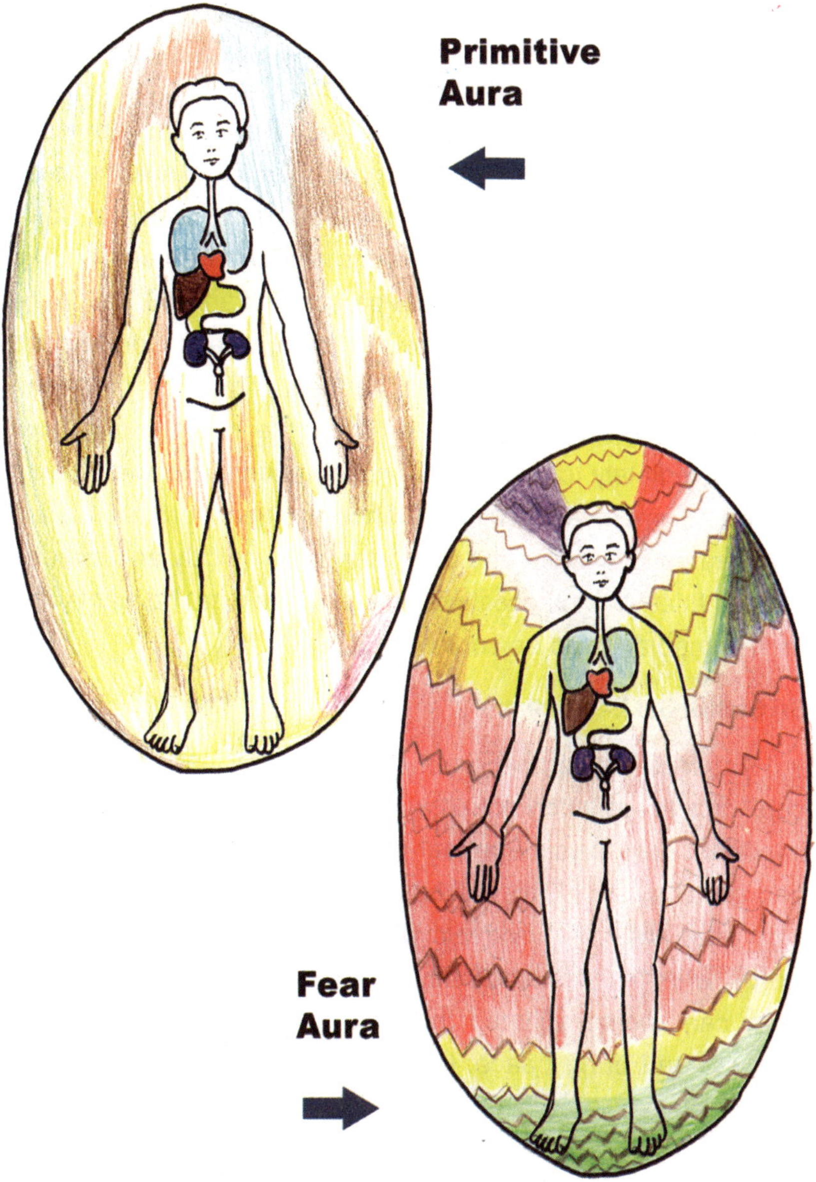

Human Values And Health ~ Diagram No. 29

Courage is an inner quality, born of faith in the Self. Take a deep breath and let your consciousness go deep within, drawing reserve strength from your inner Divinity, and then silently, or aloud if possible, repeat the name of God. Chanting the name of God is very important when we feel fear. If a terrorist comes in front of you, the name of God will come quickly and automatically to your mind. Even if the devil himself appears, face him down with calm confidence and the name of God. Remember, it is only the mind and thoughts of the person that are evil. Inside the body is the one *Atma*. Send love to them, or ask God to send love through you. If you cannot connect with this *Atmic* love, close your eyes, keep silent and bring the name and form of God immediately to your mind. The vibrations from the thought of God will improve any circumstance. If a treacherous situation accelerates, stay calm and take your leave quickly and sweetly. If it is a thief who is accosting you, give him what he wants and then immediately go on your way.

Sri Sathya Sai Baba says:

Anger is one of the great originators of fear, as it brings conflict and agitation into the *manomaya kosa*, so another important step to manage fear is to breathe deeply, keep calm and speak sweetly. This will help you to stay centered and can very often disarm individuals who are threatening you. Sweet words, whether intoned silently or aloud, carry divine vibrations. They can soothe agitated thoughts and feelings of everyone involved and bring peace. If this is impossible, simply hold a Divine silence, breathing deeply, chanting the name of God within. [44]

OTHER TREATMENTS FOR FEAR. Whenever you see anyone or anything as other than God, fear may come into you. It is only when you know that every name and every form to be found anywhere in the universe is nothing but a combination of the five elements, and that whatever form these elements take their basis and support is always God – when you are firmly grounded in this belief, then fear can gain no foothold within you and you become permanently free of fear.[45]

The Lord is the unseen foundation on which your life is built. He is the source, sustenance and strength. Without His will no leaf can turn, no blade of grass can quiver. What firmer foundation can you desire than this? Once you know that the Lord, the Omnipotent Power, is the mainspring of your life, there will be no more fear.[46]

> *I shall be ever with you, wherever you are, guarding and guiding you. March on; have no fear. Why fear when I am here?* ~ **Sri Sathya Sai Baba**

The Human Aura

When left unchecked, these inner foes fill the *manomaya kosa* of a man, making him a menace to himself and society. They form vibrational patterns, blocking out the light of man's true nature, which is divine love. When these foes are cleared through the practice of human values, the divine light evoked from within creates a healthy, loving reflection in man's outer experience.

The colour of the entire subtle body (or astral body) changes according to the state of mind, thoughts and emotions of man. The astral body can be seen as an aura, which is an oval or egg shaped emanation, projecting beyond the space occupied by the human body. There are thoughts and vibrations held within the body and around the aura, which denote the state of mind of a person. Love, devotion, hatred, rage, jealousy, envy, affection, lust, greed, compassion, fear, shame and depression, are some of the thought waves which colour the astral body. The aura is visible with Kirlian photography or to clairvoyants who have highly developed psychic powers. Previously, only sages, saints, and *Avatars* could see thoughts and vibrations, but through the technological advances of our age, experiments are being done to diagnose diseases before they appear in the physical body. An enlightened sage came to my hospital and demonstrated various auras to me. He made many diagrams, some of which I have included here. **[See Diagram No. 30]**

The Auric Colours

- ***Kama*** (lust) creates a deep wine aura.
- ***Krodha*** (anger) creates a deep dark red aura.
- ***Lobha*** (greed) creates a reddish brown aura.
- ***Moha*** (attachments) creates a smoky gray aura.
- ***Ahamkara*** (ego mind) creates a bright gray.
- ***Dwesha*** (hatred) creates a black aura.
- ***Eershya*** (revenge) creates a blackish brown aura.
- ***Mathsarya*** (jealousy) creates a deep green aura.
- ***Prema*** (love) between husband and wife creates a rose red colour, but love between mother and child creates a pink aura.
- ***Bhakti*** (devotional love for God) is from light blue to dark blue followed by light yellow to bright yellow.
- **Polite, Tolerant** and **Adaptable** nature creates a light green to bright green aura.
- A **Spiritually Great Person** will show a brilliant white sparkling aura.
- The ***Avatars*** have brilliant white, pink, blue and golden yellow sparkling auras.

Obstacles To *Atma Jnana*

While the six enemies of man need to be overcome by all who would develop into true human beings, there are other obstacles that inhibit the serious *sadhaka* (spiritual aspirant) who yearns

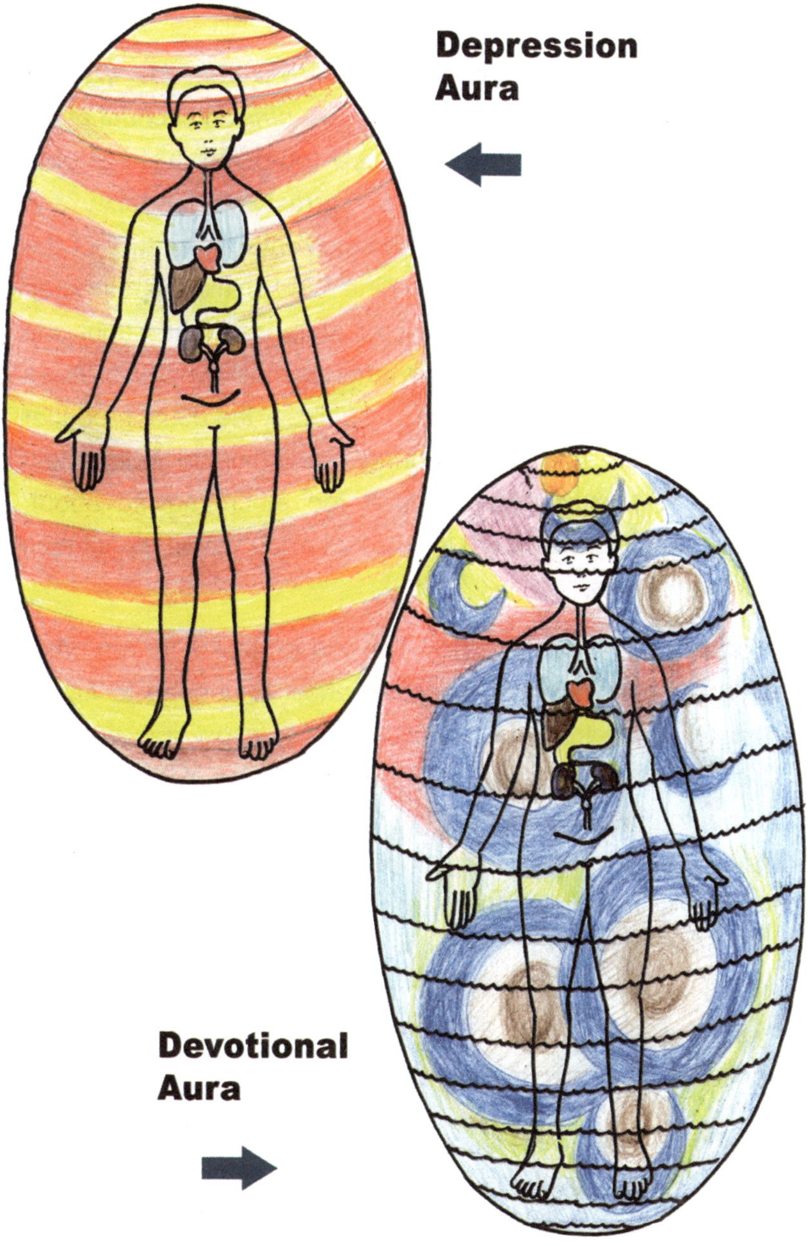

Human Values And Health ~ Diagram No. 30

for self-knowledge through meditation. Sai Baba outlines them as follows:

1. ***Laya*** (Sleep): When the mind withdraws from the external world it enters into deep sleep or *sushupthi*, on account of the overpowering influence of *samsara* (on-going cycle of birth and death) The *sadhaka* should arrest this tendency and attempt to fix the mind on the inquiry into the nature of the *Atma*. He must keep watch over the mind so that he may keep awake. He must discover the circumstances that induce the drowsiness and remove them in time. He must start the process of meditation again and again. Of course, the usual producer of drowsiness and sleep during meditation is indigestion. Overfeeding, exhaustion through too much moving about, want of sufficient sleep at night, these too cause sleepiness and drowsiness.

2. ***Vikshepa*** (Waywardness): The mind seeks to run after external objects and so constant effort is needed to turn it inwards, away from the attractions of sensory impressions. This has to be done through rigorous exercise of the Intellect, of enquiry. Discriminate and get the conviction driven into you that these are evanescent, temporary, transformable, liable to decay and therefore, unreal, not truth. Convince yourselves that what are sought after as pleasurable and avoided as painful are only the fleeting products of sensory contacts; train yourself in this way to avoid the distractions of the external world and dive deep into meditation.

3. ***Kshaya*** (Day-dreaming, scheming): The mind is drawn with immense force by all the unconscious impulses and instincts of passion and attachment towards to external world and its multitudinous attractions. It therefore experiences untold misery and might even get lost in its depths. The state of

inertia into which one is driven by despair cannot be called *Samadhi*; or one might even indulge in day-dreaming to escape from present misery; one might start building castles in the air. All this is due to attachment, to temptations of the outer world. There is another type of attachment too – attachment to the inner worlds ... the planning within oneself of various schemes to better oneself in the future as compared with the past. Both these form part of what is called *Kshaya*. The basis for both is the attraction of the outer world. Attachment brings about desire; desire leads to planning.

4. ***Rasa-Aswadana*** (Attachment to bliss): When scheming and waywardness are overcome one attains *Savikalpananda* – the bliss of the highest subject-object contact. This is the stage called "enjoyment of bliss". Even this is not the highest or supreme bliss, which one does not attain or acquire, but simply is. The *Rasa* (sweet taste) of the subject-object *samadhi* is a temptation one has to avoid for it is only second best. It is enough joy to act as a handicap. [47]

Fill The *Hridayam* With Love

To remove the wicked elements and install good qualities in their place, the only means is to foster the principle of love *(Prema Tathwa)*. When man's *Hridayam* is filled with love, all that he does will be "positive." All good deeds come out of love. *Sat-Chit-Ananda* arises from love. Compassion and kindness are born out of love. All the sublime Human Values have their origin in love. When one is filled with love, he needs no other spiritual or ritualistic practices. The *Atmic* principle is the basis for the body. All activities in life should be linked to the *Atmic* principle. Man should discard attachment to transient worldly pleasures and pursue what is eternal and everlasting.[48]

As a simple daily practice, Sri Sathya Sai Baba advises all to remember the "Four Fs":

- ***Follow the Master*** (the inner voice of the conscience)
- ***Face the Devil*** (the anti-social urges of the mind)
- ***Fight to the End*** (until one is able to overcome the six inner foes)
- ***Finish the Game*** (life on earth, gain liberation)

To this practice I add two more "F":

- ***Forgive and Forget*** (these are Divine)

---

1 *Bhagawan* Sri Sathya Sai Baba, Divine Discourse, 25/09/1998.
2 *Bhagawan* Sri Sathya Sai Baba, Divine Discourse, 11/10/1998.
3 *Bhagawan* Sri Sathya Sai Baba, Divine Discourse, 26/06/1994.
4 *Bhagawan* Sri Sathya Sai Baba, Divine Discourse, 25/02/1998.
5 *Bhagawan* Sri Sathya Sai Baba, ***Prasnottara Vahini***, Ch. 6.
6 *Bhagawan* Sri Sathya Sai Baba, recorded in **Conversations With *Bhagawan* Sri Sathya Sai Baba** by Dr. John Hislop.
7 *Bhagawan* Sri Sathya Sai Baba, **Discourses on the *Bhagavad Gita*,** Ch. 8.
8 *Bhagawan* Sri Sathya Sai Baba, recorded in **Conversations With *Bhagawan* Sri Sathya Sai Baba** by Dr. John Hislop.
9 *Bhagawan* Sri Sathya Sai Baba, **Sathya Sai Newsletter, USA,** Spring 1995.
10 *Bhagawan* Sri Sathya Sai Baba, **Discourses on the *Bhagavad Gita*,** Ch. 9, 1984.
11 *Bhagawan* Sri Sathya Sai Baba, recorded in **Conversations With *Bhagawan* Sri Sathya Sai Baba** by Dr. John Hislop.
12 *Bhagawan* Sri Sathya Sai Baba, **Sathya Sai Speaks,** Vol. 10, Ch. 1.
13 *Bhagawan* Sri Sathya Sai Baba, ***Sanathana Sarathi*,** August 1994.
14 *Bhagawan* Sri Sathya Sai Baba, **Sathya Sai Speaks,** Vol. 7.
15 *Bhagawan* Sri Sathya Sai Baba, Divine Discourse, 10/01/1993.
16 *Bhagawan* Sri Sathya Sai Baba, ***Sanathana Sarathi*,** August 1995.
17 *Bhagawan* Sri Sathya Sai Baba, **Discourses on the *Bhagavad Gita*,** Ch. 9, 1984.
18 *Bhagawan* Sri Sathya Sai Baba, **Sathya Sai Speaks,** Vol. 6, Ch. 17.
19 *Bhagawan* Sri Sathya Sai Baba, **Discourses on the *Bhagavad Gita*,** Ch. 8, 1984.
20 *Bhagawan* Sri Sathya Sai Baba, **Discourses on the *Bhagavad Gita*,** Ch. 9, 1984.
21 *Bhagawan* Sri Sathya Sai Baba, **Teachings of Sri Sathya Sai Baba.**
22 *Bhagawan* Sri Sathya Sai Baba, ***Sanathana Sarathi***, May 1995.
23 *Bhagawan* Sri Sathya Sai Baba, ***Sanathana Sarathi***, August 1993.
24 *Bhagawan* Sri Sathya Sai Baba, **Sathya Sai Speaks,** Vol. 11, Ch. 25.
25 *Bhagawan* Sri Sathya Sai Baba, **Discourses on the *Bhagavad Gita***, Ch. 23.
26 *Bhagawan* Sri Sathya Sai Baba, **Sathya Sai Speaks,** Vol. 11, Ch. 25.

27 *Bhagawan* Sri Sathya Sai Baba, **Sathya Sai Newsletter, USA**, Vol. 13.

28 *Bhagawan* Sri Sathya Sai Baba, **Baba, the Breath of Sai.**

29 *Bhagawan* Sri Sathya Sai Baba, **Sathya Sai Speaks,** Vol. 7.

30 *Bhagawan* Sri Sathya Sai Baba, ***Sanathana Sarathi,*** September 1994.

31 *Bhagawan* Sri Sathya Sai Baba, **Sathya Sai Newsletter, USA,** Summer 1995.

32 *Bhagawan* Sri Sathya Sai Baba, **Baba, the Breath of Sai.**

33 *Bhagawan* Sri Sathya Sai Baba, **Sathya Sai Newsletter, USA,** Summer 1995.

34 *Bhagawan* Sri Sathya Sai Baba, ***Jnana Vahini.***

35 *Bhagawan* Sri Sathya Sai Baba, **Discourses on the *Bhagavad Gita,*** Ch. 32.

36 *Bhagawan* Sri Sathya Sai Baba, **Discourses on the *Bhagavad Gita*** Ch. 31.

37 *Bhagawan* Sri Sathya Sai Baba, ***Sanathana Sarathi,*** October 1994.

38 *Bhagawan* Sri Sathya Sai Baba, recorded in **Conversations With *Bhagawan* Sri Sathya Sai Baba** by Dr. John Hislop.

39 *Bhagawan* Sri Sathya Sai Baba, **Teachings of Sri Sathya Sai Baba.**

40 *Bhagawan* Sri Sathya Sai Baba, Divine Discourse, 19/11/1998.

41 *Bhagawan* Sri Sathya Sai Baba, **Discourses on the *Bhagavad Gita*** Ch. 25.

42 *Bhagawan* Sri Sathya Sai Baba, Divine Discourse, 19/11/1998.

43 *Bhagawan* Sri Sathya Sai Baba, **Baba, the Breath of Sai.**

44 *Bhagawan* Sri Sathya Sai Baba, **Sathya Sai Speaks,** Vol. 9.

45 *Bhagawan* Sri Sathya Sai Baba, **Discourses on the *Bhagavad Gita*** Ch. 28.

46 *Bhagawan* Sri Sathya Sai Baba, ***Sanathana Sarathi,*** May 1995.

47 *Bhagawan* Sri Sathya Sai Baba, ***Jnana Vahini.***

48 *Bhagawan* Sri Sathya Sai Baba, Divine Discourse, 25/02/1998.

When your efforts come together with My Grace there is transformation. Bird flies with two wings. One wing is your effort, the other wing is My Grace.

~ **Sri Sathya Sai Baba**

chapter - 15

THE POTENTIAL OF HUMAN BIRTH

Sri Sathya Sai Baba explains:

> *Human birth is a rare privilege. It is highly sacred and sublime. Having been born as human beings, if men do not realise the preciousness of human life, what is the use of being born as human?*

How among all living beings, is the life of the human being supreme? Morality and good conduct govern it. The Divine has placed some limitations on the physical powers of man, but has set no limits to his mental powers. **Man can achieve whatever he resolves to achieve. He can even realise God.** This Divine power is given only to human beings. Ignorant of his limitless Divine potentialities, man suffers from various disabilities by considering himself as a mere human being.[1]

Among all types of living bodies, only a human body allows a being access to the three types of wisdom. While you have a human body you can . . .

1. Master the physical sciences.
2. Expand your scope to the science of spiritual betterment.
3. Work consistently until you experience God and become the fountain of infinite knowledge that He is. [2]

Man today is soaring in the sky as a bird and moving in the ocean like a fish. He has been able to land on the moon. But unfortunately, he is not able to live like a true human being on earth. This is indeed a matter for shame. Man can accomplish anything if he surrenders to God. When he submits himself to the will of the Divine, there is no task he cannot accomplish. Once a devotee totally surrenders to the Lord, the Divine goes to any extent to help the devotee. An insignificant little stick, by association with fire, burns brilliantly. A drop of water held in your palm evaporates in a trice. But when it is cast into the ocean, it becomes one with it. **If man wants to achieve the highest human potentialities, he has to achieve proximity to God. He has to merge in the Divine. Then he can manifest his true nature.**

Not realising the true nature of this Divine Principle, man wastes his time on rituals and religious practices of various kinds. God cannot be realised through such practices. It is only by loving God and getting close to Him that one can realise one's aspirations. *Swami* does not disapprove of *sadhana* practices. They are good activities for using time sacredly. But without service to Godly persons, they are of no use for realising freedom from the cycle of mundane existence; it is the Lord who protects one and all in innumerable ways.

There is a simple way to secure the grace of God. You must get near God. Surrender yourself to Him, become one with Him. Instead of following this easy path, man today immerses himself in petty desires and keeps away from God. Devotees should realise that God also likes to test the depth and sincerity of the devotee's love. He seeks to find out whether the devotee is filled with love of God, how intense is that love and so on. **God tests the devotee's love in various ways.** One should not be content with making offerings to God. One should love God intensely. One should pine for Him. One should lose one's self in the love of God.[3]

Churning The Ocean Of Heart *(Hridayam)*

Men today should turn their hearts towards the search for truth. The human *Hridayam* is a symbol of the Ocean of Milk (abode of Vishnu [God]). In this Ocean, the rope of wisdom is issued for churning. Some disappointments and failures may occur. Without succumbing to these failures, if man continues his efforts, he will secure precious things like Truth, Righteousness and Justice. Qualities like Forbearance and Compassion will also emerge. Man should endeavour to cultivate qualities like Tolerance, Love, Sympathy, Righteousness, Justice and Truth. People do not give any importance to this quest for Truth. The search for Truth is being directed towards worldly objects, which are ephemeral and worthless. Men should really dedicate themselves to the quest for the Truth that is eternal. All arts have originated from the search for Truth.

Hridayam is the source of all types of impulses. How is one to realise this Truth? All impulses of man arise from the *Hridayam*. When the *Hridayam* is kept pure, all our thoughts, words and actions become sweet. When the *Hridayam* is dedicated to right purposes, all our actions become righteous and our life gets redeemed. All that is good or bad in us emanates from the *Hridayam*. Good and bad are seldom separate from each other. They are inseparable. Happiness is not a separate state. It is the consummation of suffering. This oneness of the Divine subsumes everything. Humanness is the means to realise this oneness. The scriptures have declared the same Divine Spirit dwells in all beings.[4]

THE NATURE OF HUMAN BEINGS

Sri Sathya Sai Baba says:

The nature of humans can be distinguished as characteristic of three types:

1. **THE BEAST-MEN** are those who do not pay any attention to anything other than their own selfish ends. They have no trace of devotion and dedication. They do not share in helping of others. They have no concern with the sorrows and suffering of others. They do not take them to heart. They do not worry over the children they have borne or the life partner they are wedded to.

2. **THE MAN-MEN** involve themselves in the welfare of their wives and children and the small circle of their kith and kin. They spend their lives in this restricted sphere. Of course, the nature of these people is not laudable; but there is at least the possibility of the little spark of love beckoning brilliant and expansive through contacts with society, or impact of saints, or participation in some projects of selfless service. Man-men can raise themselves up into God-men.

3. **THE GOD-MEN** are described in the ***BHAGAVAD GITA*** as *Sathatham Yoginah*, "Always associated with God." They are never apart from God. They experience God in and through all things at all times. Whatever they see or do, they believe it is in God and for God.[5]

Here is humanity (*Swami* points to a line in the wall). Below is the world, above is God. Aim up, not down. You are God. There is only One. For so many lives you have been declaring that you are human, with limitations, "I am faulty … I am so and so …" That is wrong. Now say, "I am God". **Never feel or say that you are other than God.** You will show Godly qualities. You will have Godly powers. You will be God.[6]

The Types Of *Jivas* (Souls)

Sri Sathya Sai Baba tells us:

In this wide world amongst the vast humanity, we find three types of souls:

1. *Pushti Jivas* (Enjoying the Grace of God)
2. *Samashti Jivas* (Studious people reading *swadyaya* [study of spiritual texts])
3. *Pravaha Jivas* (Only engaged in worldly activities)

1. ***PUSHTI JIVAS:*** Because of the meritorious deeds in their past lives they enjoy the grace of the Divine, though they do not engage themselves now in auspicious rites, study of scriptures, making contact with saints, undertaking pilgrimages, etc. The merit of their past lives makes them always happy in the company of the Divine. They dance in delight experiencing Divine benediction. Just as you don't have need for firewood after the cooking is finished, these people don't need any spiritual *sadhana* as they have already attained the goal of all *sadhana*. You may not find this type of person doing any spiritual exercise. But he is leading a true life and experiences *Brahmananda* (supreme bliss), *Nityananda* (eternal bliss), *Advaithananda* (bliss of being the one and only), and *Paramananda* (bliss of God). There is no need for such a person to undertake any spiritual pursuit.

2. ***SAMASHTI JIVAS:*** The second type read many scriptural texts and they are keen on earning name and fame as scholars. Since they become proud of their scholarship, they do not make themselves fit to be recipients of Divine grace. When one goes on reading till the end of one's life, where is the time for practising the ideals? They may participate in seminars and meet noble souls, but they are far away from God's grace because they have no time to think of God and enshrine Him

in their *Hridayam*. This is the plight of this second type of persons termed as *Samasthi Jivas*.

3. ***PRAVAHA JIVAS:*** The third type is always engaged in mundane activities in pursuit of physical comforts and worldly pleasures. They do not think of God and think that they are capable of achieving whatever they want. At least, wicked people think of God in some difficult situations. The *Pravaha* persons have no chance of realising the Divine at all. They are born again and again. They have no chance of liberation. Some may have good feelings latent in them. However, they do not join *Satsang*, do not adhere to good conduct and righteous action, though some may be conscious of the Divine residing in the *Hridayam*.[7]

The Four *Asramas*

There are four stages of life called *Asramas*. If you know the requirements of each, you can decide which you are to fulfill, examining your own achievement, progress and aptitude. The four stages are:

1. ***BRAHMACHARYA* (STUDENT):** They keep their minds free from the delusion of the world. They are constantly engaged in thinking about God. They do not see or hear those things which are merely entertaining; they pursue only that which is in good taste. They do not yield to joy or grief; they keep their consciousness, intelligence and mind in good trim by unremitting contemplation of the formless reality.

2. ***GRIHASTA* (HOUSEHOLDER):** Being married and living with the spouse and children does not constitute being *grihasta*, as many people think. Without giving up the duties assigned to one's place in life, a householder has to treat all with equal consideration, be aware of the rights of the juniors, be full of

sympathy and willingness to help, treat everyone with loving kindness, especially dependents; grow wiser with each new experience of the world, become acquainted with scriptures and be alert to discriminate between actions which are *dharmic* and those which are *adharmic*. Householders must also rise above the eight egoisms: the conceit that develops from family, wealth, character, personal beauty, youth, scholarship, place of birth and even accomplishments in austerity. They must be conscious of the four *purusharthas* (goals of life). The householder will take no pride in material possessions, even though having them in large measure, will utilise a portion of the day in the service of others, will have no intention to harm any other household, will deserve the trust of his or her spouse, and have a trusted spouse, each understanding the other and having full faith in the other.

3. ***VANAPRASTHA* (RECLUSE OR FOREST DWELLER):** This one feels that all dualities are untrue and baseless, gives up all desires, drops all attachment to the world, dislikes living in populous places and is eager to achieve victory through prayerful repetition of a sacred text or chanting the Lord's name. He or she leads a life of austerity, eating only uncooked foods – mostly fruits and leaves – in moderation, moves in the company of sages and *maharishis* and listens to their teachings, and proceeds unfalteringly along the path of realising the Lord. The *vanaprastha* must have the approval of the spouse when moving out into solitude to lead a life of *sadhana*, and must also make sufficient provision for dependent children. If willing to go, however, the spouse must be taken along on the spiritual journey. They must henceforth live as brother and sister and not as husband and wife. Provided this new relationship is maintained, the reclusive life may be lived in the home. On the other hand, if the old life is continued, just living in the forest

does not constitute *vanaprastha*. The *vanaprasthas* must not stay in the residences of married people. They must observe the vows prescribed for each season of the year. They have to brave the rain, the sun and the cold in their season. They must be vigilant against being drawn towards physical pleasures by the fickleness of the mind. They must seek and find pleasure only in contemplation of the Lord and in dwelling upon His glory.[8]

Prepare yourselves for a celibate and spiritual discipline from the age of fifty; the five senses have to be mastered by the time five decades of your life are over. The conclusion of six decades means that you have conquered the six foes of man: lust anger, greed, attachment, pride and envy.[9]

4. ***SANYASA* (RENUNCIANT):** They are above all promptings of sensual or objective pleasure. They consider contemplation of the Lord as the very breath of life, essential to existence, and they derive joy only from this contemplation. They know that wealth and kinship, affection and attachment are all momentary. They wear the ochre robe of the mendicant; they do not live in populous places; they live on whatever little food they get; they do not decry the place where they are not given food; they do not eat twice in the same place or sleep two days in succession in the same place; they even conquer the temptation to sleep and eat. They care little for the rigors of the seasons; they are ever joyful in the company of the Lord, whom they invoke through meditation. They must be free from attachment and hatred; they do not take any interest in their surroundings; whether in a forest or town, they do not care in the least. They have no relations with others. They pay no heed to past, present or future. They move about on thorn and stone, silent, smiling to themselves, ever joyous, ever alert, seeking no comfort or shelter, seeking no place to sleep or

take food, for bliss is their food. There are great souls even today in the Himalayas, in silent caves, immersed in the bliss of knowing the God within. Not all can see them. Only your good fortune can bring you into their presence.[10,11]

THE *PURUSHA PURUSHARTHAS*

Bhagawan Baba has said the word *Purusha* did not signify the masculine gender as commonly assumed. It refers to the *Atma*, the Supreme Consciousness, which has no gender and which is immanent in all beings.

Of the two terms, *Purusha* and *Prakriti*, the latter represents the gross element in nature. It refers also to the body. *Purusha* is the Consciousness, the Indweller in the body. The two are independent.

Sri Sathya Sai Baba tells us:

The *Sastras* have declared that the body is *jada* (gross matter) and the *Atma* is *chaithanya* (consciousness) and that the body is feminine. Every being can be considered as made up of both elements and everyone, irrespective of sex, is entitled to pursue the four *purusharathas* (goals of human life):

1. ***DHARMA*:** The first one, *dharma*, is regarded in common usage as referring to actions like charity, the duties of one's *asrama* (stage in life), going on pilgrimages, and such other good deeds. But these relate only to external actions. The true *dharma* of every human being is to make every endeavour to realise the Divine. The process by which this consummation can be reached constitutes *dharma*. The observance of the duties relating to different *asramas* is incidental to the particular stage in life. These duties do not constitute *dharma* proper. *Dharma* should lead to Self-realisation.

2. ***ARTHA*:** The second term, *artha*, does not mean as commonly understood the accumulation of property and wealth. These are not our real wealth. They may well become *anartha* - calamitous. They are not lasting. The acquisition of such wealth cannot be considered a *purushartha*. The real wealth a man should acquire is the wisdom that is related to the *Purusha*.

3. ***KAMA*:** The third term, *kama*, is generally associated with worldly desires and sensual pleasures. But, when it is considered as a *purushartha*, it relates to the yearning for God and not to mundane desires.

4. ***MOKSHA:*** The fourth one, *moksha*, is generally understood as the means by which one reaches God or Heaven. But one can be in heaven only for the period earned by one's meritorious deeds and at the end will have to be reborn again. But *Moksha* in the true sense refers to a state in which nothing is lacking and there is no incoming or going out. It is a state without name or form. It is not a specific place to go to. It is the attainment of unity with the Divine.

For every human being, the tasks, among the four *purusharthas*, must be:

1. To determine what is permanent and what is transient and seek the Eternal.
2. The acquisition of Divine Wisdom as the real wealth.
3. To develop faith in God and yearn for realisation of and mergence in God.
4. *Moksha*, the state of Self-realisation in which there is no change and no movement.

The real meaning of *purushartha* is to make use of the time and circumstances as they arise for making one's life meaningful and sublime. We have to affect a remarkable, spiritual transformation in the world today. When we bring about a great spiritual transformation then there will be real peace. Such words must be used with their proper meaning; only then, there will be real peace.[12]

Man's Precious Possession

In this universe, there are *lakhs* of species, but the human is the noblest and the highest of these species. If man loses money, he can get it back; if he loses his wife, even then he can re-marry and have another wife; if he loses his share of land, he can get another, **but he cannot get back the body once it is lost.** Man does not realise the high value of precious human life and is misusing it in many ways. You must realise that once a night is passed, it won't come back. Once the river merges in the ocean, it cannot come back. When you eat a fruit you cannot get it back in its original form. Man is not knowing his own value.

Man has several capacities and faculties. These four constitute his *Sampathi* (possessions) and are enumerated as follows:

1. The first gift that a man possesses is ***Mathi*** (intellect)
2. The second is ***Sthithi*** (position)
3. The third one is ***Paristhithi*** (circumstance)
4. The fourth is ***Gathi*** (destiny)

All things that are happening to man depend on his Destiny alone. Mind is based on our conduct and it shapes our Destiny. Intellect should be sound. Everything else depends on Position and Possessions. When one understands this, one can know one's Destiny. **Everyone has to maintain the mental balance to act properly.** Suppose a person has a knife in hand. He or she cuts vegetables, cooks food and consumes it to appease hunger. On the other hand, if the person cuts the throat of another person it will lead to disastrous consequences. You must know the proper method to use any material. You must be aware of the different types of *sakti* that you are gifted with. You must know how to pass every day in the best possible way without wasting precious time. You must also know that everything happens according to the Divine Will. The Divine cannot be expected to act according to your thoughts or desires. God is fully aware of the needs of the family, country and world at large, and confers the requisite benefits at the appropriate time.[13]

Body Is An Instrument To Realise God

The human body is encased in five sheaths *Annamaya Kosa* (food or physical), *Pranamaya Kosa* (vital force), *Manomaya Kosa* (mental), *Vijnanamaya Kosa* (wisdom), and *Anandamaya Kosa* (bliss). Among the five sheaths, ***Vijnanamaya Kosa* is present only in man, and not in other beings.** Man should realise the preciousness of this gift of the wisdom sheath. It should not be misused. Man is endowed with so many noble and estimable qualities that he should not be treated as a being of no account. Forgetting all his immense potentialities and treating the physical as most important, man is leading a meaningless life. It is not the physical body that is really important. **As long as life is based on the physical alone, man can have no peace.**

Science is concerned with all the phenomena in nature. It furnishes what is required for the physical body. It is doubtlessly essential to take care of the body. But the body should not be deemed as the sole truth. However, one should devote all efforts to its maintenance and comfort. All achievements are dependent on the body. Even the Divine can be really seen through the body. **But the body is not your self.** It is only an instrument for realising God. Moreover, the Supreme *Atmic* Principle, *Paramatma*, is immanent in it. Man has many sacred qualities like love and sacrifice, but he does not put them into practice wholeheartedly.

In man the supreme Divine quality is Love. Love is God. Live in Love. Cultivate Love for all. This vast world calls for large-hearted

Love. Only then humanness will become manifest. Troubles and difficulties are incidental to human existence. But they will pass in due course. What are permanent are the values we cherish.[14]

Humanness

"A human birth is the most sacred one among the 84 *lakhs* of different living beings in this creation. To attain such a sacred birth is a great good fortune," Sathya Sai Baba tells us. The ancient texts declare that even angels, *gandharvas* and other celestial beings have to take human birth in order to realise the divine.

Sri Sathya Sai Baba says:

The human form is unique in that the divine force is as much as 80 percent present. In the animal it is only about 15 percent. Man can raise himself to union with God, whereas the animal can never be free of his natural state. The body of man is necessary because it is able to reveal the unseen God. The body serves to reveal the indwelling divinity. The expression of life on Earth is upward through the human to the Divine. By virtue of human birth, the next step is the full realisation of the Divine. Human life is sacred and must be appreciated as having the highest value. All life may aspire to human birth. But only through human birth may God be realised. To waste time is the greatest folly. Here and now is the individual. Here and now is the opportunity to realise the absolute goal of life. Who can be sure of the conditions and status of his next rebirth? Not even one moment of this life should be wasted.

> *The purpose of living is to achieve living in God. Everyone is entitled to that consecration and that consummation. You are the truth. Do not lose faith. Do not belittle yourselves. You are Divine.*[15]

---

1 *Bhagawan* Sri Sathya Sai Baba, Divine Discourse, 29/03/1998.

2 *Bhagawan* Sri Sathya Sai Baba, Divine Discourse, 25/12/1976.

3 *Bhagawan* Sri Sathya Sai Baba, Divine Discourse, 29/03/1998.

4 *Bhagawan* Sri Sathya Sai Baba, Divine Discourse, 09/07/1998.

5 *Bhagawan* Sri Sathya Sai Baba, Divine Discourse, 17/07/1981.

6 *Bhagawan* Sri Sathya Sai Baba, recorded in **Conversations with *Bhagawan* Sri Sathya Sai Baba**, by Dr. John Hislop.

7 *Bhagawan* Sri Sathya Sai Baba, Divine Discourse, 22/04/1998.

8 *Bhagawan* Sri Sathya Sai Baba, ***Prasnottara Vahini***, Ch. 3.

9 *Bhagawan* Sri Sathya Sai Baba, **Sathya Sai Speaks,** Vol. 7B, Ch. 28.

10 *Bhagawan* Sri Sathya Sai Baba, ***Prasnottara Vahini***, Ch. 3.

11 *Bhagawan* Sri Sathya Sai Baba, **Sathya Sai Newsletter, USA,** Summer, 1989.

12 *Bhagawan* Sri Sathya Sai Baba, Divine Discourse, 14/01/1985.

13 *Bhagawan* Sri Sathya Sai Baba, Divine Discourse, 22/04/1998.

14 *Bhagawan* Sri Sathya Sai Baba, Divine Discourse, 09/07/1998.

15 *Bhagawan* Sri Sathya Sai Baba, recorded in **Conversations with *Bhagawan* Sri Sathya Sai Baba**, by Dr. John Hislop.

chapter - 16

TRUE *ANANDA* IS IN LOVING ALL

Sri Sathya Sai Baba says:

Every human being seeks to enjoy *Ananda* (bliss). He aspires for a blissful life. Whether he is a scholar or an artist, a wielder of power or a man of status, he yearns for bliss. Every man strives from dawn to dusk to acquire bliss.

Man is enveloped in two screens, the **phenomenal** and the **spiritual**. His vision is affected by the material outlook and the spiritual outlook. Unable to harmonise the two, man regards them as distinct from each other. The unity of these two represents the true *Atmic* principle. Considering the material world of physical objects as the only reality, man loses himself in the pursuit of material objects. But, if the truth about these material objects is fully explored, it will be found that they have no reality at all. They have only momentary and temporal reality. They do not have the stamp of permanent reality. They do not confer enduring bliss. To realise lasting bliss, man has to make the requisite effort.[1]

Permanent Happiness Is Of The Self

When we look at a beautiful flower, happiness is generated in us. When we look at a beautiful bird or a nice house, we feel happy. We have to carefully consider whether such happiness is permanent or transient. A nice rose flower makes us feel very happy but by the evening the rose will fade away and by the next morning the petals will fall and then it does not generate as much happiness. In the same way, every object of beauty can only generate temporary happiness in us. We have to understand carefully where one can find permanent and lasting happiness. This can be found in the aspect of Self and in the thought of God. We can get permanent happiness only from things which are permanent. Out of things which are transient we can never get lasting happiness. It is only after experiencing such permanent happiness we will get true bliss. We cannot go on searching for such bliss everywhere. If we do this, it will be like going to a fish market in search of diamonds. We can find only fish in a fish market and not diamonds. Since the world is temporary and all life in it is uncertain, we cannot find permanent happiness in this world.[2]

Mental Afflictions Are Due To Bad Thoughts

The human body is prey to many ailments. Man regards all of them as bodily ailments. But not all are entirely related to the body. Ailments that are purely of the body can be treated by medicines. **But most ailments in the world today have their origin in the mind.** The aberrations of mind set up reactions in the body that cause various diseases. The mind and the body are interrelated. The influence of the mind on the body is of a negative character. Bad thoughts cause indigestion, affect the heart, and bring about variations in the blood pressure; worries are the cause of many mental diseases. Diabetes and pulmonary diseases are traceable to mental causes. This negativity is antagonistic to the experience of bliss. **It is only when bad thoughts and feelings are weeded out that man can have good health.**[3]

Happiness And Sorrow

Sri Sathya Sai Baba tells us:

Whatever trouble you may face, you must learn to feel happy in any circumstance. If you are stung by a scorpion, you must console yourself that you were not bitten by a snake, and when you are bitten by a snake, you must console yourself that it has not proved fatal. Even if you are not able to own a vehicle, be happy that you have got your legs intact that enable you to walk. Even if you are not a millionaire, be happy that you have enough resources to feed yourself and your family. This is the way to experience joy even while in adverse circumstances.[4]

Truly three-fourths of our life is filled with happiness and only one-fourth of our life is filled with pain. But we do not look at our life in that manner. We feel that three-fourths is filled with sorrow and one-fourth is filled with happiness and we get vexed and disgusted with human life and say that this human life is full of sorrow. This simply reflects man's weak state of mind.

Why do we not think of the happiness and the good that we experienced in the past? We always recall the pain and the sorrow. If at a present time of trouble, instead of remembering the pain and sorrow of the past we can recall the pleasure and happiness, then to some extent we will be relieved of the present pain. The true nature of self should be such that we recall the happiness and pleasure that has gone by and not sorrow and pain. The reason for this is that the self has the form of Bliss. Self, which is the embodiment of God, is beauty and happiness. **Sorrow is the shadow that haunts the ego; happiness is from the body. Bliss is from the Soul.**

Realise that like the waves of the sea, happiness and sorrow rise and fall; they are like the inhalation and exhalation of the breath. Ask yourself the questions: Is there a state called happiness? Can it be reached by accumulating things? No. You must teach the mind to dive into the realms of bliss.[5]

Happiness Is Man's Natural State

Man's natural state is happiness and he cannot be blamed for craving that which is his own. But man is making a serious mistake. He believes that the happiness for which he craves comes from objects which he can experience [outside himself]. The truth of the matter is that he does not experience these objects. On the contrary, these objects experience the man and in the process the man is further weakened. The eternal truth is that there is only one everlasting never failing happiness and that is God. You are God, and to drink deeply of that ever flowing spring of happiness you must turn yourself to the Divine *Atma* which, however obscured, is always the resident of your heart, the subtle truth of your being.

The *Atma*, the Lord, the Divine Happiness is not our ever-constant experience, for it is obscured by such activities of the mind as doubt, depression, hatred, jealousy, envy, craving, attachments to objects and people, and ignorance about oneself, about God and about the world. In order to expel these dangerous and harmful tendencies from one's life, one needs to engage in *sadhana*. The objective of all types of *sadhana* is purification of mind and heart. For this reason it is said that one should "do good, see good, and be good".[6]

Contentment Is The Greatest Happiness

There is no greater penance than equanimity (*santham*). Peace is the foremost prize for man. Peace confers serenity on sages. Peace is a fascinating charm of the Divine. Without such peace there can be no happiness. There is no greater happiness (*santosham*) than being contented. Man seeks happiness in various forms. But there is no happiness equal to peace (*santi*), for without peace there can be no happiness.

What greater heaven is there than contentment? There is nothing worse than desire. Contemporary man is afflicted by endless desires. These desires are the cause of innumerable diseases. There must be a limit to desires. Today desires grow limitlessly. Consequently, diseases also increase limitlessly. Owing to endless desires, man is affected mentally and this gives rise to many bodily ailments. Hence, everyone should try as far as possible to keep a check on desires.[7]

The Lord Seeks The Devotee's Love

Sri Sathya Sai Baba says:

The Lord seeks the devotee's love. People have to lead their lives based on recognition of this truth. There is only one thing God seeks from all of us: to fill our hearts with love. Offer that love to God. God does not want anything from anyone. It is enough if you develop love and share it with others. **It is only when you are happy that you can make others happy. What is happiness? It is union with God.** By chanting the name of God you will experience happiness. Good and sacred acts like worship, *japa*, meditation are useful for sanctifying time, but they are no ends in themselves. They are tinged with worldliness. But "positive" action should be dedicated to the Divine. You will then be free from disease. Only by having pure thoughts you can be hale and hearty.

Devotion does not consist merely in different forms of worship; it is the dedicated offering of yourself to the Lord with unsullied love. You have come from the Divine with love. You have to base your life on that love. That love is a gift of the Divine. You must treat it as Divine property and not as your personal possession. As long as you entertain the sense of personal property, you can never understand the *Atmic* principle. The feeling of 'I' and 'mine' is the root cause of all man's troubles. Attachment and possessiveness cannot be totally eschewed, but there should be limits. Insatiable desires are the cause of the growth of peacelessness. You should live a life of contentment, and have only one desire, the yearning for God. Devotees should not give way to doubts. Faith in God should be firm till your last breath.[8]

Everyone must learn the secret of happiness, which consists of refusing to shed tears for anything less than God.[9]

Love Of God Is *Bhakti* And Bliss

Even the man of wisdom becomes a devotee at one point in time. The greatest and the noblest path is the path of devotion. The word *Bhakti* (devotion) is derived from the root *Bhaj*, which means total surrender. Offering of total love is *Bhakti*. The worship and other rituals are only physical and worldly activities. One must have *Bhakti* to enter *Nivritti* (inward path) from this *Pravritti* (outward path).

The bliss is within you, just as precious jewels are kept in an iron chest. Likewise, *Atmic* Principle is present in this human body; God has kept many valuable jewels in this body. But one is not making any effort to realise this. God says, "O, mad cap! Why do you entertain mean and low desires? If you give up desires and offer yourself, I will give you the most valuable gifts." **When God is ready to give the limitless non-dual bliss, why should one crave for limited happiness?** Therefore, do not ask for mean things. Offer yourself to God; then God will grant you jewels of limitless eternal bliss. Just as the essence of food one partakes of gets mixed in the blood and becomes one with the body, likewise let love be unified with "My Love," then you will become "one with Me." However, in order to deserve God's grace, one's faith should grow. When faith is absent, one cannot offer oneself to God.[10]

Man deserves to enjoy peace and bliss, but does not make the necessary effort to get them. If he cultivates love and faith, he will acquire peace and bliss. If he does not have these two, his effort is as fruitless as a letter that has neither a stamp nor the proper address. With love and faith in *Swami*, you can accomplish any task. Observe three maxims: **Love of God, Fear of Sin, Morality in Society.** To develop love of God you have to see whether every act of yours pleases God or not. When you please God you will have no fear of sin. When these two are present, morality in society will follow naturally. All the ills of the world today are due to the absence of fear of sin and the decline in love for God. Decline in love for God and decline in respect for Human Values have undermined world peace.

When the Lord's name is chanted from the depths of the heart, it turns into the nectarous music of Krishna's flute, which charmed even the cows of Brindavan. The melody that flows from the devotee's heart confers ineffable bliss.[11]

The *Sat-Chit-Ananda*

Sat-Chit-Ananda (Being-Awareness-Bliss) pervades the entire universe. Every living being, from the ant onwards, is seeking this bliss, not man alone. For all living creatures, this bliss is the life-breath. People today speak about *Sat-Chit-Ananda* as a reality after hearing about the statements in the ***Vedas, Puranas*** and other scriptural texts. Such persons have no personal experience of *Sat-Chit-Ananda.* Even the scholars who expound this concept are merely relating what they have learnt from books but have no direct experience of this bliss.

Every man should seek to know what *Sat-Chit-Ananda* means. Only then will he realise his own true self. Because of the delusion caused by the phenomenal world, man regards *Sat-Chit-Ananda* as distinct from himself. This feeling arises from his attachment to the body. Everyone should find out "Who am I?" When he has found the answer to this question there will be no need for him to understand what is *Sat-Chit-Ananda*.

As long as man identifies himself with the body and his physical attributes, he will be in quest of *Sat-Chit-Ananda*. When a man has discovered the true nature of the "I", he will not go after any other thing. He will realise that he is the embodiment of *Sat-Chit-Ananda*. *Sat* is God; *Chit* is *Jiva* (individual self). The unity of *"Sat"* and *"Chit"* is *"Ananda"* (Bliss).

How To Proceed From Body To Bliss

When man constantly remembers that he is the embodiment of *Sat-Chit-Ananda*, in due course he will experience that *Ananda*. Man is covered by five *kosas* (sheaths). Man has to proceed from the gross to the subtlest sheath of bliss. The *Annamaya Kosa* sheath is the body. It is perishable, but as long as one lives the body should be kept in good health. The duties relating to the physical have to be carried out. What keep the body going are the vibrations from the vital sheath (*Pranamaya Kosa*). These vibrations are controlled by radiation from the mind (*Manomaya Kosa*).

Beyond the mind is the *Vijnanamaya Kosa*, which accounts for the "constant integrated awareness" in man. When this state is reached man can proceed next to the bliss sheath (*Anandamaya Kosa)* without much effort. Experience of bliss will be automatic. It should be evident from this that humanness has been conferred on man so that he may ascend towards his divine destiny instead of following mundane pleasures and miseries. Thereby, he will demonstrate his superiority over beast and bird.[12]

The most important duty of man is to enjoy the bliss of the *Atma*. The *Atma* is the basis for the outer world and the world within. What is meant by *Atmananda*, or the bliss of the *Atma*? Man thinks he is enjoying himself when he has all physical and bodily comforts to the fullest extent. Actually, physical bliss is very, very small. We forget ourselves and get intoxicated with these small trifling joys.

There are several types of bliss far above worldly bliss. The highest of these is the bliss of the *Atma*, which is one hundred times to the power of seven (1,000,000,000,000) or one trillion. Once you have experienced this *Atmic* bliss how can you remember anything else? We forget everything else and we merge and immerse ourselves in the bliss of the *Atma*. There is no place in the world that is not filled with this bliss. Every object in the world contains this innate bliss.[13]

Happiness And Health

Over the past several decades the medical and psychological professions have shown increasing interest in the effects of happiness, smiling and laughter on health. As we all intuitively suspect, happiness produces health.

Happiness is a physical state of the brain. When we are happy our brain produces neurochemicals that result in us wanting to eat, be more loving and even sing. Most researchers study the effects of these neurochemicals by using different measurement techniques; an FMRI (Functional Magnetic Resonance Imaging), which records blood flow that activates parts of the brain; EEG (Electroencephalogram) which monitors the electrical activity of neuronal circuits; or blood tests that measure the amount of hormones in the blood such as dopamine or serotonin.

Here are the results from some recent research on happiness, reported in the on-line journal, **Balance Magazine**:

- People who score high on psychological tests assessing happiness, produce about 50% more antibodies than the average person in response to flu vaccines.
- Individuals that test high on scales for happiness, optimism and contentment have a reduced risk of cardiovascular disease, hypertension and infections.
- Researchers found that subjects' energy levels were raised, physical health improved and they experienced less fatigue and pain when they practised acts of happiness and gratitude regularly.
- A recent study reveals that optimistic individuals reduced their risk of death by 50% over the nine years of the study.

Laughter and humour create health and well being because they:

- Reduce stress
- Boost our immune systems
- Lower our blood pressure
- Improve our brain functioning

A study at the University of Maryland Medical Centre in the USA tells us the ability to laugh in stressful situations helps the brain not to produce harmful neuro-chemicals. Laughter increases our capacity to fight various diseases by increasing our antibody production. As our bodies relax when we laugh, we reduce the risk of heart disease, hypertension, strokes, arthritis and other inflammatory diseases. Laughter reduces the levels of stress hormones like cortisol.

Laughter is also a great exercise for the body. When we laugh we work our facial, abdominal, chest, leg and back muscles. Laughing fills our lungs with oxygen which nourishes our vital organs: the brain, heart, lungs and liver.

A recent study tracked two groups of cardiac patients. One group of patients received medical care alone and the other group received medical care plus they watched 30 minutes of comedy a day. After one year, the laughing group reported fewer repeat heart attacks, fewer episodes of arrhythmia, lower blood pressures and lower levels of stress hormones.

Here are some tips on how to live a happier life:

1. **Attitude of Gratitude:** It is physiologically impossible to be grateful and experience stress at the same time. Research shows grateful individuals report having more energy and less physical complaints than their non-grateful counterparts. Studies tell us daily gratitude exercises resulted in higher levels of alertness, enthusiasm, determination, optimism and happiness.

2. **Choice:** Every moment of our lives is a choice and every choice we make has a huge ripple effect. If we choose to commit to practising happiness and optimism, we can transform our lives.

3. **Smile:** Begin the practice of intentionally smiling. A scientist studying facial expressions tells us that when a person has a smile on his/her face, he/she releases more serotonin and endorphins, happiness hormones, than a non-smiler. A smile is the first step to a life of mental, physical and spiritual health. Begin a practice of smiling to shift any situation into an optimistic opportunity.

4. **Laugh:** Laugh as often as possible to release the healing hormones, endorphins, the body's natural pain killers. Instead of buying pills for our stress, we can share a joke with friends, or even join one of the laughter clubs that can be found in many large cities around the world. Laughter lowers blood pressure, reduces stress hormones and boosts our immune function.

5. **Play:** Re-establish "childlike" qualities. Science tells us when we play it increases our immune cells that combat disease. Playfulness also increases creativity and optimism at home and at work.

6. **Health:** "Health is Wealth", Sai Baba frequently reminds us. When we care for our physical bodies we create greater possibilities for happiness. Our bodies are our greatest asset; so please care for them tenderly.

7. **Spirituality:** The vast number of happy people surveyed have developed spiritual practices that nourish their heart and soul. Our spirituality is what roots us in our lives.

8. **Selfless Service (*Seva*) and Philanthropy:** A generous soul lives a rich, abundant life. *Seva* neutralizes negative emotions that affect immune, endocrine and cardiovascular function. Acts of selflessness create a physiological response or "helper's high" that makes people feel stronger and more energetic and counters harmful effects of stress.

9. **Forgiveness:** Happy people know forgiveness sets the soul free. Someone once said, "Living with resentment is like taking poison and expecting the other person to get sick." Open your heart to the gift of happiness by letting go of pain, judgment, anger and resentment.[14]

HAPPINESS IS LOVING ALL AND SERVING ALL

Sri Sathya Sai Baba says:

One must realise: "I am you. You are in me. God is one." The sense of separation between God and the individual should go. The Divine is in every individual, but one's realisation of this depends on one's own efforts. The Divine shines according to the degree of one's spiritual awareness. To manifest the full effulgence of the Divine, one has to adhere to the path of Love. Only through Love can the Supreme Divine be attained.[15]

Where there is love, there God is certainly evident. Love more and more people, love them more and more intensely; transform the love into service and transform the service into worship. That is the highest *sadhana*. Always consider yourself to be a servant, not a leader. Real joy is found in being a servant; there is no happiness in being a leader. How can one be happy putting another into the humiliation of attending to one's personal comforts?[16]

God cannot be attained with hatred, anger or jealousy. It is because these three evil qualities are present in people that you see the marks of misery on their faces. There should be no mark of sadness on the face of one who has faith in God. This was the case with Valmiki (writer of the ***RAMAYANA***). His face was full of radiance, a radiance derived by one who is the embodiment of Love. All of you should strive to promote your effulgence and bliss by seeking oneness with the Divine. This is the primary duty of man.[17]

This is why I always say, 'Be happy, be happy, make other people happy.' **Happiness is essential for God-realisation.** It is one of the major gates to divinity. It is not just a fault if a person is not happy; it is one of the most serious of all faults. It is a barrier to realisation.[18]

Embodiments of the Divine! Develop good thoughts and feelings of sacrifice. Cherish Divine thoughts. Cultivate friendliness. To hail God as father and mother and not to have fraternal feelings towards one and all is treason to God. You should cultivate unity as the children of God and live in harmony in the company of the good and the godly. Share the nectar of love that is in you with one and all. Do not bear ill will towards anyone; speak sweetly to everyone.[19]

See God in all and love them. True *ananda* is in loving all. The act of loving gives you happiness and healing. Happiness does not come from being loved by all, but in you loving everyone. Who are you to change this world? Accept others. Change yourself. You are an atom in this world; by purifying yourself you transform at least one atom and raise the vibrations around you. This is the best service you can do to God.

Sri Sathya Sai Baba concludes:

Practise the truth that whatever gives you pain gives pain to others and whatever gives you joy gives joy to others. So do unto others as you would like them to do unto you; desist from any act in relation to others that if done by them would give you pain. Thus a kind of reciprocal relationship will grow between you and others and gradually you will reach the stage where your heart thrills with joy when others are joyful and shudders in pain when others are sad.[20]

You cannot be happy when the rest of the mankind is unhappy. You are an organic part of the human community. Share your prosperity with others; strive to alleviate the sufferings of others. That is your duty.[21]

When people view the world with the vision of love they will have peace. All diseases will be cured. Everything has a psychological basis. When a person feels that something is wrong with him he develops an illness. A healthy mind is needed for a healthy body. But it is not enough to be physically healthy. Man needs God's grace also. To acquire God's grace you have to cultivate the love of God. If you develop love disease will not come near you.[22]

---

1 *Bhagawan* Sri Sathya Sai Baba, Divine Discourse, 18/02/1998.
2 *Bhagawan* Sri Sathya Sai Baba, **Baba the Breath of Sai.**
3 *Bhagawan* Sri Sathya Sai Baba, Divine Discourse, 18/08/1995.
4 *Bhagawan* Sri Sathya Sai Baba, ***Sanathana Sarathi,*** Aug 1994.
5 *Bhagawan* Sri Sathya Sai Baba, **Baba the Breath of Sai.**
6 *Bhagawan* Sri Sathya Sai Baba, recorded by Dr. John Hislop in **My Baba and I.**
7 *Bhagawan* Sri Sathya Sai Baba, Divine Discourse, 18/02/1998.
8 *Bhagawan* Sri Sathya Sai Baba, Divine Discourse, 18/08/1995.
9 *Bhagawan* Sri Sathya Sai Baba, **Baba the Breath of Sai.**
10 *Bhagawan* Sri Sathya Sai Baba, Divine Discourse, 11/10/1998.
11 *Bhagawan* Sri Sathya Sai Baba, Divine Discourse, source unknown.
12 *Bhagawan* Sri Sathya Sai Baba, Divine Discourse, 25/02/1998.
13 *Bhagawan* Sri Sathya Sai Baba, **Sathya Sai Newsletter USA,** Vol. 13, No. 3.
14 Holden, Dr. Robert, "The Science of Happiness", **Balance Magazine**, Summer 2005. (Reprinted from internet)
15 *Bhagawan* Sri Sathya Sai Baba, **Sathya Sai Speaks,** Vol. 7.
16 *Bhagawan* Sri Sathya Sai Baba, Divine Discourse, 18/08/1995.
17 *Bhagawan* Sri Sathya Sai Baba, Divine Discourse, 18/08/1995.
18 *Bhagawan* Sri Sathya Sai Baba, recorded by Dr. John Hislop in **Conversations With *Bhagawan* Sri Sathya Sai Baba.**
19 *Bhagawan* Sri Sathya Sai Baba, Divine Discourse, 26/06/1994.
20 *Bhagawan* Sri Sathya Sai Baba, **Sathya Sai Speaks,** Vol. 1.
21 *Bhagawan* Sri Sathya Sai Baba, **Sathya Sai Speaks,** Vol. 2.
22 *Bhagawan* Sri Sathya Sai Baba, ***Sanathana Sarathi,*** July 1995.

Divine Love flows from

***Hridayam** to **Hridayam** . . .*

Divine Love is spiritual and infinitely precious. It is not fickle and changing from moment to moment. One who is immersed in the ocean of Divine Love will have no words to express its greatness and sweetness. He will speak in the language of silence. He will keep away from idle talk or debate. Those who experience the bliss of Divine Love will be filled with inner joy, whatever the external troubles they may encounter. It is only when we cultivate this kind of love that we can claim to have achieved real freedom.

~ **Sri Sathya Sai Baba**

chapter - 17

THE *PARAMA PREMA* (PURE DIVINE LOVE)

Still thy mind in Me; still thy self in Me and without doubt thou shall be united with Me, Lord of Love, dwelling in your heart.

~ ***Bhagavad Gita,*** *12.8*

The Divine Love

The year was 1516 when Mira, the princess of Rajasthan, was married to Prince Bhoja Raj of the Rajput family. From childhood, the Divine Love and Presence of Lord Krishna was firmly entrenched in her *Hridayam*. Even as a new bride, she was all the time decorating the idol of Krishna, singing *bhajans* for Him and worshiping Him in various ways. At night when her husband called for her, she would say, “Keep quiet and let Krishna sleep; then I will come.” Her husband, Ranaji asked her, “Krishna is just a statue, what kind of love can you get from him?” For one who has never been pierced through the *Hridayam* by God’s Pure Love, this is a natural question.

Mira answers her husband through a beautiful *bhajan* in Rajasthani dedicated to her Lord Krishna. In this song, Mira explains to him her experience of Pure Divine Love.

Mira Lago Ranga Hari
(Mira is drenched with the love of God)

Aur Sabhey Rang Ghata Chale (2)
(All other loves faded away)

Koye Nido Koye Bindo
(Let people critcise me in any form in any way)

Main To Gung Govinda Ke Gasha (2)
(Still I will sing the glory of my Govinda*)

Jin Marg Mira Saja Kahat Hai
(Whichever path my Beloved shows me)

Un Marg Mee Jasha (2)
(I will walk on that path only)

Giridhar Kant Katumbhi Giridhar
(Giridhar* is my husband and family)

Maata Pita Meit Bhai (2)
(He is my mother, father, friend and brother)

Tu Kaya Janeya Mera Rana
(How can you understand, my dear Ranaji?)

Kayesse Yai Preet Me Paye (2)
(What type of divine love I have received?)

Mira Lago Ranga Hari
(Mira is drenched with the love of God)

Aur Sabhey Rang Ghata Chale (2)
(All other loves fade away)

Mira Lago Ranga Hari
(Mira is drenched with the love of God)

How could anyone who has not had the experience, know of the ecstasy evoked through the Divine Union of the *Jiva* with the *Purusha* in human brain?

Jiva, or *Jivatma* is the spark of the divine consciousness, unaware of its true nature. It is located at the level of 9th, 10th

* Names for Krishna

and 11th vertebrae. *Purusha* is the embodied *Paramatma*, and is situated at the level of the limbic system of the brain. In the cosmic marriage experienced by Mira and other self-realised saints and sages, the *Jiva Sakti* becomes so enraptured by *Purusha Sakti* it flies up the spine to merge in it at the level of *Hridayam*. Physiologically, neurons fire wildly in the limbic system, setting off reactions in the pineal and pituitary bodies. The endocrine system gets to work, activating hormones, creating intense sensations in the nervous system and throughout the physical and subtle bodies, producing immense love or ecstasy. **[See Diagram No. 31]**

This experience is the culmination of developing an intense emotional relationship with God. Although there is no physical contact between the devotee and the Beloved, all of the *chakras* of the human being are activated, producing an immense physiological response of which the mundane procreative union of man and wife is but a tiny mirror. The union of *Purusha* and *Jiva* is spiritual and physical love of the highest order. It can even produce *Atmajnana*, God-Realisation, in the purified human vehicle. If the *Hridayam* has not been purified by Human Values, the nervous system may become overloaded and crack, resulting in mental illness. For this reason, working with an enlightened *Guru* is so important for the serious spiritual aspirant.

As Sathya Sai Baba says, "For the sake of human satisfaction you give name and form to the Lord, but in reality He does not have any form at all. Yet He will take on a form so that you can worship Him and feel awe, reverence and love for Him and thereby satisfy your spiritual aspirations."[1] Devotion for a particular form should be so intense that the transcendental divinity will **have** to manifest in that form which the *Bhakta* desires.

The Divine Form can be male or female and the relationship can emulate any of the physical kinships. For Mira, Krishna was truly her Divine Husband. St. Francis of Assisi viewed Jesus as Heavenly Father. In Mohammed, this merger took place with the form of pure light. More recently in the 19th century, the *jiva* in Ramakrishna *Paramahamsa*, merged with *Purusha* in the form of the Divine Mother, Kali, bringing him Self-Realisation. This is *Parama Prema* (Divine Love), which is a thousand times more glorious than worldly love can ever be. This love can never be expressed in words; it can only be experienced.

YAD BHAVA, TAD BHAVATI

"As the feeling, so the manifestation." By this I have lived my life. Thoughts are things, and when linked with strong emotion, the creative power of the universe is harnessed. It is through intense feeling that we develop our emotional relationship with God. When we pray strongly, God out-manifests in our lives in answer to our prayers. Sri Sathya Sai Baba declares that it was the power of the prayers of many saints and sages that initiated His descent as *Avatar*.

Deep emotions that come from the heart are more powerful even than any destiny or *karma*. God has to change your *karma* if you are strongly praying. Even if your *karmas* are bad, if your prayer and intention is true, He will wash out your *karma* or bestow His Grace, giving you the strength to bear with the suffering.

Sri Sathya Sai Baba says:

It may be said we are praying every day. But prayer is not the pronouncement of words. Prayer is the yearning one experiences to awaken the Divinity latent in the *Hridayam*. Prayer must emerge from the effect to the cause. The individual self has to yearn for the Supreme Self. It must emerge from a pure *Hridayam*. Prayer is like a drinking cup – it must be clean both on the outside and the inside. Prayer should not arise out of the tongue, as music

Union Of *Jiva* With *Purusha*

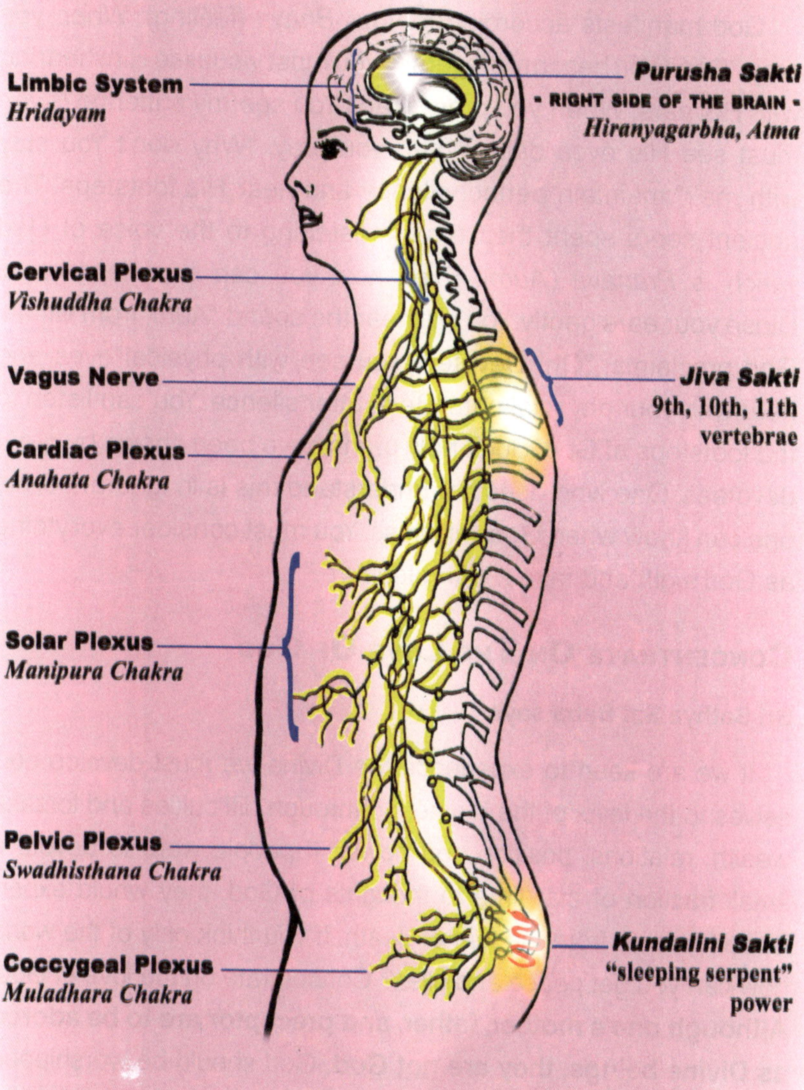

Human Values And Health ~ Diagram No. 31

Source: Divine Discourses of *Bhagawan* Sri Sathya Sai Baba

rises out of a gramophone record. When the song does not come from your depths, when you are not involved in it, how can it draw God unto you?

God manifests according to your *Bhava* (feeling). When you pray, "Can't You hear my prayers?" you must visualise Him hearing with His ears. When you pray, "Can't You see my suffering?" you must see His eyes daily. When you pray, "Why don't You stay with me?" maintain perfect silence and hear His footsteps. The ancient seers spent their time in listening to the voice of God which is *Pranava* (*Aum*). Even now you can experience this. Close your ears gently. You will hear the sound *"Aum"* from within. God proclaims, "Oh! Devotee, you see with physical eyes and hear with your physical ears. Be in utter silence. You can listen to the footsteps of God. Such holy paths have been shown by great devotees. One who does not understand this is in ignorance. No one can know when God will bless. You must consider everything as God's gift and take it with pleasure.[2]

Concentrate On The Love Of God

Sri Sathya Sai Baba says:

If we are keen to experience the Divine we must develop ourselves to the level of the Divine, go through difficulties and forsake wealth, relations, position and power. If people were to devote a small fraction of that time to thoughts of God, they would experience freedom from the fear of death. If you think only of the world how can you get peace and bliss? Concentrate on the love of God. **Although one's mother, father, and preceptor are to be adored as Divine beings, they are not God.** God should be worshipped as mother, father, preceptor, kinsman, beloved and friend. Father, Mother, and Preceptor dwell in their respective abodes. But God dwells in your *Hridayam*. Love the Lord who resides in your *Hridayam*. All other objects of love are impermanent.[3]

If a mother stands in the way of your devotion to God you must be prepared to give her up, as Bharata did when Kaikeyi sought to separate him from Rama. Mira was prepared to renounce her husband rather than give up her devotion to Krishna. Emperor Bali rejected the advice of his *Guru*, Sukracharya, when the latter advised him to retract his gift to Vamana (Vishnu). These are examples of devotees who did not flinch from any sacrifice in vindicating their devotion to God.[4]

Experiencing *Prema*

To experience real *Prema* there is no need to practise any kind of meditation, worship or rituals. ***Prema* can only be obtained by complete absorption in spirituality.**

- Sri Krishna declared in the *Gita*, "*Sarva Dharman Parithyajya*" (renouncing all *Dharmas*).
- Jesus also declared, "I am the Path."
- Buddha conveyed the same meaning and pointed out, "*Sarvaṁ Saranam Gachchaami*" (I am surrendering everything).

This means that the essence of all religions, the root of all scriptures, the goal of all virtues, is the experience of spiritual unity.[5]

Human beings have been given limited capacities and you may find it impossible to understand this divine principle. Then the easiest path to follow is the path of devotion or *Bhakti Yoga*. In teaching this to Arjuna in the ***Bhagavad Gita***, Krishna gave three steps:

1. **WORK FOR ME!** You must understand that whatever work you may perform in this physical world is already associated with the Lord, for He is the supreme master of this world. Recognising this truth, regard every activity you undertake as being done directly for the Lord.

2. **FOR MY SAKE ALONE!** Up to this point you have been thinking only about yourself. But who are you? Krishna said, "It is I who am shining in you." This word 'I' does not belong to the body. It emanates from the higher Self, from the *Atma* itself. This 'I' should not be associated with the body or the mind or the intuitive faculty or any other aspect of the individual for it transcends all these instruments. When you associate your limited self with this 'I' it is but a reflection of the one *Atma*. Whatever you have been doing has been for the satisfaction of the *Atma* alone. Not realising this sacred truth you have been swept away by delusion. Krishna told Arjuna, "Whatever you do, do it for My satisfaction, for My sake. Perform everything on My behalf. Act as My agent."

3. **BE DEVOTED ONLY TO ME!** Devotion is the expression of love. The emotion which is called love emanates from the *Atma*. Love is synonymous with *Atma*. Love has nothing at all to do with devotion; it is the very name of *Atma*. This principle of love emanating from the core of the heart must saturate every action, word and thought. This will happen when you think that everything you do, say or think is for the satisfaction of the Lord alone.[6]

Divine Love And Human Love

Prema (Divine Love) is like a most precious diamond. It will not remain ever for a single moment with selfish persons; it will not stay for even half a moment with egoistic persons. It will not remain at all with ostentatious persons. Love is alien to persons who are selfish, conceited or ostentatious.

Where, then, is this love to be found? It can be obtained only through a loving *Hridayam*. It may be asked, is not the whole world permeated with Love? Why, then is not Love readily available? **The love, with which the world is considered to be filled, is**

not real love. *Prema* cannot be associated with the body, the senses, the mind or the intellect. The *Atmic* life alone is a Love-filled life. Therefore, people must lead a spiritual life, not a life subject to the body. A life related to the body, the senses, the mind and the intellect can never be free from selfishness, conceit and ostentation.[7]

You may consider that the love within you and that the love represented by God are the same. But there is this difference. God's love is totally selfless. It is absolutely pure. It is eternal. It is flawless. Human love is self-centered and tainted; such a love cannot merge with God's love. It is only when one is free from egoism, pride, jealousy, hatred and envy that God will abide in you. **Without *tyaga*, (renunciation) if a person is immersed in worldly pleasures and leads a mundane life, all his devotion is only artificial and a kind of self-deception.** Such devotion will not lead to God. Everyone loves God for his own sake and not for the sake of God. Man seeks all things in the world for his own reasons. Even God is sought for such a reason.

To proceed from the human condition to the Divine in man, the only means is *Prematathwa* (love principle). All Indian scriptures demonstrate the power of the Lord's grace to transform the human to the state of the Divine. Although people have been taking birth after birth because of their attachment to worldly pleasures, they have not been able to get rid of their involvement with worldly concerns. Hence, they are unable to experience the bliss of oneness with the Divine. All the bad thoughts and bad actions which they have experienced in previous lives continue to prevent them from experiencing the Divine. It is only when one gets rid of these impure thoughts that he can experience Divine feeling.

God cannot be attained so easily. The *Hridayam* has only a single-seated sofa. There is room in it for only one. If you install worldly desires on that sofa, how can you expect God to sit on it? **God will enter that seat only if you empty it of all other things.**[8]

God Seeks Only Love

Everything in the world is derived from divinity. When everything comes from Him, what can you possibly offer Him? The only thing you can offer Him is your love. That is all He expects from you.[9]

By developing love one sees the Divine in all beings. It is like the wearing of coloured glasses. If you see the world through the glasses of love, you will see love everywhere. The glasses and the vision must be in harmony. Only with the eye of love can you use the glasses of love to see the loveliness of the world. There is no greater spiritual path than the path of love. It is through love that such noble qualities as kindness, compassion and sympathy are fostered. You may carry on a variety of *sadhanas*, but God does not seek your *sadhana*. Nor does He seek your devotion. **He seeks only your love.** No one should have any trouble about God. The doubting man can achieve nothing. With total faith and total love you can accomplish anything. It should be realised that proficiency in fields like music, literature and the arts is secured by the grace of the Divine. All fine arts are gifts from God. Nothing can be claimed as one's own achievement. The recipient of God's grace will lack nothing. He will have no troubles and he will commit no wrongs because he has surrendered to God. The person who considers God as his All becomes himself one with God. Hence direct your minds towards God.[10]

The Yearning

Although the Divine dwells in every person, this fact remains latent like oil in the til seed. To manifest the Divine within, you have to go through certain trials and ordeals. **Love of the Divine should grow as a result of such experiences of adversity,**

just as gold improves in brilliance the more it is heated in the crucible. Your devotion has to go through a constant purification process.[11]

Yearn to fill your heart with Him, not with 'you'. Your yearning must be warm, so warm that it can be called *Tapas*.[12]

The *chataka* bird will not shrink from being near a cloud to catch the fresh raindrops even if there is dreadful thunder and blinding lightning. It prays constantly for the pure unsullied raindrops. This is the attitude *sadhakas* should cultivate today. They must be prepared to face any kind of censure, criticism, trouble or obstacle. They should adhere to their goal regardless of anything. The *Gopikas* exemplified this type of devotion. They had no fear of any threats or abuse. They were totally unaffected. Hence, stick to your truth. Love God and fear none. Only the guilty need fear. Why fear when you are innocent? Without any fear in your hearts meditate on God. This is the royal road to the Divine in the *Kali* age. The Lord alone is the Saviour of the helpless and the forlorn. Do not waver in your faith in the Lord under any circumstance; go ahead with your tasks in faith and determination.

God tests people in many ways. They are intended only to promote your spiritual progress. None can affect God in any way. Why lose your faith in Him? It is a sign of weakness. Give no room for such unfortunate doubts. Strengthen your faith and realise God by your devotion.[13]

Your devotion must go on increasing and progressing, keeping in mind the firm belief that God is residing inside your own body. If you want to seek and search for the Lord who is residing inside you, you have to turn your vision inwards. How should you aspire for the Lord? You have to cry the same way as a calf cries for its mother who has left and gone off with the herd. You have to cry like a chaste woman who has lost her husband, wailing in pain at the separation. You have to cry out in the same way that a childless couple implores and pleads with God for a child. That is how you should pray to the Lord, full of devotion, and long to realise His presence within you.[14]

Hridaya Kamala (Lotus Of The Heart)

Sri Sathya Sai Baba tells us that:

In every human being, there are the *Chakras*. Among them, two are important. One is the Heart *Chakra,* the *Chakra* relating to the *Hridayam* [also called *Anahata*]. The other is the *Sahasrara Chakra*.

The ***Hridaya Chakra*** is described in the ***Vedas*** as *Hridaya Kamala* (the Lotus of the Heart). This Lotus has eight petals. Every petal is called *Prakriti* (Nature). All the eight petals are under the sway of the Lord. This means that God is the master (*Adipati*) of the eight petals because Krishna is the *pati* (or husband) of these petals. He is said to have eight "Queens", according to the spiritual text. Those who did not understand the esoteric meaning of all this described Krishna as having eight queens and sporting with 16,000 *Gopikas*. The real meaning of the reference to Krishna's "eight queens" is that he is the Lord of the lotus of the human *Hridayam*. As such, he holds sway over the *Hridayam*. When this is rightly understood, the supreme greatness, the Divine, will be apparent.

As regards the ***Sahasrara Chakra*** [in the head of the human body], it is a thousand-petaled lotus, each petal having sixteen *Kalas* (or phases). There are thus 16,000 *Kalas* in the *Sahasrara*. These phases are symbolically described as the wives of the Lord. The inner meaning of these expressions also should be properly understood. Going only by the superficial and literal meaning of these terms, the nature of the Divine is misconstrued and misinterpreted.[15]

We think of the play of Krishna and the *Gopikas* as some kind of game involving human enjoyment, but this is not so. Indeed this is symbolic of the sacred confluence between the *jivatma* and the *Parmatma*. The *Gopikas* were such that they provided luster to womanhood. Whether in the matter of patience or forbearance or friendship, they showed exemplary conduct. It is wrong to regard this sacred path adopted by the *Gopikas* as something trivial.

Those who are unable to grasp the glory of the *Gopis* and *Gopikas*, the *Bhakti* that melted stone and drew sobs of grief from trees, have no right to judge and pronounce a verdict. If they do they only reveal that their intelligence is more inert than rocks and boulders. Inert minds can never grasp the splendours of Krishna, who is the sovereign of the Universe, who captivates the Universe by His beauty and power.[16]

The Touch Of Divine Love

The great Sufi saint, Jalalluddin Rumi writes:

> *Jab Dil Se Dil Takrata Hai*
> (When pure love flows from *Hridayam* to *Hridayam*)
>
> *Matt Poochiya Khyo Ho Jata Hai*
> (Don't ask me what happens then)
>
> *Jhukti Hai Nazer Rukti Hai Zuban*
> (You cannot look at pure love, you cannot speak a word at that moment)
>
> *Mathe Pe Paseena Atta Hai*
> (The forehead is drenched with sweat and the face blushes)
>
> *Jab Dil Se Dil Takrata Hai*
> (When pure love flows from *Hridayam* to *Hridayam*)

On a purely human level, if a couple is sharing pure love, these same physiological changes can be observed between the two. If love can be so strongly felt between human beings, you can imagine the intensity of the love between God and *Bhakta*. During the *darshan* of *Bhagawan* Sri Sathya Sai Baba, whether the devotee is male or female, the physiological changes Rumi speaks of can be clearly seen. All eyes turn towards Baba as He passes by. Of their own volition, the hands of all *bhaktas* come together at the heart level with love and reverence, offering *namaskar* to the Lord. If Baba stops in front of a devotee, the *bhakta* starts breathing hard and their heartbeat quickens. The face of the devotee blushes, there is perspiration on the forehead. Tears roll down the cheeks of some who are overwhelmed with deep emotion. A few soft, sweet words from Him or even a glance of His can make a devotee's hands tremble or bring an uncontrollable smile to his face. Sai Baba's eyes radiate pure love. His hands transmit pure love. His serene presence exudes pure love. The eyes of the devotee shine and start transmitting the pure love of *jiva* back to *Deva*. This is *Parama Prema* – Pure Divine Love.

Surrender Earns The Lord

Sri Sathya Sai Baba says:

Dear devotees: It is not so easy to experience the Divine. You may imagine that you have comprehended the Divine. But this is a delusion. You are immersed in the affairs of the phenomenal world. This cannot lead you to the Eternal Reality. **Only those who are dedicated to the realisation of the Eternal can attain it.**[17]

For cultivating the love of an ordinary human being, you will find that you will come across several difficulties and troubles. Thus there is no surprise if to acquire the love of God you meet with many difficulties and obstructions. Because of this the *Gopikas* said they were finding a lot of trouble in the process of acquiring the love of God. The same thing has been described by Sage Vyasa who said that **if you want the love of God, you must give up love for other things.** When you give up your love for other things, it is easy to acquire the love of God. When you are bound down by several other forms of love, you will meet with lots of difficulties. The process has been described as surrender.[18]

God is all-powerful; God is everywhere; God is all knowing. Adore Him so long as you have breath, so long as you are conscious. Have no other thought than God, no other aim than knowing His command, no other activity than translating that command into action. That is what is meant by surrender. Render your self unto Him.[19]

On the path of devotion it is absolute surrender which makes the *jiva* expand and merge himself into God. It is when you relinquish your limited individuality and recognise the principle of divinity which is inherent within you, that all your weaknesses will leave you and you develop the broadness of mind that will finally culminate in your mergence with the Lord.[20]

When the Lord's Grace is won, one need not pray separately for *Moksha*. He knows best what you should get and when. He will confer what you deserve and what is beneficial. Yearn for Him. Suffer anguish for Him; there is no need to yearn for *Moksha* then. If that is done with no second thought He will destroy all sin. Hold fast to Him; He can make you immortal. Those who seek to escape from the cycle of birth and death must obey the command of the Lord and surrender to Him; then they will be crowned with success in every undertaking. They will achieve victory.[21]

Guru Nanak, First *Guru* of Sikh Religion, says:

> *Love cannot be defined in words. It can only be experienced. It is an act of complete self-surrender, an act of inner consecration, which is beyond human power to control. When we love God, we find Him in the temple of our heart and in the heart of all that lives and thus, in loving Him, we love all that exists.*[22]

---

1 *Bhagawan* Sri Sathya Sai Baba, **Discourses on the *Bhagavad Gita*,** Ch. 1, 1984.
2 *Bhagawan* Sri Sathya Sai Baba, Divine Discourse, 22/04/1998.
3 *Bhagawan* Sri Sathya Sai Baba, Divine Discourse, 09/07/1998.
4 *Bhagawan* Sri Sathya Sai Baba, ***Sanathana Sarathi,*** May 1987.
5 *Bhagawan* Sri Sathya Sai Baba, Divine Discourse, 09/07/1998.
6 *Bhagawan* Sri Sathya Sai Baba, **Discourses on the *Bhagavad Gita*,,** Ch. 2, 1984.
7 *Bhagawan* Sri Sathya Sai Baba, Divine Discourse, 21/08/1992.
8 *Bhagawan* Sri Sathya Sai Baba, Divine Discourse, 22/08/1982.
9 *Bhagawan* Sri Sathya Sai Baba, **Discourses on the *Bhagavad Gita*,** Ch. 1, 1984.
10 *Bhagawan* Sri Sathya Sai Baba, Divine Discourse, 09/07/1998.
11 *Bhagawan* Sri Sathya Sai Baba, Divine Discourse, 21/08/1992.
12 *Bhagawan* Sri Sathya Sai Baba, **Sathya Sai Speaks**, Vol. 8.
13 *Bhagawan* Sri Sathya Sai Baba, Divine Discourse, 10/01/1993.
14 *Bhagawan* Sri Sathya Sai Baba, **Discourses on the *Bhagavad Gita*,,** Ch. 5, 1984.
15 *Bhagawan* Sri Sathya Sai Baba, Divine Discourse, 10/01/1993.
16 *Bhagawan* Sri Sathya Sai Baba, ***Para Bhakthi,*** edited by Sundararaghavan Krishnaswami, 2005.
17 *Bhagawan* Sri Sathya Sai Baba, Divine Discourse, 22/08/1982.
18 *Bhagawan* Sri Sathya Sai Baba, **Summer Showers In Brindavan,** 1978.
19 *Bhagawan* Sri Sathya Sai Baba, **Sathya Sai Speaks,** Vol. 7.
20 *Bhagawan* Sri Sathya Sai Baba, **Discourses on the *Bhagavad Gita*,,** Ch. 8, 1984.
21 *Bhagawan* Sri Sathya Sai Baba, ***Geetha Vahini.***
22 Ten Sikh Gurus, ***Adi Guru Grant Sahab.***

chapter - 18

HUMAN VALUES LEAD TO *PARA BHAKTI*

Sri Sathya Sai Baba says:

It is in the experience and practise of the citizens of Bharat (India) that they generally worship God with flowers, offer *puja* and make obeisance to God, but there is something which is more sacred than this. There is a distinctive type of devotion by which you worship God with a good, clean mind and good conduct. This has been given the name of *Para Bhakti*. By worshipping God always with *puja* and flowers, the *sadhaka* (spiritual aspirant) will remain stationary in his place. This is good in a way, but to remain in one place all the time, failing to rise to a higher position, is not good. **It is a superior type of worship to worship God through good qualities, good conduct and good company**. By offering what kind of good qualities can we please God?

1. The first flower with which we can worship God is ***Ahimsa*** (non-violence).
2. The second flower is **Control of the Senses**.
3. The third flower is **Compassion** to all living beings.
4. The fourth one is ***Kshama*** (forbearance).
5. The fifth flower is ***Santi*** (peace).
6. The sixth flower is ***Tapas*** (penance or sacrifice).
7. The seventh one is the flower of ***Dhyana*** (meditation).
8. The eight is the flower of ***Sathya*** (truth).

Instead of worshipping with such worldly flowers which are impermanent and receiving impermanent rewards from God, we should worship Him with what is permanent and what is truthful, thereby attaining a higher stage. The flowers which you are using for worship have not been created by you. You are bringing flowers, which have been created by the *Sankalpa* of God on some tree or in some garden and are offering them back to the Creator Himself. What is the greatness in using the flowers created by God and giving them back to God Himself? Many people bathe in the Ganges, take the water from the Ganges into their palms and offer it back to the Ganges itself. This is not what you have created. This is not what you have the right to offer. **From the tree of your life, pick out such fruits that you have protected and have grown in the form of good qualities and offer them to God.** There is some distinctiveness in that. In order to promote good qualities, you have to undergo many troubles. So, it is through these good qualities that mind can also acquire a Divine concentration. Without good qualities and without good thoughts, how can you fix your mind in meditation?

1. The First Flower Is *Ahimsa Puspham*

We regard the word *Ahimsa* to mean not causing harm and hurt to other living things. The true meaning of the word is not to cause hurt and harm to any other living being either through your thought, word or deed. Cleansing and purifying these three: thought, word, and deed has been called *Triputi* (integral united reality of God, man and world) in spiritual parlance. This kind of flower of *Ahimsa* has been described as *Trigunam, Triputi*, *Ekabilvam* (purifying our thoughts, words and deeds). All of them should be harmonised and brought together to unite the flower.

2. The Second Flower Is the Control Of Sensory Organs

Our senses run without any control. If running horses or animals are not controlled, they pose a danger. God has created each organ of the human body for a specific purpose. It is only when we use these sensory organs along the right path for which they have been created that we will be entitled to God's grace. God has given us a nose. We should attempt to breathe in and breathe out through that nose and only accept fragrance through it. If we use such a nose to take snuff into it, the same purpose will become useless. In the same manner, He has given us a mouth and a tongue in order that we may take *Satwic* food. If we use the mouth to take in unholy food and intoxicating drinks, then we will be using the mouth for a wrong purpose. In the same manner, we should understand under what conditions and in what manner we should use each of these organs and put each one under control. Our inner strength will become less and less on account of excitement or unnecessary sorrow. The body will become ill by mental agitation and distractions. Man ages very quickly through excitement and sorrow. The reason for your not preserving this sacred instrument in sound condition is lack of control over these sensory organs. The second flower of sensory control should be used for worshipping God.

3. The Third Flower Is Compassion To All

The third flower is compassion to all living things, *Sarvabhuthe Daya Pushpam*. Looking merely and superficially at human nature, which has diverse aspects, we are forgetting God in this field. From the seed of Divinity the tree of creation has fruits and there is Divinity in the form of seed. That is why in the ***Bhagavad Gita*** Krishna has said, *"Beejam Man*

Sarvabhutanam" (I am the seed in all the living beings in the form of *Atma*). Recognising the truth that God is present in the form of *Atma* in all living beings, we say compassion to all living beings is the next flower.

4. The Fourth One Is *Kshama Pushpam*

Kshama or forbearance truly is the highest quality of a human being. But in human life because he develops narrow ideas, man wants to live in a constricted manner. He thinks "I" and "my family" are the only ones which matter. Others are all different from "me". It is not possible for us to develop the flower of forbearance as long as these ideas are in us. It is only when we love that we can have patience and forbearance. One's love should encompass all living beings. That will fructify as forbearance. Here is a small example. In our home there are our children. Along with our children there is also a servant. In the house a son may be pilfering something or the other and developing bad habits. In many ways we will try to control that son by beating, by scolding and persuading him to return to good ways, but we will never take him and hand him over to the police. In the same house, if the servant boy steals a small spoon, at once we will take him and hand him over to the police. What is the inner meaning of the situation in which we do not punish a son, even if he steals day after day, but we hand over a servant boy immediately to the police, when he steals even a small thing? The reason for this is the narrow idea that this boy is my son. Because the servant does not belong to you, there is no place for forbearance and patience. Therefore, you see that when you have the broad idea that everyone is mine, there is room for patience and forbearance. It is only then that our love will also grow.

5. The Fifth One Is *Santi Pushpam*

The fifth is the flower of *Santi* (Peace), *Santi Pushpam*. This flower of peace should not be interpreted to mean that you should be silent whosoever is attacking you, or whosoever is blaming you. It is not that. If you are unmoved and unperturbed in spite of anyone finding faults in you, this can be called real *Santi*. If you can fill your heart with love, then peace will come naturally. Peace is not something that can come to you from outside through bad qualities. To some extent we lose peace with truthful thoughts. A man will have no peace with untruthful thoughts. If you can get rid of all thoughts, you will become saint. It is only when you can be free from all thoughts that you can have peace. Your own bad thoughts are responsible for all your pain and sorrow. By good thoughts and good ideas, you will become a *Sadhu*. *Sadhu* does not mean one who merely wears an orange robe, shaves his head and wears *Rudrakshas* (prayer beads). It is he who has good thoughts and good ideas. A *Sadhu* is one who is a *Sathya Sankalpa Swarupa* (Embodiment of the expression of truth).

In the state of peace, human nature will be like the unruffled water surface. If there is water in a vessel, you will find there are ripples in a vessel, as an access of wind will make your reflection get disturbed on the surface of the water. On an impure surface our reflection is also impure. On a clear surface of water our reflection is also clear. In the same manner, although the basic truth is only one, whenever reflection takes place in a mind, which is full of *Tamo guna* (quality of ignorance, inertia) you will find there is impurity in the image of the reflection as it takes place in that mind; that will be called *Avidya*, lack of knowledge.

On the other hand, if the reflection takes place in a *Satwic* (pure) mind, that will be called *Maya* (illusion). God has *Maya* as His robe. The reflection in *Rajo guna* (passionate, active) is *Jiva,* and that in *Tamo guna* is creation. While the basic truth is one, yet the three – illusion, reflection and creation – or *Jiva* and *Maya* are not different from the basic truth. We should make an attempt to recognise the nature of the basic truth. We take a fruit. Even if it were a *neem* fruit, when it is fully ripe it becomes sweet. When you attain the totality of peace, only then you taste the sweetness of it.

6. The Sixth Flower Is *Tapas*

The sixth one is the flower of *Tapas* (penance, sacrifice), *Tapas Pushpam. Tapas* is not to give up your wife and children, go into a forest, put your head up and feet down; that is not *Tapas.* When we think of real *tapas*, one should abandon bad thoughts from the mind. The coordination of thoughts, words and deeds is *Tapas.* Whatever good thoughts sprout in your mind, to utter them as words and to put them into practise as your work – that is *Tapas.* It is in this context that is said that one is a *Mahatma* who can coordinate his thought with his word and his word with his deed. Giving up bad thoughts from your mind will become sacrifice. That sacrifice will become *Yoga.* However, giving up one's property and one's wife and going into the forest is not *Yoga.*

7. The Seventh Flower Is *Dhyana Puspam*

Today, *Dhyana* (meditation) is taking many forms. Many types of meditation that people are adopting today are against the culture and tradition of *Bharat.* To sit in *Padmasana* (lotus pose) and to make the *Kundalini Sakti* (energy at the base of the spine) rise from *Mooladhara* (root *chakra*) to *Sahasrara* (crown *chakra*) is not *Dhyana* (meditation). **True *Dhyana* consists in recognising the presence of God in all types of work.** God is present everywhere and immanent in all things.

He is the all-pervading indweller of all. To make an attempt in your *Dhyana* to confine Him (God) to one place which you choose, cannot be *Dhyana*. When you are driving a car, the car is your God. When you are doing business in a market, the market is your God. According to the culture of *Bharat*, we first make obeisance to the work, which we have to do. Before we undertake to do any work, we should regard that work as God. *Tasmai Namaha Karmana* – that is what the ***Upanishads*** are teaching us; the work I have to do, I regard as God and make obeisance to God in that form. In our daily life, from moment to moment, we are finding God in that form. Let us see the person who plays on the *Tabla*. Before he begins to play on it, he pays obeisance to the *Tabla*. The harmonium player will make obeisance to the harmonium before he starts. A dancer before she beings her dance will make obeisance to her *ghungroo* (anklets). Even a driver who is going to drive a lifeless car, before he holds the steering wheel, makes *namaskar* to the steering wheel. You do not have to go so far. While driving if the car hits another person, immediately we make *namaskar* to that person. The significance of all this is the faith and belief that God is present in all things. Thus, to regard the entire creation as the form of God and to perform your duty in that spirit is *Dhyana*.

8. The Last Flower Is *Sathya* (Truth)

If you simply speak what you feel and tell what you have done, this can be called *Loukika Satyam* – worldly truth. This cannot be called truth. Truth is that which does not change at any time. What you have seen is truth at that moment. At the next moment, it becomes untruth. All material things, which you see in this creation, are things that will decay and are bound to change. In this transient changing world, how can what you see and what you hear become truth? Truth is God. This is the eighth flower. This truth is this form of Divinity. In the world, we experience Truths of a relative nature. Let us take chemistry as an example. You take some chemicals and mix them together. They change and you get some other chemical. If in lime you mix turmeric, you get a red colour. This is chemistry. Concerning physics, if you take a three-inch needle and put it in fire, it will become a longer needle. This is the truth of physics. How long do these truths of physics and chemistry remain? These are temporary, worldly, scientific truths. But, spiritual truths are such that they will remain unchanged whatever you may do to them, whatever fires you may use, or howsoever you may change the circumstances. So, whatever does not at all change is truth. Cruelty and harshness are predominant in the world today because we are not attempting to promote such sacred qualities. Today, among believers and non-believers the same kind of attitude is developing. That day when we can promote such good qualities in the mind of the believers, the non-believers will disappear from this world.

Service To Society

We must try to rise to higher stages from natural devotion through *Para Bhakti*. Perform your *bhajans*, perform your *pujas*, but when you enter Society, recognise Society as a form of God, recognise what exists as omnipresence in Society, and thereby acquire good qualities in serving Society. Forget the agitation in the world. Then you can have peace and enjoy bliss. If you develop an idea that God, who is omnipresent and is in the entire creation and the universe, is confined in a picture which is three inches by four inches, you are narrowing your conception of God.

Broadening your heart and making it bigger and bigger, you should make it as big as God Himself. If you look at a balloon, in the initial stage, it is flat, like a human being who begins with the ideas of 'I' and 'Mine'. If you go on blowing air into the balloon, it will go on becoming bigger and bigger – like you when you ultimately move on to the place that "all are mine", "all are one". Gradually you become even broader in your vision and you burst and merge into God who is omnipresent. You should recognise the truth that man's life should consist of making the journey from the position of 'I' to the position of 'we'. If you simply stay in the place of 'I', you will remain where you are. This creation is like the bridge which connects man with God. 'I' is one hill. God is another hill. The bridge between the two is the aspect of creation. If you break and destroy the bridge you can never reach the destination. I am hoping that you plunge into creation and do service to Society and thereby use the bridge to reach God.[1]

---

1 *Bhagawan* Sri Sathya Sai Baba, Divine Discourse, June 1981.

Once we surrender our mind to

God completely, He will take

care of us in every way.

~ **Sri Sathya Sai Baba**

chapter - 19

SRI SATHYA SAI BABA, *AVATAR* OF *KALIYUGA*

Sri Sathya Sai Baba says:

> *The Scriptures declare that the Divine descends to the earth in human form to allay the sufferings of those who are sick of body or of mind. Man today seeks to have a vision of the supra-human transcendental being. This is sheer folly, because as long as one has the feeling that he is a human being, with a human form, then he is not entitled to see his transcendental form. When one transcends the sense of his humanness, he acquires the privilege to envision Transcendental Divinity. That is the reason why Rama and Krishna came as* ***Avatars*** *in human form. To claim that when you close your eyes and meditate that you see an effulgent light is only a delusion. There are innumerable things that are not visible to your naked eyes and which are beyond your ken. How do you expect to see them or know them? You know only the human form. So, at the outset, try to understand humanness. You must understand the Life-Principle and you should seek to enquire into the nature of the Divine.*[1]

In every book of mine, I include one chapter of personal experiences to illustrate *Swami*'s extraordinary omnipresence and boundless love. These incomprehensible attributes can only be present in an *Avatar*.

Swami, The Saviour

After the death of my worldly husband, Dr. A. M. Ghooi, *Swami* gave me an extensive interview in Brindavan on the morning of 31st December 1983. During this Brindavan interview, Baba, with complete accuracy, disclosed all the events that had occurred in my life during the time my husband was in a coma at the Medical College Hospital in Bhopal. When the interview was through, I was so overwhelmed that while standing up I immediately folded my hands. I was unable to hold back the tears that were flooding my eyes and cascading down my cheeks. He gave me so much assurance and said:

I Was Looking After You.
I Am Looking After You.
I Will Look After You.

This truth *Swami* has proved time and again. It is also a fact that His guiding presence has often been strongest during the most difficult times of my life.

My eldest son, Anand married Neeta in 1989, after they had both completed medical school. Sadly, their relationship soon became quarrelsome, making the home atmosphere unpleasant for everyone. After completing the E.C.F.M.G. examination, Anand was determined to take up his medical practice in America, against his wife's wishes. He had always been a sensitive, pious soul. However, the constant conflicts with his wife began to have a negative effect on his health and peace of mind. My daughter-in-law, Neeta, convinced him to accompany her to Lucknow where they could stay with her parents while Anand applied for positions in the U.S.A.

What happened there I will never know. My son did not contact me personally and whenever I called, his in-laws made some excuse to keep him away from the phone. I was deeply worried, but Anand was a grown-up adult now and it was wrong on my part to interfere in his life.

During *Guru Purnima* 1991, I took up volunteer service at the medical camp at *Puttaparthi*. I prayed hard to Beloved *Swami* for the welfare of my son and He responded. When I returned home to Bhopal I found Anand, Neeta and my grandson in the house. However, Anand had grown so sickly and pale that I could barely recognise the young man he had been. He believed he had no luck with his applications to America, so he wanted to return to Bhopal to work in our hospital. His in-laws and wife had held him a virtual prisoner in Lucknow, even hiding three acceptance letters for jobs in the U.S.A. In desperation, Anand went on fasting without even taking water. Finally, after ten days of fasting, Neeta had to agree to bring him to Bhopal. After dropping him off, she left with her son.

Immediately, I started giving him a good diet and taught him to have full faith in *Swami*. With *Swami's* continued Grace, Anand was restored to physical health. He began seeing a few patients in my hospital. I prayed continually and *Swami*, as my Divine Partner, changed Anand's lifestyle dramatically. He used to be a meat-eater as well as a drinker, who enjoyed parties. Now he threw away all alcohol, took only simple vegetarian food in small amounts and gave off wearing any lavish clothing. He began to spend long silent hours alone in his room reading spiritual texts and meditating. He showed no interest in any of my attempts to help him get established in a medical practice in my hospital. My son was leaving worldly things. I observed that his limbic system was being purified by spiritual practice and *Swami's* unseen hands. Anand now yearned only for a simple pious life.

From 1975, I was running a charitable clinic in Bhopal, the Sri Sathya Sai Homeo Clinic. We had just completed performing a *puja* there in honour of *Krishna Janma Ashtami*. Then we went to Ranjit Bhai's home for *puja*, where I received a phone call. Anand had been found lying unconscious in his room after consuming poison. My heart immediately called out to *Swami*.

I rushed back home and before even seeing my son, I ran into my *puja* room to plead with *Swami* to save his life. Anand was taken to Medical College Hospital, Bhopal and although the best of doctors treated him, he remained unconscious even after six days. In despair, I got him admitted to the I.C.C.U. at Beach Candy Hospital in Bombay. I never let up on my prayers to *Swami* and three days later Anand finally regained consciousness. When he awoke from the coma the doctors told me he might not regain full use of his right hand and right leg. Desperately, I could only beseech my Lord with full devotion to look after my son. The merciful *Swami* did answer my prayers. As soon as I entered Anand's room, he lifted his right hand to catch hold of me and moved his right leg so that I could sit by his side. To the great astonishment of all the doctors who treated him, Anand healed completely. In just a few days he could be discharged from the hospital in Bombay. Then I thanked *Swami* for his full recovery.

God Changes His Rules

After his discharge, I went with Anand and my daughter to visit my "Papa", Dr. V. K. Gokak, at his Bombay residence. Dr. V. K. Gokak advised Anand to join the Super Specialty Hospital, which would soon be opened.

Anand was not yet ready for such a spiritual opportunity. He left with his wife and sister for a rest in Pondicherry. There they saw a newspaper advertisement for Baba's hospital and sent off applications. My son was called for a job interview on 25th October 1991 and so we all met in *Puttaparthi*.

Upon arrival, we came to know that the chance of my son getting an appointment was very remote. A number of well-qualified and experienced cardiologists from all over the world had applied. But has *Swami* ever let down a devotee who has surrendered to Him fully? Only unshakeable faith is required to receive His grace and I prayed to Him fervently. Upon the advice of one physician, Anand also took the additional step of sending a wire directly to *Swami*, listing qualifications for both his wife and himself. The next morning I was informed that *Swami* Himself randomly drew several telegrams from a pile and asked the person-in-charge to appoint those individuals to the General Hospital. Among those fortunate persons were my son and daughter-in-law! In this way all the vacancies of the various departments in the General Hospital (gynecologist, dental surgeon, radiologist, surgeon, pediatrician, etc.) were filled by *Swami* without any formal advertisement or interview.

On receiving the news I went into rapture. But my joy was short lived when my daughter-in-law, Neeta, presented me with a list of grievances such as the low salary, aged colleagues, strict *ashram* rules, etc. I was prepared to sacrifice anything for the sake of my son and daughter-in-law. Nevertheless, I pleaded with my daughter-in-law to do her best to make the most of this opportunity to join Baba's Hospital. I myself had no sleep that night. I was praying to my Divine partner to help me in settling these children here in *Puttaparthi*.

Prabal Prem Ke Pale Parkar
Prabhu Ko Niyam Badalte Dekha

[Because of intense devotion,
God changes His rules]

My intense prayers throughout the night persuaded God to change all His rules. The very next day Dr. Anand and Dr. Neeta were informed that *Swami* had increased all the State pay scales to be on par with the central pay scales. As a result, they would be earning double the expected amount! Moreover, He would permit them to stay outside the *ashram* so that they could bring their son from Bhopal and enjoy certain amenities like VCR, car and more relaxed hours. *Swami* even assured them a place for their child in His school.

The Omnipresent Baba had heard all the complaints my daughter-in-law made in our flat the previous night and responded point-by-point. What better evidence can I give to emphasise that *Bhagawan* is everywhere?

The sad news is that inspite of Baba's divine generosity, Anand and Neeta chose not to join the General Hospital. They opted instead to work at the Medical College Hospital in Pondicherry, letting go of this great gift from God that would never come again.

Life Of Solitude

Even Divine intervention could not save Anand and Neeta's married life. She bitterly returned to Lucknow and Anand came home to Bhopal where he started working in our own Hospital from 1992 to 1998. Still he remained aloof. After seeing a few patients, he would take a simple meal and return to his room. There, in 1998 on *Ganesha Chaturthi*, Anand, my first-born son, passed away.

But for *Swami* I would have been shattered to pieces. My husband passed away in 1983. The eldest son was now gone forever and my two younger children had settled into medical practices and family life in the U.S.A. Blessedly their lives were happy and healthy; I could not influence them to return to India to support their anguished mother. Neeta, caught in her own despair, even launched several legal cases against me for property and money.

After the death of my son I started having telephone calls from Puttaparthi. I was informed that *Swami* had posted me to the General Hospital. Three or four times I refused. I reasoned that I had a big hospital to run in Bhopal; it just did not seem practical for me to leave this worldly responsibility.

Then one day I received a phone call from Puttaparthi which changed my mind. *Swami* ordered me to come, the doctor-in-charge reported. *Swami's* exact words to him were, **"tell her to lock the hospital and come, she is alone and unsafe."** What an illustration of *Swami's* omnipresence! Needless to say, I dropped everything, rushed to Puttaparthi and joined the General Hospital. Shortly afterwards, I escaped to the U.S.A. to visit my other children, before returning again to Bhopal. I was not yet able to leave the big hospital my husband and I had built.

Work was a comfort. During the day I was too busy to be concerned about my circumstances or to think about my loss. But when I returned to my residence, I was alone. Most of my time was spent in my *puja* room, fighting with my Divine Partner about the bad situation I found myself in. Eventually, love for *Swami* drew me back to Puttaparthi, where He graciously helped me to re-establish myself in the General Hospital.

Only with Baba's Grace did I cross this portion of my life and come to live permanently in Prasanthi Nilayam, which has truly been my "abode of peace". There are not enough words in the dictionary to express my gratitude to my *Adipati*. All I can do is to continue to serve Him with devotion and work hard to prove worthy of the position He has given me in His General Hospital.

Swami has permitted me to use alternative methods of treatment in certain cases. In every difficult case, I was writing Him letters through the Superintendent, Dr. Alreja, and getting advice. With *Swami*'s help, I was able to settle myself in Sri Sathya Sai General Hospital. With His Grace and permission, I was able to treat gynecological, obstetric and general cases with Allopathy, *Ayurvedic*, Homeopathy and *Yoga* in which I was qualified. Later I started treating sterility and fertility cases, fibroid uterus, asthma, irregular periods with cystic ovary, polycystic kidney, Lupus Erythamatosis, early cases of arthritis and osteoporosis, early cases of diabetes and all types of skin cases.

OMNISCIENT *SWAMI*

After I had settled in at the hospital, I decided to renovate the *ashram* room, given to me in 1980. It was in very bad condition because devotees had used it all the time. I wrote a long letter to *Swami* through Dr. Alreja, telling Him that I wanted changes in living room, bathroom and kitchen. In the evening, a gentleman came to my room with the letter I had written to *Swami* in his hand. He introduced himself as Mr. Prabhakar, a contractor working in *Swami*'s residence area. *Swami* had told him, "Dr. Ghooi is going tomorrow to Bhopal for ten days. Renovate her room as quickly as possible." I told him, "I'm not going to Bhopal tomorrow; I have no work in Bhopal." So he gave me his card and telephone number saying, "Whenever you go, let me know. It is *Swami*'s order and I have to obey."

He went away. As soon as he left I got a phone call from Bhopal. My assistant doctor told me, "Madam, come urgently to Bhopal as there is an income tax court case." In the morning I booked a train ticket and in the evening called Mr. Prabhakar. I said, "Sir, *Swami* was right. I got a call from Bhopal and I'm going for ten days. Please take these keys of my room and do whatever you can." It took me fifteen days to come back from Bhopal, and when I entered my room I could not recognise it. It was so beautifully done thanks to my *Adipati*, who sent his own contractor to me for renovation of my flat, and looked after my comforts so well.

My driver had brought my car to *Puttaparthi*, but it was not running well; there was a loud noise when the brakes were applied. I searched for a mechanic in *Puttaparthi* but there was nobody who could do anything. My only friend in *Puttaparthi* was *Swami*. I wrote a nice letter to Him and explained about the car, sending it through Dr. Alreja. *Swami* took the letter and continued with *darshan*. As He passed through the gents' side He called a young man from the fourteenth row, gave him my letter and asked him to see me. The man came and showed me the letter. At first I was shocked as it was addressed to *Swami*. I asked him, "From where did you get this letter?" He told me, "*Swami* Himself gave it to me, making me get up from the fourteenth row, and told me to come and see you." My next question was, "Who are you?" He said, "I am an engineer, and I have a big garage in Punjab where we renovate cars. " I told him, "Here are the keys, take my car and repair it." He took two days to complete the work and asked me to drive it. When I drove my car I was amazed. It was like driving a new car. I offered him money. He said, "No, I am a rich man in Punjab, owner of a big garage, but my labour is paid by *Bhagawan* Baba; I am so happy that out of this big crowd He knows who I am."

Then my assistant doctor in Bhopal called me, and said, "There are six court cases against you, four by your elder divorcee daughter-in-law, and two consumer court cases." By now I was so sure that *Swami* would permit me to go, and that I would win all the cases. During every trip to Bhopal I had a feeling that my *Adipati* was all the time with me. I had to take permission for leave from Dr. Alreja and *Swami*. *Swami* was very liberal in giving me holidays to look after Bhopal Hospital cum residence. By 2005, I won all the six cases because where there is Truth, God is always present.

Human Values And Health In Practice

During the five-year span, from 2000-2005 I kept a close eye on my *Hridayam* (limbic system). **I increased my efforts to purify myself at the mental and emotional levels through *namasmarana,* meditation and *yoga* exercises, cleansing my thoughts.** We all catch energy from the thoughts of other people. The thoughts may be positive or negative; the people may be near or far – **thoughts have airy wings and their vibrations directly affect the limbic system of both the sender and the receiver.** I cleaned mine by sending love to all, talking sweetly and softly, and doing good, detached actions. I did *seva* with love to everyone wherever possible in my life. This helped me to regain my health. In addition to this self-cleaning, I was also blessed to be nourished by *Swami*'s daily *darshan* and *bhajans* in the *mandir* (temple).

The latest investigations on me from the Super Specialty Hospital showed that my peptic and duodenal ulcers were healed. I have had no asthma attacks for two years. My psoriasis is better and the skin is normal. My arthritis has also improved very much and blood pressure is almost normal. No one could properly heal all the fractures in my body, but I was working normally and efficiently in the hospital by *Swami's* Grace.

Sathya Sai Baba's teachings are like an ocean in which so many pearls and precious stones are lying hidden. One should not say while standing on the shore that there is nothing in the water. You have to dive deep to attain what you need. Incarnated now is the *Avatar* of the *Kaliyuga* who has come to rescue the people on earth from sorrow through His teachings. Through practice and love you can evolve higher in your consciousness until you reach *Moksha* (liberation).

In conclusion, I would like to say that **what Sathya Sai Baba is offering is nothing other than total physical, mental, emotional, social and spiritual health, which can be acquired by practising His teachings. If we in our day-to-day life sincerely live with Human Values, then we will attain perfect health.**

Each one of us has to do cleansing of the limbic system (*Hridayam*), purifying our thoughts, emotions and actions, in order to be healthy. **Just as we clean our house daily, the *Hridayam*, which is the abode of God, must also undergo daily cleaning.** However, unlike house cleaning, this is a job no one can do for us. As I, as a human guinea pig, have done in my life, may all do, and reach His Lotus Feet!

> *Good character is a source of health. Be good, be joyful, be bold, be honest, be temperate and be patient. These are all rules of health. Good character is the most valuable source of health.*[2]
>
> ~ **Sri Sathya Sai Baba**

HELP EVER, HURT NEVER

---

1 *Bhagawan* Sri Sathya Sai Baba, Divine Discourse, 26/06/1994.

2 *Bhagawan* Sri Sathya Sai Baba, recorded in **The Life of *Bhagawan* Sri Sathya Sai Baba** by N. Kasturi, 1971.

You are living now in the dark, in ignorance. The knowledge that you are the Divine Spark, encased in the sheaths of bliss, intelligence, feelings, sensations and organic substances – this knowledge is the Light. You must light your own lamp. You cannot walk in the light of another's lamp. Earn the knowledge yourself. Even knowing it is not enough; you must experience it.

~ **Sri Sathya Sai Baba**

glossary

Adipati: God, the Divine Partner from birth to birth.

Adrenals*:* Endocrine glands located above the kidneys involved fight or flight response; corresponds to the *Swadhishthana* (abdominal) *chakra*.

Agni: Fire. One of the five basic elements, ***Panchamahabhutas***.

Aham: "I". The first word, even before *"Om"*. When *Aham* assumes a specific name and form it becomes ***Ahamkara*** – ego.

Ahamkara: Ego, egoistic consciousness. Asserts selfishness and sense of "I"-ness. Arises from the feeling of separateness.

Ahimsa: Non-violence. One of the five human values.

Aishvarya: Prosperity, wealth.

Akasa: Ether or space. One of the five basic elements (***Panchamahabhutas)*** existing everywhere, it is the highest and most subtle form of the cosmos.

Allopathy*:* The treatment of disease by modern medicine.

Amanaska: One who has transcended the mind; mindless.

Ananda: Bliss.

Anartha: Calamity.

Anatma: That which bars the vision of the ***Atma***.

Angarpanam: Offering one's limbs to the Lord, committing to use one's body only for good actions.

Angirasa: Energy present in every limb of the human body. The presiding deities of the various limbs and organs.

Antarmukham: Looking within, visualizing your own mind.

Antakarana: Inner instruments of awareness; inner sense organs. The collective name for mind, intelligence, will and ego sense.

Antaryami: The indweller who knows all, your inner self.

Anu: Atom, microcosm, the smallest particle.

Anugraha: Divine Grace.

Anuraga: Affection, mutual love.

Anushasita: One who has control over the mind. God is the only one who can control the mind.

Apsara: Beautiful women; celestial dancers.

Aradhya: The chosen God for worship.

Archana: Worship.

Archetypal Sheath: Blueprint of the body, contains all the *vasanas*, impressions, from the beginning of time, and is on right side of our brain.

Arishadvarga: Literally, 'six-fold beast'; the six energies of man: lust, anger, greed, delusion, pride, hate.

Arogya: Free from disease.

Arpitham: Total surrender to God.

Asana: *Yoga* posture.

Asrama: Stage in human life.

Astral Body: Body of light that surrounds and interpenetrates physical and subtle bodies. Projects out from the physical body 3" to 4", depending on the intensity of the individual's thoughts and emotions.

Astral World: Where seed bodies of everything exists in its subtle form.

Astrocytes: Nerve glue cells.

Atma: Divine soul, spirit. Inner motive force of everything. Spark of the ***Paramatma*** and contains the same attributes.

Aura: Emanation of energy projecting beyond the space of the human body in an egg-shape, created by the mind's emotional reaction to sensory impressions and thoughts inside the brain.

Avatar: Incarnation of God in human form.

Axon: Tentacle of a nerve cell responsible for sending signals to other neurons.

Ayurveda: Science of longevity. A branch of the *Atharva Veda* dealing with the integrated health of the body, the mind and the spirit.

Bandha: Energy locks in the body used during the practice of ***Hatha Yoga*** and ***Pranayama:***

Bhagawan: God; the Godhead; He who sustains the universe; the giver of all things.

Bhajan: Devotional singing.

Bhakti: Intense love for God. Getting rid of sense of separation from God.

Bhakta: Devotee, one who has deep love for God.

Bharat: Ancient name for India. Literally 'the land of those who have attachment (*rathi*) towards the Lord (*Bha* or ***Bhagawan***).

Bharatiya: A child of Bharat. Inheritor of the Indian culture

Bioplasmic Body: Etheric body, subtle body.

Brahma: Aspect of the One Divine Principle which governs creation. (Trinity: ***Brahma, Vishnu, Siva***).

Brahmacharya: One who seeks ***Brahman*** (God) and practises celibacy.

Brahmamayam: The supreme reality.

Brahman: Absolute, pure, infinite consciousness, Divinity; God. See ***Paramatma***.

Brahmananda: Supreme divine bliss that comes from union with God.

Buddhi: Intellect, higher mind. Place of reason, discrimination and insight. Conscience level, takes its light from the soul.

Causal Body: See ***Karana Sarira***.

Cerebral Cortex: "Gray matter"; the wrinkled outer layer of the **cerebrum**, the top portion of human brain responsible for man's higher reasoning functions.

Cerebrum: The part of the brain which is divided into two symmetrical halves (cerebral hemispheres). In humans, it is where activities including reasoning, learning, sensory perception, and emotional responses take place.

Chaitanya or ***Chaitanyam:*** Pure consciousness; the knower or seer.

Chakras: Plexuses of energy within the spinal cord and etheric body.

Chittha: Full knowledge, awareness, consciousness, beyond passion and ego.

Conscience: Divine, discriminating awareness within the body. The ***Atma***, the eternal witness.

Chinmaya: Pure, spiritual consciousness.

Conscious: Awareness, awakened state.

Consciousness: Infinite awareness. ***Chaitanaya*** (Sanskrit).

Crore: The number, ten million (10,000,000); or 100 ***lakhs***.

Dendrites: Portion of a neuron that receives electrical signals from other neurons.

Darshan: Sight of a holy person or God.

Deha: The human body.

Deva: Godly, divine being.

Deva Lokas: The higher sacred regions within the astral world.

Devotion: That which enables the unmanifested Divine principle to manifest itself if the devotee's heart is pure.

Dhairyam: Patience; courage.

Dharma: Right conduct, duty, righteousness. One of the five human values.

Dharana: Intense, single pointed concentration on a chosen object. A prelude to meditation.

Dhatus: Term used in ***ayurveda*** for elements which help in the formation of the basic structure of a body cell.

Dhyana: Meditation. One pointed attention.

Doshas: Term used in ***ayurveda*** for combinations of the ***pancha-mahabhutas*** which govern the physio-chemical and physiological activities of the body. When these elements are in balance there is health. Imbalance in these elements causes disease.
- ***Vata*** or ***Vayu*** (air and ether)
- ***Pitta*** (fire and earth)
- ***Kapha*** or *Sleshma* (earth and water)

Drasta: The seer.

Dristi: Vision, sight. Point of view.

Drisysa: The seen.

Ecstasy: A euphoric mental state or trance caused by intense religious experience in which self-awareness and self-control are lost. Rapture. Literally, outside of the self.

Ego: The false self.

Ekatma Bhava: Oneness in spirit.

Ekantham: Solitude.

Encephalon: Brain of a human or animal who possesses a vertebrae.

Endocrine System: Regulatory system of the body which secretes **hormones** through the bloodstream from seven ductless glands (pituitary, pineal, thyroid, hypothalamus, pancreas, ovaries or testes, adrenals), which correspond with the seven main ***Chakras***.

Etheric Body: The projection around the human body on the subtle level. Also called *pranic* body or **bioplasmic body**.

Ether: Another name for ***Akasa*** or space; one of the ***Panchamahabhutas***.

Gandharva: Heavenly being or angel.

Glial Cell: Nerve glue, which assists **neurons** in communication within the brain.

Gopikas: Female residents of Brindavan who had unparalleled love and devotion towards Lord Krishna. (Masculine: *Gopas*)

Guna: Quality, characteristic, attribute. There are three *gunas* which impel man's behaviour. God is only one, therefore ***nirguna***, without attributes.
- ***Satwa***: pious, divine, sacred, harmonious
- ***Rajas***: emotional, active, impatient, unlimited desires
- ***Tamas***: dull, still, lethargic, fearful

Guru: Teacher, one who dispels the darkness of ignorance.

Gyri Sulci: Ridges and foldings in the human cerebral cortex.

Hatha Yoga: *Yogic* discipline fostering good health through practices which purify the body and the mind.

Health: Man's normal condition, living in accordance with the natural laws pertaining to the body, mind, soul, and environment.

Hiranyagarbha: Literally, "golden womb"; it is the first manifestation of God, the seat of the primal consciousness from which everything is born. In man it is the spiritual heart and is spread throughout the body. The place where Divine Love originates. See ***Hridayam:***

Homeopathy: Treatment system based on law of similar curing similar.

Hormone: A chemical substance produced in the body's endocrine glands that regulates nearly all bodily functions. Literally, "to set in motion".

Hridayam or ***Hridaya:*** Spiritual heart, the seat of God and ***Sat-Chit-Ananda***, located on the right side of the human brain. Corresponds to the ***Limbic System***.

Hridaya Kamala: Lotus of the heart. The third eye.

Hypnosis: (also called hypnotism) A sleeplike condition that can be artificially induced in people by a trained practitioner, which enables access to various levels of the subconscious mind.

Hypothalamus: Endocrine gland located in the midbrain , which acts as central controller for endocrine system and regulates body temperature. Considered part of the **limbic system:**

Jagat: The moving, changing, physical world.

Jala: Water. One of the five basic elements.

Jnana: Divine knowledge, wisdom.

Jnanendriyas: Organs of perception, ears, skin, eyes, nose and tongue.

Japa: Repetition of the name of the God.

Jiva or Jivatma: Individual soul. Spark of the Divine Cosmic Self or ***Atma***. Small self, still in a state of non-realization of its Divine Self, residing in the body at the level of 9th, 10th, 11th vertebrae.

Jyothi: Light.

Kaliyuga: Iron age; age of moral decline. Present age of human evolution.

Kama: Desire; one of the six vices, or enemies of man.

Karma: Action. Law of *karma* denotes action and reaction based on cause and effect. Previous *karmas* (actions) play an important role in determining one's fate. The effects of the bad *karma* of prior births are the prime cause for many congenital diseases.

Karma Kshetra: "Field of action"; field of righteousness; the arena where all activities are sublimated into ***sadhana***.

Karmendriyas: Organs of action: vocal chords, arms, legs, genitals, excretory organs (anus, bladder)

Karana or Karanam: Cause or purpose.

Karanas: Instruments, tools.

Karana Sarira: Causal body.

Karta: The doer.

Kirlian Photography: Photographic procedure developed in Russia by which ***auras*** and energy patterns can be viewed.

Kirtanam: Singing the glory of God in groups.

Klesha: Obstacle. There are five main types that come in the way of experiencing bliss:

- ***Avidya***: Ignorance, absence of right awareness.
- ***Abinava***: Lack of mental discipline.
- ***Asthitha***: Too much interest in worldly pleasures.
- ***Raga***: Attachment to wealth and material objects.
- ***Dwesha:*** Hatred, repulsion.

Kosa: Sheath or cover for the soul. See ***Pancha Kosas:***

Krodha: Anger, one of the six vices, or enemies of man.

Kshetra: Field, region. The field of action.

Kundalini: Cosmic energy latent in the human body, concentrated at the base of the spine. Literally meaning, "coiled up", it is also called *serpent power* because it can be made to rise up through the body by means of *yoga* or meditation practices.

Lakh: One hundred thousand (100,000).

Lakshmi: Goddess of Wealth, consort of Vishnu. She dwells in the abode of Truth.

Lila: Divine play, divine sport.

Limbic System: Collective name for several interconnected structures near the brain's core. Forms a borderland between the "lower" or "animal" parts of the brain, mainly involved with instincts, drives, and automatic regulation of body processes, and the highest, uniquely human brain areas, associated with the ***Cerebral Cortex***, which permit advanced reasoning and planning. Crossroads where visceral feelings, cognition, and memory meet. Helps shape the basic motivations and emotions in human beings. Sometimes called *second brain*.

Lingam: Egg-shaped object, symbol of the first form to emerge from the formless.

Linga Sarira: The subtle body with its vital principal, subtle organs, mind, intellect and ego. When the gross body dies, the self departs, clothed in the subtle body.

Lingodbhava: Exterior manifestation of the All pervasive Divine Principle. Emergence of the lingam from the body of Sri Sathya Sai Baba.

Lobha: Greed; one of the six vices, or enemies of man.

Mada: Pride; one of the six vices, or enemies of man.

Madhava: God, master of ***maya***, master of the cosmos.

Madhura Bhakti: The sweetest, and purest love for God.

Magnetism: Principle of attraction. Magnetic power acts as a link between that which is manifest and that, which is unmanifest.

Mahabhuta: Element (see ***panchamahabhutas***).

Mahakarana: Super causal; super consciousness.

Maha Tathwa: The supreme principle which is the cause for the "being" turning into "becoming" and the orderly behaviour of the universe.

Malas: Term used in *ayurveda* for substances, which are partly utilised in the body and partly excreted in a modified form after serving their physiological functions. Waste products of the body, i.e., stool, urine, sweat.

Manas: Mind. (See ***Mind.***)

Manava: Humans. A person who has no trace of ignorance.

Manavathvam: Human existence.

Manomaya Kosa: Sheath around the human body made up of vibrations created by thoughts and emotions.

Mantra: Sacred sounds or words which, if meditated upon, create mental modification.

Marakam: Detachment, which considers God as the source and recipient of the fruits of all actions.

Marga: Path. *Pravritti Marga* = outward path. *Nivritti Marga* = inward path.

Mathsarya: Jealousy or envy; one of the six vices, or enemies of man.

Maya: Illusion

Mind: Instrument functioning through the brain, woven of desires and constantly changing thoughts.

Moksha: Liberation. Abbreviation of *"moha-kshaya"* - literally freedom from all attachments.

Moha: Attachment, delusion, fascination; one of the six vices, or enemies of man.

Mukti: Liberation.

Mystical: Divine, spiritual; that which is beyond ordinary human understanding, which can be gained only from direct experience, not religious dogma.

Nadis: Channels of energy in the subtle body of a human being that distribute ***prana*** throughout the whole body. There are said to be 72,000 throughout the subtle bodies. Three main *nadis* are represented in the caduceus of modern allopathic medicine.

- ***Ida.*** Starts from the left nostril, then moves to the crown of the head and then down to the base of the spine. As lunar energy flows through it, it is also called *Chandra-nadi.*
- ***Pingala.*** Starts from the right nostril, then moves to the crown of the head and then down to the base of the spine. As solar energy flows through it, it is also called *Surya-nadi.*
- ***Shusumna.*** Main *nadi*, situated in the spine.

Nagarasankirtan: A group of people moving in procession along the streets singing the glory of God in the morning.

Namasmarana: Remembrance of the name and form of God.

Nara: Man. A man who knows his mind, and who discriminates on reflection of what he has heard and taught.

Nara Narayana: Man and God. The inseparable Divine forces.

Narasimha: ***Avatar*** of Vishnu in the form of Man (***nara***) Lion (*simha*).

Narayana: God. The basic concept of God which is the formless and the attributeless. Another name for Vishnu, the sustainer of the universe.

Naree: Female.

Neuroglia: Cells that support neurons in the brain, sometimes referred to as "nerve glue". Also called glial cells.

Neuron: Type of cell which transmits nerve impulses throughout the nervous system. Basic unit of connection and communication within the brain.

Neuropeptides. A member of a class of protein-like molecules made in the brain. Short chains of amino acids, with some functioning as neurotransmitters and some functioning as hormones.

Neurotransmitter: A chemical that carries messages between different nerve cells or between nerve cells and muscles.

Nirguna: Formless, attributeless.

Nishkama Karma: Literally desireless action; action with no attachment to the fruits.

Nivritti Marga: The inward path.

Niyama: Various rules of righteous conduct. Purity.

Oligodendrocytes: Nerve glue cell.

Omkara: First sound, expression of the Divine Attributeless Principle. The Supreme God embodied as the form of sound.

Ovaries: Female endocrine glands located in the pelvic region responsible for reproduction; corresponds to the *Muladhara* (root) *chakra*.

Pancha: Five.

Pancha Kosas: Five sheaths surrounding the ***Atma*** or soul.

Panchamahabhutas: Five Basic Elements found in the Cosmos. They make up the animal and plant kingdoms and the human body.

Pancreas: Endocrine gland lying near the stomach which secretes insulin; corresponds to the *Manipura* (solar plexus) *chakra*.

Parakramam: Valour.

Param: Beyond, the highest.

Paramatma: Infinite universal soul. Also called ***Brahman***, *Sai Tathwa*, ***Sat-Chit-Ananda***. The embodied *paramatma* is known as ***Purusha***.

Paratathwa: The supreme principle; absolute reality.

Pineal Gland: Endocrine gland in the brain that regulates biorhythms and skin colour; corresponds to the *Ajna* (third eye) *chakra*.

Pituitary Gland: Endocrine gland at the base of the brain responsible for bone growth, genital maturation and metabolism; corresponds to the *Sahasrara* (crown) *chakra*.

Puja: Sacramental worship in which a deity is evoked and propitiated as a royal or honoured guest with offerings of fruit, food and ***Mantra***.

Prajna: Constant integrated awareness. The human being's conscious awareness of the presence of divinity within.

Prajnana: Vitality. Supreme wisdom. The principle which absorbs and interprets the messages received through the senses.

Prakriti: Nature. The gross element in nature; the sensory world. Can also refer to the human body or the feminine aspect of God [masculine: ***Purusha***].

Prana: Subtle breath, cosmic life force. Also known as *chi, orgon energy, manna*, ying-yang, ***Siva-Sakti***, vital force. The vital force in every being.

Pranayama: Control of the vital cosmic energy within the human body through concentration and regulated breathing.

Pravritti Marga: The worldly path.

Prema: Love or Divine Love. One of the five human values.

Prithivi: Earth. One of the five basic elements.

Purana: Sacred texts that elaborate the truths embodied in the ***Vedas***; also mythological stories of Bharat.

Purusha: God consciousness within the human body; the indweller. The Supreme person; the embodied ***Paramatma:*** Sometimes referred to as the masculine aspect of God [feminine: ***Prakriti***]. The term *Vedapurusha* refers to *Bhagawan* Sri Sathya Sai Baba, as God who is celebrated in the ***VEDAS***, or God of all Knowledge.

Purusharthas: Four basic goals of human life: *dharma, artha, kama* and *moksha.*

Purushotthama: The Lord of all, the supreme being. Literally, the highest of the ***Purusha***.

Pushpam: Flower offered to God.

Rasa: Taste. One of the characteristic attributes of the ***Panchmahabhutas***.

Rasul: Holy man (north Indian).

Rishi: Saint or sage.

Rita* or *Ritam: Cosmic rhythm.

Rubaiyas: Love songs to God, sprung forth spontaneously from a pure, devotion-filled heart.

Sadhaka: Spiritual aspirant.

Sadhana: Spiritual effort, spiritual discipline, spiritual practice.

Sagara: Ocean.

Saguna: With attributes and form.

Sahasam: Daring or determination.

Samadhi: State of supreme consciousness, when one is free from all duality. Communion with Divinity; absorption in the ***Atma***. Equalmindedness.

Samsara: Cycle of birth and death, ocean of illusory existence.

Samskara: The dual process of removing the dust and dirt of vice and planting the virtues and human values. (See also ***Vasanas***.)

Samyagdarshana: Seeing good, having the right vision. Literally "vision of truth".

Sankalpa: Will, plan of action, resolve, thoughts.

Sankhya: Inquiry into the nature of material objects.

Santi: Peace. One of the five human values.

Santosha: Contentment, inner peace. Limited happiness as opposed to ***Ananda*** (bliss).

Santrupthi: Contentment, satisfaction.

Sastras: Body of ancient knowledge which lays down limits and rules for orderly behaviour.

Sat-Chit-Ananda: *Sat* – eternal absolute being, *Chit* – awareness or consciousness, *Ananda* – divine bliss. Another name for God.

***Sathya*.** Truth. One of the five human values. Name and nature of *Bhagawan* Sri Sathya Sai Baba.

Satsang: Good company; gathering to celebrate the glory of God.

Satwic: Pure.

Self: Atma, the spirit.

Sakti: Power; feminine manifested aspect of the divine energy.

Sariras: Bodies. Literal meaning: "that which wastes away".

Siddhi: Wisdom or occult or yogic power won through penance or austerities, including mastery of the elements, out of body travel, mind-reading, healing, etc.

Siddha: Great being who has mastered many ***siddhis***. Divine seers.

Siva: Aspect of the One Divine Principle which governs dissolution and destruction.

Sive Netri: Third eye.

Sraddha: Faith.

Sristhi: Creation.

Subconscious Mind: Storehouse of human knowledge and experience. (***Chittha***).

Sufi: People who are self-realised; lovers of God.

Swadyaya: Reading of spiritual texts.

Swarupa: Embodiment; the true self.

Synapse: A junction between two nerve cells where the tip of a nerve fiber almost touches another in order to transmit signals.

Taijasa: The dreaming stage of existence.

Tanmataras: Five subtlenesses: sound, form, touch, taste and smell; actions of the organs of perception, ***Pancha Jnanendriyas*** inside the human brain.

Tapas: Austerity and self control. Bringing about a physical, vocal and mental unity by letting actions, words and thoughts become one.

Tathwa: Principle of a thing, its real nature.

Testes: Male endocrine glands located in the pelvic region responsible for reproduction; corresponds to the *Muladhara* (root) *chakra*.

Tharakam: Sense of possession. Attitude of attachment to outcome of actions, believing the little self to be the doer.

Third Eye: 1. Conscious connection between the physical and astral bodies in a human being that results in clairvoyant or intuitive awareness. 2. *Chakra* located on the forehead between the two eyebrows, called *Ajna* in Sanskrit.

Thymus Gland: Endocrine gland at the base of the neck involved in development of the immune system; corresponds to the *Anahata* (heart) *chakra*.

Thyroid Gland: Endocrine gland located in the neck responsible for metabolism and growth; corresponds to the *Visuddha* (throat) *chakra*.

Trikarna Shuddi: Triple purity of thought, word and action.

Turiya: Supreme causal aspect. State beyond the five ***Kosas:*** Comes after *Sushupti* (Deep sleep state). The bliss experienced in this state is true bliss and it cannot be obtained through the senses, the mind, or the intellect.

Upanishads: Sacred texts culled from the ***Vedas***, which deal with the highest spiritual truths and disciplines. Literally meaning, "to sit at the feet of the teacher".

Utthama: The highest.

Vairagya: Renunciation. Detachment.

Vaiswanara: The Divine who dwells in the body in the form of digestive fire.

Vasanas: Literally "scar". Tendencies and attachments inherited from previous births that shape desires, thoughts and actions in this birth. (Sometimes called ***Samskaras***)

Vasthu: Thing-ness, objects, substance.

Vayu: Air. One of the five basic elements.

Vedanta: Essence of the ***Vedas***; metaphysics of the Supreme Reality. Literally means "the end of the *Vedas*". The end of all knowledge. The philosophy of non-dualism.

Vedas: Name for a collection of Divine knowledge. Comes from the root word *vid*, meaning "to know". Revealed eternal truths, received by ancient *rishis* (seers) of India that have come down as four sacred scriptural texts, ***Rig Veda, Sama Veda, Atharva Veda, Yajur Veda.***

Vipaka: The taste that arises after the digestion and metabolism of a substance. One of the characteristic attributes of the ***Panchamahabhutas***.

Viratswarupa: The gross physical form assumed by the ***Atma*** in the waking state for leading a life in the world. The Cosmic Person who manifests in many forms under many names.

Virya: Potency. One of the characteristic attributes of the ***Panchamahabhutas:*** Semen.

Visvasam: Faith or confidence.

Vishnu: Aspect of the One Divine Principle which governs organization and preservation.

Vishaya Vasana: Attachment to sense objects; the urge to accumulate fortune and live in luxury.

Viveka: Discrimination, analytical intelligence, discernment.

Vyavaharika: The reflection of an object, or that which has a basis, but no permanent existence.

Yajna: Sacrificial rite; renunciation.

Yama: 1. Ethical disciplines, one of the limbs of *Asthanga Yoga*, 2. God of Death, 3. Time.

Yantra: Machine or instrument; ritual diagram or apparatus used to evoke connection with the divine.

Yoga: Union of soul with God within the human brain; from the root word *yug*, meaning "to join together". This union is reached through any one of the four main paths. ***Hatha Yoga*** is a discipline to promote good health.

- ***Bhakti Yoga.*** Path of love and devotion. Uses the emotions.
- ***Jnana Yoga***. Path of wisdom and self enquiry. Uses the intellect.
- ***Karma Yoga.*** Path of action and selfless service. Uses the body.
- ***Raja Yoga.*** Path of self control. Uses meditation and the mind.

Let the Goddess of Learning, Saraswathi herself, be the scribe to record, with all the vast material at her disposal, the immense range of ***Swami's lilas;*** *even so, the task shall forever remain unfinished.*

~ **Sri Sathya Sai Baba**

bibliography

Bhagawan Sri Sathya Sai Baba, Divine Discourses from 1962 through 2003.

Bhagawan Sri Sathya Sai Baba, ***Bhagavatha Vahini.***

Bhagawan Sri Sathya Sai Baba, ***Dhyana Vahini.***

Bhagawan Sri Sathya Sai Baba, Discourses On the ***Bhagavad Gita***, 1984.

Bhagawan Sri Sathya Sai Baba, ***Geetha Vahini.***

Bhagawan Sri Sathya Sai Baba, ***Jnana Vahini,*** reprint 1998.

Bhagawan Sri Sathya Sai Baba, ***Prasnottara Vahini***.

Bhagawan Sri Sathya Sai Baba, ***Sandheha Nivari.***

Bhagawan Sri Sathya Sai Baba, **Sathya Sai *Amrita Varshini.***

Bhagawan Sri Sathya Sai Baba, ***Sadhana*, the Inward Path.**

Bhagawan Sri Sathya Sai Baba, ***Upanishad Vahini.***

Bhagawan Sri Sathya Sai Baba, ***Vidya Vahini.***

Bhagawan Sri Sathya Sai Baba, ***Sanathana Sarathi,*** 1965 through 1995.

Bhagawan Sri Sathya Sai Baba, **Sathya Sai Speaks,** Vols. 1-23.

Bhagawan Sri Sathya Sai Baba, **Summer Showers In Brindavan,** 1978 through 2002.

Bhagawan Sri Sathya Sai Baba, **The Mind and Its Mysteries,** *Dasara* Discourses 1976.

Bhagawan Sri Sathya Sai Baba, ***Prema Dhara,*** Vol 1.

Bhagawan Sri Sathya Sai Baba, "I Am God, You Are God", pamphlet from *Chaitanya Jyothi* Museum.

Bhagawan Sri Sathya Sai Baba, ***Light of Love.***

Bhagawan Sri Sathya Sai Baba, **Sathya Sai Newsletter, USA**.

Bhagawan Sri Sathya Sai Baba, **Teachings of** *Bhagawan* **Sri Sathya Sai Baba,** 1974.

Bhagawan Sri Sathya Sai Baba, **Voice of the *Avatar.***

Atharva Veda.

Ten Sikh Gurus, ***Adi Guru Grant Sahab.***

Aurobindo, Sri, **The Life Divine.**

Vivekananda, Swami, ***Raja Yoga.***

Patanjali, Maharishi, ***Asthanga Yoga Sutras***.

Charvaka Sastra.

Besant, Annie, **The Astral Body.**

Hahnemann, Dr. Samuel, **Organon of Homeopathy.**

Vithoulkas, Dr. George, **The Science of Homeopathy.**

Kent, J. T., **Homeopathic Philosophy.**

Gopikrishna, **The Secret of *Kundalini Yoga*** and **Wonders of the Brain.**

Iyengar, B. K. S., **The Light On *Yoga* and *Pranayama*.**

Lonavala Yoga Centre, ***Pranayama***.

Lamba, Bhag Singh, **God Realization**.

Talcott, Dr. S. H., **Mental Diseases.**

Sui, Choa Kok, ***Pranic* Healing.**

Medical Research Group, **Mysteries of Healing,** Theosophical Research Center, London.

Medical Research Group, **The *Chakra*,** Theosophical Research Center, London.

Readers Digest Association, **ABC's of the Human Mind,** 1990.

Underhill, Evelyn, **Mysticism**.

American Medical Association, **Journal of Hypnosis,** 1958.

American Psychiatric Association, **Hypnosis,** 1962.

British Medical Association, **Journal of Hypnosis**,1955.

Brennan, Barbara Ann, **Hands of Light,** Bantam Books, New York, 1987.

Burks, A. J., **The Aura.**

Burnham, Sophy, **A Book of Angels.**

Coward, Harold, **Jung and Eastern Thought,** 1985.

Das, Dr. Bhagawan, ***Ayurvedic* Cure for Common Diseases.**

Grey and Wright, **Anatomy and Physiology of the Brain.**

James, William, **The Varieties of Religious Experiences.**

Joseph, R, and Harold L. Klawans, **The Transmitter to God: The Limbic System, the Soul and Spirituality,** San Jose Press.

Jung, Dr. C. G., **Physiological Reflection.**

Vinken, P. J. and C. W. Brayn, **A Handbook of Clinical Neurology,** 1969.

Kilner Walter J., M.D., **The Human Aura.**

Kramer, Kenneth, **The Sacred Art of Dying**, Paulist Press, 1988.

Newberg, Andrew, MD, Eugene D'Aquili, MD, PhD, and Vince Rause, **Why God Won't Go Away,** Ballantine Books, NY, 2001.

Leslie-Chaden, Leslie, Ed., **Compendium of the Teachings of Sathya Sai Baba,** Sai Towers Publishing, 1999.

Hislop, Dr. John, **Conversations with *Bhagawan* Sri Sathya Sai Baba,** Sri Sathya Sai Books & Publications Trust, reprint, 2005.

Hislop, Dr. John, **My Baba and I**, Sri Sathya Sai Books & Publications Trust, reprint, 2005.

Jagadeesan, J., **Journey to God, III**.

Kasturi, N., **Loving God,** Sri Sathya Sai Books & Publications Trust.

Kasturi, N., **The Life of *Bhagawan* Sri Sathya Sai Baba**, 1971.

Kasturi, N., ***Sathyam Sivam Sundaram,*** Part I-IV.

Krishnaswami, Sundararaghavan, Ed., ***Para Bhakti,*** 2005.

Kamaraju, Anil Kumar, ***Sathyopanishad***, Vol. 1, Sri Sathya Sai Books & Publications Trust.

McMartin, Grace, Ed., **Baba, the Breath of Sai**, Sri Sathya Sai Books & Publications Trust, reprint, 2001.

Sai Gita, Ed., ***Sanskrit-English Dictionary,*** Compiled from the Divine Discourses and writings of *Bhagawan* Sri Sathya Sai Baba, 2000.

Sastry, Jandhyala Venkateswara, ***Tapovanam***, Sri Sathya Sai Books and Publications Trust, 8th edition, 2005.

Students of *Bhagawan* Sri Sathya Sai Baba, ***Veda Saartham,*** 2003.

Vidyalankar, Pandit Satyakam, **The Holy *Vedas,*** Clarion Books, Delhi, Reprint 1998.

Author, ***Bhakti* and Health,** Sri Sathya Sai Books & Publications Trust, 2004.

Author, "*Pranayama*, the Only Exercise for Chronic Pulmonary Pathology", paper delivered at Asian Homeopathic Conference, Bangkok, 1989.

Author, **Spirituality and Health**, Sri Sathya Sai Books & Publications Trust, 2004.

Author, ***Vedantic* Method and Virtuous Children,** Dr. Charanjit Ghooi, 1998.

SRI SATHYA SAI BOOKS AND PUBLICATIONS TRUST
PRASANTHI NILAYAM

PIN 515 134, ANANTAPUR DISTRICT, ANDHRA PRADESH, INDIA
IMPORTER / EXPORTER CODE NO. 0990001032
RESERVE BANK OF INDIA EXPORTER CODE NO. HS-2001198

	Price Rs.	Wt. in gms.
A. BOOKS WRITTEN BY BHAGAVAN: Vahini Series		
Bhagavatha Vahini (The Glory of the Lord)	44.00	490
Dharma Vahini (Stream of Righteousness)	22.00	230
Dhyana Vahini (Stream of Meditation)	20.00	210
Geetha Vahini (The Divine Gospel)	32.00	380
Jnana Vahini (The Stream of Eternal Wisdom)	15.00	165
Leela Kaivalya Vahini (The Cosmic Play of God)	9.00	75
Prasanthi Vahini (The Supreme Bliss of Divine)	15.00	140
Prasnottara Vahini (Answers to Spiritual Questions)	15.00	140
Prema Vahini (The Stream of Divine Love)	20.00	215
Ramakatha Rasavahini Pt. 1 (Story of Rama's Glory)	48.00	705
Ramakatha Rasavahini Pt. 2 (Story of Rama's Glory)	36.00	460
Sandeha Nivarini (Clearance of Spiritual Doubts)	16.00	230
Sathya Sai Vahini (Spiritual Message of Sathya Sai)	34.00	220
Sutra Vahini (Stream of Aphorisms on Brahman)	19.00	180
Upanishad Vahini (Essence of Vedic Knowledge)	17.00	190
Vidya Vahini (Flow of Spiritual Education)	17.00	175
B. LETTERS / MESSAGES TO HIS STUDENTS / TEACHERS / OTHERS BY BHAGAVAN		
Prema Dhaara Vol.1 (Letters to His students)	16.00	130
Prema Dhaara Vol.2 (to His students / teachers / others)	29.00	335
C. DISCOURSES BY BHAGAVAN: Sathya Sai Speaks Series		
Vol. 1 (1953-60)	34.00	390
Vol. 2 (1961-62)	39.00	490
Vol. 3 (1963)	38.00	420
Vol. 4 (1964)	39.00	510
Vol. 5 (1965)	43.00	535
Vol. 6 (1966)	59.00	465
Vol. 7 (1967)	35.00	410
Vol. 8 (1968)	39.00	415
Vol. 9 (1969)	30.00	345
Vol. 10 (1970)	35.00	450
Vol. 11 (1971-72)	45.00	565
Vol. 12 (1973-74)	42.00	535
Vol. 13 (1975-77)	30.00	445
Vol. 14 Pt. 1 (78-79)	30.00	270
Vol. 14 Pt. 2 (79-80)	34.00	390
Vol. 15 Pt. 1 (1981)	32.00	330
Vol. 15 Pt. 2 (1982)	23.00	225
Vol. 16 (1983)	30.00	330
Vol. 17 (1984)	32.00	325
Vol. 18 (1985)	25.00	365
Vol. 19 (1986)	30.00	405
Vol. 20 (1987)	39.00	460
Vol. 21 (1988)	35.00	400
Vol. 22 (1989)	35.00	395
Vol. 23 (1990)	44.00	440
Vol. 24 (1991)	40.00	540
Vol. 25 (1992)	40.00	625
Vol. 26 (1993)	50.00	655
Vol. 27 (1994)	35.00	510
Vol. 28 (1995)	43.00	380
Vol. 29 (1996)	43.00	400
Vol. 30 (1997)	35.00	450
Vol. 31 (1998)	53.00	710
Vol. 32 Pt.1(1999)	27.00	380
Vol. 33 (2000)	39.00	495
Vol. 34 (2001)	38.00	462
Vol. 35 (2002)	40.00	525
Vol. 36 Pt. 1 (2003)	29.00	330
Vol. 36 Pt. 2 (2003)	23.00	250
Vol. 37 (2004)	38.00	410
Vol. 38 (2005)	29.00	330
Vol. 39 (2006)	34.00	*
Summer Showers Series (on Indian Culture and Spirituality)		
Summer Showers in Brindavan 1972	8.00	235
Summer Showers in Brindavan 1973	46.00	200
Summer Showers in Brindavan 1974 Part - I	36.00	370
Summer Showers in Brindavan 1974 Part - II	38.00	385
Summer Roses on the Blue Mountains - Ooty 1976	37.00	360
Summer Showers in Brindavan 1977	9.00	180
Summer Showers in Brindavan 1978	46.00	510
Summer Showers in Brindavan 1979	34.00	325
Summer Showers in Brindavan 1990	20.00	250
Summer Showers in Brindavan 1991	22.00	290
Summer Showers in Brindavan 1993	23.00	200
Summer Showers in Brindavan 1995	34.00	240
Summer Showers in Brindavan 1996	19.00	205

Asterisk * mark – under print

Summer Showers in Brindavan 2000	34.00	430
Summer Showers in Brindavan 2002	25.00	290

Other Discourses

Be Like Jesus	30.00	320
Benedictory Addresses (as Chancellor) (up to 2002)	26.00	350
Birthday Blessings of Bhagavan	25.00	325
Divine Discourses on Easwaramma Day	18.00	225
The Glory of Womanhood	18.00	205
Sai Echoes from Kodai Hills	20.00	235
Sree Gurucharanam (Guru Poornima Discourses 1956-98)	11.00	145
Sri Sathya Sai Veda Vani – (discourses on Veda)	50.00	560
Ati Rudra Maha Yajna – Aug 2006 (Discourses and talks by eminent scholars)	30.00	330
Bhagavad Gita Part - (I and II)	69.00	820
The Mind and its Mysteries (Dasara 1976)	14.00	170
Senses for Selfless Service (Dasara 1997)	15.00	160
Dasara Discourses 1998	19.00	200
Dasara Discourses 1999 & 2000	25.00	280
Dasara Discourses 2001	18.00	220
Dasara Discourses 2002	13.00	160
Dasara Discourses 2004	6.00	150
Dasara Discourses 2005	11.00	110

D. LIFE STORY OF BHAGAVAN

Sathyam Sivam Sundaram Vol. 1 (Birth to 1961)	60.00	595
Sathyam Sivam Sundaram Vol. 2 (1962 to 1968)	49.00	525
Sathyam Sivam Sundaram Vol. 3 (1969 to 1972)	48.00	605
Sathyam Sivam Sundaram Vol. 4 (1973 to 1979)	40.00	430
Sathyam Sivam Sundaram Vol. 5 (1980 to 1985)	55.00	660
Sathyam Sivam Sundaram Vol 1 to 5 (Deluxe Edition)	390.00	3550
His story as told by Himself	29.00	300

E. CHILDREN'S BOOKS

Chinna Katha-Part I	30.00	330
Chinna Katha-Part II	42.00	480
Chinna Katha Illustrated	21.00	80
Chinna Katha Picture Stories Vol. 1	25.00	210
Chinna Katha Picture Stories Vol. 2	25.00	210
Chinna Katha Picture Stories Vol. 3	25.00	210
Chinna Katha Picture Stories Vol. 4	25.00	210
Divine Stories Vol 1 (Human Value Stories)	35.00	430
Divine Stories Vol 2 (Human Value Stories)	30.00	375
My Life is My Message	17.00	110
Stories for Children: Part I	17.00	*
Stories for Children: Part II	28.00	325
One Single Stream of Love	41.00	210
Quiz Bhagavatam	10.00	40
Quiz Mahaabhaaratha	7.00	50
Quiz Raamaayana	7.00	50
Quiz The Bhagavath Geeta	7.00	40
Quiz Divine Life of Bhagavan Sri Sathya Sai Baba	6.00	55

Children's Books by Ms.Purnima Ray

Ramakatha Rasavahini (Pictorial) - Vol. 1	27.00	120
Ramakatha Rasavahini (Pictorial) - Vol. 2	31.00	145
Ramakatha Rasavahini (Pictorial) - Vol. 3	32.00	145

F. OUR OTHER PUBLICATIONS

A pioneering attempt at child labour elimination- A tribute to Sai Baba, The Ultimate Motivator	35.00	330
Aura of the Divine	37.00	380
Bhajanavali (in HINDI)	16.00	190
Bhagavan Uvacha Vol. 1 (7 Books)	75.00	*
Bhagavan Uvacha Vol. 2 (7 Books)	70.00	460
Bhagavan Uvacha Vol. 3 (7 Books)	85.00	*
Divine Memories - Diana Baskin	47.00	485
Faith and Devotion – Compiled by Prem Luthra	21.00	210
Food for Thought	40.00	475

Gems of Wisdom	53.00	610
Guidelines to Active workers of SSSS Organisations from Bhagavan Baba (Qs & As)	19.00	200
Garland of 108 Precious Gems (108 Holy Names of Bhagavan)	20.00	160
Message of the Lord	185.00	1400
Nama Mahima - Compilations	16.00	160
Namasmarana - Dr.B.Mavinkurve	8.00	55
Ocean of Love (Pictorial)	500.00	1880
Prasanthi Nilayam Information Booklet	12.00	100
Raso Vai Sah - Brahmananda Panda	48.00	450
Sadhana - The Inward Path	43.00	475
Sai Advent - Compiled by Harendra Singh	11.00	85
Sai Baba and You - Practical Spirituality - Mark and Barbara Gardner	27.00	295
Sai Bhajanamala	45.00	600
Sai Study Circle Manual – Cheruvu S.Murthy	20.00	210
Sathya Sai Education in Human Values – Loraine Burrows	25.00	240
Sathya Sai Samarchanam - Jandyala V. Sastry	10.00	160
Sri Sathya Sai Anandadayi - Karunamba Ramamurthy	48.00	600
Suggestions for Study Groups and Individuals use of the Ceiling on Desires Programme	10.00	75
The Mission of Sathya Sai at a Glance (Pictorial)	75.00	430
The Essential Sai – Sainet Editorial Committee	39.00	410
Thought for the Day (Desktop)	30.00	260
Tribute - Messages & Articles by eminent persons	70.00	760
Truth is Only One – Ann Cleveland	32.00	370
The Direct Flight to Divinity – Sai Anoos	22.00	205
To my Father - Justice Padma Khastgir	13.00	165
Unforgettable Baba - Joyce Darlene Barker	40.00	335
Who is a Devotee of the Lord	12.00	85
Books by Prof. T.K. Sudarshan		
Grama Seva is Rama Seva	20.00	220
Master the Mind and Be A Master Mind	28.00	*
Books by Dr. John S. Hislop		
Conversation with Bhagavan Sri Sathya Sai Baba	29.00	375
My Baba and I	42.00	415
Seeking Divinity	32.00	385
Books by Ranvir Singh		
Fundamentals of Sri Sathya Sai Educare Vol. I	60.00	520
Fundamentals of Sri Sathya Sai Educare Vol. II	60.00	520
Fundamentals of Sri Sathya Sai Educare Vol. III	49.00	625
Fundamental s of Sri Sathya Sai Educare Vol. IV	64.00	635
Books by Grace J.Mc Martin		
Baba - The Breath of Sai	46.00	485
Seva: A flower At His Lotus Feet	29.00	325
A Recapitulation of Baba's Divine Teachings	35.00	*
Books by Dr. (Mrs) Charanjit Ghooi		
Bhakthi and Health	30.00	270
Human Values and Health (Hard bound)	94.00	*
Spirituality and Health (Hard bound)	60.00	650
Books by Sri. P.P. Arya		
End of the Endless Search	28.00	265
Sri Sathya Sai Gita – All about Spirituality Qs & As	45.00	485
Books by Prof. N. Kasturi		
Loving God	52.00	600
Easwaramma The chosen mother	24.00	285
Pathway to Peace Prasanthi	21.00	235
Siva Sakthi Swarupa	13.00	130
The Light of Love (Bhagavan's East Africa visit)	18.00	225
Books by Rita Bruce		
Love of Conscience	29.00	305
Sathya Sai Parenting	33.00	400
Vision of Sai I	47.00	470
Vision of Sai II	48.00	465
Books by Joy Thomas		
Life is a Game Play It	42.00	450

Life is a Challenge Meet It	26.00	290
Life is Love Enjoy It	29.00	345
Life is a Dream Realise It	32.00	305
Books by John Goldthwait, Ph.D		
Purifying the Heart	20.00	225
A Practice for Purifying the Heart	8.00	75
Books by Phyllis Krystal		
Sai Baba-The Ultimate Experience	35.00	385
Reconnecting the Love Energy (for sale in India)	25.00	265
Taming our Monkey Mind - (for sale in India)	28.00	320
Suggestions for Study Groups and Individuals use of the Ceiling on Desires Programme (for sale in India)	10.00	75
Books by Dr.Samuel H. Sandweiss		
Sai Baba - The Holyman and Psychiatrist	58.00	425
Spirit and the Mind	46.00	545
With Love Man is God (for sale in India)	115.00	755
Book by Lieut Gen. (Retd) Dr. M.L. Chibber		
Sai Baba's Mahavakya on Leadership (Hard Bound)	52.00	480
Sai Baba's Mahavakya on Leadership (HB. – Dlx. Ed.)	75.00	*
Books by Prof. K. Anil Kumar		
Rays of Radiance - Service, Adoration, Illumination	37.00	425
Sai Chology	45.00	475
Sai Sandesh	43.00	275
Universal and Practical Teachings of Bhagavan	26.00	300
Books by Judy Warner		
The Dharmic Challenge	25.00	280
Transformation of the Heart (for sale in India)	28.00	240
Books by Don Mario Mazzoleni		
A Catholic Priest Meets Sai Baba (for sale in India)	37.00	490
The Wish-Fulfilling Tree	44.00	490
Books by Jonathan Roof		
Pathways to God Vol. I (for sale in India)	26.00	360
Pathways to God Vol. II (for sale in India)	39.00	400
Pathways to God Vol. III (for sale in India)	45.00	430

Rates indicated are the prevailing rates. They are liable to change.

INLAND / OVERSEAS BOOK ORDERS

Books are despatched by Regd. Book Post only subject to availability. Indents and remittances within India should be received by Money Order/Indian Postal Order/Account Payee Cheques/Bank Drafts.

REMITTANCES

Remittances from Overseas towards Book Orders can be sent by A/C payee Bank Cheque / Demand Draft / International Money Order in **FOREIGN CURRENCY ONLY AND NOT IN INDIAN RUPEES.** Sending Cash Currency is liable to be confiscated by Government.

All remittances should be in favour of **THE CONVENER, SRI SATHYA SAI BOOKS AND PUBLICATIONS TRUST, PRASANTHI NILAYAM, ANANTAPUR DISTRICT, ANDHRA PRADESH, INDIA, PIN CODE - 515 134,** payable at State Bank of India, Prasanthi Nilayam (Branch Code No. 2786) mentioning full address in capitals with Area Pin Code, Zip Code No., where the books are to be despatched.

The approximate postage + packing + forwarding charges for Overseas Sea Mail and Inland per packet are indicated below:

Wt. of Packets	Overseas		Inland
	APPU Countries	Others	
Up to 500 gms.	Rs.78/-	Rs.82/-	Rs.37/-
Above 500 gms. - Below 1 kg	Rs.93/-	Rs.100/-	Rs.42/-
Above 1 kg - Below 2 kg	Rs.109/-	Rs.118/-	Rs.52/-
Above 2 kg - Below 3 kg	Rs.135/-	Rs.150/-	Rs.72/-
Above 3 kg - Below 4 kg	Rs.162/-	Rs.180/-	Rs.82/-
Above 4 kg - Below 5 kg	Rs.188/-	Rs.212/-	Rs.92/-

N.B. Maximum weight allowed per packet is 5 kgs. Weight of packing materials *per packet* to be added to the weight of books – Overseas – 300 gms.

Inland up to 2 kgs – 100 gms. Above 2 kgs and up to 5 kgs – 300 gms.

APPU Countries: Afghanistan, Australia, Brunei, Cambodia, China (People's Republic), Fiji, Indonesia, Iran, Japan, Korea (Rep.), Laos (Rep.) Malaysia, Maldives, Myanmar, Naura, Papua New Guinea, Philippines, Solomon Island, Sri Lanka, Thailand, Vietnam, New Zealand, Singapore.